BOLLINGEN SERIES XX

———————————

THE COLLECTED WORKS

OF

C. G. JUNG

VOLUME 9, PART II

EDITORS

†SIR HERBERT READ

MICHAEL FORDHAM, M.D., M.R.C.P.

GERHARD ADLER, PH.D.

WILLIAM MCGUIRE, *executive editor*

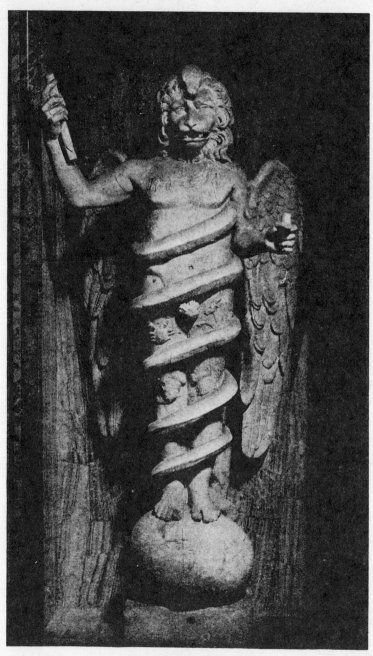

The Mithraic god Aion
Roman, 2nd–3rd century

AION

RESEARCHES INTO THE

PHENOMENOLOGY OF THE SELF

C. G. JUNG

SECOND EDITION

TRANSLATED BY R. F. C. HULL

BOLLINGEN SERIES XX

PRINCETON UNIVERSITY PRESS

Second hardcover edition, with corrections and minor revisions, 1968
Fifth hardcover printing, with additional corrections, 1978
First Princeton / Bollingen Paperback printing, 1979

This book is a paperback reprint of Volume 9, part ii, of the Collected Works of C. G. Jung. All the volumes comprising the Collected Works constitute number XX in Bollingen Series, under the editorship of Herbert Read (d. 1968), Michael Fordham, and Gerhard Adler; executive editor, William McGuire.

Translated from the first part of *Aion: Untersuchungen zur Symbolgeschichte* (Psychologische Abhandlungen, VIII), published by Rascher Verlag, Zurich, 1951.

ISBN 0-691-01826-X (paperback edition)
ISBN 0-691-09775-5 (hardcover edition)
LIBRARY OF CONGRESS CATALOG CARD NUMBER 75-156

EDITORIAL NOTE

Volume 9 of the Collected Works is devoted to studies of the specific archetypes of the collective unconscious. Part I, entitled *The Archetypes and the Collective Unconscious*, is composed of shorter essays; Part II, *Aion*, is a long monograph on the archetype of the self. The author has agreed to a modification of the sub-title of *Aion*, which in the Swiss edition appeared in two forms, "Researches into the History of Symbols" and "Contributions to the Symbolism of the Self." The first five chapters were previously published, with small differences, in *Psyche and Symbol: A Selection from the Writings of C. G. Jung*, edited by Violet S. de Laszlo (Anchor Books, Garden City, New York, 1958).

EDITORIAL NOTE TO THE SECOND EDITION

For this edition corrections have been made in the text and footnotes and the bibliographical references have been brought up to date in relation to the *Collected Works*. The translation has been corrected in light of further experience of translating Jung's works.

TRANSLATOR'S NOTE

Grateful acknowledgment is made to the following persons, whose translations have been consulted during the preparation of the present work: Mr. William H. Kennedy, for extensive use of his translation of portions of chapters 2 and 3, issued as "Shadow, Animus, and Anima" by the Analytical Psychology Club of New York, 1950; Dr. Hildegarde Nagel, for reference to her translation of the original *Eranos-Jahrbuch* version (1949) of "Concerning the Self," in *Spring*, 1951, which original version the author later expanded into *Aion*, chapters 4 and 5; and Miss Barbara Hannah and Dr. Marie-Louise von Franz, for helpful advice with the remaining chapters. Especial thanks are due to Mr. A. S. B. Glover, who (unless otherwise noted) translated the Latin and Greek texts throughout. References to published sources are given for the sake of completeness.

TABLE OF CONTENTS

EDITORIAL NOTES   V

TRANSLATOR'S NOTE   vi

LIST OF PLATES   viii

FOREWORD   ix

I. The Ego   3

II. The Shadow   8

III. The Syzygy: Anima and Animus   11

IV. The Self   23

V. Christ, a Symbol of the Self   36

VI. The Sign of the Fishes   72

VII. The Prophecies of Nostradamus   95

VIII. The Historical Significance of the Fish 103

IX. The Ambivalence of the Fish Symbol   118

X. The Fish in Alchemy   126
     1. *The Medusa*, 126 — 2. *The Fish*, 137 — 3. *The Fish Symbol of the Cathars*, 145

XI. The Alchemical Interpretation of the Fish 154

XII. Background to the Psychology of Christian Alchemical Symbolism   173

XIII. Gnostic Symbols of the Self   184

XIV. The Structure and Dynamics of the Self 222

XV. Conclusion   266

BIBLIOGRAPHY   271

INDEX   301

LIST OF PLATES

The Mithraic god Aion
Roman, 2nd–3rd century. Museo Profano, Vatican. P: Alinari.
frontispiece

I. The Four Elements
Michael Maier, *Scrutinium chymicum* (1687), Emblema XVII, p. 49.
following page　250

II. The Trinity
From a manuscript by Joachim of Flora. Graphics Collection, Zurich
Central Library, B x 606.　　*following page*　254

FOREWORD

The theme of this work [1] is the idea of the Aeon (Greek, *Aion*). My investigation seeks, with the help of Christian, Gnostic, and alchemical symbols of the self, to throw light on the change of psychic situation within the "Christian aeon." Christian ·tradition from the outset is not only saturated with Persian and Jewish ideas about the beginning and end of time, but is filled with intimations of a kind of enantiodromian reversal of dominants. I mean by this the dilemma of Christ and Antichrist. Probably most of the historical speculations about time and the division of time were influenced, as the Apocalypse shows, by astrological ideas. It is therefore only natural that my reflections should gravitate mainly round the symbol of the *Fishes,* for the Pisces aeon is the synchronistic concomitant of two thousand years of Christian development. In this time-period not only was the figure of the Anthropos (the "Son of Man") progressively amplified symbolically, and thus assimilated psychologically, but it brought with it changes in man's attitude that had already been anticipated by the expectation of the Antichrist in the ancient texts. Because these texts relegate the appearance of Antichrist to the end of time, we are justified in speaking of a "Christian aeon," which, it was presupposed, would find its end with the Second Coming. It seems as if this expectation coincides with the astrological conception of the "Platonic month" of the Fishes.

1 [In the Swiss edition, this foreword begins as follows: "In this volume (VIII of the Psychologische Abhandlungen) I am bringing out two works which, despite their inner and outer differences, belong together in so far as they both treat of the great theme of this book, namely the idea of the Aeon (Greek, *Aion*). While the contribution of my co-worker, Dr. Marie-Louise von Franz, describes the psychological transition from antiquity to Christianity by analysing the Passion of St. Perpetua, my own investigation seeks, with the help of" etc., as above. Dr. von Franz's "Die Passio Perpetuae" is omitted from the present volume. —EDITORS.]

The immediate occasion for my proposing to discuss these historical questions is the fact that the archetypal image of wholeness, which appears so frequently in the products of the unconscious, has its forerunners in history. These were identified very early with the figure of Christ, as I have shown in my book *Psychology and Alchemy*.[2] I have been requested so often by my readers to discuss the relations between the traditional Christ-figure and the natural symbols of wholeness, or the self, that I finally decided to take this task in hand. Considering the unusual difficulties of such an undertaking, my decision did not come easily to me, for, in order to surmount all the obstacles and possibilities of error, a knowledge and caution would be needed which, unfortunately, are vouchsafed me only in limited degree. I am moderately certain of my observations on the empirical material, but I am fully aware of the risk I am taking in drawing the testimonies of history into the scope of my reflections. I think I also know the responsibility I am taking upon myself when, as though continuing the historical process of assimilation, I add to the many symbolical amplifications of the Christ-figure yet another, the psychological one, or even, so it might seem, reduce the Christ-symbol to a psychological image of wholeness. My reader should never forget, however, that I am not making a confession of faith or writing a tendentious tract, but am simply considering how certain things could be understood from the standpoint of our modern consciousness—things which I deem it valuable to understand, and which are obviously in danger of being swallowed up in the abyss of incomprehension and oblivion; things, finally, whose understanding would do much to remedy our philosophic disorientation by shedding light on the psychic background and the secret chambers of the soul. The essence of this book was built up gradually, in the course of many years, in countless conversations with people of all ages and all walks of life; with people who in the confusion and uprootedness of our society were likely to lose all contact with the meaning of European culture and to fall into that state of suggestibility which is the occasion and cause of the Utopian mass-psychoses of our time.

I write as a physician, with a physician's sense of responsibility, and not as a proselyte. Nor do I write as a scholar,

[2] [Ch. 5, "The Lapis-Christ Parallel."]

otherwise I would wisely barricade myself behind the safe walls of my specialism and not, on account of my inadequate knowledge of history, expose myself to critical attack and damage my scientific reputation. So far as my capacities allow, restricted as they are by old age and illness, I have made every effort to document my material as reliably as possible and to assist the verification of my conclusions by citing the sources.

C. G. JUNG

May 1950

AION

RESEARCHES INTO THE PHENOMENOLOGY
OF THE SELF

These things came to pass, they say, that Jesus might be made the first sacrifice in the discrimination of composite natures.

HIPPOLYTUS, *Elenchos*, VII, 27, 8

I

THE EGO

1   Investigation of the psychology of the unconscious confronted me with facts which required the formulation of new concepts. One of these concepts is the *self*. The entity so denoted is not meant to take the place of the one that has always been known as the *ego,* but includes it in a supraordinate concept. We understand the ego as the complex factor to which all conscious contents are related. It forms, as it were, the centre of the field of consciousness; and, in so far as this comprises the empirical personality, the ego is the subject of all personal acts of consciousness. The relation of a psychic content to the ego forms the criterion of its consciousness, for no content can be conscious unless it is represented to a subject.

2   With this definition we have described and delimited the *scope* of the subject. Theoretically, no limits can be set to the field of consciousness, since it is capable of indefinite extension. Empirically, however, it always finds its limit when it comes up against the *unknown*. This consists of everything we do not know, which, therefore, is not related to the ego as the centre of the field of consciousness. The unknown falls into two groups of objects: those which are outside and can be experienced by the senses, and those which are inside and are experienced immediately. The first group comprises the unknown in the outer world; the second the unknown in the inner world. We call this latter territory the *unconscious*.

3   The ego, as a specific content of consciousness, is not a simple or elementary factor but a complex one which, as such, cannot be described exhaustively. Experience shows that it rests on two seemingly different bases: the *somatic* and the *psychic*. The somatic basis is inferred from the totality of endosomatic perceptions, which for their part are already of a psychic nature and are associated with the ego, and are therefore conscious. They are produced by endosomatic stimuli, only some of which

3

cross the threshold of consciousness. A considerable proportion of these stimuli occur unconsciously, that is, subliminally. The fact that they are subliminal does not necessarily mean that their status is merely physiological, any more than this would be true of a psychic content. Sometimes they are capable of crossing the threshold, that is, of becoming perceptions. But there is no doubt that a large proportion of these endosomatic stimuli are simply incapable of consciousness and are so elementary that there is no reason to assign them a psychic nature—unless of course one favours the philosophical view that all life-processes are psychic anyway. The chief objection to this hardly demonstrable hypothesis is that it enlarges the concept of the psyche beyond all bounds and interprets the life-process in a way not absolutely warranted by the facts. Concepts that are too broad usually prove to be unsuitable instruments because they are too vague and nebulous. I have therefore suggested that the term "psychic" be used only where there is evidence of a will capable of modifying reflex or instinctual processes. Here I must refer the reader to my paper "On the Nature of the Psyche," [1] where I have discussed this definition of the "psychic" at somewhat greater length.

4   The somatic basis of the ego consists, then, of conscious and unconscious factors. The same is true of the psychic basis: on the one hand the ego rests on the *total field of consciousness,* and on the other, on the *sum total of unconscious contents.* These fall into three groups: first, temporarily subliminal contents that can be reproduced voluntarily (memory); second, unconscious contents that cannot be reproduced voluntarily; third, contents that are not capable of becoming conscious at all. Group two can be inferred from the spontaneous irruption of subliminal contents into consciousness. Group three is hypothetical; it is a logical inference from the facts underlying group two. It contains contents which have *not yet* irrupted into consciousness, or which never will.

5   When I said that the ego "rests" on the total field of consciousness I do not mean that it *consists* of this. Were that so, it would be indistinguishable from the field of consciousness as a whole. The ego is only the latter's point of reference, grounded on and limited by the somatic factor described above.

1 Pars. 371ff.

6   Although its bases are in themselves relatively unknown and unconscious, the ego is a conscious factor par excellence. It is even acquired, empirically speaking, during the individual's lifetime. It seems to arise in the first place from the collision between the somatic factor and the environment, and, once established as a subject, it goes on developing from further collisions with the outer world and the inner.

7   Despite the unlimited extent of its bases, the ego is never more and never less than consciousness as a whole. As a conscious factor the ego could, theoretically at least, be described completely. But this would never amount to more than a picture of the *conscious personality;* all those features which are unknown or unconscious to the subject would be missing. A total picture would have to include these. But a total description of the personality is, even in theory, absolutely impossible, because the unconscious portion of it cannot be grasped cognitively. This unconscious portion, as experience has abundantly shown, is by no means unimportant. On the contrary, the most decisive qualities in a person are often unconscious and can be perceived only by others, or have to be laboriously discovered with outside help.

8   Clearly, then, the *personality as a total phenomenon* does not coincide with the ego, that is, with the conscious personality, but forms an entity that has to be distinguished from the ego. Naturally the need to do this is incumbent only on a psychology that reckons with the fact of the unconscious, but for such a psychology the distinction is of paramount importance. Even for jurisprudence it should be of some importance whether certain psychic facts are conscious or not—for instance, in adjudging the question of responsibility.

9   I have suggested calling the total personality which, though present, cannot be fully known, the *self.* The ego is, by definition, subordinate to the self and is related to it like a part to the whole. Inside the field of consciousness it has, as we say, free will. By this I do not mean anything philosophical, only the well-known psychological fact of "free choice," or rather the subjective feeling of freedom. But, just as our free will clashes with necessity in the outside world, so also it finds its limits outside the field of consciousness in the subjective inner world, where it comes into conflict with the facts of the self. And just as

circumstances or outside events "happen" to us and limit our freedom, so the self acts upon the ego like an *objective occurrence* which free will can do very little to alter. It is, indeed, well known that the ego not only can do nothing against the self, but is sometimes actually assimilated by unconscious components of the personality that are in the process of development and is greatly altered by them.

¹⁰ It is, in the nature of the case, impossible to give any general description of the ego except a formal one. Any other mode of observation would have to take account of the *individuality* which attaches to the ego as one of its main characteristics. Although the numerous elements composing this complex factor are, in themselves, everywhere the same, they are infinitely varied as regards clarity, emotional colouring, and scope. The result of their combination—the ego—is therefore, so far as one can judge, individual and unique, and retains its identity up to a certain point. Its stability is relative, because far-reaching changes of personality can sometimes occur. Alterations of this kind need not always be pathological; they can also be developmental and hence fall within the scope of the normal.

¹¹ Since it is the point of reference for the field of consciousness, the ego is the subject of all successful attempts at adaptation so far as these are achieved by the will. The ego therefore has a significant part to play in the psychic economy. Its position there is so important that there are good grounds for the prejudice that the ego is the centre of the personality, and that the field of consciousness is the psyche *per se*. If we discount certain suggestive ideas in Leibniz, Kant, Schelling, and Schopenhauer, and the philosophical excursions of Carus and von Hartmann, it is only since the end of the nineteenth century that modern psychology, with its inductive methods, has discovered the foundations of consciousness and proved empirically the existence of a psyche outside consciousness. With this discovery the position of the ego, till then absolute, became relativized; that is to say, though it retains its quality as the centre of the field of consciousness, it is questionable whether it is the centre of the personality. It is part of the personality but not the whole of it. As I have said, it is simply impossible to estimate how large or how small its share is; how free or how dependent it is on the qualities of this "extra-conscious" psyche. We can only say that

its freedom is limited and its dependence proved in ways that are often decisive. In my experience one would do well not to underestimate its dependence on the unconscious. Naturally there is no need to say this to persons who already overestimate the latter's importance. Some criterion for the right measure is afforded by the psychic consequences of a wrong estimate, a point to which we shall return later on.

12   We have seen that, from the standpoint of the psychology of consciousness, the unconscious can be divided into three groups of contents. But from the standpoint of the psychology of the personality a twofold division ensues: an "extra-conscious" psyche whose contents are *personal,* and an "extra-conscious" psyche whose contents are *impersonal* and *collective.* The first group comprises contents which are integral components of the individual personality and could therefore just as well be conscious; the second group forms, as it were, an omnipresent, unchanging, and everywhere identical *quality or substrate of the psyche per se.* This is, of course, no more than a hypothesis. But we are driven to it by the peculiar nature of the empirical material, not to mention the high probability that the general similarity of psychic processes in all individuals must be based on an equally general and impersonal principle that conforms to law, just as the instinct manifesting itself in the individual is only the partial manifestation of an instinctual substrate common to all men.

II

THE SHADOW

¹³   Whereas the contents of the personal unconscious are acquired during the individual's lifetime, the contents of the collective unconscious are invariably archetypes that were present
from the beginning. Their relation to the instincts has been discussed elsewhere.[1] The archetypes most clearly characterized
from the empirical point of view are those which have the most
frequent and the most disturbing influence on the ego. These
are the *shadow,* the *anima,* and the *animus.*[2] The most accessible
of these, and the easiest to experience, is the shadow, for its
nature can in large measure be inferred from the contents of the
personal unconscious. The only exceptions to this rule are those
rather rare cases where the positive qualities of the personality
are repressed, and the ego in consequence plays an essentially
negative or unfavourable role.

¹⁴   The shadow is a moral problem that challenges the whole
ego-personality, for no one can become conscious of the shadow
without considerable moral effort. To become conscious of it
involves recognizing the dark aspects of the personality as present and real. This act is the essential condition for any kind of
self-knowledge, and it therefore, as a rule, meets with considerable resistance. Indeed, self-knowledge as a psychotherapeutic
measure frequently requires much painstaking work extending
over a long period.

¹⁵   Closer examination of the dark characteristics—that is, the
inferiorities constituting the shadow—reveals that they have an
emotional nature, a kind of autonomy, and accordingly an ob-
sessive or, better, possessive quality. Emotion, incidentally, is

---

[1] "Instinct and the Unconscious" and "On the Nature of the Psyche," pars. 397ff.
[2] The contents of this and the following chapter are taken from a lecture delivered to the Swiss Society for Practical Psychology, in Zurich, 1948. The material
was first published in the *Wiener Zeitschrift für Nervenheilkunde und deren
Grenzgebiete,* I (1948) : 4.

not an activity of the individual but something that happens to him. Affects occur usually where adaptation is weakest, and at the same time they reveal the reason for its weakness, namely a certain degree of inferiority and the existence of a lower level of personality. On this lower level with its uncontrolled or scarcely controlled emotions one behaves more or less like a primitive, who is not only the passive victim of his affects but also singularly incapable of moral judgment.

16   Although, with insight and good will, the shadow can to some extent be assimilated into the conscious personality, experience shows that there are certain features which offer the most obstinate resistance to moral control and prove almost impossible to influence. These resistances are usually bound up with *projections,* which are not recognized as such, and their recognition is a moral achievement beyond the ordinary. While some traits peculiar to the shadow can be recognized without too much difficulty as one's own personal qualities, in this case both insight and good will are unavailing because the cause of the emotion appears to lie, beyond all possibility of doubt, in the *other person.* No matter how obvious it may be to the neutral observer that it is a matter of projections, there is little hope that the subject will perceive this himself. He must be convinced that he throws a very long shadow before he is willing to withdraw his emotionally-toned projections from their object.

17   Let us suppose that a certain individual shows no inclination whatever to recognize his projections. The projection-making factor then has a free hand and can realize its object—if it has one—or bring about some other situation characteristic of its power. As we know, it is not the conscious subject but the unconscious which does the projecting. Hence one meets with projections, one does not make them. The effect of projection is to isolate the subject from his environment, since instead of a real relation to it there is now only an illusory one. Projections change the world into the replica of one's own unknown face. In the last analysis, therefore, they lead to an autoerotic or autistic condition in which one dreams a world whose reality remains forever unattainable. The resultant *sentiment d'incomplétude* and the still worse feeling of sterility are in their turn explained by projection as the malevolence of the environment, and by means of this vicious circle the isolation is intensified. The more

projections are thrust in between the subject and the environment, the harder it is for the ego to see through its illusions. A forty-five-year-old patient who had suffered from a compulsion neurosis since he was twenty and had become completely cut off from the world once said to me: "But I can never admit to myself that I've wasted the best twenty-five years of my life!"

18   It is often tragic to see how blatantly a man bungles his own life and the lives of others yet remains totally incapable of seeing how much the whole tragedy originates in himself, and how he continually feeds it and keeps it going. Not *consciously*, of course—for consciously he is engaged in bewailing and cursing a faithless world that recedes further and further into the distance. Rather, it is an unconscious factor which spins the illusions that veil his world. And what is being spun is a cocoon, which in the end will completely envelop him.

19   One might assume that projections like these, which are so very difficult if not impossible to dissolve, would belong to the realm of the shadow—that is, to the negative side of the personality. This assumption becomes untenable after a certain point, because the symbols that then appear no longer refer to the same but to the opposite sex, in a man's case to a woman and vice versa. The source of projections is no longer the shadow—which is always of the same sex as the subject—but a contrasexual figure. Here we meet the animus of a woman and the anima of a man, two corresponding archetypes whose autonomy and unconsciousness explain the stubbornness of their projections. Though the shadow is a motif as well known to mythology as anima and animus, it represents first and foremost the personal unconscious, and its content can therefore be made conscious without too much difficulty. In this it differs from anima and animus, for whereas the shadow can be seen through and recognized fairly easily, the anima and animus are much further away from consciousness and in normal circumstances are seldom if ever realized. With a little self-criticism one can see through the shadow—so far as its nature is personal. But when it appears as an archetype, one encounters the same difficulties as with anima and animus. In other words, it is quite within the bounds of possibility for a man to recognize the relative evil of his nature, but it is a rare and shattering experience for him to gaze into the face of absolute evil.

III

THE SYZYGY: ANIMA AND ANIMUS

20   What, then, is this projection-making factor? The East calls
it the "Spinning Woman" [1]—Maya, who creates illusion by her
dancing. Had we not long since known it from the symbolism
of dreams, this hint from the Orient would put us on the right
track: the enveloping, embracing, and devouring element points
unmistakably to the mother,[2] that is, to the son's relation to the
real mother, to her imago, and to the woman who is to become
a mother for him. His Eros is passive like a child's; he hopes to
be caught, sucked in, enveloped, and devoured. He seeks, as it
were, the protecting, nourishing, charmed circle of the mother,
the condition of the infant released from every care, in which
the outside world bends over him and even forces happiness
upon him. No wonder the real world vanishes from sight!

21   If this situation is dramatized, as the unconscious usually
dramatizes it, then there appears before you on the psychological
stage a man living regressively, seeking his childhood and his
mother, fleeing from a cold cruel world which denies him understanding. Often a mother appears beside him who apparently
shows not the slightest concern that her little son should become
a man, but who, with tireless and self-immolating effort, neglects
nothing that might hinder him from growing up and marrying.
You behold the secret conspiracy between mother and son, and
how each helps the other to betray life.

22   Where does the guilt lie? With the mother, or with the son?
Probably with both. The unsatisfied longing of the son for life
and the world ought to be taken seriously. There is in him a

1 Erwin Rousselle, "Seelische Führung im lebenden Taoismus," Pl. I, pp. 150, 170.
Rousselle calls the spinning woman the "animal soul." There is a saying that
runs, "The spinner sets in motion." I have defined the anima as a personification
of the unconscious.
2 Here and in what follows, the word "mother" is not meant in the literal sense
but as a symbol of everything that functions as a mother.

desire to touch reality, to embrace the earth and fructify the field of the world. But he makes no more than a series of fitful starts, for his initiative as well as his staying power are crippled by the secret memory that the world and happiness may be had as a gift—from the mother. The fragment of world which he, like every man, must encounter again and again is never quite the right one, since it does not'fall into his lap, does not meet him half way, but remains resistant, has to be conquered, and submits only to force. It makes demands on the masculinity of a man, on his ardour, above all on his courage and resolution when it comes to throwing his whole being into the scales. For this he would need a faithless Eros, one capable of forgetting his mother and undergoing the pain of relinquishing the first love of his life. The mother, foreseeing this danger, has carefully inculcated into him the virtues of faithfulness, devotion, loyalty, so as to protect him from the moral disruption which is the risk of every life adventure. He has learnt these lessons only too well, and remains true to his mother. This naturally causes her the deepest anxiety (when, to her greater glory, he turns out to be a homosexual, for example) and at the same time affords her an unconscious satisfaction that is positively mythological. For, in the relationship now reigning between them, there is consummated the immemorial and most sacred archetype of the marriage of mother and son. What, after all, has commonplace reality to offer, with its registry offices, pay envelopes, and monthly rent, that could outweigh the mystic awe of the *hieros gamos*? Or the star-crowned woman whom the dragon pursues, or the pious obscurities veiling the marriage of the Lamb?

23   This myth, better than any other, illustrates the nature of the collective unconscious. At this level the mother is both old and young, Demeter and Persephone, and the son is spouse and sleeping suckling rolled into one. The imperfections of real life, with its laborious adaptations and manifold disappointments, naturally cannot compete with such a state of indescribable fulfilment.

24   In the case of the son, the projection-making factor is identical with the mother-imago, and this is consequently taken to be the real mother. The projection can only be dissolved when the son sees that in the realm of his psyche there is an imago not only of the mother but of the daughter, the sister, the beloved,

the heavenly goddess, and the chthonic Baubo. Every mother and every beloved is forced to become the carrier and embodiment of this omnipresent and ageless image, which corresponds to the deepest reality in a man. It belongs to him, this perilous image of Woman; she stands for the loyalty which in the interests of life he must sometimes forgo; she is the much needed compensation for the risks, struggles, sacrifices that all end in disappointment; she is the solace for all the bitterness of life. And, at the same time, she is the great illusionist, the seductress, who draws him into life with her Maya—and not only into life's reasonable and useful aspects, but into its frightful paradoxes and ambivalences where good and evil, success and ruin, hope and despair, counterbalance one another. Because she is his greatest danger she demands from a man his greatest, and if he has it in him she will receive it.

25   This image is "My Lady Soul," as Spitteler called her. I have suggested instead the term "anima," as indicating something specific, for which the expression "soul" is too general and too vague. The empirical reality summed up under the concept of the anima forms an extremely dramatic content of the unconscious. It is possible to describe this content in rational, scientific language, but in this way one entirely fails to express its living character. Therefore, in describing the living processes of the psyche, I deliberately and consciously give preference to a dramatic, mythological way of thinking and speaking, because this is not only more expressive but also more exact than an abstract scientific terminology, which is wont to toy with the notion that its theoretic formulations may one fine day be resolved into algebraic equations.

26   The projection-making factor is the anima, or rather the unconscious as represented by the anima. Whenever she appears, in dreams, visions, and fantasies, she takes on personified form, thus demonstrating that the factor she embodies possesses all the outstanding characteristics of a feminine being.[3] She is not an invention of the conscious, but a spontaneous product of the

---

[3] Naturally, she is a typical figure in *belles-lettres*. Recent publications on the subject of the anima include Linda Fierz-David, *The Dream of Poliphilo*, and my "Psychology of the Transference." The anima as a psychological idea first appears in the 16th-cent. humanist Richardus Vitus. Cf. my *Mysterium Coniunctionis*, pars. 91ff.

unconscious. Nor is she a substitute figure for the mother. On the contrary, there is every likelihood that the numinous qualities which make the mother-imago so dangerously powerful derive from the collective archetype of the anima, which is incarnated anew in every male child.

27   Since the anima is an archetype that is found in men, it is reasonable to suppose that an equivalent archetype must be present in women; for just as the man is compensated by a feminine element, so woman is compensated by a masculine one. I do not, however, wish this argument to give the impression that these compensatory relationships were arrived at by deduction. On the contrary, long and varied experience was needed in order to grasp the nature of anima and animus empirically. Whatever we have to say about these archetypes, therefore, is either directly verifiable or at least rendered probable by the facts. At the same time, I am fully aware that we are discussing pioneer work which by its very nature can only be provisional.

28   Just as the mother seems to be the first carrier of the projection-making factor for the son, so is the father for the daughter. Practical experience of these relationships is made up of many individual cases presenting all kinds of variations on the same basic theme. A concise description of them can, therefore, be no more than schematic.

29   Woman is compensated by a masculine element and therefore her unconscious has, so to speak, a masculine imprint. This results in a considerable psychological difference between men and women, and accordingly I have called the projection-making factor in women the animus, which means mind or spirit. The animus corresponds to the paternal Logos just as the anima corresponds to the maternal Eros. But I do not wish or intend to give these two intuitive concepts too specific a definition. I use Eros and Logos merely as conceptual aids to describe the fact that woman's consciousness is characterized more by the connective quality of Eros than by the discrimination and cognition associated with Logos. In men, Eros, the function of relationship, is usually less developed than Logos. In women, on the other hand, Eros is an expression of their true nature, while their Logos is often only a regrettable accident. It gives rise to misunderstandings and annoying interpretations in the family

circle and among friends. This is because it consists of *opinions* instead of reflections, and by opinions I mean *a priori* assumptions that lay claim to absolute truth. Such assumptions, as everyone knows, can be extremely irritating. As the animus is partial to argument, he can best be seen at work in disputes where both parties know they are right. Men can argue in a very womanish way, too, when they are anima-possessed and have thus been transformed into the animus of their own anima. With them the question becomes one of personal vanity and touchiness (as if they were females); with women it is a question of *power,* whether of truth or justice or some other "ism"—for the dressmaker and hairdresser have already taken care of their vanity. The "Father" (i.e., the sum of conventional opinions) always plays a great role in female argumentation. No matter how friendly and obliging a woman's Eros may be, no logic on earth can shake her if she is ridden by the animus. Often the man has the feeling—and he is not altogether wrong—that only seduction or a beating or rape would have the necessary power of persuasion. He is unaware that this highly dramatic situation would instantly come to a banal and unexciting end if he were to quit the field and let a second woman carry on the battle (his wife, for instance, if she herself is not the fiery war horse). This sound idea seldom or never occurs to him, because no man can converse with an animus for five minutes without becoming the victim of his own anima. Anyone who still had enough sense of humour to listen objectively to the ensuing dialogue would be staggered by the vast number of commonplaces, misapplied truisms, clichés from newspapers and novels, shopsoiled platitudes of every description interspersed with vulgar abuse and brain-splitting lack of logic. It is a dialogue which, irrespective of its participants, is repeated millions and millions of times in all the languages of the world and always remains essentially the same.

30   This singular fact is due to the following circumstance: when animus and anima meet, the animus draws his sword of power and the anima ejects her poison of illusion and seduction. The outcome need not always be negative, since the two are equally likely to fall in love (a special instance of love at first sight). The language of love is of astonishing uniformity, using the well-worn formulas with the utmost devotion and fidelity,

so that once again the two partners find themselves in a banal collective situation. Yet they live in the illusion that they are related to one another in a most individual way.

31   In both its positive and its negative aspects the anima/animus relationship is always full of "animosity," i.e., it is emotional, and hence collective. Affects lower the level of the relationship and bring it closer to the common instinctual basis, which no longer has anything individual about it. Very often the relationship runs its course heedless of its human performers, who afterwards do not know what happened to them.

32   Whereas the cloud of "animosity" surrounding the man is composed chiefly of sentimentality and resentment, in woman it expresses itself in the form of opinionated views, interpretations, insinuations, and misconstructions, which all have the purpose (sometimes attained) of severing the relation between two human beings. The woman, like the man, becomes wrapped in a veil of illusions by her demon-familiar, and, as the daughter who alone understands her father (that is, is eternally right in everything), she is translated to the land of sheep, where she is put to graze by the shepherd of her soul, the animus.

33   Like the anima, the animus too has a positive aspect. Through the figure of the father he expresses not only conventional opinion but—equally—what we call "spirit," philosophical or religious ideas in particular, or rather the attitude resulting from them. Thus the animus is a psychopomp, a mediator between the conscious and the unconscious and a personification of the latter. Just as the anima becomes, through integration, the Eros of consciousness, so the animus becomes a Logos; and in the same way that the anima gives relationship and relatedness to a man's consciousness, the animus gives to woman's consciousness a capacity for reflection, deliberation, and self-knowledge.

34   The effect of anima and animus on the ego is in principle the same. This effect is extremely difficult to eliminate because, in the first place, it is uncommonly strong and immediately fills the ego-personality with an unshakable feeling of rightness and righteousness. In the second place, the cause of the effect is projected and appears to lie in objects and objective situations. Both these characteristics can, I believe, be traced back to the peculiarities of the archetype. For the archetype, of course, exists

16

a priori. This may possibly explain the often totally irrational yet undisputed and indisputable existence of certain moods and opinions. Perhaps these are so notoriously difficult to influence because of the powerfully suggestive effect emanating from the archetype. Consciousness is fascinated by it, held captive, as if hypnotized. Very often the ego experiences a vague feeling of moral defeat and then behaves all the more defensively, defiantly, and self-righteously, thus setting up a vicious circle which only increases its feeling of inferiority. The bottom is then knocked out of the human relationship, for, like megalomania, a feeling of inferiority makes mutual recognition impossible, and without this there is no relationship.

35   As I said, it is easier to gain insight into the shadow than into the anima or animus. With the shadow, we have the advantage of being prepared in some sort by our education, which has always endeavoured to convince people that they are not one-hundred-per-cent pure gold. So everyone immediately understands what is meant by "shadow," "inferior personality," etc. And if he has forgotten, his memory can easily be refreshed by a Sunday sermon, his wife, or the tax collector. With the anima and animus, however, things are by no means so simple. Firstly, there is no moral education in this respect, and secondly, most people are content to be self-righteous and prefer mutual vilification (if nothing worse!) to the recognition of their projections. Indeed, it seems a very natural state of affairs for men to have irrational moods and women irrational opinions. Presumably this situation is grounded on instinct and must remain as it is to ensure that the Empedoclean game of the hate and love of the elements shall continue for all eternity. Nature is conservative and does not easily allow her courses to be altered; she defends in the most stubborn way the inviolability of the preserves where anima and animus roam. Hence it is much more difficult to become conscious of one's anima/animus projections than to acknowledge one's shadow side. One has, of course, to overcome certain moral obstacles, such as vanity, ambition, conceit, resentment, etc., but in the case of projections all sorts of purely intellectual difficulties are added, quite apart from the contents of the projection which one simply doesn't know how to cope with. And on top of all this there arises a profound doubt as to whether one is not meddling too much with nature's

17

business by prodding into consciousness things which it would have been better to leave asleep.

36   Although there are, in my experience, a fair number of people who can understand without special intellectual or moral difficulties what is meant by anima and animus, one finds very many more who have the greatest trouble in visualizing these empirical concepts as anything concrete. This shows that they fall a little outside the usual range of experience. They are unpopular precisely because they seem unfamiliar. The consequence is that they mobilize prejudice and become taboo like everything else that is unexpected.

37   So if we set it up as a kind of requirement that projections should be dissolved, because it is wholesomer that way and in every respect more advantageous, we are entering upon new ground. Up till now everybody has been convinced that the idea "my father," "my mother," etc., is nothing but a faithful reflection of the real parent, corresponding in every detail to the original, so that when someone says "my father" he means no more and no less than what his father is in reality. This is actually what he supposes he does mean, but a supposition of identity by no means brings that identity about. This is where the fallacy of the *enkekalymmenos* ('the veiled one') comes in.[4] If one includes in the psychological equation X's picture of his father, which he takes for the real father, the equation will not work out, because the unknown quantity he has introduced does not tally with reality. X has overlooked the fact that his idea of a person consists, in the first place, of the possibly very incomplete picture he has received of the real person and, in the second place, of the subjective modifications he has imposed upon this picture. X's idea of his father is a complex quantity for which the real father is only in part responsible, an indefinitely larger share falling to the son. So true is this that every time he criticizes or praises his father he is unconsciously hitting back at himself, thereby bringing about those psychic consequences that overtake people who habitually disparage or overpraise themselves. If, however, X carefully compares his reactions with reality, he stands a chance of noticing that he has miscalculated

[4] The fallacy, which stems from Eubulides the Megarian, runs: "Can you recognize your father?" Yes. "Can you recognize this veiled one?" No. "This veiled one is your father. Hence you can recognize your father and not recognize him."

somewhere by not realizing long ago from his father's behaviour that the picture he has of him is a false one. But as a rule X is convinced that he is right, and if anybody is wrong it must be the other fellow. Should X have a poorly developed Eros, he will be either indifferent to the inadequate relationship he has with his father or else annoyed by the inconsistency and general incomprehensibility of a father whose behaviour never really corresponds to the picture X has of him. Therefore X thinks he has every right to feel hurt, misunderstood, and even betrayed.

8   One can imagine how desirable it would be in such cases to dissolve the projection. And there are always optimists who believe that the golden age can be ushered in simply by telling people the right way to go. But just let them try to explain to these people that they are acting like a dog chasing its own tail. To make a person see the shortcomings of his attitude considerably more than mere "telling" is needed, for more is involved than ordinary common sense can allow. What one is up against here is the kind of fateful misunderstanding which, under ordinary conditions, remains forever inaccessible to insight. It is rather like expecting the average respectable citizen to recognize himself as a criminal.

9   I mention all this just to illustrate the order of magnitude to which the anima/animus projections belong, and the moral and intellectual exertions that are needed to dissolve them. Not all the contents of the anima and animus are projected, however. Many of them appear spontaneously in dreams and so on, and many more can be made conscious through active imagination. In this way we find that thoughts, feelings, and affects are alive in us which we would never have believed possible. Naturally, possibilities of this sort seem utterly fantastic to anyone who has not experienced them himself, for a normal person "knows what he thinks." Such a childish attitude on the part of the "normal person" is simply the rule, so that no one without experience in this field can be expected to understand the real nature of anima and animus. With these reflections one gets into an entirely new world of psychological experience, provided of course that one succeeds in realizing it in practice. Those who do succeed can hardly fail to be impressed by all that the ego does not know and never has known. This increase in self-knowledge is still very rare nowadays and is usually

paid for in advance with a neurosis, if not with something worse.

40   The autonomy of the collective unconscious expresses itself in the figures of anima and animus. They personify those of its contents which, when withdrawn from projection, can be integrated into consciousness. To this extent, both figures represent *functions* which filter the contents of the collective unconscious through to the conscious mind. They appear or behave as such, however, only so long as the tendencies of the conscious and unconscious do not diverge too greatly. Should any tension arise, these functions, harmless till then, confront the conscious mind in personified form and behave rather like systems split off from the personality, or like part souls. This comparison is inadequate in so far as nothing previously belonging to the ego-personality has split off from it; on the contrary, the two figures represent a disturbing accretion. The reason for their behaving in this way is that though the *contents* of anima and animus can be integrated they themselves cannot, since they are archetypes. As such they are the foundation stones of the psychic structure, which in its totality exceeds the limits of consciousness and therefore can never become the object of direct cognition. Though the effects of anima and animus can be made conscious, they themselves are factors transcending consciousness and beyond the reach of perception and volition. Hence they remain autonomous despite the integration of their contents, and for this reason they should be borne constantly in mind. This is extremely important from the therapeutic standpoint, because constant observation pays the unconscious a tribute that more or less guarantees its co-operation. The unconscious as we know can never be "done with" once and for all. It is, in fact, one of the most important tasks of psychic hygiene to pay continual attention to the symptomatology of unconscious contents and processes, for the good reason that the conscious mind is always in danger of becoming one-sided, of keeping to well-worn paths and getting stuck in blind alleys. The complementary and compensating function of the unconscious ensures that these dangers, which are especially great in neurosis, can in some measure be avoided. It is only under ideal conditions, when life is still simple and unconscious enough to follow the serpentine path of instinct without hesitation or misgiving, that the compensation works with entire success. The more civilized, the more con-

scious and complicated a man is, the less he is able to follow his instincts. His complicated living conditions and the influence of his environment are so strong that they drown the quiet voice of nature. Opinions, beliefs, theories, and collective tendencies appear in its stead and back up all the aberrations of the conscious mind. Deliberate attention should then be given to the unconscious so that the compensation can set to work. Hence it is especially important to picture the archetypes of the unconscious not as a rushing phantasmagoria of fugitive images but as constant, autonomous factors, which indeed they are.

41   Both these archetypes, as practical experience shows, possess a fatality that can on occasion produce tragic results. They are quite literally the father and mother of all the disastrous entanglements of fate and have long been recognized as such by the whole world. Together they form a divine pair,[5] one of whom, in accordance with his Logos nature, is characterized by *pneuma* and *nous,* rather like Hermes with his ever-shifting hues, while the other, in accordance with her Eros nature, wears the features of Aphrodite, Helen (Selene), Persephone, and Hecate. Both of them are unconscious powers, "gods" in fact, as the ancient world quite rightly conceived them to be. To call them by this name is to give them that central position in the scale of psychological values which has always been theirs whether consciously acknowledged or not; for their power grows in proportion to the degree that they remain unconscious. Those who do not see them are in their hands, just as a typhus epidemic flourishes best when its source is undiscovered. Even in Christianity the divine syzygy has not become obsolete, but occupies the highest place as Christ and his bride the Church.[6] Parallels like these prove extremely helpful in our attempts to find the right

5 Naturally this is not meant as a psychological definition, let alone a metaphysical one. As I pointed out in "The Relations between the Ego and the Unconscious" (pars. 296ff.), the syzygy consists of three elements: the femininity pertaining to the man and the masculinity pertaining to the woman; the experience which man has of woman and vice versa; and, finally, the masculine and feminine archetypal image. The first element can be integrated into the personality by the process of conscious realization, but the last one cannot.

6 "For the Scripture says, God made man male and female; the male is Christ, the female is the Church."—Second Epistle of Clement to the Corinthians, xiv, 2 (trans. by Lake, I, p. 151). In pictorial representations, Mary often takes the place of the Church.

criterion for gauging the significance of these two archetypes. What we can discover about them from the conscious side is so slight as to be almost imperceptible. It is only when we throw light into the dark depths of the psyche and explore the strange and tortuous paths of human fate that it gradually becomes clear to us how immense is the influence wielded by these two factors that complement our conscious life.

42   Recapitulating, I should like to emphasize that the integration of the shadow, or the realization of the personal unconscious, marks the first stage in the analytic process, and that without it a recognition of anima and animus is impossible. The shadow can be realized only through a relation to a partner, and anima and animus only through a relation to a partner of the opposite sex, because only in such a relation do their projections become operative. The recognition of the anima gives rise, in a man, to a triad, one third of which is transcendent: the masculine subject, the opposing feminine subject, and the transcendent anima. With a woman the situation is reversed. The missing fourth element that would make the triad a quaternity is, in a man, the archetype of the Wise Old Man, which I have not discussed here, and in a woman the Chthonic Mother. These four constitute a half immanent and half transcendent quaternity, an archetype which I have called the *marriage quaternio*.[7] The marriage quaternio provides a schema not only for the self but also for the structure of primitive society with its cross-cousin marriage, marriage classes, and division of settlements into quarters. The self, on the other hand, is a God-image, or at least cannot be distinguished from one. Of this the early Christian spirit was not ignorant, otherwise Clement of Alexandria could never have said that he who knows himself knows God.[8]

[7] "The Psychology of the Transference," pars. 425ff. Cf. infra, pars. 358ff., the Naassene *quaternio*.
[8] Cf. infra, par. 347.

IV

THE SELF [1]

43   We shall now turn to the question of whether the increase in self-knowledge resulting from the withdrawal of impersonal projections—in other words, the integration of the contents of the collective unconscious—exerts a specific influence on the ego-personality. To the extent that the integrated contents are *parts of the self,* we can expect this influence to be considerable. Their assimilation augments not only the area of the field of consciousness but also the importance of the ego, especially when, as usually happens, the ego lacks any critical approach to the unconscious. In that case it is easily overpowered and becomes identical with the contents that have been assimilated. In this way, for instance, a masculine consciousness comes under the influence of the anima and can even be possessed by her.

44   I have discussed the wider effects of the integration of unconscious contents elsewhere [2] and can therefore omit going into details here. I should only like to mention that the more numerous and the more significant the unconscious contents which are assimilated to the ego, the closer the approximation of the ego to the self, even though this approximation must be a never-ending process. This inevitably produces an inflation of the ego,[3] unless a critical line of demarcation is drawn between it and the unconscious figures. But this act of discrimination yields practical results only if it succeeds in fixing reasonable boundaries to the ego and in granting the figures of the unconscious—the self, anima, animus, and shadow—relative autonomy and reality

---

1 The material for this chapter is drawn from a paper, "Über das Selbst," published in the *Eranos-Jahrbuch 1948.*
2 "The Relations between the Ego and the Unconscious."
3 In the sense of the words used in I Cor. 5 : 2: "Inflati estis [πεφυσιώμενοι] et non magis luctum habuistis" (And you are puffed up, and have not rather mourned)—with reference to a case of tolerated incest with the mother ("that a man should have his father's wife").

(of a psychic nature). To psychologize this reality out of existence either is ineffectual, or else merely increases the inflation of the ego. One cannot dispose of facts by declaring them unreal. The projection-making factor, for instance, has undeniable reality. Anyone who insists on denying it becomes identical with it, which is not only dubious in itself but a positive danger to the well-being of the individual. Everyone who has dealings with such cases knows how perilous an inflation can be. No more than a flight of steps or a smooth floor is needed to precipitate a fatal fall. Besides the "pride goeth before a fall" motif there are other factors of a no less disagreeable psychosomatic and psychic nature which serve to reduce "puffed-up-ness." This condition should not be interpreted as one of conscious self-aggrandizement. Such is far from being the rule. In general we are not directly conscious of this condition at all, but can at best infer its existence indirectly from the symptoms. These include the reactions of our immediate environment. Inflation magnifies the blind spot in the eye, and the more we are assimilated by the projection-making factor, the greater becomes the tendency to identify with it. A clear symptom of this is our growing disinclination to take note of the reactions of the environment and pay heed to them.

45   It must be reckoned a psychic catastrophe when the *ego is assimilated by the self.* The image of wholeness then remains in the unconscious, so that on the one hand it shares the archaic nature of the unconscious and on the other finds itself in the psychically relative space-time continuum that is characteristic of the unconscious as such.[4] Both these qualities are numinous and hence have an unlimited determining effect on ego-consciousness, which is differentiated, i.e., separated, from the unconscious and moreover exists in an absolute space and an absolute time. It is a vital necessity that this should be so. If, therefore, the ego falls for any length of time under the control of an unconscious factor, its adaptation is disturbed and the way opened for all sorts of possible accidents.

46   Hence it is of the greatest importance that the ego should be anchored in the world of consciousness and that consciousness should be reinforced by a very precise adaptation. For this, certain virtues like attention, conscientiousness, patience, etc.,

4 Cf. "On the Nature of the Psyche," pars. 414ff., 439ff.

are of great value on the moral side, just as accurate observation of the symptomatology of the unconscious and objective self-criticism are valuable on the intellectual side.

7   However, accentuation of the ego personality and the world of consciousness may easily assume such proportions that the figures of the unconscious are psychologized and the *self consequently becomes assimilated to the ego*. Although this is the exact opposite of the process we have just described it is followed by the same result: inflation. The world of consciousness must now be levelled down in favour of the reality of the unconscious. In the first case, reality had to be protected against an archaic, "eternal" and "ubiquitous" dream-state; in the second, room must be made for the dream at the expense of the world of consciousness. In the first case, mobilization of all the virtues is indicated; in the second, the presumption of the ego can only be damped down by moral defeat. This is necessary, because otherwise one will never attain that median degree of modesty which is essential for the maintenance of a balanced state. It is not a question, as one might think, of relaxing morality itself but of making a moral effort in a different direction. For instance, a man who is not conscientious enough has to make a moral effort in order to come up to the mark; while for one who is sufficiently rooted in the world through his own efforts it is no small moral achievement to inflict defeat on his virtues by loosening his ties with the world and reducing his adaptive performance. (One thinks in this connection of Brother Klaus, now canonized, who for the salvation of his soul left his wife to her own devices, along with numerous progeny.)

48   Since real moral problems all begin where the penal code leaves off, their solution can seldom or never depend on precedent, much less on precepts and commandments. The real moral problems spring from *conflicts of duty*. Anyone who is sufficiently humble, or easy-going, can always reach a decision with the help of some outside authority. But one who trusts others as little as himself can never reach a decision at all, unless it is brought about in the manner which Common Law calls an "Act of God." The Oxford Dictionary defines this concept as the "action of uncontrollable natural forces." In all such cases there is an unconscious authority which puts an end to doubt by creating a *fait accompli*. (In the last analysis this is true also of

25

those who get their decision from a higher authority, only in more veiled form.) One can describe this authority either as the "will of God" or as an "action of uncontrollable natural forces," though psychologically it makes a good deal of difference how one thinks of it. The rationalistic interpretation of this inner authority as "natural forces" or the instincts satisfies the modern intellect but has the great disadvantage that the apparent victory of instinct offends our moral self-esteem; hence we like to persuade ourselves that the matter has been decided solely by the rational motions of the will. Civilized man has such a fear of the "crimen laesae maiestatis humanae" that whenever possible he indulges in a retrospective coloration of the facts in order to cover up the feeling of having suffered a moral defeat. He prides himself on what he believes to be his self-control and the omnipotence of his will, and despises the man who lets himself be outwitted by mere nature.

49   If, on the other hand, the inner authority is conceived as the "will of God" (which implies that "natural forces" are divine forces), our self-esteem is benefited because the decision then appears to be an act of obedience and the result a divine intention. This way of looking at it can, with some show of justice, be accused not only of being very convenient but of cloaking moral laxity in the mantle of virtue. The accusation, however, is justified only when one is in fact knowingly hiding one's own egoistic opinion behind a hypocritical façade of words. But this is by no means the rule, for in most cases instinctive tendencies assert themselves for or against one's subjective interests no matter whether an outside authority approves or not. The inner authority does not need to be consulted first, as it is present at the outset in the intensity of the tendencies struggling for decision. In this struggle the individual is never a spectator only; he takes part in it more or less "voluntarily" and tries to throw the weight of his feeling of moral freedom into the scales of decision. Nevertheless, it remains a matter of doubt how much his seemingly free decision has a causal, and possibly unconscious, motivation. This may be quite as much an "act of God" as any natural cataclysm. The problem seems to me unanswerable, because we do not know where the roots of the feeling of moral freedom lie; and yet they exist no less surely than the instincts, which are felt as compelling forces.

50   All in all, it is not only more beneficial but more "correct" psychologically to explain as the "will of God" the natural forces that appear in us as instincts. In this way we find ourselves living in harmony with the *habitus* of our ancestral psychic life; that is, we function as man has functioned at all times and in all places. The existence of this habitus is proof of its viability, for, if it were not viable, all those who obeyed it would long since have perished of maladaptation. On the other hand, by conforming to it one has a reasonable life expectancy. When an habitual way of thinking guarantees as much as this there is not only no ground for declaring it incorrect but, on the contrary, every reason to take it as "true" or "correct" in the psychological sense. Psychological truths are not metaphysical insights; they are habitual modes of thinking, feeling, and behaving which experience has proved appropriate and useful.

51   So when I say that the impulses which we find in ourselves should be understood as the "will of God," I wish to emphasize that they ought not to be regarded as an arbitrary wishing and willing, but as absolutes which one must learn how to handle correctly. The will can control them only in part. It may be able to suppress them, but it cannot alter their nature, and what is suppressed comes up again in another place in altered form, but this time loaded with a resentment that makes the otherwise harmless natural impulse our enemy. I should also like the term "God" in the phrase "the will of God" to be understood not so much in the Christian sense as in the sense intended by Diotima, when she said: "Eros, dear Socrates, is a mighty daemon." The Greek words *daimon* and *daimonion* express a determining power which comes upon man from outside, like providence or fate, though the ethical decision is left to man. He must know, however, what he is deciding about and what he is doing. Then, if he obeys he is following not just his own opinion, and if he rejects he is destroying not just his own invention.

52   The purely biological or scientific standpoint falls short in psychology because it is, in the main, intellectual only. That this should be so is not a disadvantage, since the methods of natural science have proved of great heuristic value in psychological research. But the psychic phenomenon cannot be grasped in its totality by the intellect, for it consists not only of *meaning* but also of *value*, and this depends on the intensity of the

accompanying feeling-tones. Hence at least the two "rational" functions [5] are needed in order to map out anything like a complete diagram of a given psychic content.

53   If, therefore, in dealing with psychic contents one makes allowance not only for intellectual judgments but for value judgments as well, not only is the result a more complete picture of the content in question, but one also gets a better idea of the particular position it holds in the hierarchy of psychic contents in general. The feeling-value is a very important criterion which psychology cannot do without, because it determines in large measure the role which the content will play in the psychic economy. That is to say, the affective value gives the measure of the intensity of an idea, and the intensity in its turn expresses that idea's energic tension, its effective potential. The shadow, for instance, usually has a decidedly negative feeling-value, while the anima, like the animus, has more of a positive one. Whereas the shadow is accompanied by more or less definite and describable feeling-tones, the anima and animus exhibit feeling qualities that are harder to define. Mostly they are felt to be fascinating or numinous. Often they are surrounded by an atmosphere of sensitivity, touchy reserve, secretiveness, painful intimacy, and even absoluteness. The relative autonomy of the anima- and animus-figures expresses itself in these qualities. In order of affective rank they stand to the shadow very much as the shadow stands in relation to ego-consciousness. The main affective emphasis seems to lie on the latter; at any rate it is able, by means of a considerable expenditure of energy, to repress the shadow, at least temporarily. But if for any reason the unconscious gains the upper hand, then the valency of the shadow and of the other figures increases proportionately, so that the scale of values is reversed. What lay furthest away from waking consciousness and seemed unconscious assumes, as it were, a threatening shape, and the affective value increases the higher up the scale you go: ego-consciousness, shadow, anima, self. This reversal of the conscious waking state occurs regularly during the transition from waking to sleeping, and what then emerge most vividly are the very things that were unconscious by day. Every *abaissement du niveau mental* brings about a relative reversal of values.

[5] Cf. *Psychological Types*, Defs., "Rational" and "Irrational."

28

54   I am speaking here of the *subjective* feeling-value, which is subject to the more or less periodic changes described above. But there are also *objective* values which are founded on a *consensus omnium*—moral, aesthetic, and religious values, for instance, and these are universally recognized ideals or feeling-toned collective ideas (Lévy-Bruhl's "représentations collectives").[6] The subjective feeling-tones or "value quanta" are easily recognized by the kind and number of constellations, or symptoms of disturbance,[7] they produce. Collective ideals often have no subjective feeling-tone, but nevertheless retain their feeling-value. This value, therefore, cannot be demonstrated by subjective symptoms, though it may be by the attributes attaching to these collective ideas and by their characteristic symbolism, quite apart from their suggestive effect.

55   The problem has a practical aspect, since it may easily happen that a collective idea, though significant in itself, is—because of its lack of subjective feeling-tone—represented in a dream only by a subsidiary attribute, as when a god is represented by his theriomorphic attribute, etc. Conversely, the idea may appear in consciousness lacking the affective emphasis that properly belongs to it, and must then be transposed back into its archetypal context—a task that is usually discharged by poets and prophets. Thus Hölderlin, in his "Hymn to Liberty," lets this concept, worn stale by frequent use and misuse, rise up again in its pristine splendour:

> Since her arm out of the dust has raised me,
> Beats my heart so boldly and serene;
> And my cheek still tingles with her kisses,
> Flushed and glowing where her lips have been.
> Every word she utters, by her magic
> Rises new-created, without flaw;
> Hearken to the tidings of my goddess,
> Hearken to the Sovereign, and adore! [8]

56   It is not difficult to see here that the idea of liberty has been changed back to its original dramatic state—into the shining

---

6 *Les Fonctions mentales dans les sociétés inférieures.*
7 "On Psychic Energy," pars. 14ff., 20ff.
8 *Sämtliche Werke*, I, p. 126.

figure of the anima, freed from the weight of the earth and the tyranny of the senses, the psychopomp who leads the way to the Elysian fields.

57 The first case we mentioned, where the collective idea is represented in a dream by a lowly aspect of itself, is certainly the more frequent: the "goddess" appears as a black cat, and the Deity as the *lapis exilis* (stone of no worth). Interpretation then demands a knowledge of certain things which have less to do with zoology and mineralogy than with the existence of an historical *consensus omnium* in regard to the object in question. These "mythological" aspects are always present, even though in a given case they may be unconscious. If for instance one doesn't happen to recall, when considering whether to paint the garden gate green or white, that green is the colour of life and hope, the symbolic aspect of "green" is nevertheless present as an unconscious *sous-entendu*. So we find something which has the highest significance for the life of the unconscious standing lowest on the scale of conscious values, and vice versa. The figure of the shadow already belongs to the realm of bodiless phantoms—not to speak of anima and animus, which do not seem to appear at all except as projections upon our fellow human beings. As for the self, it is completely outside the personal sphere, and appears, if at all, only as a religious mythologem, and its symbols range from the highest to the lowest. Anyone who identifies with the daylight half of his psychic life will therefore declare the dreams of the night to be null and void, notwithstanding that the night is as long as the day and that all consciousness is manifestly founded on unconsciousness, is rooted in it and every night is extinguished in it. What is more, psychopathology knows with tolerable certainty what the unconscious can do to the conscious, and for this reason devotes to the unconscious an attention that often seems incomprehensible to the layman. We know, for instance, that what is small by day is big at night, and the other way round; thus we also know that besides the small by day there always looms the big by night, even when it is invisible.

58 This knowledge is an essential prerequisite for any integration—that is to say a content can only be integrated when its double aspect has become conscious and when it is grasped not merely intellectually but understood according to its feeling-

value. Intellect and feeling, however, are difficult to put into one harness—they conflict with one another by definition. Whoever identifies with an intellectual standpoint will occasionally find his feeling confronting him like an enemy in the guise of the anima; conversely, an intellectual animus will make violent attacks on the feeling standpoint. Therefore, anyone who wants to achieve the difficult feat of realizing something not only intellectually, but also according to its feeling-value, must for better or worse come to grips with the anima/animus problem in order to open the way for a higher union, a *coniunctio oppositorum*. This is an indispensable prerequisite for wholeness.

59 Although "wholeness" seems at first sight to be nothing but an abstract idea (like anima and animus), it is nevertheless empirical in so far as it is anticipated by the psyche in the form of spontaneous or autonomous symbols. These are the quaternity or mandala symbols, which occur not only in the dreams of modern people who have never heard of them, but are widely disseminated in the historical records of many peoples and many epochs. Their significance as *symbols of unity and totality* is amply confirmed by history as well as by empirical psychology. What at first looks like an abstract idea stands in reality for something that exists and can be experienced, that demonstrates its *a priori* presence spontaneously. Wholeness is thus an objective factor that confronts the subject independently of him, like anima or animus; and just as the latter have a higher position in the hierarchy than the shadow, so wholeness lays claim to a position and a value superior to those of the syzygy. The syzygy seems to represent at least a substantial portion of it, if not actually two halves of the totality formed by the royal brother-sister pair, and hence the tension of opposites from which the divine child [9] is born as the symbol of unity.

60 Unity and totality stand at the highest point on the scale of objective values because their symbols can no longer be distinguished from the *imago Dei*. Hence all statements about the God-image apply also to the empirical symbols of totality. Experience shows that individual mandalas are symbols of *order*, and that they occur in patients principally during times of psychic

---

[9] Cf. my "Psychology of the Child Archetype"; also *Psychology and Alchemy,* index, s.v. "filius Philosophorum," "child," "hermaphrodite."

disorientation or re-orientation. As magic circles they bind and subdue the lawless powers belonging to the world of darkness, and depict or create an order that transforms the chaos into a cosmos.[10] The mandala at first comes into the conscious mind as an unimpressive point or dot,[11] and a great deal of hard and painstaking work as well as the integration of many projections are generally required before the full range of the symbol can be anything like completely understood. If this insight were purely intellectual it could be achieved without much difficulty, for the world-wide pronouncements about the God within us and above us, about Christ and the *corpus mysticum,* the personal and suprapersonal atman, etc., are all formulations that can easily be mastered by the philosophic intellect. This is the common source of the illusion that one is then in possession of the thing itself. But actually one has acquired nothing more than its name, despite the age-old prejudice that the name magically represents the thing, and that it is sufficient to pronounce the name in order to posit the thing's existence. In the course of the millennia the reasoning mind has been given every opportunity to see through the futility of this conceit, though that has done nothing to prevent the intellectual mastery of a thing from being accepted at its face value. It is precisely our experiences in psychology which demonstrate as plainly as could be wished that the intellectual "grasp" of a psychological fact produces no more than a concept of it, and that a concept is no more than a name, a *flatus vocis.* These intellectual counters can be bandied about easily enough. They pass lightly from hand to hand, for they have no weight or substance. They sound full but are hollow; and though purporting to designate a heavy task and obligation, they commit us to nothing. The intellect is undeniably useful in its own field, but is a great cheat and illusionist outside of it whenever it tries to manipulate values.

61   It would seem that one can pursue any science with the intellect alone except psychology, whose subject—the psyche—has more than the two aspects mediated by sense-perception and thinking. The function of value—feeling—is an integral part of our conscious orientation and ought not to be missing in a psychological judgment of any scope, otherwise the model we are trying to build of the real process will be incomplete. Every

---

[10] Cf. *Psychology and Alchemy,* Part II, ch. 3.   [11] [Cf. infra, par. 340.]

psychic process has a value quality attached to it, namely its feeling-tone. This indicates the degree to which the subject is *affected* by the process or how much it means to him (in so far as the process reaches consciousness at all). It is through the "affect" that the subject becomes involved and so comes to feel the whole weight of reality. The difference amounts roughly to that between a severe illness which one reads about in a textbook and the real illness which one has. In psychology one possesses nothing unless one has experienced it in reality. Hence a purely intellectual insight is not enough, because one knows only the words and not the substance of the thing from inside.

62　　There are far more people who are afraid of the unconscious than one would expect. They are even afraid of their own shadow. And when it comes to the anima and animus, this fear turns to panic. For the syzygy does indeed represent the psychic contents that irrupt into consciousness in a psychosis (most clearly of all in the paranoid forms of schizophrenia).[12] The overcoming of this fear is often a moral achievement of unusual magnitude, and yet it is not the only condition that must be fulfilled on the way to a real experience of the self.

63　　The shadow, the syzygy, and the self are psychic factors of which an adequate picture can be formed only on the basis of a fairly thorough experience of them. Just as these concepts arose out of an experience of reality, so they can be elucidated only by further experience. Philosophical criticism will find everything to object to in them unless it begins by recognizing that they are concerned with *facts,* and that the "concept" is simply an abbreviated description or definition of these facts. Such criticism has as little effect on the object as zoological criticism on a duck-billed platypus. It is not the concept that matters; the concept is only a word, a counter, and it has meaning and use only because it stands for a certain sum of experience. Unfortunately I cannot pass on this experience to my public. I have tried in a number of publications, with the help of case material, to present the nature of these experiences and also the method of obtaining them. Wherever my methods were really applied the facts I give have been confirmed. One could see the

12 A classic case is the one published by Nelken: "Analytische Beobachtungen über Phantasien eines Schizophrenen." Another is Schreber's *Memoirs of My Nervous Illness.*

moons of Jupiter even in Galileo's day if one took the trouble to use his telescope.

64   Outside the narrower field of professional psychology these figures meet with understanding from all who have any knowledge of comparative mythology. They have no difficulty in recognizing the shadow as the adverse representative of the dark chthonic world, a figure whose characteristics are universal. The syzygy is immediately comprehensible as the psychic prototype of all divine couples. Finally the self, on account of its empirical peculiarities, proves to be the *eidos* behind the supreme ideas of unity and totality that are inherent in all monotheistic and monistic systems.

65   I regard these parallels as important because it is possible, through them, to relate so-called *metaphysical* concepts, which have lost their root connection with natural experience, to living, universal psychic processes, so that they can recover their true and original meaning. In this way the connection is reestablished between the ego and projected contents now formulated as "metaphysical" ideas. Unfortunately, as already said, the fact that metaphysical ideas exist and are believed in does nothing to prove the actual existence of their content or of the object they refer to, although the coincidence of idea and reality in the form of a special psychic state, a state of grace, should not be deemed impossible, even if the subject cannot bring it about by an act of will. Once metaphysical ideas have lost their capacity to recall and evoke the original experience they have not only become useless but prove to be actual impediments on the road to wider development. One clings to possessions that have once meant wealth; and the more ineffective, incomprehensible, and lifeless they become the more obstinately people cling to them. (Naturally it is only sterile ideas that they cling to; living ideas have content and riches enough, so there is no need to cling to them.) Thus in the course of time the meaningful turns into the meaningless. This is unfortunately the fate of metaphysical ideas.

66   Today it is a real problem what on earth such ideas can mean. The world—so far as it has not completely turned its back on tradition—has long ago stopped wanting to hear a "message"; it would rather be told what the message means. The words that resound from the pulpit are incomprehensible and cry for an

explanation. How has the death of Christ brought us redemption when no one feels redeemed? In what way is Jesus a God-man and what is such a being? What is the Trinity about, and the parthenogenesis, the eating of the body and the drinking of the blood, and all the rest of it? What connection can there be between the world of such concepts and the everyday world, whose material reality is the concern of natural science on the widest possible scale? At least sixteen hours out of twenty-four we live exclusively in this everyday world, and the remaining eight we spend preferably in an unconscious condition. Where and when does anything take place to remind us even remotely of phenomena like angels, miraculous feedings, beatitudes, the resurrection of the dead, etc.? It was therefore something of a discovery to find that during the unconscious state of sleep intervals occur, called "dreams," which occasionally contain scenes having a not inconsiderable resemblance to the motifs of mythology. For myths are miracle tales and treat of all those things which, very often, are also objects of belief.

67 In the everyday world of consciousness such things hardly exist; that is to say, until 1933 only lunatics would have been found in possession of living fragments of mythology. After this date the world of heroes and monsters spread like a devastating fire over whole nations, proving that the strange world of myth had suffered no loss of vitality during the centuries of reason and enlightenment. If metaphysical ideas no longer have such a fascinating effect as before, this is certainly not due to any lack of primitivity in the European psyche, but simply and solely to the fact that the erstwhile symbols no longer express what is now welling up from the unconscious as the end-result of the development of Christian consciousness through the centuries. This end-result is a true *antimimon pneuma*, a false spirit of arrogance, hysteria, woolly-mindedness, criminal amorality, and doctrinaire fanaticism, a purveyor of shoddy spiritual goods, spurious art, philosophical stutterings, and Utopian humbug, fit only to be fed wholesale to the mass man of today. That is what the post-Christian spirit looks like.

V

CHRIST, A SYMBOL OF THE SELF

68   The dechristianization of our world, the Luciferian development of science and technology, and the frightful material and
moral destruction left behind by the second World War have
been compared more than once with the *eschatological* events
foretold in the New Testament. These, as we know, are concerned with the coming of the Antichrist: "This is Antichrist,
who denieth the Father and the Son." [1] "Every spirit that dis-
solveth Jesus . . . is Antichrist . . . of whom you have heard
that he cometh." [2] The Apocalypse is full of expectations of terrible things that will take place at the end of time, before the
marriage of the Lamb. This shows plainly that the *anima christiana* has a sure knowledge not only of the existence of an
adversary but also of his future usurpation of power.

69   Why—my reader will ask—do I discourse here upon Christ
and his adversary, the Antichrist? Our discourse necessarily
brings us to Christ, because he is the still living myth of our
culture. He is our culture hero, who, regardless of his historical
existence, embodies the myth of the divine Primordial Man, the
mystic Adam. It is he who occupies the centre of the Christian
mandala, who is the Lord of the Tetramorph, i.e., the four symbols of the evangelists, which are like the four columns of his
throne. He is in us and we in him. His kingdom is the pearl of
great price, the treasure buried in the field, the grain of mustard seed which will become a great tree, and the heavenly

---

[1] I John 2 : 22 (DV).

[2] I John 4 : 3 (DV). The traditional view of the Church is based on II Thessalonians 2 : 3ff., which speaks of the apostasy, of the ἄνθρωπος τῆς ἀνομίας (man of
lawlessness) and the υἱὸς τῆς ἀπωλείας (son of perdition) who herald the coming of
the Lord. This "lawless one" will set himself up in the place of God, but will
finally be slain by the Lord Jesus "with the breath of his mouth." He will work
wonders κατ' ἐνέργειαν τοῦ σατανᾶ (according to the working of Satan). Above all,
he will reveal himself by his *lying and deceitfulness.* Daniel 11 : 36ff. is regarded
as a prototype.

city.[3] As Christ is in us, so also is his heavenly kingdom.[4]
These few, familiar references should be sufficient to make
the psychological position of the Christ symbol quite clear.
Christ exemplifies the archetype of the self.[5] He represents a
totality of a divine or heavenly kind, a glorified man, a son of
God *sine macula peccati*, unspotted by sin. As *Adam secundus*
he corresponds to the first Adam before the Fall, when the latter
was still a pure image of God, of which Tertullian (d. 222) says:
"And this therefore is to be considered as the image of God in
man, that the human spirit has the same motions and senses as
God has, though not in the same way as God has them." [6] Origen
(185–254) is very much more explicit: The *imago Dei* imprinted
on the soul, not on the body,[7] is an image of an image, "for my
soul is not directly the image of God, but is made after the likeness of the former image." [8] Christ, on the other hand, is the

3 For "city" cf. *Psychology and Alchemy*, pp. 104ff.

4 Ἡ βασιλεία τοῦ θεοῦ ἐντὸς ὑμῶν ἔστιν (The kingdom of God is within you [or
"among you"]). "The kingdom of God cometh not with observation: neither shall
they say, Lo here! or, lo there!" for it is within and everywhere. (Luke 17 : 20f.)
"It is not of this [external] world." (John 18 : 36.) The likeness of the kingdom
of God to man is explicitly stated in the parable of the sower (Matthew 13 : 24.
Cf. also Matthew 13 : 45, 18 : 23, 22 : 2). The papyrus fragments from Oxyrhynchus say: . . . ἡ βασ[ιλεία τῶν οὐρανῶν] ἐντὸς ὑμῶν [ἐ]στι [καὶ ὅστις ἂν ἑαυτὸν]
γνῷ ταύτην εὑρή[σει] ἑαυτοὺς γνώσεσθε κτλ. (The kingdom of heaven is within you,
and whosoever knoweth himself shall find it. Know yourselves.) Cf. James, *The
Apocryphal New Testament*, p. 26, and Grenfell and Hunt, *New Sayings of
Jesus*, p. 15.

5 Cf. my observations on Christ as archetype in "A Psychological Approach to the
Dogma of the Trinity," pars. 226ff.

6 "Et haec ergo imago censenda est Dei in homine, quod eosdem motus et sensus
habeat humanus animus, quos et Deus, licet non tales quales Deus" (*Adv. Marcion.*, II, xvi; in Migne, *P.L.*, vol. 2, col. 304).

7 *Contra Celsum*, VIII, 49 (Migne, *P.G.*, vol. 11, col. 1590): "In anima, non in
corpore impressus sit imaginis conditoris character" (The character of the image
of the Creator is imprinted on the soul, not on the body). (Cf. trans. by H. Chadwick, p. 488.)

8 *In Lucam homilia*, VIII (Migne, *P.G.*, vol. 13, col. 1820): "Si considerem Dominum Salvatorem imaginem esse invisibilis Dei, et videam animam meam factam
ad imaginem conditoris, ut imago esset imaginis: neque enim anima mea spe-
cialiter imago est Dei, sed ad similitudinem imaginis prioris effecta est" (If I
consider that the Lord and Saviour is the image of the invisible God, I see that
my soul is made after the image of the Creator, so as to be an image of an image;
for my soul is not directly the image of God, but is made after the likeness of the
former image).

true image of God,[9] after whose likeness our inner man is made, invisible, incorporeal, incorrupt, and immortal.[10] The God-image in us reveals itself through "prudentia, iustitia, moderatio, virtus, sapientia et disciplina."[11]

71   St. Augustine (354–430) distinguishes between the God-image which is Christ and the image which is implanted in man as a means or possibility of becoming like God.[12] The God-image is not in the corporeal man, but in the *anima rationalis*, the possession of which distinguishes man from animals. "The God-image is within, not in the body. . . . Where the understanding is, where the mind is, where the power of investigating truth is, there God has his image."[13] Therefore we should remind ourselves, says Augustine, that we are fashioned after the image of God nowhere save in the understanding: ". . . but where man knows himself to be made after the image of God,

[9] *De principiis*, I, ii, 8 (Migne, *P.G.*, vol. 11, col. 156): "Salvator figura est substantiae vel subsistentiae Dei" (The Saviour is the figure of the substance or subsistence of God). *In Genesim homilia*, I, 13 (Migne, *P.G.*, vol. 12, col. 156): "Quae est ergo alia imago Dei ad cuius imaginis similitudinem factus est homo, nisi Salvator noster, qui est primogenitus omnis creaturae?" (What else therefore is the image of God after the likeness of which image man was made, but our Saviour, who is the first born of every creature?) *Selecta in Genesim*, IX, 6 (Migne, *P.G.*, vol. 12, col. 107): "Imago autem Dei invisibilis salvator" (But the image of the invisible God is the saviour).

[10] *In Gen. hom.*, I, 13 (Migne, *P.G.*, vol. 12, col. 155): "Is autem qui ad imaginem Dei factus est et ad similitudinem, interior homo noster est, invisibilis et incorporalis, et incorruptus atque immortalis" (But that which is made after the image and similitude of God is our inner man, invisible, incorporeal, incorrupt, and immortal).

[11] *De princip.*, IV, 37 (Migne, *P.G.*, vol. 11, col. 412).

[12] *Retractationes*, I, xxvi (Migne, *P.L.*, vol. 32, col. 626): "(Unigenitus) . . . tantummodo imago est, non ad imaginem" (The Only-Begotten . . . alone is the image, not after the image).

[13] *Enarrationes in Psalmos*, XLVIII, Sermo II (Migne, *P.L.*, vol. 36, col. 564): "Imago Dei intus est, non est in corpore . . . ubi est intellectus, ubi est mens, ubi ratio investigandae veritatis etc. ibi habet Deus imaginem suam." Also ibid., Psalm XLII, 6 (Migne, *P.L.*, vol. 36, col. 480): "Ergo intelligimus habere nos aliquid ubi imago Dei est, mentem scilicet atque rationem" (Therefore we understand that we have something in which the image of God is, namely mind and reason). Sermo XC, 10 (Migne, *P.L.*, vol. 38, col. 566): "Veritas quaeritur in Dei imagine" (Truth is sought in the image of God), but against this the *Liber de vera religione* says: "in interiore homine habitat veritas" (truth dwells in the inner man). From this it is clear that the *imago Dei* coincides with the *interior homo*.

there he knows there is something more in him than is given to the beasts." [14] From this it is clear that the God-image is, so to speak, identical with the *anima rationalis*. The latter is the higher spiritual man, the *homo coelestis* of St Paul.[15] Like Adam before the Fall, Christ is an embodiment of the God-image,[16] whose totality is specially emphasized by St. Augustine. "The Word," he says, "took on complete manhood, as it were in its fulness: the soul and body of a man. And if you would have me put it more exactly—since even a beast of the field has a 'soul' and a body—when I say a human soul and human flesh, I mean he took upon him a complete human soul." [17]

72   The God-image in man was not destroyed by the Fall but was only damaged and corrupted ("deformed"), and can be restored through God's grace. The scope of the integration is suggested by the *descensus ad inferos*, the descent of Christ's soul to hell, its work of redemption embracing even the dead. The psychological equivalent of this is the integration of the collective unconscious which forms an essential part of the individuation process. St. Augustine says: "Therefore our end must be our perfection, but our perfection is Christ," [18] since he is the perfect God-image. For this reason he is also called "King." His bride (*sponsa*) is the human soul, which "in an inwardly hidden spiritual mystery is joined to the Word, that two may be in one flesh," to correspond with the mystic marriage of Christ and the Church.[19] Concurrently with the continuance of this *hieros*

14 *Enarr. in Ps.*, LIV, 3 (Migne, *P.L.*, vol. 36, col. 629): ". . . ubi autem homo ad imaginem Dei factum se novit, ibi aliquid in se agnoscit amplius esse quam datum est pecoribus."
15 I Cor. 15 : 47.
16 *In Joannis Evangelium*, Tract. LXXVIII, 3 (Migne, *P.L.*, vol. 35, col. 1896): "Christus est Deus, anima rationalis et caro" (Christ is God, a rational soul and a body).
17 Sermo CCXXXVII, 4 (Migne, *P.L.*, vol. 38, col. 1124): "(Verbum) suscepit totum quasi plenum hominem, animam et corpus hominis. Et si aliquid scrupulosius vis audire; quia animam et carnem habet et pecus, cum dico animam humanam et carnem humanam, totam animam humanam accepit."
18 *Enarr. in Ps.*, LIV, 1 (Migne, *P.L.*, vol. 36, col. 628).
19 *Contra Faustum*, XXII, 38 (Migne, *P.L.*, vol. 42, col. 424): "Est enim et sancta Ecclesia Domino Jesu Christo in occulto uxor. Occulte quippe atque intus in abscondito secreto spirituali anima humana inhaeret Verbo Dei, ut sint duo in carne una." Cf. St. Augustine's *Reply to Faustus the Manichaean* (trans. by Richard Stothert, p. 433): "The holy Church, too, is in secret the spouse of the

gamos in the dogma and rites of the Church, the symbolism developed in the course of the Middle Ages into the alchemical conjunction of opposites, or "chymical wedding," thus giving rise on the one hand to the concept of the *lapis philosophorum*, signifying totality, and on the other hand to the concept of chemical combination.

73   The God-image in man that was damaged by the first sin can be "reformed"[20] with the help of God, in accordance with Romans 12 : 2: "And be not conformed to this world, but be transformed by the renewal of your mind, that you may prove what is . . . the will of God" (RSV). The totality images which the unconscious produces in the course of an individuation process are similar "reformations" of an *a priori* archetype (the mandala).[21] As I have already emphasized, the spontaneous symbols of the self, or of wholeness, cannot in practice be distinguished from a God-image. Despite the word μεταμορφοῦσθε ('be transformed') in the Greek text of the above quotation, the "renewal" (ἀνακαίνωσις, *reformatio*) of the mind is not meant as an actual alteration of consciousness, but rather as the restoration of an original condition, an apocatastasis. This is in exact agreement with the empirical findings of psychology, that there is an ever-present archetype of wholeness[22] which may easily disappear from the purview of consciousness or may never be perceived at all until a consciousness illuminated by conversion recognizes it in the figure of Christ. As a result of this "anamnesis" the original state of oneness with the God-image is restored. It brings about an integration, a bridging of the split in the personality caused by the instincts striving apart in different and mutually contradictory directions. The only time the split

---

Lord Jesus Christ. For it is secretly, and in the hidden depths of the spirit, that the soul of man is joined to the word of God, so that they are two in one flesh." St. Augustine is referring here to Eph. 5 : 31f.: "For this cause shall a man leave his father and mother, and shall be joined unto his wife, and they two shall be one flesh. This is a great mystery: but I speak concerning Christ and the Church."

[20] Augustine, *De Trinitate*, XIV, 22 (Migne, *P.L.*, vol. 42, col. 1053): "Reformamini in novitate mentis vostrae, ut incipiat illa imago ab illo reformari, a quo formata est" (Be reformed in the newness of your mind; the beginning of the image's reforming must come from him who first formed it) (trans. by John Burnaby, p. 120).

[21] Cf. "Concerning Mandala Symbolism," in Part I of vol. 9.

[22] *Psychology and Alchemy*, pars. 323ff.

does not occur is when a person is still as legitimately unconscious of his instinctual life as an animal. But it proves harmful and impossible to endure when an artificial unconsciousness— a repression—no longer reflects the life of the instincts.

74   There can be no doubt that the original Christian conception of the *imago Dei* embodied in Christ meant an all-embracing totality that even includes the animal side of man. Nevertheless the Christ-symbol lacks wholeness in the modern psychological sense, since it does not include the dark side of things but specifically excludes it in the form of a Luciferian opponent. Although the exclusion of the power of evil was something the Christian consciousness was well aware of, all it lost in effect was an insubstantial shadow, for, through the doctrine of the *privatio boni* first propounded by Origen, evil was characterized as a mere diminution of good and thus deprived of substance. According to the teachings of the Church, evil is simply "the accidental lack of perfection." This assumption resulted in the proposition "omne bonum a Deo, omne malum ab homine." Another logical consequence was the subsequent elimination of the devil in certain Protestant sects.

75   Thanks to the doctrine of the *privatio boni,* wholeness seemed guaranteed in the figure of Christ. One must, however, take evil rather more substantially when one meets it on the plane of empirical psychology. There it is simply the opposite of good. In the ancient world the Gnostics, whose arguments were very much influenced by psychic experience, tackled the problem of evil on a broader basis than the Church Fathers. For instance, one of the things they taught was that Christ "cast off his shadow from himself." [23] If we give this view the weight it

23 Irenaeus (*Adversus haereses*, II, 5, 1) records the Gnostic teaching that when Christ, as the demiurgic Logos, created his mother's being, he "cast her out of the Pleroma—that is, he cut her off from knowledge." For creation took place outside the pleroma, in the shadow and the void. According to Valentinus (*Adv. haer.*, I, 11, 1), Christ did not spring from the Aeons of the pleroma, but from the mother who was outside it. She bore him, he says, "not without a kind of shadow." But he, "being masculine,' cast off the shadow from himself and returned to the Pleroma (καὶ τοῦτον [Χριστὸν] μὲν ἅτε ἄρρενα ὑπάρχοντα ἀποκόψαντα ἀφ' ἑαυτοῦ τὴν σκιάν, ἀναδραμεῖν εἰς τὸ Πλήρωμα κτλ.), while his mother, "being left behind in the shadow, and deprived of spiritual substance,' there gave birth to the real "Demiurge and Pantokrator of the lower world.' But the shadow which lies over the world is, as we know from the Gospels, the *princeps huius mundi*, the devil. Cf. *The Writings of Irenaeus*, I, pp. 45f.

deserves, we can easily recognize the cut-off counterpart in the figure of Antichrist. The Antichrist develops in legend as a perverse imitator of Christ's life. He is a true ἀντίμιμον πνεῦμα, an imitating spirit of evil who follows in Christ's footsteps like a shadow following the body. This complementing of the bright but one-sided figure of the Redeemer—we even find traces of it in the New Testament—must be of especial significance. And indeed, considerable attention was paid to it quite early.

76   If we see the traditional figure of Christ as a parallel to the psychic manifestation of the self, then the Antichrist would correspond to the shadow of the self, namely the dark half of the human totality, which ought not to be judged too optimistically. So far as we can judge from experience, light and shadow are so evenly distributed in man's nature that his psychic totality appears, to say the least of it, in a somewhat murky light. The psychological concept of the self, in part derived from our knowledge of the whole man, but for the rest depicting itself spontaneously in the products of the unconscious as an archetypal quaternity bound together by inner antinomies, cannot omit the shadow that belongs to the light figure, for without it this figure lacks body and humanity. In the empirical self, light and shadow form a paradoxical unity. In the Christian concept, on the other hand, the archetype is hopelessly split into two irreconcilable halves, leading ultimately to a metaphysical dualism—the final separation of the kingdom of heaven from the fiery world of the damned.

77   For anyone who has a positive attitude towards Christianity the problem of the Antichrist is a hard nut to crack. It is nothing less than the counterstroke of the devil, provoked by God's Incarnation; for the devil attains his true stature as the adversary of Christ, and hence of God, only after the rise of Christianity, while as late as the Book of Job he was still one of God's sons and on familiar terms with Yahweh.[24] Psychologically the case is clear, since the dogmatic figure of Christ is so sublime and spotless that everything else turns dark beside it. It is, in fact, so one-sidedly perfect that it demands a psychic complement to restore the balance. This inevitable opposition led very early to the doctrine of the two sons of God, of whom the elder

24 Cf. R. Schärf, "Die Gestalt des Satans im Alten Testament."

was called Satanaël.[25] The coming of the Antichrist is not just a prophetic prediction—it is an inexorable psychological law whose existence, though unknown to the author of the Johannine Epistles, brought him a sure knowledge of the impending enantiodromia. Consequently he wrote as if he were conscious of the inner necessity for this transformation, though we may be sure that the idea seemed to him like a divine revelation. In reality every intensified differentiation of the Christ-image brings about a corresponding accentuation of its unconscious complement, thereby increasing the tension between above and below.

8   In making these statements we are keeping entirely within the sphere of Christian psychology and symbolism. A factor that no one has reckoned with, however, is the fatality inherent in the Christian disposition itself, which leads inevitably to a reversal of its spirit—not through the obscure workings of chance but in accordance with psychological law. The ideal of spirituality striving for the heights was doomed to clash with the materialistic earth-bound passion to conquer matter and master the world. This change became visible at the time of the "Renaissance." The word means "rebirth," and it referred to the renewal of the antique spirit. We know today that this spirit was chiefly a mask; it was not the spirit of antiquity that was reborn, but the spirit of medieval Christianity that underwent strange pagan transformations, exchanging the heavenly goal for an earthly one, and the vertical of the Gothic style for a horizontal perspective (voyages of discovery, exploration of the world and of nature). The subsequent developments that led to the Enlightenment and the French Revolution have produced a worldwide situation today which can only be called "antichristian" in a sense that confirms the early Christian anticipation of the "end of time." It is as if, with the coming of Christ, opposites that were latent till then had become manifest, or as if a pendulum had swung violently to one side and were now carrying out the complementary movement in the opposite direction. No tree, it is said, can grow to heaven unless its roots reach down to hell. The double meaning of this movement lies in the nature of the pendulum. Christ is without spot, but right at the beginning of his career there occurs the encounter with Satan, the

25 "The Spirit Mercurius," par. 271.

Adversary, who represents the counterpole of that tremendous tension in the world psyche which Christ's advent signified. He is the "mysterium iniquitatis" that accompanies the "sol iustitiae" as inseparably as the shadow belongs to the light, in exactly the same way, so the Ebionites [26] and Euchites [27] thought, that one brother cleaves to the other. Both strive for a kingdom: one for the kingdom of heaven, the other for the "principatus huius mundi." We hear of a reign of a "thousand years" and of a "coming of the Antichrist," just as if a partition of worlds and epochs had taken place between two royal brothers. The meeting with Satan was therefore more than mere chance; it was a link in the chain.

79   Just as we have to remember the gods of antiquity in order to appreciate the psychological value of the anima/animus archetype, so Christ is our nearest analogy of the self and its meaning. It is naturally not a question of a collective value artificially manufactured or arbitrarily awarded, but of one that is effective and present *per se,* and that makes its effectiveness felt whether the subject is conscious of it or not. Yet, although the attributes of Christ (consubstantiality with the Father, co-eternity, filiation, parthenogenesis, crucifixion, Lamb sacrificed between opposites, One divided into Many, etc.) undoubtedly mark him out as an embodiment of the self, looked at from the psychological angle he corresponds to only one half of the archetype. The other half appears in the Antichrist. The latter is just as much a manifestation of the self, except that he consists of its dark aspect. Both are Christian symbols, and they have the same meaning as the image of the Saviour crucified between two thieves. This great symbol tells us that the progressive development and differentiation of consciousness leads to an ever more menacing awareness of the conflict and involves nothing less than a crucifixion of the ego, its agonizing suspension between irreconcilable opposites.[28] Naturally there can be no question

[26] Jewish Christians who formed a Gnostic-syncretistic party.

[27] A Gnostic sect mentioned in Epiphanius, *Panarium adversus octoginta haereses,* LXXX, 1–3, and in Michael Psellus, *De daemonibus* (in Marsilius Ficinus, *Auctores Platonici* [*Iamblichus de mysteriis Aegyptiorum*], Venice, 1497).

[28] "Oportuit autem ut alter illorum extremorum isque optimus appellaretur Dei filius propter suam excellentiam; alter vero ipsi *ex diametro oppositus,* mali daemonis, Satanae diabolique filius diceretur" (But it is fitting that one of these two extremes, and that the best, should be called the Son of God because of his excel-

of a total extinction of the ego, for then the focus of consciousness would be destroyed, and the result would be complete unconsciousness. The relative abolition of the ego affects only
those supreme and ultimate decisions which confront us in
situations where there are insoluble conflicts of duty. This
means, in other words, that in such cases the ego is a suffering
bystander who decides nothing but must submit to a decision and
surrender unconditionally. The "genius" of man, the higher
and more spacious part of him whose extent no one knows, has
the final word. It is therefore well to examine carefully the psychological aspects of the individuation process in the light of
Christian tradition, which can describe it for us with an exact-
ness and impressiveness far surpassing our feeble attempts, even
though the Christian image of the self—Christ—lacks the shadow
that properly belongs to it.

30   The reason for this, as already indicated, is the doctrine of
the Summum Bonum. Irenaeus says very rightly, in refuting the

---

lence, and the other, *diametrically opposed* to him, the son of the evil demon, of
Satan and the devil) (Origen, *Contra Celsum*, VI, 45; in Migne, *P.G.*, vol. 11, col.
1367; cf. trans. by Chadwick, p. 362). The opposites even condition one another:
"Ubi quid malum est . . . ibi necessario bonum esse malo contrarium. . . .
Alterum ex altero sequitur: proinde aut utrumque tollendum est negandumque
bona et mala esse; aut admisso altero maximeque malo, bonum quoque admissum
oportet." (Where there is evil . . . there must needs be good contrary to the
evil. . . . The one follows from the other; hence we must either do away with
both, and deny that good and evil exist, or if we admit the one, and particularly
evil, we must also admit the good.) (*Contra Celsum*, II, 51; in Migne, *P.G.*, vol. 11,
col. 878; cf. trans. by Chadwick, p. 106.) In contrast to this clear, logical statement
Origen cannot help asserting elsewhere that the "Powers, Thrones, and Prin-
cipalities" down to the evil spirits and impure demons "do not have it—the contrary virtue—substantially" ("non substantialiter id habeant scl. virtus adversaria"),
and that they were not created evil but chose the condition of wickedness
("malitiae gradus") of their own free will. (*De principiis*, I, VIII, 4; in Migne, *P.G.*,
vol. 11, col. 179.) Origen is already committed, at least by implication, to the
definition of God as the Summum Bonum, and hence betrays the inclination to
deprive evil of substance. He comes very close to the Augustinian conception of
the *privatio boni* when he says: "Certum namque est malum esse bono carere"
(For it is certain that to be evil means to be deprived of good). But this sentence
is immediately preceded by the following: "Recedere autem a bono, non aliud est
quam effici in malo" (To turn aside from good is nothing other than to be perfected in evil) (*De principiis*, II, IX, 2; in Migne, *P.G.*, vol. 11, cols. 226–27). This
shows clearly that an increase in the one means a diminution of the other, so
that good and evil represent equivalent halves of an opposition.

45

Gnostics, that exception must be taken to the "light of their Father," because it "could not illuminate and fill even those things which were within it,"[29] namely the shadow and the void. It seemed to him scandalous and reprehensible to suppose that within the pleroma of light there could be a "dark and formless void." For the Christian neither God nor Christ could be a paradox; they had to have a single meaning, and this holds true to the present day. No one knew, and apparently (with a few commendable exceptions) no one knows even now, that the hybris of the speculative intellect had already emboldened the ancients to propound a philosophical definition of God that more or less obliged him to be the Summum Bonum. A Protestant theologian has even had the temerity to assert that "God *can* only be good." Yahweh could certainly have taught him a thing or two in this respect, if he himself is unable to see his intellectual trespass against God's freedom and omnipotence. This forcible usurpation of the Summum Bonum naturally has its reasons, the origins of which lie far back in the past (though I cannot enter into this here). Nevertheless, it is the effective source of the concept of the *privatio boni,* which nullifies the reality of evil and can be found as early as Basil the Great (330–79) and Dionysius the Areopagite (2nd half of the 4th century), and is fully developed in Augustine.

81 The earliest authority of all for the later axiom "Omne bonum a Deo, omne malum ab homine" is Tatian (2nd century), who says: "Nothing evil was created by God; we ourselves have produced all wickedness."[30] This view is also adopted by Theophilus of Antioch (2nd century) in his treatise *Ad Autolycum.*[31]

82 Basil says:

You must not look upon God as the author of the existence of evil, nor consider that evil has any subsistence in itself [ἰδίαν ὑπόστασιν τοῦ κακοῦ εἶναι]. For evil does not subsist as a living being does, nor can we set before our eyes any substantial essence [οὐσίαν ἐνυπόστατον] thereof. For evil is the privation [στέρησις] of good. . . . And thus evil does not inhere in its own substance [ἐν ἰδίᾳ ὑπάρξει], but arises

29 *Adv. haer.,* II, 4, 3.   30 *Oratio ad Graecos* (Migne, *P.G.,* vol. 6, col. 829).
31 Migne, *P.G.,* vol. 6, col. 1080.

from the mutilation [πηρώμασιν] of the soul.[32] Neither is it uncreated, as the wicked say who set up evil for the equal of good . . . nor is it created. For if all things are of God, how can evil arise from good? [33]

83   Another passage sheds light on the logic of this statement. In the second homily of the *Hexaemeron*, Basil says:

It is equally impious to say that evil has its origin from God, because the contrary cannot proceed from the contrary. Life does not engender death, darkness is not the origin of light, sickness is not the maker of health. . . . Now if evil is neither uncreated nor created by God, whence comes its nature? That evil exists no one living in the world will deny. What shall we say, then? That evil is not a living and animated entity, but a condition [διάθεσις] of the soul opposed to virtue, proceeding from light-minded [ῥαθύμοις] persons on account of their falling away from good. . . . Each of us should acknowledge that he is the first author of the wickedness in him.[34]

84   The perfectly natural fact that when you say "high" you immediately postulate "low" is here twisted into a causal relationship and reduced to absurdity, since it is sufficiently obvious that darkness produces no light and light produces no darkness. The idea of good and evil, however, is the premise for any moral judgment. They are a logically equivalent pair of opposites and, as such, the *sine qua non* of all acts of cognition. From the empirical standpoint we cannot say more than this. And from this standpoint we would have to assert that good and evil, being coexistent halves of a moral judgment, do not derive from one another but are always there together. Evil, like good, belongs to the category of human values, and we are the authors of moral value judgments, but only to a limited degree are we authors of the facts submitted to our moral judgment. These facts are called by one person good and by another evil. Only in capital cases is there anything like a *consensus generalis*. If we hold with Basil that man is the author of evil, we are saying in the same breath that he is also the author of good. But man is first and

32 Basil thought that the darkness of the world came from the shadow cast by the body of heaven. *Hexaemeron*, II, 5 (Migne, *P.G.*, vol. 29, col. 40).
33 *Homilia: Quod Deus non est auctor malorum* (Migne, *P.G.*, vol. 31, col. 341).
34 *De spiritu sancto* (Migne, *P.G.*, vol. 29, col. 37). Cf. *Nine Homilies of the Hexaemeron*, trans. by Blomfield Jackson, pp. 61f.

foremost the author merely of judgments; in relation to the facts judged, his responsibility is not so easy to determine. In order to do this, we would have to give a clear definition of the extent of his free will. The psychiatrist knows what a desperately difficult task this is.

85   For these reasons the psychologist shrinks from metaphysical assertions but must criticize the admittedly human foundations of the *privatio boni*. When therefore Basil asserts on the one hand that evil has no substance of its own but arises from a "mutilation of the soul," and if on the other hand he is convinced that evil really exists, then the relative reality of evil is grounded on a real "mutilation" of the soul which must have an equally real cause. If the soul was originally created good, then it has really been corrupted and by something that is real, even if this is nothing more than carelessness, indifference, and frivolity, which are the meaning of the word ῥαθυμία. When something —I must stress this with all possible emphasis—is traced back to a psychic condition or fact, it is very definitely not reduced to nothing and thereby nullified, but is shifted on to the plane of *psychic reality*, which is very much easier to establish empirically than, say, the reality of the devil in dogma, who according to the authentic sources was not invented by man at all but existed long before he did. If the devil fell away from God of his own free will, this proves firstly that evil was in the world before man, and therefore that man cannot be the sole author of it, and secondly that the devil already had a "mutilated" soul for which we must hold a real cause responsible. The basic flaw in Basil's argument is the *petitio principii* that lands him in insoluble contradictions: it is laid down from the start that the independent existence of evil must be denied even in face of the eternity of the devil as asserted by dogma. The historical reason for this was the threat presented by Manichaean dualism. This is especially clear in the treatise of Titus of Bostra (d. *c.* 370), entitled *Adversus Manichaeos*,[35] where he states in refutation of the Manichaeans that, so far as substance is concerned, there is no such thing as evil.

86   John Chrysostom (*c.* 344–407) uses, instead of στέρησις (*privatio*), the expression ἐκτροπὴ τοῦ καλοῦ (deviation, or turning away,

[35] Migne, *P.G.*, vol. 18, cols. 1132f.

from good). He says: "Evil is nothing other than a turning away from good, and therefore evil is secondary in relation to good." [36]

87   Dionysius the Areopagite gives a detailed explanation of evil in the fourth chapter of *De divinis nominibus*. Evil, he says, cannot come from good, because if it came from good it would not be evil. But since everything that exists comes from good, everything is in some way good, but "evil does not exist at all" (τὸ δὲ κακὸν οὔτε ὄν ἐστιν).

88   Evil in its nature is neither a thing nor does it bring anything forth.

Evil does not exist at all and is neither good nor productive of good [οὐκ ἔστι καθόλου τὸ κακὸν οὔτε ἀγαθὸν οὔτε ἀγαθοποιόν].

All things which are, by the very fact that they are, are good and come from good; but in so far as they are deprived of good, they are neither good nor do they exist.

That which has no existence is not altogether evil, for the absolutely non-existent will be nothing, unless it be thought of as subsisting in the good superessentially [κατὰ τὸ ὑπερούσιον]. Good, then, as absolutely existing and as absolutely non-existing, will stand in the foremost and highest place [πολλῷ πρότερον ὑπεριδρύμενον], while evil is neither in that which exists nor in that which does not exist [τὸ δὲ κακὸν οὔτε ἐν τοῖς οὖσιν, οὔτε ἐν τοῖς μὴ οὖσιν].[37]

89   These quotations show with what emphasis the reality of evil was denied by the Church Fathers. As already mentioned, this hangs together with the Church's attitude to Manichaean dualism, as can plainly be seen in St. Augustine. In his polemic against the Manichaeans and Marcionites he makes the following declaration:

For this reason all things are good, since some things are better than others and the goodness of the less good adds to the glory of the better. . . . Those things we call evil, then, are defects in good things, and quite incapable of existing in their own right outside good things. . . . But those very defects testify to the natural goodness of things. For what is evil by reason of a defect must obviously be good of its own nature. For a defect is something contrary to nature, something which damages the nature of a thing—and it can

---

36 *Responsiones ad orthodoxas* (Migne, *P.G.*, vol. 6, cols. 1313–14).
37 Migne, *P.G.*, vol. 3, cols. 716–18. Cf. the *Works of Dionysius the Areopagite*, trans. by John Parker, I, pp. 53ff.

do so only by diminishing that thing's goodness. *Evil therefore is nothing but the privation of good.* And thus it can have no existence anywhere except in some good thing. . . . So there can be things which are good without any evil in them, such as God himself, and the higher celestial beings; but there can be no evil things without good. For if evils cause no damage to anything, they are not evils; if they do damage something, they diminish its goodness; and if they damage it still more, it is because it still has some goodness which they diminish; and if they swallow it up altogether, nothing of its nature is left to be damaged. And so there will be no evil by which it can be damaged, since there is then no nature left whose goodness any damage can diminish.[38]

90   The *Liber Sententiarum ex Augustino* says (CLXXVI): "Evil is not a substance,[39] for as it has not God for its author, it

[38] "Nunc vero ideo sunt omnia bona, quia sunt aliis alia meliora, et bonitas inferiorum addit laudibus meliorum. . . . Ea vero quae dicuntur mala, aut vitia sunt rerum bonarum, quae omnino extra res bonas per se ipsa alicubi esse non possunt. . . . Sed ipsa quoque vitia testimonium perhibent bonitati naturarum. Quod enim malum est per vitium, profecto bonum est per naturam. Vitium quippe contra naturam est, quia naturae nocet; nec noceret, nisi bonum eius minueret. *Non est ergo malum nisi privatio boni.* Ac per hoc nusquam est nisi in re aliqua bona. . . . Ac per hoc bona sine malis esse possunt, sicut ipse Deus, et quaeque superiora coelestia; mala vero sine bonis esse non possunt. Si enim nihil nocent, mala non sunt; si autem nocent, bonum minuunt; et si amplius nocent, habent adhuc bonum quod minuant; et si totum consumunt, nihil naturae remanebit qui noceatur; ac per hoc nec malum erit a quo noceatur, quando natura defuerit, cuius bonum nocendo minuatur." (*Contra adversarium legis et prophetarum,* I, 4f.; in Migne, *P.L.,* vol. 42, cols. 606–7.) Although the *Dialogus Quaestionum LXV* is not an authentic writing of Augustine's, it reflects his standpoint very clearly. Quaest. XVI: "Cum Deus omnia bona creaverit, nihilque sit quod non ab illo conditum sit, unde malum? Resp. Malum natura non est; sed *privatio boni* hoc nomen accepit. Denique bonum potest esse sine malo, sed malum non potest esse sine bono, nec potest esse malum ubi non fuerit bonum. . . . Ideoque quando dicimus bonum, naturam laudamus; quando dicimus malum, non naturam sed vitium, quod est bonae naturae contrarium reprehendimus." (Question XVI: Since God created all things good and there is nothing which was not created by him, whence arises evil? Answer: Evil is not a natural thing, it is rather the name given to the privation of good. Thus there can be good without evil, but there cannot be evil without good, nor can there be evil where there is no good. . . . Therefore, when we call a thing good, we praise its inherent nature; when we call a thing evil, we blame not its nature, but some defect in it contrary to its nature, which is good.)

[39] "Iniquity has no substance" (CCXXVIII). "There is a nature in which there is no evil—in which, indeed, there can be no evil. But it is impossible for a nature to exist in which there is no good" (CLX).

does not exist; and so the defect of corruption is nothing else than the desire or act of a misdirected will." [40] Augustine agrees with this when he says: "The steel is not evil; but the man who uses the steel for a criminal purpose, he is evil." [41]

These quotations clearly exemplify the standpoint of Dionysius and Augustine: evil has no substance or existence in itself, since it is merely a diminution of good, which alone has substance. Evil is a *vitium,* a bad use of things as a result of erroneous decisions of the will (blindness due to evil desire, etc.). Thomas Aquinas, the great theoretician of the Church, says with reference to the above quotation from Dionysius:

One opposite is known through the other, as darkness is known through light. Hence also what evil is must be known from the nature of good. Now we have said above that good is everything appetible; and thus, since every nature desires its own being and its own perfection, it must necessarily be said that the being and perfection of every created thing is essentially good. Hence it cannot be that evil signifies a being, or any form or nature. Therefore it must be that by the name of evil is signified the absence of good.[42]
Evil is not a being, whereas good is a being.[43]
That every agent works for an end clearly follows from the fact that every agent tends to something definite. Now that to which an agent tends definitely must needs be befitting to that agent, since the latter would not tend to it save on account of some fittingness thereto. But that which is befitting to a thing is good for it. Therefore every agent works for a good.[44]

St. Thomas himself recalls the saying of Aristotle that "the thing is the whiter, the less it is mixed with black," [45] without mentioning, however, that the reverse proposition: "the thing is the blacker, the less it is mixed with white," not only has the same validity as the first but is also its logical equivalent. He

[40] *Augustini Opera omnia,* Maurist edn., X, Part 2, cols. 2561–2618.
[41] *Sermones supposititii,* Sermo I, 3, Maurist edn., V, col. 2287.
[42] *Summa theologica,* I, q. 48, ad 1 (trans. by the Fathers of the English Dominican Province, II, p. 264).   [43] Ibid., I, q. 48, ad 3 (trans., p. 268).
[44] ". . . Quod autem conveniens est alicui est illi bonum. Ergo omne agens agit propter bonum" (*Summa contra Gentiles,* III, ch. 3, trans. by the English Dominican Fathers, vol. III, p. 7).
[45] *Summa theologica,* I, q. 48, ad 2 (trans., II, p. 266, citing Aristotle's *Topics,* iii, 4).

might also have mentioned that not only darkness is known through light, but that, conversely, light is known through darkness.

93   As only that which works is real, so, according to St. Thomas, only good is real in the sense of "existing." His argument, however, introduces a good that is tantamount to "convenient, sufficient, appropriate, suitable." One ought therefore to translate "omne agens agit propter bonum" as: "Every agent works for the sake of what suits it." That's what the devil does too, as we all know. He too has an "appetite" and strives after perfection— not in good but in evil. Even so, one could hardly conclude from this that his striving is "essentially good."

94   Obviously evil can be represented as a diminution of good, but with this kind of logic one could just as well say: The temperature of the Arctic winter, which freezes our noses and ears, is relatively speaking only a little below the heat prevailing at the equator. For the Arctic temperature seldom falls much lower than 230° C. above absolute zero. All things on earth are "warm" in the sense that nowhere is absolute zero even approximately reached. Similarly, all things are more or less "good," and just as cold is nothing but a diminution of warmth, so evil is nothing but a diminution of good. The *privatio boni* argument remains a euphemistic *petitio principii* no matter whether evil is regarded as a lesser good or as an effect of the finiteness and limitedness of created things. The false conclusion necessarily follows from the premise "Deus = Summum Bonum," since it is unthinkable that the perfect good could ever have created evil. It merely created the good and the less good (which last is simply called "worse" by laymen).[46] Just as we freeze miserably despite a temperature of 230° above absolute zero, so there are people and things that, although created by God, are good only to the minimal and bad to the maximal degree.

95   It is probably from this tendency to deny any reality to evil that we get the axiom "Omne bonum a Deo, omne malum ab homine." This is a contradiction of the truth that he who created the heat is also responsible for the cold ("the goodness of the less good"). We can certainly hand it to Augustine that

[46] In the Decrees of the 4th Lateran Council we read: "For the devil and the other demons as created by God were naturally good, but became evil of their own motion." Denzinger and Bannwart, *Enchiridion symbolorum*, p. 189.

all natures are good, yet just not good enough to prevent their badness from being equally obvious.

*

96   One could hardly call the things that have happened, and still happen, in the concentration camps of the dictator states an "accidental lack of perfection"—it would sound like mockery.

97   Psychology does not know what good and evil are in themselves; it knows them only as judgments about relationships. "Good" is what seems suitable, acceptable, or valuable from a certain point of view; evil is its opposite. If the things we call good are "really" good, then there must be evil things that are "real" too. It is evident that psychology is concerned with a more or less subjective judgment, i.e., with a psychic antithesis that cannot be avoided in naming value relationships: "good" denotes something that is not bad, and "bad" something that is not good. There are things which from a certain point of view are extremely evil, that is to say dangerous. There are also things in human nature which are very dangerous and which therefore seem proportionately evil to anyone standing in their line of fire. It is pointless to gloss over these evil things, because that only lulls one into a sense of false security. Human nature is capable of an infinite amount of evil, and the evil deeds are as real as the good ones so far as human experience goes and so far as the psyche judges and differentiates between them. Only unconsciousness makes no difference between good and evil. Inside the psychological realm one honestly does not know which of them predominates in the world. We hope, merely, that good does—i.e., what seems suitable to us. No one could possibly say what the general good might be. No amount of insight into the relativity and fallibility of our moral judgment can deliver us from these defects, and those who deem themselves beyond good and evil are usually the worst tormentors of mankind, because they are twisted with the pain and fear of their own sickness.

98   Today as never before it is important that human beings should not overlook the danger of the evil lurking within them. It is unfortunately only too real, which is why psychology must insist on the reality of evil and must reject any definition that regards it as insignificant or actually non-existent. Psychology is an empirical science and deals with realities. As a psychologist,

therefore, I have neither the inclination nor the competence to mix myself up with metaphysics. Only, I have to get polemical when metaphysics encroaches on experience and interprets it in a way that is not justified empirically. My criticism of the *privatio boni* holds only so far as psychological experience goes. From the scientific point of view the *privatio boni*, as must be apparent to everyone, is founded on a *petitio principii*, where what invariably comes out at the end is what you put in at the beginning. Arguments of this kind have no power of conviction. But the fact that such arguments are not only used but are undoubtedly believed is something that cannot be disposed of so easily. It proves that there is a tendency, existing right from the start, to give priority to "good," and to do so with all the means in our power, whether suitable or unsuitable. So if Christian metaphysics clings to the *privatio boni*, it is giving expression to the tendency always to increase the good and diminish the bad. The *privatio boni* may therefore be a metaphysical truth. I presume to no judgment on this matter. I must only insist that in our field of experience white and black, light and dark, good and bad, are equivalent opposites which always predicate one another.

99   This elementary fact was correctly appreciated in the so-called Clementine Homilies,[47] a collection of Gnostic-Christian writings dating from about A.D. 150. The unknown author understands good and evil as the right and left hand of God, and views the whole of creation in terms of syzygies, or pairs of opposites. In much the same way the follower of Bardesanes, Marinus, sees good as "light" and pertaining to the right hand (δεξιόν), and evil as "dark" and pertaining to the left hand (ἀριστερόν).[48] The left also corresponds to the feminine. Thus in Irenaeus (*Adv. haer.*, I, 30, 3), Sophia Prounikos is called Sinistra. Clement finds this altogether compatible with the idea of God's unity.

[47] Harnack (*Lehrbuch der Dogmengeschichte*, p. 332) ascribes the Clementine Homilies to the beginning of the 4th cent. and is of the opinion that they contain "no source that could be attributed with any certainty to the 2nd century." He thinks that Islam is far superior to this theology. Yahweh and Allah are un-reflected God-images, whereas in the Clementine Homilies there is a psychological and reflective spirit at work. It is not immediately evident why this should bring about a disintegration of the God-concept, as Harnack thinks. Fear of psychology should not be carried too far.

[48] *Der Dialog des Adamantius*, III, 4 (ed. by van de Sande Bakhuyzen, p. 119).

Provided that one has an anthropomorphic God-image—and every God-image is anthropomorphic in a more or less subtle way—the logic and naturalness of Clement's view can hardly be contested. At all events this view, which may be some two hundred years older than the quotations given above, proves that the reality of evil does not necessarily lead to Manichaean dualism and so does not endanger the unity of the God-image. As a matter of fact, it guarantees that unity on a plane beyond the crucial difference between the Yahwistic and the Christian points of view. Yahweh is notoriously unjust, and injustice is not good. The God of Christianity, on the other hand, is *only* good. There is no denying that Clement's theology helps us to get over this contradiction in a way that fits the psychological facts.

100   It is therefore worth following up Clement's line of thought a little more closely. "God," he says, "appointed two kingdoms [βασιλείας] and two ages [αἰῶνας], determining that the present world should be given over to evil [πονηρῷ], because it is small and passes quickly away. But he promised to preserve the future world for good, because it is great and eternal." Clement goes on to say that this division into two corresponds to the structure of man: the body comes from the female, who is characterized by emotionality; the spirit comes from the male, who stands for rationality. He calls body and spirit the "two triads." [49]

Man is a compound of two mixtures [φυραμάτων, lit. 'pastes'], the female and the male. Wherefore also two ways have been laid before him—those of obedience and of disobedience to law; and two kingdoms have been established—the one called the kingdom of heaven, and the other the kingdom of those who are now rulers upon earth. . . . Of these two, the one does violence to the other. Moreover these two rulers are the swift hands of God.

That is a reference to Deuteronomy 32 : 39: "I will kill and I will make to live" (DV). He kills with the left hand and saves with the right.

[49] The female or somatic triad consist of ἐπιθυμία (desire), ὀργή (anger), and λύπη (grief); the male, of λογισμός (reflection), γνῶσις (knowledge), and φόβος (fear). Cf. the triad of functions in "The Phenomenology of the Spirit in Fairy-tales," Part I of vol. 9, pars. 425ff.

These two principles have not their substance outside of God, for there is no other primal source [ἀρχή]. Nor have they been sent forth from God as animals, for they were of the same mind [ὁμόδοξοι] with him. . . . But from God were sent forth the four first elements—hot and cold, moist and dry. In consequence of this, he is the Father of every substance [οὐσίας], but not of the knowledge which arises from the mixing of the elements.[50] For when these were combined from without, choice [προαίρεσις] was begotten in them as a child.[51]

That is to say, through the mixing of the four elements inequalities arose which caused uncertainty and so necessitated decisions or acts of choice. The four elements form the fourfold substance of the body (τετραγενὴς τοῦ σώματος οὐσία) and also of evil (τοῦ πονηροῦ). This substance was "carefully discriminated and sent forth from God, but when it was combined from without, according to the will of him who sent it forth, there arose, as a result of the combination, the preference which rejoices in evils [ἡ κακοῖς χαίρουσα προαίρεσις]."[52]

101   The last sentence is to be understood as follows: The fourfold substance is eternal (οὖσα ἀεί) and God's child. But the tendency to evil was added from outside to the mixture willed by God (κατὰ τὴν τοῦ θεοῦ βούλησιν ἔξω τῇ κράσει συμβέβηκεν). Thus evil is not created by God or by any one else, nor was it projected out of him, nor did it arise of itself. Peter, who is engaged in these reflections, is evidently not quite sure how the matter stands.

102   It seems as if, without God's intending it (and possibly without his knowing it) the mixture of the four elements took a wrong turning, though this is rather hard to square with Clement's idea of the opposite hands of God "doing violence to one another." Obviously Peter, the leader of the dialogue, finds it rather difficult to attribute the cause of evil to the Creator in so many words.

103   The author of the Homilies espouses a Petrine Christianity distinctly "High Church" or ritualistic in flavour. This, taken

---

[50] P. de Lagarde (Clementina, p. 190) has here . . . πάσης οὐσίας . . . οὔσης γνώμης. The reading οὐ τῆς seems to me to make more sense.
[51] Ch. III: τῆς μετὰ τὴν κρᾶσιν.
[52] The Clementine Homilies and the Apostolical Constitutions, trans. by Thomas Smith et al., pp. 312ff. (slightly modified).

together with his doctrine of the dual aspect of God, brings him into close relationship with the early Jewish-Christian Church, where, according to the testimony of Epiphanius, we find the Ebionite notion that God had two sons, an elder one, Satan, and a younger one, Christ.[53] Michaias, one of the speakers in the dialogue, suggests as much when he remarks that if good and evil were begotten in the same way they must be brothers.[54]

104   In the (Jewish-Christian?) apocalypse, the "Ascension of Isaiah," we find, in the middle section, Isaiah's vision of the seven heavens through which he was rapt.[55] First he saw Sammaël and his hosts, against whom a "great battle" was raging in the firmament. The angel then wafted him beyond this into the first heaven and led him before a throne. On the right of the throne stood angels who were more beautiful than the angels on the left. Those on the right "all sang praises with *one* voice," but the ones on the left sang *after* them, and their singing was not like the singing of the first. In the second heaven all the angels were more beautiful than in the first heaven, and there was no difference between them, either here or in any of the higher heavens. Evidently Sammaël still has a noticeable influence on the first heaven, since the angels on the left are not so beautiful there. Also, the lower heavens are not so splendid as the upper ones, though each surpasses the other in splendour. The devil, like the Gnostic archons, dwells in the firmament, and he and his angels presumably correspond to astrological gods and influences. The gradation of splendour, going all the way up to the topmost heaven, shows that his sphere interpenetrates with the divine sphere of the Trinity, whose light in turn filters down as far as the lowest heaven. This paints a picture of complementary opposites balancing one another like right and left hands. Significantly enough, this vision, like the Clementine Homilies, belongs to the pre-Manichaean period (second century), when there was as yet no need for Christianity to fight against its Manichaean competitors. It might easily be a descrip-

[53] *Panarium*, ed. by Oehler, I, p. 267.
[54] *Clement. Hom.* XX, ch. VII. Since there is no trace in pseudo-Clement of the defensive attitude towards Manichaean dualism which is so characteristic of the later writers, it is possible that the Homilies date back to the beginning of the 3rd cent., if not earlier.
[55] Hennecke, *Neutestamentliche Apokryphen*, pp. 309ff.

tion of a genuine yang-yin relationship, a picture that comes closer to the actual truth than the *privatio boni*. Moreover, it does not damage monotheism in any way, since it unites the opposites just as yang and yin are united in Tao (which the Jesuits quite logically translated as "God"). It is as if Manichaean dualism first made the Fathers conscious of the fact that until then, without clearly realizing it, they had always believed firmly in the substantiality of evil. This sudden realization might well have led them to the dangerously anthropomorphic assumption that what man cannot unite, God cannot unite either. The early Christians, thanks to their greater unconsciousness, were able to avoid this mistake.

105   Perhaps we may risk the conjecture that the problem of the Yahwistic God-image, which had been constellated in men's minds ever since the Book of Job, continued to be discussed in Gnostic circles and in syncretistic Judaism generally, all the more eagerly as the Christian answer to this question—namely the unanimous decision in favour of God's goodness [56]—did not satisfy the conservative Jews. In this respect, therefore, it is significant that the doctrine of the two antithetical sons of God originated with the Jewish Christians living in Palestine. Inside Christianity itself the doctrine spread to the Bogomils and Cathars; in Judaism it influenced religious speculation and found lasting expression in the two sides of the cabalistic Tree of the Sephiroth, which were named *hesed* (love) and *din* (justice). A rabbinical scholar, Zwi Werblowsky, has been kind enough to put together for me a number of passages from Hebrew literature which have bearing on this problem.

106   R. Joseph taught: "What is the meaning of the verse, 'And none of you shall go out at the door of his house until the morning?' (Exodus 12 : 22.) [57] Once permission has been granted to the destroyer, he does not distinguish between the righteous and the wicked. Indeed, he even begins with the righteous." [58] Commenting on Exodus 33 : 5 ("If for a single moment I should go up among you, I would consume you"), the midrash says: "Yahweh means he could wax wroth with you for a moment—

[56] Cf. Matt. 19 : 17 and Mark 10 : 18.
[57] A reference to the slaying of the first-born in Egypt.
[58] *Nezikin* I, Baba Kamma 60 (in *The Babylonian Talmud*, trans. and ed. by Isidore Epstein, p. 348 [hereafter abbr. *BT*]; slightly modified).

for that is the length of his wrath, as is said in Isaiah 26 : 20, 'Hide yourselves for a little moment until the wrath is past'—and destroy you." Yahweh gives warning here of his unbridled irascibility. If in this moment of divine wrath a curse is uttered, it will indubitably be effective. That is why Balaam, "who knows the thoughts of the Most High," [59] when called upon by Balak to curse Israel, was so dangerous an enemy, because he knew the moment of Yahweh's wrath.[60]

07   God's love and mercy are named his right hand, but his justice and his administration of it are named his left hand. Thus we read in I Kings 22 : 19: "I saw the Lord sitting on his throne, and all the host of heaven standing beside him on his right hand and on his left." The midrash comments: "Is there right and left on high? This means that the intercessors stand on the right and the accusers on the left." [61] The comment on Exodus 15 : 6 ("Thy right hand, O Lord, glorious in power, thy right hand, O Lord, shatters the enemy") runs: "When the children of Israel perform God's will, they make the left hand his right hand. When they do not do his will, they make even the right hand his left hand." [62] "God's left hand dashes to pieces; his right hand is glorious to save." [63]

08   The dangerous aspect of Yahweh's justice comes out in the following passage: "Even so said the Holy One, blessed be He: If I create the world on the basis of mercy alone, its sins will be great; but on the basis of justice alone the world cannot exist. Hence I will create it on the basis of justice and mercy, and may it then stand!" [64] The midrash on Genesis 18 : 23 (Abraham's plea for Sodom) says (Abraham speaking): "If thou desirest the world to endure, there can be no absolute justice, while if thou desirest absolute justice, the world cannot endure. Yet thou wouldst hold the cord by both ends, desiring both the world and absolute justice. Unless thou forgoest a little, the world cannot endure." [65]

59 Numbers 24 : 16.   60 *Zera'im* I, Berakoth 7a (*BT*, p. 31).
61 *Midrash Tanchuma Shemoth* XVII.
62 Cf. *Pentateuch with Targum Onkelos . . . and Rashi's Commentary*, trans. by M. Rosenbaum and A. M. Silbermann, II, p. 76.
63 Midrash on Song of Sol. 2 : 6.
64 *Bereshith Rabba* XII, 15 (*Midrash Rabbah translated into English*, ed. by H. Freedman and M. Simon, I, p. 99; slightly modified).
65 Ibid. XXXIX, 6 (p. 315).

109   Yahweh prefers the repentant sinners even to the righteous, and protects them from his justice by covering them with his hand or by hiding them under his throne.[66]

110   With reference to Habakkuk 2 : 3 ("For still the vision awaits its time. . . . If it seem slow, wait for it"), R. Jonathan says: "Should you say, *We* wait [for his coming] but *He* does not, it stands written (Isaiah 30 : 18), 'Therefore will the Lord wait, that he may be gracious unto you.' . . . But since we wait and he waits too. what delays his coming? Divine justice delays it." [67] It is in this sense that we have to understand the prayer of R. Jochanan: "May it be thy will, O Lord our God, to look upon our shame and behold our evil plight. Clothe thyself in thy mercies, cover thyself in thy strength, wrap thyself in thy loving-kindness, and gird thyself with thy graciousness, and may thy goodness and gentleness come before thee." [68] God is properly exhorted to remember his good qualities. There is even a tradition that God prays to himself: "May it be My will that My mercy may suppress My anger, and that My compassion may prevail over My other attributes." [69] This tradition is borne out by the following story:

R. Ishmael the son of Elisha said: I once entered the innermost sanctuary to offer incense, and there I saw Akathriel [70] Jah Jahweh Zebaoth [71] seated upon a high and exalted throne. He said to me, Ishmael, my son, bless me! And I answered him: May it be Thy will that Thy mercy may suppress Thy anger, and that Thy compassion may prevail over Thy other attributes, so that Thou mayest deal with Thy children according to the attribute of mercy and stop short of the limit of strict justice! And He nodded to me with His head.[72]

111   It is not difficult to see from these quotations what was the effect of Job's contradictory God-image. It became a subject for religious speculation inside Judaism and, through the medium

---

[66] *Mo'ed* IV, Pesahim 119 (*BT*, p. 613); *Nezikin* VI, Sanhedrin II, 103 (*BT*, pp. 698ff.).   [67] *Nezikin* VI, Sanhedrin II, 97 (*BT*, p. 659; modified).

[68] *Zera'im* I, Berakoth 16b (*BT*, p. 98; slightly modified).   [69] Ibid. 7a (p. 30).

[70] "Akathriel" is a made-up word composed of *ktr = kether* (throne) and *el*, the name of God.

[71] A string of numinous God names, usually translated as "the Lord of Hosts."

[72] *Zera'im* I, Berakoth 7 (*BT*, p. 30; slightly modified).

of the Cabala, it evidently had an influence on Jakob Böhme. In his writings we find a similar ambivalence, namely the love and the "wrath-fire" of God, in which Lucifer burns for ever.[73]

112   Since psychology is not metaphysics, no metaphysical dualism can be derived from, or imputed to, its statements concerning the equivalence of opposites.[74] It knows that equivalent opposites are necessary conditions inherent in the act of cognition, and that without them no discrimination would be possible. It is not exactly probable that anything so intrinsically bound up with the act of cognition should be at the same time a property of the object. It is far easier to suppose that it is primarily our consciousness which names and evaluates the differences between things, and perhaps even creates distinctions where no differences are discernible.

113   I have gone into the doctrine of the *privatio boni* at such length because it is in a sense responsible for a too optimistic conception of the evil in human nature and for a too pessimistic view of the human soul. To offset this, early Christianity, with unerring logic, balanced Christ against an Antichrist. For how can you speak of "high" if there is no "low," or "right" if there is no "left," of "good" if there is no "bad," and the one is as real as the other? Only with Christ did a devil enter the world as the real counterpart of God, and in early Jewish-Christian circles Satan, as already mentioned, was regarded as Christ's elder brother.

114   But there is still another reason why I must lay such critical stress on the *privatio boni.* As early as Basil we meet with the tendency to attribute evil to the disposition (διάθεσις) of the soul, and at the same time to give it a "non-existent" character. Since, according to this author, evil originates in human frivolity

---

73 *Aurora,* trans. by John Sparrow, p. 423.
74 My learned friend Victor White, O.P., in his *Dominican Studies* (II, p. 399), thinks he can detect a Manichaean streak in me. I don't go in for metaphysics, but ecclesiastical philosophy undoubtedly does, and for this reason I must ask what are we to make of hell, damnation, and the devil, if these things are eternal? Theoretically they consist of nothing, and how does that square with the dogma of eternal damnation? But if they consist of something, that something can hardly be good. So where is the danger of dualism? In addition to this my critic should know how very much I stress the unity of the self, this central archetype which is a *complexio oppositorum* par excellence, and that my leanings are therefore towards the very reverse of dualism.

and therefore owes its existence to mere negligence, it exists, so to speak, only as a by-product of psychological oversight, and this is such a *quantité négligeable* that evil vanishes altogether in smoke. Frivolity as a cause of evil is certainly a factor to be taken seriously, but it is a factor that can be got rid of by a change of attitude. We *can* act differently, if we want to. Psychological causation is something so elusive and seemingly unreal that everything which is reduced to it inevitably takes on the character of futility or of a purely accidental mistake and is thereby minimized to the utmost. It is an open question how much of our modern undervaluation of the psyche stems from this prejudice. This prejudice is all the more serious in that it causes the psyche to be suspected of being the birthplace of all evil. The Church Fathers can hardly have considered what a fatal power they were ascribing to the soul. One must be positively blind not to see the colossal role that evil plays in the world. Indeed, it took the intervention of God himself to deliver humanity from the curse of evil, for without his intervention man would have been lost. If this paramount power of evil is imputed to the soul, the result can only be a negative inflation —i.e., a daemonic claim to power on the part of the unconscious which makes it all the more formidable. This unavoidable consequence is anticipated in the figure of the Antichrist and is reflected in the course of contemporary events, whose nature is in accord with the Christian aeon of the Fishes, now running to its end.

115   In the world of Christian ideas Christ undoubtedly represents the self.[75] As the apotheosis of individuality, the self has the attributes of uniqueness and of occurring once only in time. But since the psychological self is a transcendent concept, expressing the totality of conscious and unconscious contents, it

[75] It has been objected that Christ cannot have been a valid symbol of the self, or was only an illusory substitute for it. I can agree with this view only if it refers strictly to the present time, when psychological criticism has become possible, but not if it pretends to judge the pre-psychological age. Christ did not merely *symbolize* wholeness, but, as a psychic phenomenon, he *was* wholeness. This is proved by the symbolism as well as by the phenomenology of the past, for which— be it noted—evil was a *privatio boni*. The idea of totality is, at any given time, as total as one is oneself. Who can guarantee that our conception of totality is not equally in need of completion? The mere concept of totality does not by any means posit it.

can only be described in antinomial terms; [76] that is, the above attributes must be supplemented by their opposites if the transcendental situation is to be characterized correctly. We can do this most simply in the form of a quaternion of opposites:

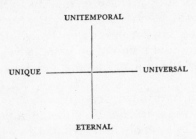

UNITEMPORAL

UNIQUE ——————— UNIVERSAL

ETERNAL

116   This formula expresses not only the psychological self but also the dogmatic figure of Christ. As an historical personage Christ is unitemporal and unique; as God, universal and eternal. Likewise the self: as the essence of individuality it is unitemporal and unique; as an archetypal symbol it is a God-image and therefore universal and eternal.[77] Now if theology describes Christ as simply "good" and "spiritual," something "evil" and "material"—or "chthonic"—is bound to arise on the other side, to represent the Antichrist. The resultant quaternion of opposites is united on the psychological plane by the fact that the self is not deemed exclusively "good" and "spiritual"; consequently its shadow turns out to be much less black. A further result is that the opposites of "good" and "spiritual" need no longer be separated from the whole:

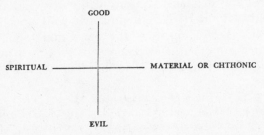

GOOD

SPIRITUAL ——————— MATERIAL OR CHTHONIC

EVIL

76 Just as the transcendent nature of light can only be expressed through the image of waves *and* particles.
77 Cf. *Psychology and Alchemy*, pars. 323ff., and "The Relations between the Ego and the Unconscious," pars. 398ff.

117   This *quaternio* characterizes the psychological self. Being a totality, it must by definition include the light and dark aspects, in the same way that the self embraces both masculine and feminine and is therefore symbolized by the marriage *quaternio*.[78] This last is by no means a new discovery, since according to Hippolytus it was known to the Naassenes.[79] Hence individuation is a "mysterium coniunctionis," the self being experienced as a nuptial union of opposite halves [80] and depicted as a composite whole in mandalas that are drawn spontaneously by patients.

118   It was known, and stated, very early that the man Jesus, the son of Mary, was the *principium individuationis*. Thus Basilides [81] is reported by Hippolytus as saying: "Now Jesus became the first sacrifice in the discrimination of the natures [φυλοκρίνησις], and the Passion came to pass for no other reason than the discrimination of composite things. For in this manner, he says, the sonship that had been left behind in a formless state [ἀμορφία] . . . needed separating into its components [φυλοκρινηθῆναι], in the same way that Jesus was separated." [82] According to the rather complicated teachings of Basilides, the "non-existent" God begot a threefold sonship (υἱότης). The first "son," whose nature was the finest and most subtle, remained up above with the Father. The second son, having a grosser (παχυμερέστερα) nature, descended a bit lower, but received "some such wing as that with which Plato . . . equips the soul in his *Phaedrus*." [83] The third son, as his nature needed purifying (ἀποκαθάρσις), fell deepest into "formlessness." This third "sonship" is obviously the grossest and heaviest because of its impurity. In these three emanations or manifestations of the non-existent God it is not hard to see the trichotomy of spirit, soul, and body (πνευματικόν, ψυχικόν, σαρκικόν). Spirit is the finest and highest; soul, as the *ligamentum spiritus et corporis*, is grosser than spirit, but has "the wings of an eagle,"[84] so that it may lift its heaviness up to

---

78 Cf. "The Psychology of the Transference," pars. 425ff.
79 *Elenchos*, V, 8, 2 (trans. by F. Legge, I, p. 131). Cf. infra, pars. 358ff.
80 *Psychology and Alchemy*, par. 334, and "The Psychology of the Transference," pars. 457ff.   81 Basilides lived in the 2nd cent.
82 *Elenchos*, VII, 27, 12 (cf. Legge trans., II, p. 79).
83 Ibid., VII, 22, 10 (cf. II, pp. 69–70).
84 Ibid., VII, 22, 15 (II, p. 70). The eagle has the same significance in alchemy.

the higher regions. Both are of a "subtle" nature and dwell, like the ether and the eagle, in or near the region of light, whereas the body, being heavy, dark, and impure, is deprived of the light but nevertheless contains the divine seed of the third sonship, though still *unconscious and formless*. This seed is as it were awakened by Jesus, purified and made capable of ascension (ἀναδρομή),[85] by virtue of the fact that the opposites were separated in Jesus through the Passion (i.e., through his division into four).[86] Jesus is thus the prototype for the awakening of the third sonship slumbering in the darkness of humanity. He is the "spiritual inner man." [87] He is also a complete trichotomy in himself, for Jesus the son of Mary represents the incarnate man, but his immediate predecessor is the second Christ, the son of the highest archon of the hebdomad, and his first prefiguration is Christ the son of the highest archon of the ogdoad, the demiurge Yahweh.[88] This trichotomy of Anthropos figures corresponds exactly to the three sonships of the non-existing God and to the division of human nature into three parts. We have therefore three trichotomies:

[85] This word also occurs in the well-known passage about the *krater* in Zosimos. (Berthelot, *Alch. grecs*, III, li, 8: ἀναδραμε ἐπὶ τὸ γένος τὸ σόν.

[86] I must say a word here about the *horos* doctrine of the Valentinians in Irenaeus (*Adv. haer*, I, 2, 2ff.) Horos (boundary) is a "power" or numen identical with Christ, or at least proceeding from him. It has the following synonyms: ὁροθέτης (boundary-fixer), μεταγωγεύς (he who leads across), καρπιστής (emancipator), λυτρώτης (redeemer), σταυρός (cross). In this capacity he is the regulator and mainstay of the universe, like Jesus. When Sophia was "formless and shapeless as an embryo, Christ took pity on her, stretched her out through his Cross and gave her form through his power," so that at least she acquired substance (*Adv. haer.*, I, 4). He also left behind for her an "intimation of immortality." The identity of the Cross with Horos, or with Christ, is clear from the text, an image that we find also in Paulinus of Nola:

> ". . . regnare deum super omnia Christum,
> qui cruce dispensa per quattuor extima ligni
> quattuor adtingit dimensum partibus orbem,
> ut trahat ad uitam populos ex omnibus oris."

(Christ reigns over all things as God, who, on the outstretched cross, reaches out through the four extremities of the wood to the four parts of the wide world, that he may draw unto life the peoples from all lands.) (*Carmina*, ed. by Wilhelm Hartel, Carm. XIX, 639ff., p. 140.) For the Cross as God's "lightning" cf. "A Study in the Process of Individuation," pars. 535f.

[87] *Elenchos*, VII, 27, 5 (Legge trans., II, p. 78).

[88] Ibid., VII, 26, 5 (II, p. 75).

I	II	III
First sonship	Christ of the Ogdoad	Spirit
Second sonship	Christ of the Hebdomad	Soul
Third sonship	Jesus the Son of Mary	Body

119   It is in the sphere of the dark, heavy body that we must look for the ἀμορφία, the "formlessness" wherein the third sonship lies hidden. As suggested above, this formlessness seems to be practically the equivalent of "unconsciousness." G. Quispel has drawn attention to the concepts of ἀγνωσία in Epiphanius [89] and ἀνόητον in Hippolytus,[90] which are best translated by "unconscious." Ἀμορφία, ἀγνωσία, and ἀνόητον all refer to the initial state of things, to the potentiality of unconscious contents, aptly formulated by Basilides as οὐκ ὂν σπέρμα τοῦ κόσμου πολύμορφον ὁμοῦ καὶ πολυούσιον (the non-existent, many-formed, and all-empowering seed of the world).[91]

120   This picture of the third sonship has certain analogies with the medieval *filius philosophorum* and the *filius macrocosmi*, who also symbolize the world-soul slumbering in matter.[92] Even with Basilides the body acquires a special and unexpected significance, since in it and its materiality is lodged a third of the revealed Godhead. This means nothing less than that matter is predicated as having considerable numinosity in itself, and I see this as an anticipation of the "mystic" significance which matter subsequently assumed in alchemy and—later on—in natural science. From a psychological point of view it is par-

[89] *Panarium*, XXXI, 5 (Oehler edn., I, p. 314).
[90] *Elenchos*, VII, 22, 16 (Legge trans., II, p. 71). Cf. infra, pars. 298ff.
[91] Ibid., 20, 5 (cf. II, p. 66). Quispel, "Note sur 'Basilide'."
[92] With reference to the psychological nature of Gnostic sayings, see Quispel's "Philo und die altchristliche Häresie," p. 432, where he quotes Irenaeus (*Adv. haer.*, II, 4, 2): "Id quod extra et quod intus dicere eos secundum agnitionem et ignorantiam, sed non secundum localem sententiam" (In speaking of what is outward and what is inward, they refer, not to place, but to what is known and what is not known). (Cf. Legge, I, p. 127.) The sentence that follows immediately after this—"But in the Pleroma, or in that which is contained by the Father, everything that the demiurge or the angels have created is contained by the unspeakable greatness, as the centre in a circle"—is therefore to be taken as a description of unconscious contents. Quispel's view of projection calls for the critical remark that projection does not do away with the *reality* of a psychic content. Nor can a fact be called "unreal" merely because it cannot be described as other than "psychic." Psyche is reality par excellence.

ticularly important that Jesus corresponds to the third sonship and is the prototype of the "awakener" because the opposites were separated in him through the Passion and so became conscious, whereas in the third sonship itself they remain unconscious so long as the latter is formless and undifferentiated. This amounts to saying that in unconscious humanity there is a latent seed that corresponds to the prototype Jesus. Just as the man Jesus became conscious only through the light that emanated from the higher Christ and separated the natures in him, so the seed in unconscious humanity is awakened by the light emanating from Jesus, and is thereby impelled to a similar discrimination of opposites. This view is entirely in accord with the psychological fact that the archetypal image of the self has been shown to occur in dreams even when no such conceptions exist in the conscious mind of the dreamer.[93]

*

21   I would not like to end this chapter without a few final remarks that are forced on me by the importance of the material we have been discussing. The standpoint of a psychology whose subject is the phenomenology of the psyche is evidently something that is not easy to grasp and is very often misunderstood. If, therefore, at the risk of repeating myself, I come back to fundamentals, I do so only in order to forestall certain wrong impressions which might be occasioned by what I have said, and to spare my reader unnecessary difficulties.

22   The parallel I have drawn here between Christ and the self is not to be taken as anything more than a psychological one, just as the parallel with the fish is mythological. There is no question of any intrusion into the sphere of metaphysics, i.e., of faith. The images of God and Christ which man's religious fantasy projects cannot avoid being anthropomorphic and are admitted to be so; hence they are capable of psychological elucidation like any other symbols. Just as the ancients believed that they had said something important about Christ with their fish symbol, so it seemed to the alchemists that their parallel with the stone served to illuminate and deepen the meaning of the Christ-image. In the course of time, the fish symbolism

93 Cf. *Psychology and Alchemy*, pars. 52ff., 122ff., and "A Study in the Process of Individuation," pars. 542, 550, 581f.

disappeared completely, and so likewise did the *lapis philosophorum*. Concerning this latter symbol, however, there are plenty of statements to be found which show it in a special light —views and ideas which attach such importance to the stone that one begins to wonder whether, in the end, it was Christ who was taken as a symbol of the stone rather than the other way round. This marks a development which—with the help of certain ideas in the epistles of John and Paul—includes Christ in the realm of immediate inner experience and makes him appear as the figure of the total man. It also links up directly with the psychological evidence for the existence of an archetypal content possessing all those qualities which are characteristic of the Christ-image in its archaic and medieval forms. Modern psychology is therefore confronted with a question very like the one that faced the alchemists: Is the self a symbol of Christ, or is Christ a symbol of the self?

123   In the present study I have affirmed the latter alternative. I have tried to show how the traditional Christ-image concentrates upon itself the characteristics of an archetype—the archetype of the self. My aim and method do not purport to be anything more in principle than, shall we say, the efforts of an art historian to trace the various influences which have contributed towards the formation of a particular Christ-image. Thus we find the concept of the archetype in the history of art as well as in philology and textual criticism. The psychological archetype differs from its parallels in other fields only in one respect: it refers to a living and ubiquitous psychic fact, and this naturally shows the whole situation in a rather different light. One is then tempted to attach greater importance to the immediate and living presence of the archetype than to the idea of the historical Christ. As I have said, there is among certain of the alchemists, too, a tendency to give the *lapis* priority over Christ. Since I am far from cherishing any missionary intentions, I must expressly emphasize that I am not concerned here with confessions of faith but with proven scientific facts. If one inclines to regard the archetype of the self as the real agent and hence takes Christ as a symbol of the self, one must bear in mind that there is a considerable difference between *perfection* and *completeness*. The Christ-image is as good as perfect (at least it is meant to be so), while the archetype (so far as known) denotes completeness

but is far from being perfect. It is a paradox, a statement about something indescribable and transcendental. Accordingly the realization of the self, which would logically follow from a recognition of its supremacy, leads to a fundamental conflict, to a real suspension between opposites (reminiscent of the crucified Christ hanging between two thieves), and to an approximate state of wholeness that lacks perfection. To strive after teleiosis in the sense of perfection is not only legitimate but is inborn in man as a peculiarity which provides civilization with one of its strongest roots. This striving is so powerful, even, that it can turn into a passion that draws everything into its service. Natural as it is to seek perfection in one way or another, the archetype fulfils itself in completeness, and this is a τελείωσις of quite another kind. Where the archetype predominates, completeness is *forced* upon us against all our conscious strivings, in accordance with the archaic nature of the archetype. The individual may strive after perfection ("Be you therefore perfect—τέλειοι— as also your heavenly Father is perfect." [94]) but must suffer from the opposite of his intentions for the sake of his completeness. "I find then a law, that, when I would do good, evil is present with me." [95]

24 The Christ-image fully corresponds to this situation: Christ is the perfect man who is crucified. One could hardly think of a truer picture of the goal of ethical endeavour. At any rate the transcendental idea of the self that serves psychology as a working hypothesis can never match that image because, although it is a symbol, it lacks the character of a revelatory historical event. Like the related ideas of *atman* and *tao* in the East, the idea of the self is at least in part a product of cognition, grounded neither on faith nor on metaphysical speculation but on the experience that under certain conditions the unconscious spontaneously brings forth an archetypal symbol of wholeness. From this we must conclude that some such archetype occurs universally and is endowed with a certain numinosity. And there is in fact any amount of historical evidence as well as modern case material to prove this.[96] These naïve and completely uninfluenced pictorial representations of the symbol show that it is given central and supreme importance precisely because it

94 Matt. 5 : 48 (DV).   95 Rom. 7 : 21 (AV).
96 Cf. the last two papers in Part I of vol. 9.

stands for the conjunction of opposites. Naturally the conjunction can only be understood as a paradox, since a union of opposites can be thought of only as their annihilation. Paradox is a characteristic of all transcendental situations because it alone gives adequate expression to their indescribable nature.

125   Whenever the archetype of the self predominates, the inevitable psychological consequence is a state of conflict vividly exemplified by the Christian symbol of crucifixion—that acute state of unredeemedness which comes to an end only with the words "consummatum est." Recognition of the archetype, therefore, does not in any way circumvent the Christian mystery; rather, it forcibly creates the psychological preconditions without which "redemption" would appear meaningless. "Redemption" does not mean that a burden is taken from one's shoulders which one was never meant to bear. Only the "complete" person knows how unbearable man is to himself. So far as I can see, no relevant objection could be raised from the Christian point of view against anyone accepting the task of individuation imposed on us by nature, and the recognition of our wholeness or completeness, as a binding personal commitment. If he does this consciously and intentionally, he avoids all the unhappy consequences of repressed individuation. In other words, if he voluntarily takes the burden of completeness on himself, he need not find it "happening" to him against his will in a negative form. This is as much as to say that anyone who is destined to descend into a deep pit had better set about it with all the necessary precautions rather than risk falling into the hole backwards.

126   The irreconcilable nature of the opposites in Christian psychology is due to their moral accentuation. This accentuation seems natural to us, although, looked at historically, it is a legacy from the Old Testament with its emphasis on righteousness in the eyes of the law. Such an influence is notably lacking in the East, in the philosophical religions of India and China. Without stopping to discuss the question of whether this exacerbation of the opposites, much as it increases suffering, may not after all correspond to a higher degree of truth, I should like merely to express the hope that the present world situation may be looked upon in the light of the psychological rule alluded to above. Today humanity, as never before, is split into two apparently irrec-

oncilable halves. The psychological rule says that when an inner situation is not made conscious, it happens outside, as fate. That is to say, when the individual remains undivided and does not become conscious of his inner opposite, the world must perforce act out the conflict and be torn into opposing halves.

VI

THE SIGN OF THE FISHES

[127]   The figure of Christ is not as simple and unequivocal as one could wish. I am not referring here to the enormous difficulties arising out of a comparison of the Synoptic Christ with the Johannine Christ, but to the remarkable fact that in the hermeneutic writings of the Church Fathers, which go right back to the days of primitive Christianity, Christ has a number of symbols or "allegories" in common with the devil. Of these I would mention the lion, snake (*coluber*, 'viper'), bird (devil = *nocturna avis*), raven (Christ = *nycticorax*, 'night-heron'), eagle, and fish. It is also worth noting that Lucifer, the Morning Star, means Christ as well as the devil.[1] Apart from the snake, the fish is one of the oldest allegories. Nowadays we would prefer to call them symbols, because these synonyms always contain more than mere allegories, as is particularly obvious in the case of the fish symbol. It is unlikely that Ἰχθῦς is simply an anagrammatic abbreviation of Ἰ[ησοῦς] Χ[ριστὸς] Θ[εοῦ] Υ[ἱὸς] Σ[ωτήρ],[2] but rather

---

[1] Early collections of such allegories in the *Ancoratus* of Epiphanius, and in Augustine, *Contra Faustum*. For *nycticorax* and *aquila* see Eucherius, *Liber formularum spiritalis intelligentiae*, cap. 5 (Migne, *P.L.*, vol. 50, col. 740).

[2] Augustine (*City of God*, trans. by J. Healey, II, p. 196) relates how the former proconsul Flaccianus, with whom he had a conversation about Jesus, produced a book containing the songs of the Erythraean Sibyl, and showed him the passage where the above words, forming the acrostic Ἰχθῦς, are themselves the acrostic for a whole poem, an apocalyptic prophecy of the Sibyls:

> "Iudicii signum tellus sudore madescet,
> E coelo Rex adveniet per saecla futurus:
> Scilicet in carne praesens ut iudicet orbem.
> Unde Deum cernent incredulus atque fidelis
> Celsum cum Sanctis, aevi iam termino in ipso.
> Sic animae cum carne aderunt quas judicat ipse . . ."
> (In sign of doomsday the whole earth shall sweat.
> Ever to reign a king in heavenly seat
> Shall come to judge all flesh. The faithful and
> Unfaithful too before this God shall stand,
> Seeing him high with saints in time's last end.

the symbolical designation for something far more complex. (As I have frequently pointed out in my other writings, I do not regard the symbol as an allegory or a sign, but take it in its proper sense as the best possible way of describing and formulating an object that is not completely knowable. It is in this sense that the creed is called a "symbolum.") The order of the words gives one more the impression that they were put together for the purpose of explaining an already extant and widely disseminated "Ichthys."[3] For the fish symbol, in the Near and Middle East especially, has a long and colourful prehistory, from the Babylonian fish-god Oannes and his priests who clothed themselves in fish-skins, to the sacred fish-meals in the cult of the Phoenician goddess Derceto-Atargatis and the obscurities of the Abercius inscription.[4] The symbol ranges from the redeemer-fish of Manu in farthest India to the Eucharistic fish-feast celebrated by the "Thracian riders" in the Roman Empire.[5] For our purpose it is hardly necessary to go into this voluminous material more closely. As Doelger and others have shown, there are plenty of occasions for fish symbolism within the original, purely Christian world of ideas. I need only mention the regeneration in the font, in which the baptized swim like fishes.[6]

In view of this wide distribution of the fish symbol, its appearance at a particular place or at a particular moment in the history of the world is no cause for wonder. But the sudden activation of the symbol, and its identification with Christ even in the early days of the Church, lead one to conjecture a second

---

Corporeal shall he sit, and thence extend
His doom on souls . . .) (Ibid., p. 437.)

The Greek original is in *Oracula Sibyllina*, ed. John Geffcken, p. 142. [For Augustine's explanation of the discrepancy in the acrostic, see Healey trans., II, p. 196.—EDITORS.]

3 Cf. Jeremias, *The Old Testament in the Light of the Ancient East*, I, p. 76, n. 2.

4 From this inscription I will cite only the middle portion, which says: "Everywhere I had a travelling companion, since I had Paul sitting in the chariot. But everywhere Faith drew me onward, and everywhere he set before me for food a fish from the source, exceeding great and pure, which a holy virgin had caught. And he offered this fish to the friends to eat, having good wine, a mixed drink with bread." See Ramsay, "The Cities and Bishoprics of Phrygia," p. 424.

5 Cf. the material in Goodenough, *Jewish Symbols in the Greco-Roman Period*, V, pp. 13ff.

6 Doelger, 'ΙΧΘΥΣ: *Das Fischsymbol in frühchristlicher Zeit*.

source. This source is astrology, and it seems that Friedrich Muenter [7] was the first to draw attention to it. Jeremias [8] adopts the same view and mentions that a Jewish commentary on Daniel, written in the fourteenth century, expected the coming of the Messiah in the sign of the Fishes. This commentary is mentioned by Muenter in a later publication [9] as stemming from Don Isaac Abarbanel, who was born in Lisbon in 1437 and died in Venice in 1508.[10] It is explained here that the House of the Fishes (♓) is the house of justice and of brilliant splendour (♃ in ♓). Further, that in *anno mundi* 2365,[11] a great conjunction of Saturn (♄) and Jupiter (♃) took place in Pisces.[12] These two great planets, he says, are also the most important for the destiny of the world, and especially for the destiny of the Jews. The conjunction took place three years before the birth of Moses. (This is of course legendary.) Abarbanel expects the coming of the Messiah when there is a conjunction of Jupiter and Saturn in Pisces. He was not the first to express such expectations. Four hundred years earlier we find similar pronouncements; for instance, Rabbi Abraham ben Hiyya, who died about 1136, is said to have decreed that the Messiah was to be expected in 1464, at the time of the great conjunction in Pisces; and the same is reported of Solomon ben Gabirol (1020–70).[13] These astrological ideas are quite understandable when one considers that Saturn is the star of Israel, and that Jupiter means the "king" (of justice). Among the territories ruled by the Fishes, the house of Jupiter, are Mesopotamia, Bactria, the Red Sea, and Palestine.[14] Chiun (Saturn) is mentioned in Amos 5 : 26

---

[7] *Sinnbilder und Kunstvorstellungen der alten Christen* (1825), p. 49. Muenter mentions Abrabanel (sic) here, "who in all probability drew on older sources."

[8] Op. cit., p. 76.

[9] *Der Stern der Weisen* (1827), pp. 54ff.

[10] Isaac Abravanel (Abarbanel) ben Jehuda, *Ma'yene ha-Yeshu'ah* ("Sources of Salvation"—A Commentary on Daniel. Ferrara, 1551).

[11] Corresponding to 1396 B.C.

[12] Actually the conjunction took place in Sagittarius (♐). The *coniunctiones magnae* of the water trigon (♋, ♏, ♓) fall in the years 1800 to 1600 and 1000 to 800 B.C.

[13] Anger, "Der Stern der Weisen und das Geburtsjahr Christi," p. 396, and Gerhardt, *Der Stern des Messias*, pp. 54f.

[14] Gerhardt, p. 57. Ptolemy and, following him, the Middle Ages associate Palestine with Aries.

as "the star of your god."[15] James of Sarug (d. 521) says the Israelites worshipped Saturn. The Sabaeans called him the "god of the Jews."[16] The Sabbath is Saturday, Saturn's Day. Albumasar[17] testifies that Saturn is the star of Israel.[18] In medieval astrology Saturn was believed to be the abode of the devil.[19] Both Saturn and Ialdabaoth, the demiurge and highest archon, have lion's faces. Origen elicits from the diagram of Celsus that Michael, the first angel of the Creator, has "the shape of a lion."[20] He obviously stands in the place of Ialdabaoth, who is identical with Saturn, as Origen points out.[21] The demiurge of the Naassenes is a "fiery god, the fourth by number."[22] According to the teachings of Apelles, who had connections with Marcion, there was a "third god who spoke to Moses, a fiery one, and there was also a fourth, the author of evil."[23] Between the god of the Naassenes and the god of Apelles there is evidently a close relationship, and also, it appears, with Yahweh, the demiurge of the Old Testament.

9   Saturn is a "black" star,[24] anciently reputed a "maleficus." "Dragons, serpents, scorpions, vipères, renards, chats et souris, oiseaux nocturnes et autres engeances sournoises sont le lot de Saturne," says Bouché-Leclercq.[25] Remarkably enough, Saturn's animals also include the ass,[26] which on that account was rated

[15] "Ye have borne Siccuth your king and Chiun your images, the star of your god, which ye made to yourselves" (RV). Stephen refers to this in his defence (Acts 7 : 43): "And you took unto you the tabernacle of Moloch and the star of your god Rempham." "Rempham" ('Ρομφά), is a corruption of Kewan (Chiun).

[16] Dozy and de Goeje, "Nouveaux documents pour l'étude de la religion des Harraniens," p. 350.   [17] Abu Ma'shar, d. 885.

[18] Gerhardt, p. 57. Also Pierre d'Ailly, Concordantia astronomie cum theologia, etc., fol. g4 (Venice, 1490): "But Saturn, as Messahali says, has a meaning which concerns the Jewish people or their faith."

[19] Reitzenstein, Poimandres, p. 76.

[20] Contra Celsum, VI, 30 (trans. by H. Chadwick, p. 345).

[21] Ibid., VI, 31: "But they say that this angel like unto a lion has a necessary connection with the star Saturn." Cf. Pistis Sophia, trans. by Mead, p. 47, and Bousset, Hauptprobleme der Gnosis, pp. 352ff.

[22] Hippolytus, Elenchos, V, 7, 30 (Legge trans., I, p. 128).

[23] Ibid., VII, 38, 1 (cf. Legge trans., II, p. 96).

[24] Hence the image of Saturn worshipped by the Sabaeans was said to be made of lead or black stone. (Chwolsohn, Die Ssabier und der Ssabismus, II, p. 383.)

[25] L'Astrologie grecque, p. 317.

[26] Bouché-Leclercq (p. 318) conjectures one of the known classical "etymologies," namely an onos (ass) contained in Kronos (Saturn), based on a joke aimed at the

a theriomorphic form of the Jewish god. A pictorial representation of it is the well-known mock crucifixion on the Palatine.[27] Similar traditions can be found in Plutarch,[28] Diodorus, Josephus,[29] and Tacitus.[30] Sabaoth, the seventh archon, has the form of an ass.[31] Tertullian is referring to these rumours when he says: "You are under the delusion that our God is an ass's head," and that "we do homage only to an ass." [32] As we have indicated, the ass is sacred to the Egyptian Set.[33] In the early texts, however, the ass is the attribute of the sun-god and only later became an emblem of the underworldly Apep and of evil (Set).[34]

130   According to medieval tradition, the religion of the Jews originated in a conjunction of Jupiter with Saturn, Islam in ♃ ☌ ♀, Christianity in ♃ ☌ ☿, and the Antichrist in ♃ ☌ ☽.[35]

Megarian philosopher Diodoros. But the reason for the Saturn-ass analogy probably lies deeper, that is, in the nature of the ass itself, which was regarded as a "cold, intractable, slow-witted, long-lived animal." (From the Greek bestiary cited by Bouché-Leclercq.) In Polemon's bestiary I find the following description of the wild ass: "Given to flight, timid, stupid, untamed, lustful, jealous, killing its females" (*Scriptores physiognomici graeci et latini*, I, p. 182).

[27] A possible model might be the Egyptian tradition of the martyrdom of Set, depicted at Denderah. He is shown tied to the "slave's post," has an ass's head, and Horus stands before him with a knife in his hand. (Mariette, *Dendérah*, plates vol. IV, pl. 56.)   [28] *Quaestiones convivales*, IV, 5.

[29] *Contra Apionem*, II, 7–8 (8off.). (Cf. trans. by H. St. J. Thackeray and R. Marcus, I, pp. 325ff.)   [30] *The Histories*, trans. by W. H. Fyfe, II, pp. 204ff.

[31] Epiphanius, *Panarium*, ed. Oehler, I, p. 184.

[32] *Apologeticus adversus gentes*, XVI (Migne, *P.L.*, vol. 1, cols. 364–65; cf. trans. by S. Thelwall, I, pp. 84f.).

[33] Plutarch, *De Iside et Osiride*, in *Moralia*, pp. 77, 123. In ch. 31 Plutarch states that the legend of Set's flight on an ass and of the fathering of his two sons Hierosolymus and Judaeus is not Egyptian, but pertained to the 'Ιουδαϊκά.

[34] In the Papyrus of Ani (ed. E. A. W. Budge, p. 248) a hymn to Ra says: "May I advance upon the earth; may I smite the Ass; may I crush the evil one (Sebau); may I destroy Apep in his hour."

[35] Albumasar, Lib. II, *De magnis coniunctionibus*, tract. I, diff. 4, p. a8ʳ (1489): "If (Jupiter) is in conjunction with Saturn, it signifies that the faith of the citizens thereof is Judaism. . . . And if the moon is in conjunction with Saturn it signifies doubt and revolution and change, and this by reason of the speed of the corruption of the moon and the rapidity of its motion and the shortness of its delay in the sign." Cf. also Pierre d'Ailly, *Concordantia*, etc., fol. d8ʳ. J. H. Heidegger (*Quaestiones ad textum Lucae VII, 12–17*, 1655) says in ch. IX that Abu Mansor (= Albumasar), in his sixth tractate, in the *Introductio maior*, connects the life of Christ, like that of Mahomet, with the stars. Cardan ascribes ☿ ☌ ♃

Unlike Saturn, Jupiter is a beneficent star. In the Iranian view Jupiter signifies life, Saturn death.[36] The conjunction of the two therefore signifies the *union of extreme opposites*. In the year 7 B.C. this famed conjunction took place no less than three times in the sign of the Fishes. The greatest approximation occurred on May 29 of that year, the planets being only 0.21 degrees apart, less than half the width of the full moon.[37] The conjunction took place in the middle of the commissure, "near the bend in the line of the Fishes." From the astrological point of view this conjunction must appear especially significant, because the approximation of the two planets was exceptionally large and of an impressive brilliance. In addition, seen heliocentrically, it took place near the equinoctial point, which at that time was located between ♈ and ♓, that is, between fire and water.[38] The conjunction was characterized by the important fact that Mars was in opposition (♂ ☍ ♃ ♄), which means, astrologically, that the planet correlated with the instincts stood in a hostile relationship to it, which is peculiarly characteristic of Christianity. If we accept Gerhardt's calculation that the conjunction took place on May 29, in the year 7 B.C., then the position of the sun—especially important in a man's nativity—at Christ's birth would be in the double sign of the *Twins*.[39] One

---

to Christianity, ☿ ☌ ♄ to Judaism, ☿ ☌ ♂ to Islam, and according to him ☿ ☌ ♀ signifies idolatry ("Commentarium in Ptolemaeum De astrorum Judiciis," p. 188).
[36] Christensen, *Le Premier Homme et le premier roi dans l'histoire légendaire des Iraniens*, part 1, p. 24.   [37] Gerhardt, *Stern des Messias*, p. 74.
[38] Calculated on the basis of Peters and Knobel, *Ptolemy's Catalogue of Stars*.
[39] Medieval astrologers cast a number of ideal horoscopes for Christ. Albumasar and Albertus Magnus took Virgo as the ascendent; Pierre d'Ailly (1356–1420), on the other hand, took Libra, and so did Cardan. Pierre d'Ailly says: "For Libra is the human sign, that is, of the Liberator of men, [the sign] of a prudent and just and spiritual man" (*Concordantia*, etc., cap. 2). Kepler, in his *Discurs von der grossen Conjunction* (1623; p. 701), says that God himself marked "such great conjunctions as these with extraordinary and marvellous stars visible in high heaven, also with notable works of his divine Providence." He continues: "Accordingly he appointed the birth of his Son Christ our Saviour exactly at the time of the great conjunction in the signs of the Fishes and the Ram, near the equinoctial point." Seen heliocentrically, the conjunction took place just in front of the equinoctial point, and this gives it a special significance astrologically. Pierre d'Ailly (*Concordantia*, etc., fol. br) says: "But a great conjunction is that of Saturn and Jupiter in the beginning of the Ram." These con-

thinks involuntarily of the ancient Egyptian pair of hostile brothers, Horus and Set, the sacrificer and the sacrificed (cf. n. 27, on Set's "martyrdom"), who in a sense prefigure the drama of the Christian myth. In the Egyptian myth it is the evil one who is sacrificed on the "slave's post." [40] But the pair of brothers Heru-ur (the "older Horus") and Set are sometimes pictured as having one body with two heads. The planet Mercury is correlated with Set, and this is interesting in view of the tradition that Christianity originated in a conjunction of Jupiter with Mercury. In the New Kingdom (XIXth dynasty) Set appears as Sutech in the Nile delta. In the new capital built by Rameses II, one district was dedicated to Amon, the other to Sutech. [41] It was here that the Jews were supposed to have done slave-labour.

131   In considering the double aspect of Christ, mention might be made of the legend of Pistis Sophia (3rd cent.), which also originated in Egypt. Mary says to Jesus:

When thou wert a child, before the spirit had descended upon thee, when thou wert in the vineyard with Joseph, the spirit came down from the height, and came unto me in the house, like unto thee, and I knew him not, but thought that he was thou. And he said unto me, "Where is Jesus, my brother, that I may go to meet him?" And when he had said this unto me, I was in doubt, and thought it was a phantom tempting me. I seized him and bound him to the foot of the bed which was in my house, until I had gone to find you in the field, thee and Joseph; and I found you in the vineyard, where Joseph was putting up the vine-poles. And it came to pass, when thou didst hear me saying this thing unto Joseph, that thou didst understand, and thou wert joyful, and didst say, "Where is

junctions occur every 20 years and take place every 200 years in the same trigon. But the same position can only recur every 800 years. The most significant positions are those between two trigons. Albumasar (*De magnis coniunc.*, tract. 3, diff. 1, fol. D 8ʳ) says they manifest themselves "in changes of parties and offices and in changes of the laws and . . . in the coming of prophets and of prophesying and of miracles in parties and offices of state."

[40] Crucifixion was a well-known punishment for slaves. The Cross with a snake on it, instead of the Crucified, is often found in medieval times [*Psychology and Alchemy*, fig. 217], and also in the dreams and fantasy-images of modern people who know nothing of this tradition. A characteristic dream of this sort is the following: *The dreamer was watching a Passion play in the theatre. On the way to Golgotha, the actor taking the part of the Saviour suddenly changed into a snake or crocodile.*   [41] Erman, *Die Religion der Ägypter*, p. 137.

he, that I may see him?" And it came to pass, when Joseph heard thee say these words, that he was disturbed. We went up together, entered into the house and found the spirit bound to the bed, and we gazed upon thee and him, and found that thou wert like unto him. And he that was bound to the bed was unloosed, he embraced thee and kissed thee, and thou also didst kiss him, and you became one.[42]

2   It appears from the context of this fragment that Jesus is the "truth sprouting from the earth," whereas the spirit that resembled him is "justice [δικαιοσύνη] looking down from heaven." The text says: "Truth is the power which issued from thee when thou wast in the lower regions of chaos. For this cause thy power hath said through David, 'Truth hath sprouted out of the earth,' because thou wert in the lower regions of chaos."[43] Jesus, accordingly, is conceived as a double personality, part of which rises up from the chaos or *hyle,* while the other part descends as pneuma from heaven.

3   One could hardly find the φυλοκρίνησις, or 'discrimination of the natures' that characterizes the Gnostic Redeemer, exemplified more graphically than in the astrological determination of time. The astrological statements that were quite possible in antiquity all point to the prominent double aspect [44] of the birth that occurred at this particular moment of time, and one can understand how plausible was the astrological interpretation of the Christ-Antichrist myth when it entered into manifestation at the time of the Gnostics. A fairly old authority, earlier anyway than the sixth century, which bears striking witness to the antithetical nature of the Fishes is the Talmud. This says:

Four thousand two hundred and ninety-one years after the Creation [A.D. 530], the world will be orphaned. There will follow the war of the *tanninim* [sea-monsters], the war of Gog and Magog,[45] and then

42 *Pistis Sophia,* Mead trans., pp. 118f., slightly modified.
43 Cf. the fish that Augustine says was "drawn from the deep."
44 In this connection mention should be made of the "Saviour of the twins" (σωτῆρες) in *Pistis Sophia* (Mead trans., pp. 2, 17, and elsewhere).
45 Also mentioned in the *Chronique* of Tabari (I, ch. 23, p. 67). There Antichrist is the king of the Jews, who appears with Gog and Magog. This may be an allusion to Rev. 20 : 7f.: "And when the thousand years are expired, Satan shall be loosed out of his prison, and shall go out to deceive the nations which are

the Messianic era; only after seven thousand years will the Holy One, blessed be He, set up his world anew. R. Abba, the son of Raba, said, It was taught: after five thousand years.[46]

The Talmud commentator Solomon ben Isaac, alias Rashi (1039–1105), remarks that the *tanninim* are fishes, presumably basing himself on an older source, since he does not give this as his own opinion, as he usually does. This remark is important, firstly because it takes the battle of the fishes as an eschatological event (like the fight between Behemoth and Leviathan), and secondly because it is probably the oldest testimony to the antithetical nature of the fishes. From about this period, too—the eleventh century—comes the apocryphal text of a Johannine Genesis in which the two fishes are mentioned, this time in unmistakably astrological form.[46a] Both documents fall within the critical epoch that opened with the second millennium of the Christian era, about which I shall have more to say in due course.

---

in the four corners of the earth, Gog and Magog, to gather them together to battle" (AV).

Graf von Wackerbarth (*Merkwürdige Geschichte der weltberühmten Gog und Magog*, p. 19) relates from an English "History of the World," which came out in German in 1760, that the Arab writers say the "Yajui" were "of more than ordinary size," whereas the "Majui" were "not more than three spans high." This story, despite the obscurity of its origins, points to the antithetical nature of Gog and Magog, who thus form a parallel to the Fishes. Augustine interprets "the nations which are in the four corners of the earth, Gog and Magog" as, respectively (Gog), *tectum*, 'roof' or 'house,' and (Magog) *de tecto*, 'he that comes out of the house': "Ut illae sint tectum, ipse de tecto." That is to say the nations are the house, but the devil dwells in the house and comes out of it. (*City of God*, Healey trans., II, p. 286.) On Augustine is based the *Compendium theologicae veritatis* (Venice, 1492), which was attributed in turn to Albertus Magnus, Hugh of Strasbourg, and John of Paris. It is our main source for the Antichrist legend. With reference to Augustine it says (Libell. 7, cap. 11) that Gog means "occultatio" (concealment), Magog "detectio" (revelation). This corroborates the antithetical nature of Gog and Magog at least for the Middle Ages. It is another instance of the motif of the hostile brothers, or of duplication. Albumasar (tract. 4, diff. 12, f. 8r) calls the sixth "clima" (inclination towards the Pole) that of Gog and Magog, and correlates it with Gemini and Virgo.

[46] *Nezikin* VI, Sanhedrin II (*BT*, p. 658). R. Hanan ben Tahlifa, into whose mouth this prophecy is put, is mentioned in the list of Amoraim (teachers of the Talmud) and lived in the 2nd cent. A.D.   [46a] Cf. infra, pars. 225ff.

4   The year 531 is characterized astronomically by a conjunction of ♃ and ♄ in Gemini. This sign stands for a pair of brothers, and they too have a somewhat antithetical nature. The Greeks interpreted them as the Dioscuri ('boys of Zeus'), the sons of Leda who were begotten by the swan and hatched out of an egg. Pollux was immortal, but Castor shared the human lot. Another interpretation takes them as representing Apollo and Heracles or Apollo and Dionysus. Both interpretations suggest a certain polarity. Astronomically, at any rate, the air sign Gemini stands in a quartile and therefore unfavourable aspect to the conjunction that took place in the year 7 B.C. The inner polarity of ♊ may perhaps shed light on the prophecy about the war of the *tanninim,* which Rashi interprets as fishes. From the dating of Christ's birth it would appear, as said, that the sun was in Gemini. The motif of the brothers is found very early in connection with Christ, for instance among the Jewish Christians and Ebionites.[47]

35   From all this we may risk the conjecture that the Talmudic prophecy was based on astrological premises.

36   The precession of the equinoxes was a fact well known to the astrologers of antiquity. Origen, helped out by the observations and calculations of Hipparchus,[48] uses it as a cogent argument against an astrology based on the so-called "morphomata" (the actual constellations).[49] Naturally this does not apply to the distinction already drawn in ancient astrology between the morphomata and the ζῳδιὰ νοητά (the fictive signs of the zodiac).[50] If we take the 7,000 years mentioned in the prophecy as *anno mundi* 7000, the year denoted would be A.D. 3239. By then the

---

47 Epiphanius, *Panarium,* XXX (Oehler edn., I, pp. 240ff.).

48 Hipparchus is supposed to have discovered the precession. Cf. Boll, *Sphaera,* p. 199, n. 1.

49 Origen, *Commentaria in Genesim,* tom. III, i, 14, 11 (Migne, *P.G.,* vol. 12, col. 79): "There is indeed a theory that the zodiacal circle, just like the planets, is carried back from setting to rising [or: from west to east], within a century by one degree; . . . since the twelfth part [1 zodion] is one thing when conceived in the mind, another when perceived by the senses; yet from that which is conceived only in the mind, and can scarcely, or not even scarcely, be held for certain, the truth of the matter appears." The Platonic year was then reckoned as 36,000 years. Tycho Brahe reckoned it at 24,120 years. The constant for the precession is 50.3708 seconds and the total cycle (360°) takes 25,725.6 years.

50 Bouché-Leclercq, p. 591, n. 2; Knapp, *Antiskia;* Boll, *Sphaera.*

spring-point will have moved from its present position 18 degrees into Aquarius, the next aeon, that of the Water Carrier. As an astrologer of the second or third century would be acquainted with the precession, we may surmise that these dates were based on astrological considerations. At all events the Middle Ages were much concerned with the calculation of *coniunctiones maximae* and *magnae,* as we know from Pierre d'Ailly and Cardan.[51] Pierre d'Ailly reckoned that the first *coniunctio maxima* ($\mathrm{2\!\!\!\!L}$ δ $\hbar$ in Υ) after the creation of the world took place in 5027 B.C., while Cardan relegated the tenth conjunction to A.D. 3613.[52] Both of them assumed the lapse of too large an interval between conjunctions in the same sign. The correct astronomical interval is about 795 years. Cardan's conjunction would accordingly take place in the year A.D. 3234. For astrological speculation this date is naturally of the greatest importance.

137   As to the 5,000 years, the date we get is A.D. 1239. This was an epoch noted for its spiritual instability, revolutionary heresies and chiliastic expectations, and at the same time it saw the founding of the mendicant orders, which injected new life into monasticism. One of the most powerful and influential voices to announce the coming of a "new age of the spirit" was Joachim of Flora (d. 1202), whose teachings were condemned by the Fourth Lateran Council in 1215. He expected the opening of the seventh seal in the fairly near future, the advent of the "everlasting gospel" and the reign of the "intellectus spiritualis," the age of the Holy Ghost. This third aeon, he says, had already begun with St. Benedict, the founder of the Benedictine Order (the first monastery was supposed to have been built a few years after 529). One of Joachim's followers, the Franciscan friar Gerard of Borgo San Donnino, proclaimed in his *Introductorius in evangelium aeternum,* which appeared in 1254 in Paris, that Joachim's three main treatises were in fact the everlasting gospel, and that in the year 1260 this would replace the

---

[51] The theory of the conjunctions was set down in writing by the Arabs about the middle of the 9th cent., more particularly by Messahala. Cf. Strauss, *Die Astrologie des Johannes Kepler.*

[52] With his estimate of 960 years between two *coniunctiones maximae,* Pierre d'Ailly would also arrive at A.D. 3613.

gospel of Jesus Christ.[53] As we know, Joachim saw monasticism as the true vehicle of the Holy Ghost and for this reason he dated the secret inception of the new era from the lifetime of St. Benedict, whose founding of the Benedictine Order revived monasticism in the West.

38   To Pierre d'Ailly the time of Pope Innocent III (1198–1216) had already seemed significant. About the year 1189, he says, the revolutions of Saturn were once again completed ("completae anno Christi 1189 vel circiter"). He complains that the Pope had condemned a treatise of Abbot Joachim,[54] and also the heretical doctrine of Almaricus.[55] This last is the theological philosopher Amalric of Bene (d. 1204), who took part in the widespread Holy Ghost movement of that age. It was then, too, he says, that the Dominican and Franciscan mendicant orders came into existence, "which was a great and wonderful thing for the Christian church." Pierre d'Ailly thus lays stress on the same phenomena that struck us as being characteristic of the time, and further regards this epoch as having been foretold in astrology.

39   The date for the founding of the monastery of Monte Cassino brings us very close to the year 530, which the Talmud prophesied would be a critical one. In Joachim's view not only does a new era begin then, but a new "status" of the world—the age of monasticism and the reign of the Holy Ghost. Its beginning still comes within the domain of the Son, but Joachim surmises in a psychologically correct manner that a new status— or, as we would say, a new attitude—would appear first as a more or less latent preliminary stage, which would then be followed by the *fructificatio,* the flower and the fruit. In Joachim's day the fruition was still in abeyance, but one could observe far and wide an uncommon agitation and commotion of men's spirits. Everyone felt the rushing wind of the pneuma; it was an age of new and unprecedented ideas which were blazoned abroad by the Cathari, Patarenes, Concorricci, Waldenses, Poor Men of

---

[53] This period around the year 1240 would, from the astrological standpoint, be characterized by the great conjunction of Jupiter and Saturn in Libra, in 1246. Libra is another double sign with a pneumatic nature (air trigon), like Gemini, and for this reason it was taken by Pierre d'Ailly as Christ's ascendent.

[54] At the Lateran Council, 1215. Cf. Denziger and Bannwart, *Enchiridion symbolorum,* pp. 190ff.

[55] "His teaching is to be held not so much heretical as insane," says the decree.

Lyons, Beghards, Brethren of the Free Spirit, "Bread through God," [56] and whatever else these movements were called. Their visible beginnings all lay in the early years of the eleventh century. The contemporary documents amassed by Hahn throw a revealing light on the ideas current in these circles:

Item, they believe themselves to be God by nature without distinction . . . and that they are eternal. . . .

Item, that they have no need of God or the Godhead.

Item, that they constitute the kingdom of heaven.

Item, that they are immutable in the new rock, that they rejoice in naught and are troubled by naught.

Item, that a man is bound to follow his inner instinct rather than the truth of the Gospel which is preached every day. . . . They say that they believe the Gospel to contain poetical matters which are not true. [57]

140   These few examples may suffice to show what kind of spirit animated these movements. They were made up of people who identified themselves (or were identified) with God, who deemed themselves supermen, had a critical approach to the gospels, followed the promptings of the inner man, and understood the kingdom of heaven to be within. In a sense, therefore, they were modern in their outlook, but they had a religious inflation instead of the rationalistic and political psychosis that is the affliction of our day. We ought not to impute these extremist ideas to Joachim, even though he took part in that great movement of the spirit and was one of its outstanding figures. One must ask oneself what psychological impulse could have moved

[56] Hahn, *Geschichte der Ketzer im Mittelalter*, II, p. 779: ". . . some who under the name of a false and pretended religious order, whom the common folk call Beghards and Schwestrones or 'Brod durch Gott'; but they call themselves Little Brethren and Sisters of the fellowship of the Free Spirit and of Voluntary Poverty."

[57] "Item credunt se esse Deum per naturam sine distinctione . . . se esse aeternos . . .

"Item quod nullo indigent nec Deo nec Deitate.

"Item quod sunt ipsum regnum coelorum.

"Item quod sunt etiam immutabiles in nova rupe, quod de nullo gaudent, et de nullo turbantur.

"Item quod homo magis tenetur sequi instinctum interiorem quam veritatem Evangelii quod cottidie praedicatur . . . dicunt, se credere ibi (in Evangelio) esse poëtica quae non sunt vera." (Hahn, II, pp. 779f.)

him and his adherents to cherish such bold expectations as the substitution of the "everlasting gospel" for the Christian message or the supersession of the second Person in the Godhead by the third, who would reign over the new era. This thought is so heretical and subversive that it could never have occurred to him had he not felt himself supported and swept along by the revolutionary currents of the age. He felt it as a revelation of the Holy Ghost, whose life and procreative power no church could bring to a stop. The numinosity of this feeling was heightened by the temporal coincidence—"synchronicity"—of the epoch he lived in with the beginning of the sphere of the "antichristian" fish in Pisces. In consequence, one might feel tempted to regard the Holy Ghost movement and Joachim's central ideas as a direct expression of the antichristian psychology that was then dawning. At any rate the Church's condemnation is thoroughly understandable, for in many ways his attitude to the Church of Jesus Christ comes very close to open insurrection, if not downright apostasy. But if we allow some credence to the conviction of these innovators that they were moved by the Holy Ghost, then another interpretation becomes not only possible but even probable.

That is to say, just as Joachim supposed that the status of the Holy Ghost had secretly begun with St. Benedict, so we might hazard the conjecture that a new status was secretly anticipated in Joachim himself. Consciously, of course, he thought he was bringing the status of the Holy Ghost into reality, just as it is certain that St. Benedict had nothing else in mind than to put the Church on a firm footing and deepen the meaning of the Christian life through monasticism. But, unconsciously—and this is psychologically what probably happened—Joachim could have been seized by the archetype of the spirit. There is no doubt that his activities were founded on a numinous experience, which is, indeed, characteristic of all those who are gripped by an archetype. He understood the spirit in the dogmatic sense as the third Person of the Godhead, for no other way was possible, but not in the sense of the empirical archetype. This archetype is not of uniform meaning, but was originally an ambivalent dualistic figure [58] that broke through again

[58] Cf. "The Phenomenology of the Spirit in Fairytales," pars. 396ff.

in the alchemical concept of spirit after engendering the most contradictory manifestations within the Holy Ghost movement itself. The Gnostics in their day had already had clear intimations of this dualistic figure. It was therefore very natural, in an age which coincided with the beginning of the second Fish and which was, so to speak, forced into ambiguity, that an espousal of the Holy Ghost in its Christian form should at the same time help the archetype of the spirit to break through in all its characteristic ambivalence. It would be unjust to class so worthy a personage as Joachim with the bigoted advocates of that revolutionary and anarchic turbulence, which is what the Holy Ghost movement turned into in so many places. We must suppose, rather, that he himself unwittingly ushered in a new "status," a religious attitude that was destined to bridge and compensate the frightful gulf that had opened out between Christ and Antichrist in the eleventh century. The antichristian era is to blame that the spirit became non-spiritual and that the vitalizing archetype gradually degenerated into rationalism, intellectualism, and doctrinairism, all of which leads straight to the tragedy of modern times now hanging over our heads like a sword of Damocles. In the old formula for the Trinity, as Joachim knew it, the dogmatic figure of the devil is lacking, for then as now he led a questionable existence somewhere on the fringes of theological metaphysics, in the shape of the *mysterium iniquitatis*. Fortunately for us, the threat of his coming had already been foretold in the New Testament—for the less he is recognized the more dangerous he is. Who would suspect him under those high-sounding names of his, such as public welfare, lifelong security, peace among the nations, etc.? He hides under idealisms, under -isms in general, and of these the most pernicious is doctrinairism, that most unspiritual of all the spirit's manifestations. The present age must come to terms drastically with the facts as they are, with the absolute opposition that is not only tearing the world asunder politically but has planted a schism in the human heart. We need to find our way back to the original, living spirit which, because of its ambivalence, is also a mediator and uniter of opposites,[59] an idea that preoccupied the alchemists for many centuries.

[59] "The Spirit Mercurius," pars. 284ff., and "A Psychological Approach to the Dogma of the Trinity," pars. 257ff.

If, as seems probable, the aeon of the fishes is ruled by the archetypal motif of the hostile brothers, then the approach of the next Platonic month, namely Aquarius, will constellate the problem of the union of opposites. It will then no longer be possible to write off evil as the mere privation of good; its real existence will have to be recognized. This problem can be solved neither by philosophy, nor by economics, nor by politics, but only by the individual human being, via his experience of the living spirit, whose fire descended upon Joachim, one of many, and, despite all contemporary misunderstandings, was handed onward into the future. The solemn proclamation of the *Assumptio Mariae* which we have experienced in our own day is an example of the way symbols develop through the ages. The impelling motive behind it did not come from the ecclesiastical authorities, who had given clear proof of their hesitation by postponing the declaration for nearly a hundred years,[60] but from the Catholic masses, who have insisted more and more vehemently on this development. Their insistence is, at bottom, the urge of the archetype to realize itself.[61]

The repercussions of the Holy Ghost movement spread, in the years that followed, to four minds of immense significance for the future. These were Albertus Magnus (1193–1280); his pupil Thomas Aquinas, the philosopher of the Church and an adept in alchemy (as also was Albertus); Roger Bacon (*c.* 1214–*c.* 1294), the English forerunner of inductive science; and finally Meister Eckhart (*c.* 1260–1327), the independent religious thinker, now enjoying a real revival after six hundred years of obscurity. Some people have rightly seen the Holy Ghost movement as the forerunner of the Reformation. At about the time of the twelfth and thirteenth centuries we find also the beginnings of Latin alchemy, whose philosophical and spiritual content I have tried to elucidate in my book *Psychology and Alchemy*. The image mentioned above (par. 139) of "immutability in the new rock" bears a striking resemblance to the central idea of philosophical alchemy, the *lapis philosophorum*, which is used as a parallel to Christ, the "rock," the "stone," the "corner-

---

60 [Although Mary's Immaculate Conception was declared *de fide* by Pope Pius IX in 1854, by the bull *Ineffabilis Deus*, her Assumption was not defined as part of divine revelation until 1950.—EDITORS.]

61 [Cf. "Psychology and Religion," par. 122, and "Answer to Job," pars. 748ff.]

stone." Priscillian (4th cent.) says: "We have Christ for a rock, Jesus for a cornerstone." [62] An alchemical text speaks of the "rock which is smitten thrice with Moses' rod, so that the waters flow forth freely." [63] The *lapis* is called a "sacred rock" and is described as having four parts.[64] St. Ambrose says the water from the rock is a prefiguration of the blood that flowed from Christ's side.[65] Another alchemical text mentions the "water from the rock" as the equivalent of the universal solvent, the *aqua permanens*.[66] Khunrath, in his somewhat florid language, even speaks of the "Petroleum sapientum." [67] By the Naassenes, Adam was called the "rock" and the "cornerstone." [68] Both these allegories of Christ are mentioned by Epiphanius in his *Ancoratus,* and also by Firmicus Maternus.[69] This image, common to ecclesiastical and alchemical language alike, goes back to I Corinthians 10 : 4 and I Peter 2 : 4.

144   The new rock, then, takes the place of Christ, just as the everlasting gospel was meant to take the place of Christ's message. Through the descent and indwelling of the Holy Ghost the υἱότης, sonship, is infused into every individual, so that everybody who possesses the Holy Ghost will be a new rock, in accordance with I Peter 2 : 5: "Be you also as living stones built up." [70] This is a logical development of the teaching about the

62 *Opera,* ed. G. Schepps, p. 24.

63 Cf. *Aurora Consurgens* (ed. von Franz), p. 127: "this great and wide sea smote the rock and the metallic waters flowed forth."

64 *Musaeum hermeticum* (1678), p. 212: "Our stone is called the sacred rock, and is understood or signified in four ways." Cf. Ephesians 3 : 18. The Pyramid Text of Pepi I mentions a god of resurrection with four faces: "Homage to thee, O thou who hast four faces. . . . Thou art endowed with a soul, and thou dost rise (like the sun) in thy boat . . . carry thou this Pepi with thee in the cabin of thy boat, for this Pepi is the son of the Scarab." (Budge, *Gods of the Egyptians,* I, p. 85.)

65 *Explanationes in Psalmos,* XXXVIII: "In the shadow there was water from the rock, as it were the blood of Christ."

66 Mylius, *Philosophia reformata* (1622), p. 112: "Whence the philosopher brought forth water from the rock and oil out of the flinty stone."

67 *Von hylealischen Chaos* (1597), p. 272.

68 Hippolytus, *Elenchos,* V, 7, 34f. (Legge trans., I, p. 129). Reference is also made here to the "stone cut from the mountain without hands" (Daniel 2 : 45), a metaphor used by the alchemists.

69 *De errore profanarum religionum,* 20, 1.

70 Cf. the building of the seamless tower (church) with "living stones" in the "Shepherd" of Hermas.

Paracletc and the filiation, as stated in Luke 6 : 35: "You shall be sons of the Highest," and John 10 : 34: "Is it not written in your law: I said, you are gods?" The Naassenes, as we know, had already made use of these allusions and thus anticipated a whole tract of historical development—a development that led via monasticism to the Holy Ghost movement, via the *Theologia Germanica* direct to Luther, and via alchemy to modern science.

Let us now turn back to the theme of Christ as the fish. According to Doelger, the Christian fish symbol first appeared in Alexandria around A.D. 200; [71] similarly, the baptismal bath was described as a *piscina* (fish-pond) quite early. This presupposes that the believers were fishes, as is in fact suggested by the gospels (for instance Matt. 4 : 19). There Christ wants to make Peter and Andrew "fishers of men," and the miraculous draught of fishes (Luke 5 : 10) is used by Christ himself as a paradigm for Peter's missionary activity.

A direct astrological aspect of Christ's birth is given us in Matthew 2 : 1ff. The Magi from the East were star-gazers who, beholding an extraordinary constellation, inferred an equally extraordinary birth. This anecdote proves that Christ, possibly even at the time of the apostles, was viewed from the astrological standpoint or was at least brought into connection with

[71] Doelger, ΙΧΘΥΣ: *Das Fischsymbol*, I, p. 18. Though the Abercius inscription, which dates from the beginning of the 3rd cent. (after A.D. 216), is of importance in this connection, it is of doubtful Christian origin. Dieterich (*Die Grabschrift des Aberkios*), in the course of a brilliant argument, demonstrates that the "holy shepherd" mentioned in the inscription is Attis, the Lord of the sacred Ram and the thousand-eyed shepherd of glittering stars. One of his special forms was Elogabal of Emera, the god of the emperor Heliogabalus, who caused the *hieros gamos* of his god to be celebrated with Urania of Carthage, also called *Virgo coelestis*. Heliogabalus was a *gallus* (priest) of the Great Mother, whose fish only the priests might eat. The fish had to be caught by a virgin. It is conjectured that Abercius had this inscription written in commemoration of his journey to Rome to the great *hieros gamos*, sometime after A.D. 216. For the same reasons there are doubts about the Christianity of the Pectorios inscription at Autun, in which the fish figures too: Ἔσθιε πν . . . , ἰχθὺν ἔχων παλάμαις Ἰχθύϊ χόρταξ ἄρα λιλαίω δέσποτα σῶτερ: "Eat . . . (reading uncertain), holding the fish in the hands. Nourish now with the fish, I yearn, Lord Saviour." Probable reading: πινάων instead of πεινάων. Cf. Cabrol and Leclercq, *Dictionnaire d'archéologie chrétienne*, XIII, cols. 2884ff., "Pectorios." The first three distichs of the inscription make the acrostic Ichthys. Dating is uncertain (3rd–5th cent.). Cf. Doelger, I, pp. 12ff.

astrological myths. The latter alternative is fully confirmed when we consider the apocalyptic utterances of St. John. Since this exceedingly complex question has been discussed by those who are more qualified than I, we can support our argument on the well-attested fact that glimpses of astrological mythology may be caught behind the stories of the worldly and other-worldly life of the Redeemer.[72]

147   Above all it is the connections with the age of the Fishes which are attested by the fish symbolism, either contemporaneously with the gospels themselves ("fishers of men," fishermen as the first disciples, miracle of loaves and fishes), or immediately afterwards in the post-apostolic era. The symbolism shows Christ and those who believe in him as fishes, fish as the food eaten at the Agape,[73] baptism as immersion in a fish-pond, etc. At first sight, all this points to no more than the fact that the fish symbols and mythologems which have always existed had assimilated the figure of the Redeemer; in other words, it was a symptom of Christ's assimilation into the world of ideas prevailing at that time. But, to the extent that Christ was regarded as the new aeon, it would be clear to anyone acquainted with astrology that he was born as the first fish of the Pisces era, and was doomed to die as the last ram [74] (ἀρνίον, lamb) of the declining Aries era.[75] Matthew 27 : 15ff. hands down this mythologem in

[72] I refer particularly to Boll, *Aus der Offenbarung Johannis*. The writings of Arthur Drews have treated the astrological parallels with—one can well say—monomaniacal thoroughness, not altogether to the advantage of this idea. See *Der Sternenhimmel in der Dichtung und Religion der alten Völker und des Christentums.*

[73] Religious meal. According to Tertullian (*Adversus Marcionem*, I, cap. XIV; Migne, *P.L.*, vol. 2, col. 262) the fish signifies "the holier food." Cf. also Goodenough, *Jewish Symbols*, V, pp. 41ff.

[74] Origen, *In Genesim hom.* VIII, 9 (Migne, *P.G.*, vol. 12, col. 208): "We said . . . that Isaac bore the form of Christ, but that the *ram* also seems no less to bear the form of Christ." Augustine (*City of God*, XVI, 32, 1) asks: "Who was that ram by the offering whereof was made a complete sacrifice in typical blood . . . who was prefigured thereby but Jesus . . . ?" For the Lamb as Aries in the Apocalypse see Boll, *Aus der Offenbarung Johannis.*

[75] Eisler, *Orpheus—The Fisher*, pp. 51ff. There is also a wealth of material in Eisler's paper "Der Fisch als Sexualsymbol," though it contains little that would help to interpret the fish-symbol, since the question puts the cart before the horse. It has long been known that *all the instinctual forces of the psyche* are involved in the formation of symbolic images, hence sexuality as well. Sex is not

the form of the old sacrifice of the seasonal god. Significantly enough, Jesus's partner in the ceremony is called Barabbas, "son of the father." There would be some justification for drawing a parallel between the tension of opposites in early Christian psychology and the fact the zodiacal sign for Pisces (♓) frequently shows two fishes moving in opposite directions, but only if it could be proved that their contrary movement dates from pre-Christian times or is at least contemporary with Christ. Unfortunately, I know of no pictorial representation from this period that would give us any information about the position of the fishes. In the fine bas-relief of the zodia from the Little Metropolis in Athens, Pisces and Aquarius are missing. There is one representation of the fishes, near the beginning of our era, that is certainly free from Christian influence. This is the globe of the heavens from the Farnese Atlas in Naples. The first fish, depicted north of the equator, is vertical, with its head pointing to the celestial Pole; the second fish, south of the equator, is horizontal, with its head pointing West. The picture follows the astronomical configuration and is therefore naturalistic.[76] The zodiac from the temple of Hathor at Denderah (1st cent. B.C.) shows the fishes, but they both face the same way. The planisphere of Timochares,[77] mentioned by Hipparchus, has only *one* fish where Pisces should be. On coins and gems from the time of the emperors, and also on Mithraic monuments,[78] the fishes are shown either facing the same way or moving in opposite directions.[79] The polarity which the fishes later acquired may perhaps be due to the fact that the astronomical constellation shows the first (northerly) fish as vertical, and the second (southerly) fish as horizontal. They move almost at right

---

"symbolized" in these images, but leaps to the eye, as Eisler's material clearly shows. In whatsoever a man is involved, there his sexuality will appear too. The indubitably correct statement that St. Peter's is made of stone, wood, and metal hardly helps us to interpret its meaning, and the same is true of the fish symbol if one continues to be astonished that this image, like all others, has its manifest sexual components. With regard to the terminology, it should be noted that something known is never "symbolized," but can only be expressed *allegorically* or *semiotically*.   [76] Thiele, *Antike Himmelsbilder*, p. 29.
[77] Boll, *Sphaera*, Pl. I, and Eisler, *The Royal Art of Astrology*, Pl. 5, following p. 164.   [78] Gaedechens, *Der Marmorne Himmelsglobus*.
[79] Cumont, *Textes et monuments*, II.

angles to one another and hence form a cross. This counter-movement, which was unknown to the majority of the oldest sources, was much emphasized in Christian times, and this leads one to suspect a certain tendentiousness.[80]

148   Although no connection of any kind can be proved between the figure of Christ and the inception of the astrological age of the fishes, the simultaneity of the fish symbolism of the Redeemer with the astrological symbol of the new aeon seems to me important enough to warrant the emphasis we place upon it. If we try to follow up the complicated mythological ramifications of this parallel, we do so with intent to throw light on the multifarious aspects of an archetype that manifests itself on the one hand in a *personality,* and on the other hand synchronistically, in a moment of time determined in advance, before Christ's birth. Indeed, long before that, the archetype had been written in the heavens by projection, so as then, "when the time was fulfilled," to coincide with the symbols produced by the new era. The fish, appropriately enough, belongs to the winter rainy season, like Aquarius and Capricorn (αἰγόκερως, the goat-fish).[81] As a zodiacal sign, therefore, it is not in the least remarkable. It becomes a matter for astonishment only when, through the precession of the equinoxes, the spring-point moves into this sign and thus inaugurates an age in which the "fish" was used as a name for the God who became a man, who was born as a fish and was sacrificed as a ram, who had fishermen for disciples and wanted to make them fishers of men, who fed the multitude with miraculously multiplying fishes, who was himself eaten as a fish, the "holier food," and whose followers are little fishes, the "pisciculi." Assume, if you like, that a fairly widespread knowledge of astrology would account for at least some of this sym-

---

[80] See the two fishes in Lambspringk's symbols (*Mus. herm.,* p. 343), representing at the same time the opposites to be united. Aratus (*Phaenomena,* Mair trans., p. 401) mentions only the higher position of the northern fish as compared with the southern one, without emphasizing their duality or opposition. Their double character is, however, stressed in modern astrological speculation. (E. M. Smith, *The Zodia,* p. 279.) Senard (*Le Zodiaque,* p. 446) says: "The fish . . . swimming from above downwards symbolizes the movement of involution of Spirit in Matter; that . . . which swims from below upwards, the movement of evolution of the Spirit-Matter composite returning to its Unique Principle."
[81] Capricorn ♑ or ♑.

bolism in certain Gnostic-Christian circles.[82] But this assumption does not apply when it comes to eyewitness accounts in the synoptic gospels. There is no evidence of any such thing. We have no reason whatever to suppose that those stories are disguised astrological myths. On the contrary, one gets the impression that the fish episodes are entirely natural happenings and that there is nothing further to be looked for behind them. They are "Just So" stories, quite simple and natural, and one wonders whether the whole Christian fish symbolism may not have come about equally fortuitously and without premeditation. Hence one could speak just as well of the seemingly fortuitous coincidence of this symbolism with the name of the new aeon, the more so as the age of the fishes seems to have left no very clear traces in the cultures of the East. I could not maintain with any certainty that this is correct, because I know far too little about Indian and Chinese astrology. As against this, the fact that the traditional fish symbolism makes possible a verifiable prediction that had already been made in the New Testament is a somewhat uncomfortable proposition to swallow.

49   The northerly, or easterly, fish, which the spring-point entered at about the beginning of our era,[83] is joined to the southerly, or westerly, fish by the so-called commissure. This consists of a band of faint stars forming the middle sector of the constellation, and the spring-point gradually moved along its southern edge. The point where the ecliptic intersects with the meridian at the tail of the second fish coincides roughly with the sixteenth century, the time of the Reformation, which as we know is so extraordinarily important for the history of Western symbols. Since then the spring-point has moved along the southern edge of the second fish, and will enter Aquarius in the

---

82 A clear reference to astrology can be found in *Pistis Sophia*, where Jesus converses with the "ordainers of the nativity": "But Jesus answered and said to Mary: If the ordainers of the nativity find Heimarmene and the Sphere turned to the left in accordance with their first circulation, then their words will be true, and they will say what must come to pass. But if they find Heimarmene or the Sphere turned to the right, then they will not say anything true, because I have changed their influences and their squares and their triangles and their octants." (Cf. Mead trans., p. 29.)

83 The meridian of the star "O" in the commissure passed through the spring-point in A.D. 11, and that of the star "a 113" in 146 B.C. Calculated on the basis of Peters and Knobel, *Ptolemy's Catalogue of Stars*.

course of the third millennium.[84] Astrologically interpreted, the designation of Christ as one of the fishes identifies him with the first fish, the vertical one. Christ is followed by the Antichrist, at the end of time. The beginning of the enantiodromia would fall, logically, midway between the two fishes. We have seen that this is so. The time of the Renaissance begins in the immediate vicinity of the second fish, and with it comes that spirit which culminates in the modern age.[85]

[84] Since the delimitation of the constellations is known to be somewhat arbitrary, this date is very indefinite. It refers to the actual constellation of fixed stars, not to the *zodion noeton*, i.e., the zodiac divided into sectors of 30° each. Astrologically the beginning of the next aeon, according to the starting-point you select, falls between A.D. 2000 and 2200. Starting from star "O" and assuming a Platonic month of 2,143 years, one would arrive at A.D. 2154 for the beginning of the Aquarian Age, and at A.D. 1997 if you start from star "a 113." The latter date agrees with the longitude of the stars in Ptolemy's Almagest.

[85] Modern astrological speculation likewise associates the Fishes with Christ: "The fishes . . . the inhabitants of the waters, are fitly an emblem of those whose life being hid with Christ in God, come out of the waters of judgment without being destroyed [an allusion to the fishes which were *not* drowned in the Deluge!—C.G.J.] and shall find their true sphere where life abounds and death is not: where, for ever surrounded with the living water and drinking from its fountain, they 'shall not perish, but have everlasting life.' . . . Those who shall dwell for ever in the living water are one with Jesus Christ the Son of God, the Living One." (Smith, *The Zodia,* pp. 28of.)

VII

THE PROPHECIES OF NOSTRADAMUS

150   The course of our religious history as well as an essential part of our psychic development could have been predicted more or less accurately, both as regards time and content, from the precession of the equinoxes through the constellation of Pisces. The prediction, as we saw, was actually made and coincides with the fact that the Church suffered a schism in the sixteenth century. After that an enantiodromian process set in which, in contrast to the "Gothic" striving *upwards* to the heights, could be described as a horizontal movement *outwards,* namely the voyages of discovery and the conquest of Nature. The vertical was cut across by the horizontal, and man's spiritual and moral development moved in a direction that grew more and more obviously antichristian, so that today we are confronted with a crisis of Western civilization whose outcome appears to be exceedingly dubious.

151   With this background in mind, I would like to mention the astrological prophecies of Nostradamus, written in a letter [1] to Henry II of France, on June 27, 1558. After detailing a year characterized, among other things, by ♃ ☌ ☿ with ♂ □ ☿,[2] he says:

---

[1] Printed in the Amsterdam edition of the *Vrayes Centuries et Prophéties de Maistre Michel Nostredame* (1667), pp. 96ff.

[2] According to the old tradition the conjunction of Jupiter and Mercury, as mentioned above, is characteristic of Christianity. The quartile aspect between Mercury and Mars "injures" Mercury by "martial" violence. According to Cardan, ☿ ☌ ♂ signifies "the law of Mahomet" (*Comment. in Ptol.*, p. 188). This aspect could therefore indicate an attack by Islam. Albumasar regards ♃ ☌ ♂ in the same way: "And if Mars shall be in conjunction with him (Jupiter), it signifies the fiery civilization and the pagan faith" (*De magn. coniunct.*, tract. I, diff. 4, p. a8r). On the analogy of history the evil events to come are ascribed to the crescent moon, but one never reflects that the opponent of Christianity dwells in the European unconscious. History repeats itself.

95

Then the beginning of that year shall see a greater persecution against the Christian Church than ever was in Africa,[3] and it shall be in the year 1792, at which time everyone will think it a renovation of the age. . . . And at that time and in those countries the infernal power shall rise against the Church of Jesus Christ. This shall be the second Antichrist, which shall persecute the said Church and its true vicar by means of the power of temporal kings, who through their ignorance shall be seduced by tongues more sharp than any sword in the hands of a madman. . . . The persecution of the clergy shall have its beginning in the power of the Northern Kings joined by the Eastern ones. And that persecution shall last eleven years, or a little less, at which time the chief Northern king shall fail.[4]

152   However, Nostradamus thinks that "a united Southern king" will outlast the Northern one by three years. He sees a return of paganism ("the sanctuary destroyed by paganism"), the Bible will be burned, and an immense blood-bath will take place: "So great tribulations as ever did happen since the first foundation of the Christian Church." All Latin countries will be affected by it.

153   There are historical determinants that may have moved Nostradamus to give the year 1792 as the beginning of the new aeon. For instance, Cardinal Pierre d'Ailly, basing himself on Albumasar, writes in his *Concordantia* [5] on the eighth *coniunctio maxima* ($\u2643\ \u260d\ \u2644$ in $\u2648$), which had been calculated for 1693:

And after that shall be the fulfilment of ten revolutions of Saturn in the year 1789, and this will happen after the said conjunction, in the course of ninety-seven years or thereabouts. . . . This being so, we say that if the world shall endure until then, which God alone knows, then there will be many and great and marvellous changes and transformations of the world, especially as concerns law-giving and religious sects, for the said conjunction and the revolutions of Saturn will coincide with the revolution or reversal of the upper orb, i.e., the eighth sphere, and from these and other premises the change of sects will be known. . . . Whence it may

[3] Where Roman Christendom succumbed to Islam.
[4] *The Complete Prophecies of Nostradamus*, trans. and ed. by H. C. Roberts, pp. 231ff.
[5] D 7ᵛ to 8ʳ, div. 2, cap. 60 and 61. Cf. also Thorndike, *A History of Magic and Experimental Science*, IV, p. 102.

be concluded with some probability that this is the time when the Antichrist shall come with his law and his damnable sects, which are utterly contrary and inimical to the law of Christ; for, being human, we can have no certainty with regard to the time and the moment of his coming. . . . Yet, despite the indeterminate statement that he will come at approximately that time, it is possible to have a probable conjecture and a credible hypothesis in accordance with the astronomical indications. If, therefore, the astronomers say that a change of sects will occur about that time, then, according to them, a Mighty One will come after Mahomet, who will set up an evil and magical law. Thus we may surmise with credible probability that after the sect of Mahomet none other will come save the law of the Antichrist.[6]

4   In connection with the calculation of the year 1693, Pierre d'Ailly quotes Albumasar as saying that the first *coniunctio maxima* of Saturn and Jupiter took place *anno mundi* 3200. To this Albumasar added 960 years, which brings us to A.D. 1693 as the year of the eighth *coniunctio maxima*.[7] In Part III of his book, chapter 17, Pierre d'Ailly criticizes this view and calls it a "false deduction." In his treatise against "superstitiosos astronomos," 1410, he maintains that the Christian religion should not be brought under astrological laws. He was alluding in particular to Roger Bacon, who had revived the theory that Christianity was under the influence of the planet Mercury. Pierre d'Ailly

---

6 "Et post illam erit complementum 10 revolutionum saturnalium anno Christi 1789 et hoc erit post dictam coniunctionem per annos 97 vel prope. . . . His itaque praesuppositis dicimus quod si mundus usque ad illa tempora duraverit, quod solus deus novit, multae tunc et magnae et mirabiles alterationes mundi et mutationes futurae sunt, et *maxime circa leges et sectas*, nam cum praedicta coniunctione et illis revolutionibus Saturni ad hoc concurret revolutio seu reversio superioris orbis, id est, octavae sphaerae per quam et per alia praemissa cognoscitur sectarum mutatio . . . Unde ex his probabiliter concluditur quod forte circa illa tempora veniet *Antichristus* cum lege sua vel secta damnabili, quae maxime adversa erit et contraria legi Christi; nam licet de adventu sui determinato tempore vel momento haberi non possit humanitus certitudo. . . . Tamen indeterminate loquendo quod circa illa tempora venturus sit potest haberi probabilis coniectura et verisimilis suspicio per astronomica iudicia. Cum enim dictum sit secundum astronomos circa illa tempora fieri mutationem sectarum et secundum eos post *machometum* erit aliquis potens, qui legem foedam et magicam constituet. Ideo verisimili probabilitate credi potest, quod post sectam machometi nulla secta veniet, nisi lex antichristi."

7 *Concordantia*, etc., fol. b 5.

held that only superstitions and heretical opinions were astrologically influenced, and especially the coming of the Antichrist.[8]

155   We are probably right in assuming that these calculations were known to Nostradamus, who proposed 1792 as an improvement on 1789. Both dates are suggestive, and a knowledge of subsequent events confirms that the things that happened around that time were significant forerunners of developments in our own day. The enthronement of the "Déesse Raison" was, in fact, an anticipation of the antichristian trend that was pursued from then onwards.

156   The "renovation of the age" might mean a new aeon, and it coincides in a remarkable way with the new system of dating, the revolutionary calendar, which began with September 22, 1792, and had a distinctly antichristian character.[9] What had been brewing up long beforehand then became a manifest event; in the French Revolution men witnessed the enantiodromia that had set in with the Renaissance and ran parallel with the astrological fish symbol. The time seemed a significant one astrologically, for a variety of reasons. In the first place this was the moment when the precession of the equinoxes reached the tail of the second fish.[10] Then, in the year 1791, Saturn was in ♈, a fiery sign. Besides that, tradition made use of the theory of maximal conjunctions [11] and regarded the year of the eighth *coniunctio maxima*—1693—as a starting-point for future calculations.[12] This critical year was combined with another

---

[8] Cf. Thorndike, IV, p. 103.

[9] In classical usage *renovatio* can have the meaning of the modern word "revolution," whereas even in late Latin *revolutio* still retains its original meaning of "revolving." As the text shows, Nostradamus thought of this moment (1791) as the climax of a long-standing persecution of the Church. One is reminded of Voltaire's "écrasez l'infâme!"

[10] There is nothing to suggest that a conscious attempt was made to prophesy on the basis of the precession.

[11] Conjunctions in Aries were regarded as such, at least as a rule. 0° Aries is the spring-point.

[12] I cannot claim to have understood Pierre d'Ailly's argument. Here is the text (Second treatise, ch. 60, "De octava coniunctione maxima"): "Et post illam erit complementum 10 revolutionum saturnalium anno Christi 1789 et hoc erit post dictam coniunctionem per annos 97 vel prope et inter dictam coniunctionem et illud complementum dictarum 10 revolutionum erit status octavae sphaerae circiter per annos 25 quod sic patet: quia status octavae sphaerae erit

tradition basing itself on periods of ten revolutions of Saturn, each period taking three hundred years. Pierre d'Ailly cites Albumasar, who says in his *Magnae coniunctiones:* "They said that the change shall come when ten revolutions of Saturn have been completed, and that the permutation of Saturn is particularly appropriate to the movable signs" (♈, ♋, ♎, ♑).[13] According to Pierre d'Ailly, a Saturn period came to an end in 11 B.C., and he connects this with the appearance of Christ. Another period ended in A.D. 289: this he connects with Manichaeism. The year 589 foretells Islam, and 1189 the significant reign of Pope Innocent III; 1489 announces a schism of the Church, and 1789 signalizes—by inference—the coming of the Antichrist. Fantasy could do the rest, for the archetype had long been ready and was only waiting for the time to be fulfilled. That a usurper from the North would seize power [14] is easily understood when we consider that the Antichrist is something infernal, the devil or the devil's son, and is therefore Typhon or Set, who has his fiery abode in the North. Typhon's power is triadic, possessing two confederates, one in the East and one in the South. This power corresponds to the "lower triad." [15]

57   Nostradamus, the learned physician and astrologer, would certainly have been familiar with the idea of the North as the region of the devil, unbelievers, and all things evil. The idea,

---

anno 444 post situm augmentationum [reading uncertain], quae secundum tabulas astronomicas sunt adaequatae ad annum Christi 1320 perfectum, et ideo anno Christi 1764, quibus annis si addas 25, sunt anni 1789 quos praediximus. Unde iterum patet quod ab hoc anno Christi 1414 usque ad statum octavae sphaerae erunt anni 253 perfecti." (And after that shall be the fulfilment of 10 revolutions of Saturn to the year 1789, and this shall be after the said conjunction for 97 years or thereabouts, and between the said conjunction and that fulfilment of the 10 revolutions there shall be a standstill of the eighth sphere for about 25 years, which is evident from this: that the standstill of the eighth sphere shall be in the 444th year after the position of the augmentations, which according to the astronomical tables are assigned to the end of the year of Christ 1320, that is the year of Christ 1764, and if you add 25 years to this, you arrive at the year 1789 aforesaid. Hence it is again evident that from this year of Christ 1414 to the standstill of the eighth sphere there will be 253 complete years.)

13 Fol. d 6.

14 It is not clear from the text whether the same "persecution" is meant, or a new one. The latter would be possible.

15 Cf. "The Phenomenology of the Spirit in Fairytales," pars. 425f., 436ff.

as St. Eucherius of Lyons (d. 450) remarks,[16] goes back to Jeremiah 1 : 14: "From the north shall an evil wind break forth upon all the inhabitants of the land," [17] and other passages such as Isaiah 14 : 12f.:

How art thou fallen from heaven, O Lucifer, son of the morning! how art thou cut down to the ground, which didst weaken the nations! For thou hast said in thine heart, I will ascend into heaven, I will exalt my throne above the stars of God, I will sit on the mount of assembly in the far north.[18]

The Benedictine monk Rhabanus Maurus (d. 856) says that "the north wind is the harshness of persecution" and "a figure of the old enemy." [19] The north wind, he adds, signifies the devil, as is evident from Job 26 : 7: "He stretcheth out the north over the empty space, and hangeth the earth upon nothing." [20] Rhabanus interprets this as meaning that "God allows the devil to rule the minds of those who are empty of his grace." [21] St. Augustine says: "Who is that north wind, save him who said: I will set up my seat in the north, I will be like the most High? The devil held rule over the wicked, and possessed the nations," etc.[22]

158   The Victorine monk Garnerius says that the "malign spirit" was called Aquilo, the north wind. Its coldness meant the "frigidity of sinners." [23] Adam Scotus imagined there was a frightful dragon's head in the north from which all evil comes. From its mouth and snout it emitted smoke of a triple nature,[24] the "threefold ignorance, namely of good and evil, of true and

[16] Migne, *P.L.*, vol. 50, col. 740.
[17] "Ab Aquilone pendetur malum super omnes habitatores terrae" (DV).
[18] "Quomodo cecidisti de coelo, Lucifer, qui mane oriebaris? corruisti in terram qui vulnerabas gentes? Qui dicebas in corde tuo: in caelum conscendam, super astra Dei exaltabo solium meum, sedebo in monte testamenti, in lateribus Aquilonis" (trans. is AV; last line RSV).
[19] Migne, *P.L.*, vol. 112, col. 860.
[20] This is an obvious analogy of the pneuma brooding on the face of the deep.
[21] ". . . quod illorum mentibus, qui gratia sua vacui, diabolum Deus dominari permittit."
[22] *Enar. in Ps.* XLVII, 3; Migne, *P.L.*, vol. 36, col. 534.
[23] *Sancti Victoris Parisiensis Gregorianum;* Migne, *P.L.*, vol. 193, cols. 59f.
[24] Allusion to the lower triad.

false, of fitting and unfitting." [25] "That is the smoke," says Adam Scotus, "which the prophet Ezekiel, in his vision of God, saw coming from the north," [26] the "smoke" of which Isaiah speaks. [27] The pious author never stops to think how remarkable it is that the prophet's vision of God should be blown along on the wings of the north wind, wrapped in this devilish smoke of threefold ignorance. Where there is smoke, there is fire. Hence the "great cloud" had "brightness round about it, and fire flashing forth continually, and in the midst of the fire, as it were gleaming bronze." [28] The north wind comes from the region of fire and, despite its coldness, is a "ventus urens" (burning wind), as Gregory the Great calls it, referring to Job 27 : 21. [29] This wind is the malign spirit, "who rouses up the flames of lust in the heart" and kindles every living thing to sin. "Through the breath of evil incitement to earthly pleasures he makes the hearts of the wicked to burn." As Jeremiah 1 : 13 says, "I see a boiling pot, facing away from the north." In these quotations from Gregory we hear a faint echo of the ancient idea of the fire in the north, which is still very much alive in Ezekiel, whose cloud of fire appears from the north, whence "an evil shall break forth upon all the inhabitants of the land." [30]

In these circumstances it is hardly surprising that Nostradamus warns against the usurper from the north when foretelling the coming of the Antichrist. Even before the Reformation the Antichrist was a popular figure in folklore, as the numerous editions of the "Entkrist" [31] in the second half of the

25 *De tripartito tabernaculo*, III, c. 9; Migne, *P.L.*, vol. 198, col. 761. Adam Scotus speaks of the "darkness of the smoke from the north." Pseudo-Clement (*Homilies*, XIX, 22) stresses "the sins of unconsciousness" (*agnoia*). Honorius of Autun (*Speculum de mysteriis ecclesiae*; Migne, *P.L.*, vol. 172, col. 833) says: "By the north, where the sun lies hidden under the earth, Matthew is meant, who describes the divinity of Christ hidden under the flesh." This confirms the chthonic nature of the triad.
26 Ezek. 1 : 4: "And I saw, and behold a whirlwind came out of the north, and a great cloud . . ."
27 Isaiah 14 : 31: "Howl, O gate, cry, O city, all Philistia is thrown down, for a smoke shall come from the north, and there is none that shall escape his troop."
28 Ezek. 1 : 4.
29 "A burning wind shall take him up and carry him away; and as a whirlwind shall snatch him from his place" (*In Expositionem beati Job Moralia*; Migne, *P.L.*, vol. 76, cols. 54, 55).
30 Jer. 1 : 13f.   31 Cf. *Symbols of Transformation*, par. 565.

fifteenth century show.[32] This is quite understandable in view of the spiritual events then impending: the Reformation was about to begin. Luther was promptly greeted as the Antichrist, and it is possible that Nostradamus calls the Antichrist who was to appear after 1792 the "second Antichrist" because the first had already appeared in the guise of the German reformer, or much earlier with Nero or Mohammed.[33] We should not omit to mention in this connection how much capital the Nazis made out of the idea that Hitler was continuing and completing the work of reformation which Luther had left only half finished.

160   From the existing astrological data, therefore, and from the possibilities of interpreting them it was not difficult for Nostradamus to predict the imminent enantiodromia of the Christian aeon; indeed, by making this prediction, he placed himself firmly in the antichristian phase and served as its mouthpiece.

161   After this excursion, let us turn back to our fish symbolism.

[32] The text of the various mss. is supposed to go back to the *Compendium theologicae veritatis* of Hugh of Strasbourg (13th cent.). Cf. Kelchner, *Der Enndkrist*, p. 7.

[33] So in Giovanni Nanni (1432–1502). See Thorndike, IV, pp. 263ff.

VIII

THE HISTORICAL SIGNIFICANCE
OF THE FISH

162 In addition to the "pisciculi Christianorum," the shepherd and the lamb play, as we know only too well, an almost greater role in Christian allegory, and Hermes Kriophoros (the "ram-bearer") became the prototype of the "good shepherd," the tutelary god of flocks. Another prototype, in his capacity as shepherd, was Orpheus.[1] This aspect of the Poimen gave rise to a figure of similar name in the mystery cults, who was popularized in the "Shepherd" of Hermas (2nd century). Like the "giant fish" mentioned in the Abercius inscription,[2] the shepherd probably has connections with Attis, both temporally and regionally. Reitzenstein even conjectures that the "Shepherd" of Hermas derives from the Poimandres writings, which are of purely pagan origin.[3] Shepherd, ram, and lamb symbolism coincides with the expiring aeon of Aries. In the first century of our era the two aeons overlap, and the two most important mystery gods of this period, Attis and Christ, are both characterized as shepherds, rams, and fishes. The Poimen symbolism has undergone such thorough elaboration at the hands of Reitzenstein that I am in no position to add anything illuminating in this respect. The case is somewhat different with the fish symbol. Not only are the sources more copious, but the very nature of the symbol, and in particular its dual aspects, give rise to definite psychological questions which I should like to go into more closely.

163 Like every hero, Christ had a childhood that was threatened (massacre of the innocents, flight into Egypt). The astrological "interpretation" of this can be found in Revelation 12 : 1: "A woman clothed with the sun, with the moon under her feet,

---

[1] Eisler, *Orpheus—The Fisher*, pp. 51ff.   [2] [Cf. par. 127, n. 4.]
[3] *Poimandres*, pp. 32ff.

103

and on her head a crown of twelve stars." She is in the pangs of birth and is pursued by a dragon. She will give birth to a man-child who shall "rule the nations with a rod of iron." This story carries echoes of numerous kindred motifs in East and West, for instance that of Leto and Python, of Aphrodite and her son, who, when pursued, leapt into the Euphrates and were changed into fishes,[4] and of Isis and Horus in Egypt. The Syrian Greeks identified Derceto-Atargatis and her son Ichthys with the constellation of the Fishes.[5]

164   The mother-goddess—and the star-crowned woman of the Apocalypse counts as one—is usually thought of as a virgin (παρθένος, *virgo*). The Christmas message, Ἡ παρθένος τέτοκεν, αὔξει φῶς (the virgin has brought forth, the light increases), is pagan. Speaking of the so-called Korion in Alexandria, Epiphanius[6] says that on the night of the Epiphany (January 5/6) the pagans held a great festival:

They stay up the whole night singing songs and playing the flute, offering these to the images of the gods; and, when the revelries of the night are over, after cock-crow, they go down with torches into a subterranean sanctuary and bring up a carved wooden image, which is laid naked on a litter. On its forehead it has the sign of the cross, in gold, and on both its hands two other signs of the same shape, and two more on its knees; and the five signs are all fashioned in gold. They carry this carved image seven times round the middle of the temple precincts, to the sound of flutes and tambourines and hymns, and after the procession they carry it down again into the crypt. But if you ask them what this mysterious performance means, they answer: Today, at this hour, the Kore, that is to say the virgin, has given birth to the Aeon.

165   Epiphanius expressly states that he is not telling this of a Christian sect, but of the worshippers of idols, and he does so in order to illustrate the idea that even the pagans bear involuntary witness to the truth of Christianity.

---

[4] Eisler, *The Royal Art of Astrology*, p. 107.

[5] Bouché-Leclercq, *L'Astrologie grecque*, p. 147. For the relation of the *gyne* (woman) to the zodiacal sign Virgo see Boll, *Aus der Offenbarung Johannis*, p. 122.

[6] *Panarium*, LI, 22, Oehler edn., Part 3, pp. 632f. This passage is not in the older editions of the *Panarium*, since it was discovered only recently in a ms. at Venice.

66   Virgo, the zodiacal sign, carries either a wheat-sheaf or a child. Some authorities connect her with the "woman" of the Apocalypse.[7] At any rate, this woman has something to do with the prophecy of the birth of a Messiah at the end of time. Since the author of the Apocalypse was supposed to be a Christian, the question arises: To whom does the woman refer who is interpreted as the mother of the Messiah, or of Christ? And to whom does the son of the woman refer who (translating the Greek literally) shall "pasture ($\pi o\iota\mu\alpha i\nu\epsilon\iota\nu$) the pagans with an iron staff"?

67   As this passage contains an allusion on the one hand to the Messianic prophecy in Isaiah 66 : 7,[8] and on the other to Yahweh's wrath (Psalm 2 : 9[9]), it would seem to refer in some way to the future rebirth of the Messiah. But such an idea is quite impossible in the Christian sphere. Boll[10] says of the description of the "lamb" in Revelation 5 : 6ff.: "This remarkably bizarre figure with seven horns and seven eyes cannot possibly be explained in Christian terms." Also, the "lamb" develops some very unexpected peculiarities: he is a *bellicose* lamb, a conqueror (Rev. 17 : 14). The mighty ones of the earth will have to hide from his *wrath* (Rev. 6 : 15ff.). He is likened to the "*lion* of the tribe of Judah" (Rev. 5 : 5). This lamb, who is reminiscent of Psalm 2 : 9 ("Thou shalt break them with a rod of iron, thou shalt dash them in pieces like a potter's vessel"), rather gives one the sinister impression of a daemonic ram,[11] and not at all of a lamb who is led meekly to the slaughter. The lamb of the Apocalypse belongs, without doubt, to the category of horned monsters mentioned in these prophecies. One must therefore consider the question whether the author of the Apocalypse was influenced by an idea that was in some sense antithetical to Christ, perhaps by a psychological shadow-figure,

7 Boll, pp. 121ff.

8 "Before she travailed, she brought forth; before her pain came, she was delivered of a man child."

9 "Thou shalt break them with a rod of iron; thou shalt dash them in pieces like a potter's vessel."   10 Boll, p. 44.

11 His eyes signify the "seven Spirits of God" (Rev. 5 : 6) or the "seven eyes of the Lord" (Zech. 4 : 10). The Lamb stands with the seven angels before God's throne, as Satan did with the sons of God (Job 1 : 6), so that God is described under the aspect of Ezekiel's vision and is thought of in Yahwistic terms—an "umbra in lege"!

an "umbra Jesu" which was united at the end of time with the triumphant Christ, through an act of rebirth. This hypothesis would explain the repetition of the birth myth and also the curious fact that so important an eschatological expectation as the coming of the Antichrist receives but scant mention in the Apocalypse. The seven-horned ram is just about everything that Jesus appears not to be.[12] He is a real shadow-figure, but he could not be described as the Antichrist, who is a creature of Satan. For although the monstrous, warlike lamb is a shadow-figure in the sense that he is the counterpart of the lamb who was sacrificed, he is not nearly so irreconcilable with Christ as the Antichrist would have to be. The duplication of the Christ-figure cannot, therefore, be traced back to this split between Christ and Antichrist, but is due rather to the anti-Roman resentment felt by the Jewish Christians, who fell back on their god of vengeance and his warlike Messiah. The author of the Apocalypse may have been acquainted with Jewish speculations known to us through later tradition. We are told in the *Bereshith Rabbati* of Moses ha-Darshan that Elias found in Bethlehem a young woman sitting before her door with a newborn child lying on the ground beside her, flecked with blood. She explained that her son had been born at an evil hour, just when the temple was destroyed. Elias admonished her to look after the child. When he came back again five weeks later, he asked about her son. "He neither walks, nor sees, nor speaks, nor hears, but lies there like a stone," said the woman. Suddenly a wind blew from the four corners of the earth, bore the child away, and plunged him into the sea. Elias lamented that it was now all up with the salvation of Israel, but a *bath kol* (voice) said to him:

It is not so. He will remain in the great sea for four hundred years, and eighty years in the rising smoke of the children of Korah,[13] eighty years under the gates of Rome, and the rest of the time he will wander round in the great cities until the end of the days comes.[14]

168   This story describes a Messiah who, though born in Bethlehem, is wafted by divine intervention into the Beyond (sea = unconscious). From the very beginning his childhood is so

[12] That is, if we disregard passages like Matt. 21 : 19 and 22 : 7 and Luke 19 : 27.
[13] [Cf. Num. 16.—EDITORS.]   [14] Wünsche, *Die Leiden des Messias*, p. 91.

threatened that he is scarcely able to live. The legend is symptomatic of an extraordinary weakness of the Messianic element in Judaism and the dangers attending it, which would explain the delay in the Messiah's appearance. For 560 years he remains latent, and only then does his missionary work begin. This interlude is not so far off the 530 years mentioned in the Talmudic prophecy (cf. par. 133), near enough anyway for us to compare them, if we take this legend as referring to Christ. In the limitless sea of Jewish speculation mutual contacts of this sort are more likely to have occurred than not. Thus the deadly threat to the Messiah and his death by violence is a motif that repeats itself in other stories, too. The later, mainly Cabalistic tradition speaks of two Messiahs, the Messiah ben Joseph (or ben Ephraim) and the Messiah ben David. They were compared to Moses and Aaron, also to two roes, and this on the authority of the Song of Solomon 4 : 5: "Thy two breasts are like two young roes that are twins." [15] Messiah ben Joseph is, according to Deuteronomy 33 : 17, the "firstling of his bullock," and Messiah ben David rides on an ass.[16] Messiah ben Joseph is the first, Messiah ben David the second.[17] Messiah ben Joseph must die in order to "atone with his blood for the children of Yahweh." [18] He will fall in the fight against Gog and Magog, and Armilus will kill him. Armilus is the Anti-Messiah, whom Satan begot on a block of marble.[19] He will be killed by Messiah ben David in his turn. Afterwards, ben David will fetch the new Jerusalem down from heaven and bring ben Joseph back to life.[20] This ben Joseph plays a strange role in later tradition. Tabari, the commentator on the Koran, mentions that the Antichrist will be a king of the Jews,[21] and in Abarbanel's *Mashmi'a Yeshu'ah* the Messiah ben Joseph actually is the Antichrist. So he is not only characterized as the suffering Messiah in contrast to

---

[15] Targum on Canticles 4 : 5 in *The Targum to The Song of Songs*, p. 50. Wünsche, p. 111. In the *Zohar* the Messiah is called "Mother." Schoettgen, *Horae Hebraicae et Talmudicae*, II, p. 10. Cf. also the "Saviour of the twins" in *Pistis Sophia* (above, par. 133, n. 44).

[16] *Zohar*, trans. by H. Sperling and M. Simon, II, p. 358: "Hence it is written of him [the Messiah] that he will be 'poor and riding on an ass . . .' (Zech. 12 : 9)." Also Wünsche, p. 100.   [17] Ibid., p. 114.   [18] Ibid., p. 115.

[19] Armilus or Armillus = 'Ρωμύλος, the Antichrist. Methodius: "Romulus, who is also Armaeleus."   [20] Wünsche, p. 120.

[21] *Chronique* of Tabari, I, ch. 23, p. 67.

the victorious one, but is ultimately thought of as his antagonist.[22]

169   As these traditions show, the above-mentioned weakness of the Messianic element consists in a split which in the end becomes a complete polarity. This development is foreshadowed in Persian religious literature, in the pre-Christian idea of an enantiodromia of the great time-periods, and the deterioration of goodness. The Bahman Yast calls the fourth Iron Age "the evil sovereignty of the demons with dishevelled hair of the race of Wrath."[23] On the other hand, the splitting of the Messiah into two is an expression of an inner disquiet with regard to the character of Yahweh, whose injustice and unreliability must have shocked every thoughtful believer ever since the time of Job.[24] Job puts the problem in unequivocal terms, and Christianity gave an equally unequivocal answer. Jewish mysticism, on the other hand, went its own way, and its speculations hover over depths which Christian thinkers have done their utmost to cover up. I do not want to elaborate this theme here, but will mention as an example a story told by Ibn Ezra. In Spain, he says, there was a great sage who was reputed to be unable to read the Eighty-ninth Psalm because it saddened him too much. The verses in question are:

> I will not remove from him my steadfast love,
>   or be false to my faithfulness.
> I will not violate my covenant,
>   or alter the word that went forth from my lips.
> Once for all I have sworn my holiness:
>   I will not lie to David.
> His line shall endure for ever,
>   his throne as long as the sun before me.
> Like the moon it shall be established for ever;
>   the witness in the skies is sure. Selah!
> But now thou hast cast off and rejected,
>   thou art full of wrath against thy anointed.
> Thou hast renounced the covenant with thy servant;
>   thou hast trodden his crown in the dust.

[22] Bousset, *The Antichrist Legend*, p. 111.
[23] *Pahlavi Texts*, trans. by E. W. West, p. 193.
[24] Cf. the opposition between mercy and justice in God's nature, supra, pars. 108ff.

Thou hast breached all his walls;
thou hast laid his strongholds in ruins.[25]

70   It is the same problem as in Job. As the highest value and supreme dominant in the psychic hierarchy, the God-image is immediately related to, or identical with, the self, and everything that happens to the God-image has an effect on the latter. Any uncertainty about the God-image causes a profound uneasiness in the self, for which reason the question is generally ignored because of its painfulness. But that does not mean that it remains unasked in the unconscious. What is more, it is answered by views and beliefs like materialism, atheism, and similar substitutes, which spread like epidemics. They crop up wherever and whenever one waits in vain for the legitimate answer. The *ersatz* product represses the real question into the unconscious and destroys the continuity of historical tradition which is the hallmark of civilization. The result is bewilderment and confusion. Christianity has insisted on God's goodness as a loving Father and has done its best to rob evil of substance. The early Christian prophecy concerning the Antichrist, and certain ideas in late Jewish theology, could have suggested to us that the Christian answer to the problem of Job omits to mention the corollary, the sinister reality of which is now being demonstrated before our eyes by the splitting of our world: *the destruction of the God-image is followed by the annulment of the human personality.* Materialistic atheism with its utopian chimeras forms the religion of all those rationalistic movements which delegate the freedom of personality to the masses and thereby extinguish it. The advocates of Christianity squander their energies in the mere preservation of what has come down to them, with no thought of building on to their house and making it roomier. Stagnation in these matters is threatened in the long run with a lethal end.

71   As Bousset has plausibly suggested, the duality of the apocalyptic Christ is the outcome of Jewish-Gnostic speculations whose echoes we hear in the traditions mentioned above. The intensive preoccupation of the Gnostics with the problem of evil stands out in startling contrast to the peremptory nullification of it by the Church fathers, and shows that this question

25 Psalm 89 : 33ff. (RSV).

had already become topical at the beginning of the third century. In this connection we may recall the view expressed by Valentinus,[26] that Christ was born "not without a kind of shadow" and that he afterwards "cast off the shadow from himself." [27] Valentinus lived sometime in the first half of the second century, and the Apocalypse was probably written about A.D. 90, under Domitian. Like other Gnostics, Valentinus carried the gospels a stage further in his thinking, and for this reason it does not seem to me impossible that he understood the "shadow" as the Yahwistic law under which Christ was born. The Apocalypse and other things in the New Testament could easily have prompted him to such a view, quite apart from the more or less contemporaneous ideas about the demiurge and the prime Ogdoad that consists of light and shadow.[28] It is not certain whether Origen's doubt concerning the ultimate fate of the devil was original; [29] at all events, it proves that the possibility of the devil's reunion with God was an object of discussion in very early times, and indeed had to be if Christian philosophy was not to end in dualism. One should not forget that the theory of the *privatio boni* does not dispose of the eternity of hell and damnation. God's humanity is also an expression of dualism, as the controversy of the Monophysites and Dyopnysites in the early Church shows. Apart from the religious significance of the decision in favour of a complete union of both natures, I would mention in passing that the Monophysite dogma has a noteworthy psychological aspect: it tells us (in psychological parlance) that since Christ, as a man, corresponds to the ego, and, as God, to the self, he is at once both ego and self, part and whole. Empirically speaking, consciousness can never compre-

26 He was, it seems, a cleric, who is said to have been a candidate for the episcopal see in Rome.

27 Irenaeus, *Adv. haer.*, I, 11, 1 (Roberts/Rambaut trans., I, p. 46).

28 Doctrine of the Valentinian Secundus (ibid., I, p. 46).

29 *De oratione*, 27: ". . . so that that supreme sinner and blasphemer against the Holy Ghost may be kept from sin through all this present age, and hereafter in the age to come from its beginning to its end be treated I know not how" (. . . ita ut summus ille peccator et in Spiritum sanctum blasphemus per totum hoc praesens saeculum a peccato detineatur, et post haec in futuro ab initio ad finem sit nescio quomodo tractandus), thus giving rise to the view that "even the devil will some day be saved." [Cf. alternative trans. by J. E. L. Oulton and H. Chadwick, p. 304.]

hend the whole, but it is probable that the whole is unconsciously present in the ego. This would be equivalent to the
highest possible state of τελείωσις (completeness or perfection).

I have dwelt at some length on the dualistic aspects of the
Christ-figure because, through the fish symbolism, Christ was
assimilated into a world of ideas that seems far removed from
the gospels—a world of pagan origin, saturated with astrological
beliefs to an extent that we can scarcely imagine today. Christ
was born at the beginning of the aeon of the Fishes. It is by no
means ruled out that there were educated Christians who knew
of the *coniunctio maxima* of Jupiter and Saturn in Pisces in
the year 7 B.C., just as, according to the gospel reports, there
were Chaldaeans who actually found Christ's birthplace. The
Fishes, however, are a double sign.

At midnight on Christmas Eve, when (according to the old
time-reckoning) the sun enters Capricorn, Virgo is standing on
the eastern horizon, and is soon followed by the Serpent held
by Ophiuchus, the "Serpent-bearer." This astrological coincidence seems to me worth mentioning, as also the view that the
two fishes are mother and son. The latter idea has a quite special
significance because this relationship suggests that the two fishes
were originally one. In fact, Babylonian and Indian astrology
know of only one fish.[30] Later, this mother evidently gave birth
to a son, who was a fish like her. The same thing happened to
the Phoenician Derceto-Atargatis, who, half fish herself, had a
son called Ichthys. It is just possible that "the sign of the prophet
Jonah"[31] goes back to an older tradition about an heroic night
sea journey and conquest of death, where the hero is swallowed
by a fish ("whale-dragon") and is then reborn.[32] The redemp-
tory name Joshua[33] (Yehoshua, Yeshua, Gr. *Iesous*) is connected with the fish: Joshua is the son of Nun, and Nun means
'fish.' The Joshua ben Nun of the Khidr legend had dealings
with a fish that was meant to be eaten but was revived by a drop
of water from the fountain of life.[34]

30 Namely *Piscis Austrinus*, the "Southern Fish," which merges with Pisces and
whose principal star is Fomalhaut.   31 Matt. 12 : 39, 16 : 4; Luke 11 : 29f.
32 Cf. Frobenius, *Das Zeitalter des Sonnengottes*, and my *Symbols of Transformation*, pars. 308ff.   33 "Yahweh is salvation."
34 Koran, Sura 18. Cf. "Concerning Rebirth," pars. 244f., and Vollers, "Chidher,"
p. 241.

174   The mythological Great Mothers are usually a danger to their sons. Jeremias mentions a fish representation on an early Christian lamp, showing one fish devouring the other.[35] The name of the largest star in the constellation known as the Southern Fish—Fomalhaut, 'the fish's mouth'—might be interpreted in this sense, just as in fish symbolism every conceivable form of devouring *concupiscentia* is attributed to fishes, which are said to be "ambitious, libidinous, voracious, avaricious, lascivious"—in short, an emblem of the vanity of the world and of earthly pleasures ("voluptas terrena").[36] They owe these bad qualities most of all to their relationship with the mother- and love-goddess Ishtar, Astarte, Atargatis, or Aphrodite. As the planet Venus, she has her "exaltatio" in the zodiacal sign of the fishes. Thus, in astrological tradition as well as in the history of symbols, the fishes have always had these opprobrious qualities attached to them,[37] while on the other hand laying claim to a special and higher significance. This claim is based—at least in astrology—on the fact that anyone born under Pisces may expect to become a fisherman or a sailor, and in that capacity to catch fishes or hold dominion over the sea—an echo of the primitive totemistic identity between the hunter and his prey. The Babylonian culture-hero Oannes was himself a fish, and the Christian Ichthys is a fisher of men par excellence. Symbologically, he is actually the hook or bait on God's fishing-rod with which the Leviathan—death or the devil—is caught.[38] In Jewish tradition the Leviathan is a sort of eucharistic food stored up for the

[35] Jeremias, *The Old Testament in the Light of the Ancient East*, p. 76. This lamp has never been traced.

[36] Picinellus, *Mundus symbolicus* (1680–81), Lib. VI, cap. I.

[37] Bouché-Leclercq, p. 147.

[38] How closely the negative and the positive meanings are related can be seen from the fish-hook motif, attributed to St. Cyprian: "Like a fish which darts at a baited hook, and not only does not lay hold of the bait along with the hook, but is itself hauled up out of the sea; so he who had the power of death did indeed snatch away the body of Jesus unto death, but did not observe that the hook of the Godhead was concealed therein, until he had devoured it; and thereupon remained fixed thereto."

Stephen of Canterbury (*Liber allegoricus in Habacuc*, unavailable to me) says: "It is the bait of longed-for enjoyment that is displayed in the hook, but the tenacious hidden hook is consumed along with the bait. So in fleshly concupiscence the devil displays the bait of pleasure, but the sting of sin lies hid therein." In this regard see Picinellus, Lib. VI, cap. 1.

faithful in Paradise. After death, they clothe themselves in fish-robes.[39] Christ is not only a fisher but the fish that is "eucharistically" eaten.[40] Augustine says in his *Confessions:* "But [the earth] eats the fish that was drawn from the deep, at the table which you have prepared for them that believe; for the fish was drawn from the deep in order to nourish the needy ones of the earth." [41] St. Augustine is referring to the meal of fishes eaten by the disciples at Emmaus (Luke 24 : 43). We come across the "healing fish" in the story of Tobit: the angel Raphael helps Tobit to catch the fish that is about to eat him, and shows him how to make a magic "smoke" against evil spirits from the heart and liver of the fish, and how he can heal his father's blindness with its gall (Tobit 6 : 1ff.).

75   St. Peter Damian (d. 1072) describes monks as fishes, because all pious men are little fishes leaping in the net of the Great Fisher.[42] In the Pectorios inscription (beginning of the fourth century), believers are called the "divine descendants of the heavenly fish." [43]

76   The fish of Manu is a saviour,[44] identified in legend with Vishnu, who had assumed the form of a small goldfish. He begs Manu to take him home, because he was afraid of being de-

---

39 Scheftelowitz, "Das Fisch-Symbol im Judentum und Christentum," p. 365.
40 Cf. Goodenough, *Jewish Symbols*, V, pp. 41ff.
41 Lib. XIII, cap. XXI. (Cf. trans. by F. J. Sheed, p. 275, modified.)
42 "The cloister of a monastery is indeed a fishpond of souls, and fish live therein" (Picinellus, *Mundus*).
      An Alexandrian hymn from the 2nd cent. runs:
              "Fisher of men, whom Thou to life dost bring!
              From the evil sea of sin
              And from the billowy strife
              Gathering pure fishes in,
              Caught with sweet bait of life."

(*Writings of Clement of Alexandria*, trans. by W. Wilson, I, p. 344.) Cf. Doelger, ΊΧΘΥΣ, I, p. 4. Tertullian (*De baptismo*, cap. I) says: "But we little fishes, after the example of our ΊΧΘΥΣ Jesus Christ, are born in water, nor have we safety in any other way than by permanently abiding in (that) water." (Trans. by S. Thelwall, I, pp. 231–32.) The disciples of Gamaliel the Elder (beginning of 1st cent.) were named after various kinds of fishes. (*Abot de Rabbi Nathan*, cap. 40 [cf. trans. by J. Goldin, p. 166], cited in Scheftelowitz, p. 5.)
43 Pohl, *Das Ichthysmonument von Autun*, and Doelger, I, pp. 12ff.
44 "I will save thee." Shatapatha Brahmana (trans. by J. Eggeling, I [i.e., XII], p. 216).

voured by the water monsters.[45] He then grows mightily, fairy-tale fashion, and in the end rescues Manu from the great flood.[46] On the twelfth day of the first month of the Indian year a golden fish is placed in a bowl of water and invoked as follows: "As thou, O God, in the form of a fish, hast saved the Vedas that were in the underworld, so save me also, O Keshava!"[47] De Gubernatis and other investigators after him tried to derive the Christian fish from India.[48] Indian influence is not impossible, since relations with India existed even before Christ and various spiritual currents from the East made themselves felt in early Christianity, as we know from the reports of Hippolytus and Epiphanius. Nevertheless, there is no serious reason to derive the fish from India, for Western fish symbolism is so rich and at the same time so archaic that we may safely regard it as autochthonous.

177   Since the Fishes stand for mother and son, the mythological tragedy of the son's early death and resurrection is already implicit in them. Being the twelfth sign of the Zodiac, Pisces denotes the end of the astrological year and also a new beginning. This characteristic coincides with the claim of Christianity to be the beginning and end of all things, and with its eschatological expectation of the end of the world and the coming of God's kingdom.[49] *Thus the astrological characteristics of the fish contain essential components of the Christian myth; first, the cross; second, the moral conflict and its splitting into the figures of Christ and Antichrist; third, the motif of the son of a virgin; fourth, the classical mother-son tragedy; fifth, the danger at birth; and sixth, the saviour and bringer of healing.* It is therefore not beside the point to relate the designation of Christ as a fish to the new aeon then dawning. If this relationship existed even in antiquity, it must obviously have been a tacit

[45] De Gubernatis, *Zoological Mythology*, II, pp. 334f.

[46] Shatapatha Brahmana (Eggeling trans., pp. 216ff.).

[47] Doelger, I, p. 23. Keshava means 'having much or fine hair,' a cognomen of Vishnu.   [48] Ibid., pp. 21ff.

[49] Origen (*De oratione*, cap. 27): ". . . as the last month is the end of the year, after which the beginning of another month ensues, so it may be that, since several ages complete as it were a year of ages, the present age is 'the end,' after which certain 'ages to come' will ensue, of which the age to come is the beginning, and in those coming ages God will 'shew the riches of his grace in kindness' [Eph. 2 : 7]" (Oulton/Chadwick trans., p. 304).

assumption or one that was purposely kept secret; for, to my knowledge, there is no evidence in the old literature that the Christian fish symbolism was derived from the zodiac. Moreover, the astrological evidence up to the second century A.D. is by no means of such a kind that the Christ/Antichrist antithesis could be derived *causally* from the polarity of the Fishes, since this, as the material we have cited shows, was not stressed as in any way significant. Finally, as Doelger rightly emphasizes, the Ichthys was always thought of as only *one* fish, though here we must point out that in the astrological interpretation Christ is in fact only one of the fishes, the role of the other fish being allotted to the Antichrist. There are, in short, no grounds whatever for supposing that the zodion of the Fishes could have served as the Ichthys prototype.

78   Pagan fish symbolism plays in comparison a far greater role.[50] The most important is the Jewish material collected by Scheftelowitz. The Jewish "chalice of benediction"[51] was sometimes decorated with pictures of fishes, for fishes were the food of the blessed in Paradise. The chalice was placed in the dead man's grave as a funerary gift.[52] Fishes have a wide distribution as sepulchral symbols. The Christian fish occurs mainly in this connection. Devout Israelites who live "in the water of the doctrine" are likened to fishes. This analogy was self-evident around A.D. 100.[53] The fish also has a Messianic significance.[54] According to the Syrian Apocalypse of Baruch, Leviathan shall rise from the sea with the advent of the Messiah.[55] This is probably the "very great fish" of the Abercius inscription, corresponding to the "fish from the fountain" mentioned in a

---

[50] Especially noteworthy is the cult of the dove and the fish in the Syrian area. There too the fish was eaten as "Eucharistic" food. (Cumont, *Les Religions orientales dans le paganisme romain*, pp. 108–9, 255–57.) The chief deity of the Philistines was called Dagon, derived from *dag*, 'fish.'

[51] τὸ ποτήριον τῆς εὐλογίας: *calix benedictionis* (I Cor. 10 : 16, DV).

[52] Scheftelowitz, p. 375.   [53] Ibid., p. 3.

[54] Cf. Goodenough, V, pp. 35ff.

[55] At the same time "Behemoth shall be revealed from his place . . . and then they shall be food for all that are left." (Charles, *Apocrypha and Pseudepigrapha*, II, p. 497.) The idea of Leviathan rising from the sea also links up with the vision in II Esdras 13 : 25, of the "man coming up from the midst of the sea." Cf. Charles, II, p. 579, and Wischnitzer-Bernstein, *Symbole und Gestalten der jüdischen Kunst*, pp. 122f. and 134f.

religious debate at the court of the Sassanids (5th century). The fountain refers to the Babylonian Hera, but in Christian language it means Mary, who in orthodox as well as in Gnostic circles (Acts of Thomas) was invoked as πηγή, 'fountain.' Thus we read in a hymn of Synesius (c. 350): Παγὰ παγῶν, ἀρχῶν ἀρχά, ῥιζῶν ῥίζα, μονὰς εἶ μονάδων, κτλ. (Fountain of fountains, source of sources, root of roots, monad of monads art thou.) [56] The fountain of Hera was also said to contain the one fish (μόνον ἰχθύν) that is caught by the "hook of divinity" and "feeds the whole world with its flesh." [57] In a Boeotian vase-painting the "lady of the beasts" [58] is shown with a fish between her legs, or in her body,[59] presumably indicating that the fish is her son. Although, in the Sassanid debate, the legend of Mary was transferred to Hera, the "one fish" that is hooked does not correspond to the Christian symbol, for in Christian symbology the crucifix is the hook or bait with which God catches Leviathan,[60] who is either death or the devil ("that ancient serpent") but not the Messiah. In Jewish tradition, on the other hand, the *pharmakon athanasias* is the flesh of Leviathan, the "Messianic fish," as Scheftelowitz says. The Talmud Sanhedrin says that the Messiah "will not come until a fish is sought for an invalid and cannot be procured." [61] According to the Apocalypse of Baruch, Behemoth as well as Leviathan [62] is a eucharistic food. This is assiduously overlooked. As I have explained elsewhere,[63] Yahweh's two prehistoric monsters seem to represent a pair of opposites, the one being unquestionably a land animal, and the other aquatic.

[56] Wirth, *Aus orientalischen Chroniken*, p. 199.

[57] Ibid., pp. 161, 19f.

[58] [Cf. Neumann, *The Great Mother*, ch. 14 and pl. 134.—EDITORS.]

[59] Eisler, *Orpheus—The Fisher*, Pl. LXIV.

[60] See *Psychology and Alchemy*, fig. 28.

[61] Scheftelowitz, p. 9; from the Talmud *Nezikin* VI, Sanhedrin II (*BT*, p. 662). Cf. the ἐσθίε πινάων in the Pectorios inscription, supra, p. 89n.

[62] A passage in Moses Maimonides (*Guide for the Perplexed*, trans. by M. Friedlander, p. 303) has bearing on the interpretation of Leviathan. Kirchmaier (*Disputationes Zoologicae*, 1736, p. 73) cites it as follows: "Speaking of these same things Rabbi Moses Maimon says that Leviathan possesses a [universal] combination (*complexum generalem*) of bodily peculiarities found separate in different animals." Although this rationalistic author dismisses the idea as "nugatory," it nevertheless seems to me to hint at an archetype ("complexum generalem") of the "spirit of gravity."

[63] *Psychological Types*, pars. 456ff.

'9   Since olden times, not only among the Jews but all over the Near East, the birth of an outstanding human being has been identified with the rising of a star. Thus Balaam prophesies (Num. 24 : 17):

> I shall see him, but not now,
> I shall behold him, but not nigh;
> a star shall come forth out of Jacob. . . .

'30   Always the hope of a Messiah is connected with the appearance of a star. According to the Zohar, the fish that swallowed Jonah died, but revived after three days and then spewed him out again. "Through the fish we shall find a medicament for the whole world." [64] This text is medieval but comes from a trustworthy source. The "very great [65] and pure fish from the fountain" mentioned in the Abercius inscription is, in the opinion of Scheftelowitz,[66] none other than Leviathan, which is not only the biggest fish but is held to be pure, as Scheftelowitz shows by citing the relevant passages from Talmudic literature. In this connection we might also mention the "one and only fish" (εἶς μόνος ἰχθῦς) recorded in the "Happenings in Persia." [67]

[64] Scheftelowitz, p. 10. Cf. Matt. 12 : 39 and 16 : 4, where Christ takes the sign of the prophet Jonah as a sign of the Messianic age and a prefiguration of his own fate. Cf. also Goodenough, *Jewish Symbols*, V, pp. 47ff.

[65] Παμμεγέθης.   [66] Pp. 7f.

[67] Τὰ ἐν Περσίδι πραχθέντα (Wirth, p. 151).

IX

THE AMBIVALENCE OF THE FISH SYMBOL

According to the Syrian Apocalypse of Baruch (29 : 1ff.), the time preceding the coming of the Messiah falls into twelve parts, and the Messiah will appear in the twelfth. As a time-division, the number twelve points to the zodia, of which the twelfth is the Fishes. Leviathan will then rise out of the sea. "The two great sea monsters which I created on the fifth day of creation and which I have preserved until that time shall then be food for all who are left." [1] Since Behemoth is unquestionably not a sea-animal, but one which, as a midrash says, "pastures on a thousand mountains," [2] the two "sea monsters" must be a duplication of Leviathan. And as a matter of fact, he does appear to be divided as to sex, for there is a male and a female of the species. [3] A similar duplication is suggested in Isaiah 27 : 1: "In that day, the Lord with his sore and great strong sword shall punish Leviathan the piercing serpent, even Leviathan that crooked serpent, and he shall slay the dragon [Vulgate: whale] that is in the sea." This duplication gave rise in medieval alchemy to the idea of two serpents fighting each other, one winged, the other wingless. [4] In the Book of Job, where Leviathan appears only in the singular, the underlying polarity comes to light in his opposite number, Behemoth. A poem by Meir ben Isaac describes the battle between Leviathan and Behemoth at the end of time, in which the two monsters wound each other to death. Yahweh then cuts them up and serves them

[1] Charles, II, p. 497, modified.
[2] *Midrash Tanchuma*, Lev. 11 : 2 and Deut. 29 : 9; cited in Scheftelowitz, pp. 39f.
[3] Talmud, *Nezikin* III, Baba Bathra (*BT*, I, p. 296). The *female* Leviathan has already been killed by Yahweh, salted, and preserved for the end of time. The male he castrated, for otherwise they would have multiplied and swamped the earth.
[4] A typical pair of opposites. Cf. the struggle between the two dragons in hexagram 2, line 6, in the *I Ching* (Wilhelm/Baynes trans., 1967, p. 15).

as food to the devout.[5] This idea is probably connected with the old Jewish Passover, which was celebrated in the month of Adar, the fish. In spite of the distinct duplication of Leviathan in the later texts, it is very likely that originally there was only one Leviathan, authenticated at a very early date in the Ugarit texts from Ras Shamra (c. 2000 B.C.). Virolleaud gives the following translation:

> Quand tu frapperas Ltn, le serpent brḥ
> Tu achèveras le serpent ʿqltn,
> Le puissant aux sept têtes.

82   He comments: "It is remarkable that the two adjectives brḥ and ʿqltn are the ones which qualify, in Isaiah 27 : 1, a particularly dangerous species of serpent which we call Leviathan, in Hebrew Liviatan."[6] From this period, too, there are pictures of a fight between Baal and the serpent Ltn,[7] remarkable in that the conflict is between a god and a monster and not between two monsters, as it was later.

83   We can see from the example of Leviathan how the great "fish" gradually split into its opposite, after having itself been the opposite of the highest God and hence his shadow, the embodiment of his evil side.[8]

84   With this splitting of the monster into a new opposite, its original opposition to God takes a back seat, and the monster is now in conflict either with itself or with an equivalent monster (e.g., Leviathan and Behemoth). This relieves God of his own inner conflict, which now appears outside him in the form of a hostile pair of brother monsters. In later Jewish tradition the Leviathan that Yahweh fought with in Isaiah develops a tendency, on the evidence cited by Scheftelowitz, to become "pure" and be eaten as "eucharistic" food, with the result that, if one wanted to derive the Ichthys symbol from this source, Christ as

5 Cf. the *Midrash Tanchuma*.

6 "Note complémentaire sur le poème de Mot et Aleïn," p. 357.

7 Virolleaud, "La légende de Baal, dieu des Phéniciens," p. ix.

8 Perhaps an echo of this psychological development may be found in the views of Moses Maimonides, who writes that in the Book of Job (ch. 41) Yahweh "dwells longest on the nature of the Leviathan, which possesses a combination of bodily peculiarities found separate in different animals, in those that walk, those that swim, and those that fly" (*Guide for the Perplexed*, p. 303). Accordingly Leviathan is a kind of super-animal, just as Yahweh is a kind of superman.

a fish would appear in place of Leviathan, the monstrous animals of tradition having meanwhile faded into mere attributes of death and the devil.

185   This split corresponds to the doubling of the shadow often met with in dreams, where the two halves appear as different or even as antagonistic figures. This happens when the conscious ego-personality does not contain all the contents and components that it could contain. Part of the personality then remains split off and mixes with the normally unconscious shadow, the two together forming a double—and often antagonistic—personality. If we apply this experience from the domain of practical psychology to the mythological material under discussion, we find that God's monstrous antagonist produces a double because the God-image is incomplete and does not contain everything it logically ought to contain. Whereas Leviathan is a fishlike creature, primitive and cold-blooded, dwelling in the depths of the ocean, Behemoth is a warm-blooded quadruped, presumably something like a bull, who roams the mountains (at least in later tradition). Hence he is related to Leviathan as a higher, superior creature to a lower, inferior one, rather like the winged and the wingless dragon in alchemy. All winged beings are "volatile," i.e., vapours and gases, in other words pneuma. Just as in Augustine Christ the fish is "drawn from the deep," [9] so in II Esdras 13 : 2ff. the "man" came out of the sea like a wind. His appearance was heralded by an eagle and a lion, theriomorphic symbols which greatly affrighted the prophet in the same way that Behemoth inspired chiefly terror in Job. The fish drawn from the deep has a secret connection with Leviathan: he is the bait with which Leviathan is lured and caught. This fish is probably a duplication of the great fish and stands for its pneumatic aspect. It is evident that Leviathan has such an aspect, because he, like the Ichthys, is eucharistic food.[10] That this doubling represents an act of conscious realization is clear from Job 26 : 12, where we are told that Yahweh smote Rahab "by his understanding" (tebūnā). Rahab, the sea monster, is cousin german to Tiamat, whom Marduk split asunder by filling her up with Imhullu, the north wind.[11] The word tebūnā comes

---

[9] *Confessions,* Sheed trans., p. 275.   [10] Cf. Goodenough, V, pp. 51ff.
[11] The motif of splitting is closely related to that of penetration and perforation in alchemy. Cf. also Job 26 : 13: "His hand pierced the fleeing serpent" (RSV).

from *bīn*, 'to separate, split, part asunder'—in other words, to discriminate, which is the essence of conscious realization.[12] In this sense Leviathan and Behemoth represent stages in the development of consciousness whereby they become assimilated and humanized. The fish changes, via the warm-blooded quadruped, into a human being, and in so far as the Messiah became, in Christianity, the second Person of the Trinity, the human figure split off from the fish hints at God's incarnation.[13] What was previously missing in the God-image, therefore, was the human element.

86   The role of the fish in Jewish tradition probably has some connections with the Syrophoenician fish cult of Atargatis. Her temples had pools with sacred fishes in them which no one was allowed to touch.[14] Similarly, meals of fish were ritually eaten in the temples. "This cult and these customs, which originated in Syria, may well have engendered the Ichthys symbolism in Christian times," says Cumont.[15] In Lycia they worshipped the divine fish Orphos or Diorphos, the son of Mithras and the "sacred stone," Cybele.[16] This god is a variant of the Semitic fish-deities we have already mentioned, such as Oannes, the Babylonian Nun, Dagon, and Adonis, whom the Greeks called Ichthys. Fish offerings were made to Tanit in Carthage and to Ea and Nina in Babylon. Traces of a fish cult can be found in Egypt too. The Egyptian priests were forbidden to eat fish, for fishes were held to be as unclean as Typhon's sea. "All abstain from sea-fish," observes Plutarch. According to Clement of Alexandria, the inhabitants of Syene, Elephantine, and Oxyrhynchus worshipped a fish. Plutarch [17] says it was the custom to eat a broiled fish before the door of one's house on the ninth day of the first month. Doelger inclines to the view that this custom paved the way for the eucharistic fish in Christianity.[18]

187   The ambivalent attitude towards the fish is an indication of its double nature. It is unclean and an emblem of hatred on the one hand, but on the other it is an object of veneration. It

---

12 For this information I am indebted to Dr. Riwkah Schärf.

13 II Esdras is a Jewish text written at the end of the 1st cent. A.D.

14 Cumont, *Les Religions orientales*, p. 255.

15 Ibid., pp. 108-9, 256.   16 Eisler, *Orpheus—The Fisher*, p. 20.

17 *De Iside et Osiride*, cap. VII (Babbitt trans., V, p. 19).

18 ΊΧΘΥΣ, I, p. 126. The risen Christ ate of a broiled fish (Luke 24 : 42).

even seems to have been regarded as a symbol for the soul, if we are to judge by a painting on a late Hellenistic sarcophagus. The mummy lies on a lion-shaped bier, and under the bier are the four Canopic jars, the lids representing the four sons of Horus, three of them with animal heads and one with a human head. Over the mummy there floats a fish,[19] instead of the usual soul-bird. It is clear from the painting that the fish is an oxyrhynchus, or barbel, one of the three most abominated fishes, which was said to have devoured the phallus of Osiris after he had been dismembered by Typhon (Set).[20] Barbels were sacred to Typhon, who is "that part of the soul which is passionate, impulsive, irrational, and truculent."[21] Because of their voraciousness, fishes were regarded in the Middle Ages as an allegory of the damned.[22] The fish as an Egyptian soul-symbol is therefore all the more remarkable. The same ambivalence can be seen in the figure of Typhon/Set. In later times he was a god of death, destruction, and the desert, the treacherous opponent of his brother Osiris. But earlier he was closely connected with Horus and was a friend and helper of the dead. In one of the Pyramid Texts he and Heru-ur (the "older Horus") help Osiris to climb up to heaven. The floor of heaven consists of an iron plate, which in places is so close to the tops of the mountains that one can climb up to heaven with the help of a ladder. The four corners of the iron plate rest on four pillars, corresponding to the four cardinal points. In the Pyramid Texts of Pepi I, a song of praise is addressed to the "ladder of the twin gods," and the Unas text says: "Unas cometh forth upon the Ladder which his father Ra hath made for him, and Horus and Set take the hand of Unas, and they lead him into the Tuat."[23] Other texts show that there was enmity between Heru-ur and Set because one was a god of the day and the other a god of the night. The hieroglyph for Set has as a determinative the sign for a stone, or else

[19] Spiegelberg, "Der Fisch als Symbol der Seele," p. 574. Cf. Goodenough, V, fig. 9, where the mummy appears in the form of a fish.

[20] The oxyrhynchus fish was regarded as sacred all over Egypt. Cf. Budge, *The Gods of the Egyptians*, II, p. 382; Plutarch, *De Iside*, cap. XLIX (Babbitt trans., V, p. 19).

[21] Ibid. (pp. 120f.).

[22] Picinellus, *Mundus symbolicus*, Lib. VI, cap. I.

[23] Budge, II, pp. 241f. Cf. Christ's transfiguration in the presence of Moses and Elias (Matt. 17 : 4), and the "Saviour of the twins" in *Pistis Sophia*.

the unidentified Set-animal with long ears. There are paintings showing the heads of Heru-ur and Set growing out of the same body, from which we may infer the identity of the opposites they represent. Budge says: "The attributes of Heru-ur changed somewhat in early dynastic times, but they were always the opposite of those of Set, whether we regard the two gods as personifications of two powers of nature, i.e., Light and Darkness, Day and Night, or as Kosmos and Chaos, or as Life and Death, or as Good and Evil."[24]

88   This pair of gods represent the latent opposites contained in Osiris, the higher divinity, just as Behemoth and Leviathan do in relation to Yahweh. It is significant that the opposites have to work together for a common purpose when it comes to helping the *one* god, Osiris, to reach the heavenly quaternity. This quaternity is also personified by the four sons of Horus: Mestha, Hapi, Tuamutef, and Qebhsennuf, who are said to dwell "behind the thigh of the northern heaven," that is, behind the thigh of Set, whose seat is in the constellation of the Great Bear. The four sons of Horus are Set's enemies, but on the other hand they are closely connected with him. They are an analogy of the four pillars of heaven which support the four-cornered iron plate. Since three of the sons are often shown with animal heads, and one with a human head, we may point to a similar state of affairs in the visions of Ezekiel, from whose cherubim-figures the well-known symbols of the evangelists (three animals, one angel) are derived.[25] Ezekiel says, furthermore (1 : 22): "Over the heads of the living creatures [the cherubim] there was the likeness of a solid plate, shining like terrible crystal, spread out above their heads," and (1 : 26, RSV): "And above the solid plate that was over their heads there was the likeness of a throne, in appearance like sapphire; and seated above the likeness of a throne was a likeness as it were of a human form."

89   In view of the close ties between Israel and Egypt an intermingling of symbols is not unlikely. What is remarkable, however, is that in Arab tradition the region round the heavenly Pole is seen in the form of a *fish*. Qazvini says: "The Pole can

24 Budge, II, p. 243.
25 Daniel 3 : 25 may be of relevance in this connection: the three men in the burning fiery furnace, who were joined by a fourth, a "son of God."

be seen. Round it are the smaller *Benat na'sh* [26] and dark stars, which together form the picture of a fish, and in its midst is the Pole." [27] This means that the Pole, which in ancient Egypt denoted the region of Set and was at the same time the abode of the four sons of Horus, was contained, so to speak, in the body of a fish. According to Babylonian tradition Anu has his seat in the northern heaven; likewise Marduk, as the highest god, world-creator and ruler of its courses, is the Pole. The *Enuma Elish* says of him: "He who fixes the course of the stars of heaven, like sheep shall pasture the gods all together." [28]

190   At the northern point of the ecliptic is the region of fire (purgatory and the entrance to the Anu-heaven). Hence the northern corner of the temple built around the tower at Nippur was called the *kibla* (point of orientation). In like manner the Sabaeans and Mandaeans, when praying, turn towards the north.[29] We might also mention the Mithraic liturgy in this connection: in the final vision Mithras appears, "holding the golden shoulder of a young bull. This is the constellation of the Bear, which moves and turns the heavens round." The text piles endless fire-attributes on this god, who obviously hails from the north.[30]

191   These Babylonian ideas about the significance of the north make it easier for us to understand why Ezekiel's vision of God came from that quarter, despite the fact that it is the birthplace of all evil. The coincidence of opposites is the normal thing in a primitive conception of God, since God, not being an object of reflection, is simply taken for granted. At the level of conscious reflection, however, the coincidence of opposites becomes a major problem, which we do everything possible to circumvent. That is why the position of the devil in Christian dogma is so very unsatisfactory. When there are such gaps in our collective ideas, in the dominants of our conscious orientation, we can count with absolute certainty on the existence of complementary or—to be more precise—compensatory developments in the unconscious. These compensating ideas can be found in the speculations of alchemy. We can hardly suppose that ideas of

---

[26] Lit., 'daughters of the bier', presumably mourning women who walk ahead of the coffin. Cf. Ideler, *Untersuchungen über den Ursprung und die Bedeutung der Sternnamen,* p. 11.   [27] Ibid., p. 15.   [28] Jeremias, p. 22.
[29] Ibid., p. 33.   [30] Dieterich, *Eine Mithrasliturgie,* pp. 8ff.

this sort remained totally unconscious so far as the adepts were concerned. What they were aiming at was a more or less conscious restoration of the primitive God-image. Hence they were able to propound paradoxes as shocking as that of God's love glowing in the midst of hell-fire,[31] which is represented as being no more than the Christian conception of God in a new but necessary relation to everything hell stands for. Above all it was Jakob Böhme who, influenced by alchemy and the Cabala equally, envisaged a paradoxical God-image in which the good and the bad aspects appertain to the same divine being in a way that bears comparison with the views of Clement of Rome.

192   Ancient history gives us a divided picture of the region to the north: it is the seat of the highest gods and also of the adversary; thither men direct their prayers, and from thence blows an evil pneuma, the Aquilo, "by the name whereof is to be understood the evil spirit"; [32] and finally, it is the navel of the world and at the same time hell. Bernard of Clairvaux apostrophizes Lucifer thus: "And dost thou strive perversely towards the north? The more thou dost hasten toward the heights, the more speedily shalt thou go down to thy setting." [33] The "king of the North" in Nostradamus has to be understood in the light of this passage. At the same time, it is clear from St. Bernard's words that the heights of power to which Lucifer strives are still associated with the north.[34]

31 Cf. *Psychology and Alchemy,* par. 446.
32 Garnerius, in Migne, *P.L.,* vol. 193, col. 49.
33 *Tractatus de gradibus superbiae,* in Migne, *P.L.,* vol. 182, col. 961.
34 One of the bad qualities of the north wind ("The north wind numbs with cold" = the numbness of the evil spirit, who "hardens the hearts of the wicked"), was responsible for an alchemical hypothesis concerning the formation of coral: "The coral is a kind of vegetable which comes into being in the sea, and has roots and branches, and in its original state is moist. But when the wind blows north, it hardens, and turns into a red substance, which the seafarer sees under the water and cuts off; then, when it comes out of the water, it turns into a stone, of a red colour." ("Allegoriae super librum Turbae," *Art. aurif.,* 1593, I, p. 143.)

X

THE FISH IN ALCHEMY

1. The Medusa

193   Michel Nostradamus, physician and astrologer, must surely have been acquainted with alchemy, since this art was practised mainly by physicians. Whether he knew that the fish was a symbol for the arcane substance and the *lapis* is perhaps questionable, but it is more than likely that he had read the classics of alchemy. Of these one of the greatest authorities is the *Turba philosophorum,* which had been translated very early (11th–12th cent.) from the Arabic into Latin. At about the same time, or a little later, its appendices were also translated, namely the "Allegoriae super librum Turbae," the "Allegoriae sapientum supra librum Turbae XXIX distinctiones," [1] together with the "Aenigmata ex Visione Arislei" and "In Turbam philosophorum exercitationes." The *Turba* belongs to the same sphere of thought as the *Tabula smaragdina,* and hence is one of those late Hellenistic products that were transmitted to us by the Arabs, mainly, perhaps, through the Neoplatonic school of Harran (Thabit ibn Qurrah and others), which flourished at the beginning of the eleventh century.[2] The ideas preserved in these treatises are "Alexandrian," and the recipes, particularly those set forth in the "Allegoriae super librum Turbae," adhere closely to the spirit and letter of the *Papyri Graecae Magicae.*[3]

194   Now these "Allegoriae"[4] are our earliest source for the alchemical fish symbolism. For this reason we may assign a

[1] This treatise was not printed together with the *Turba,* like the others, but it appears to belong to the same category. The 28th Distinctio contains the "Dicta Belini" (Belinus = Apollonius of Tyana).

[2] Cf. Ruska, *Turba Philosophorum.*

[3] Cf. the edn. of Preisendanz.

[4] Printed in *Artis auriferae* (1593), I, pp. 139ff.; *Theatrum chemicum,* V, pp. 64ff.; and Manget, *Bibliotheca chemica curiosa* (1702), I, pp. 494ff.

fairly early date to the alchemical fish—before the eleventh century, in any case.[5] There is nothing to suggest that it is of Christian origin. That, however, did not prevent it from becoming—through the transformation of the arcane substance which it had at first represented—a symbol of the *lapis,* the latter term denoting the *prima materia* as well as the end product of the process, variously called *lapis philosophorum, elixir vitae, aurum nostrum, infans, puer, filius philosophorum, Hermaphroditus,* and so on. This *filius,* as I have shown elsewhere, was regarded as a parallel of Christ. Thus, by an indirect route, the alchemical fish attains the dignity of a symbol for the *Salvator mundi.* Its father is God, but its mother is the *Sapientia Dei,* or Mercurius as Virgo. The *filius philosophorum* (or *macrocosmi*), otherwise the *lapis,* means nothing other than the self, as I have explained in a detailed examination of its various attributes and peculiarities.

95   The text containing the earliest reference to the fish runs: "There is in the sea a round fish, lacking bones and cortex, and having in itself a fatness, a wondrous virtue, which, if it is cooked on a slow fire until its fatness and moisture entirely disappear . . . is saturated with sea-water until it begins to shine."[6] This recipe is repeated in another, possibly later, treatise of the same kind, the "Aenigmata philosophorum."[7] Here the "piscis" has become a "pisciculus," and "lucescat" has become "candescat." Common to both treatises is the ironic conclusion of the recipe: When the *citrinitas* (*xanthosis,* 'yellowing') appears, "there is formed the *collyrium* [eyewash] of the philosophers." If they wash their eyes with it, they will easily understand the secrets of the philosophy.

96   This round fish is certainly not a fish in the modern sense, but an invertebrate. This is borne out by the absence of bones and "cortex," which in medieval Latin simply means a mussel-

5 I am not counting the fish as technical alchemical material, in which capacity it was of course known even to the Greek alchemists. I would mention, for instance, the "procedure of Salmanas" (Berthelot, *Alch. grecs,* V, viii, 5) for producing the "round pearl." Fish-glue was often used as an agglutinant.
6 "Allegoriae," in *Art. aurif.,* I, p. 141: "Est in mari piscis rotundus, ossibus et corticibus carens, et habet in se pinguedinem, mirificam virtutem, quae si lento igne coquatur, donec eius pinguedo et humor prorsus recedit . . . et quousque lucescat, aqua maris imbuatur."
7 "Aenigmata," in *Art. aurif.,* I, p. 149.

shell or mollusc.[8] At all events, it is some kind of round organism that lives in the sea, presumably a scyphomedusa or jellyfish, which abounded in the seas of the ancient world. Its free-swimming form, the acrospedote medusa, has a round, bell- or disc-shaped body of radial construction, which as a rule is divided into eight sections by means of four perradials and four interradials (whose angles may again be halved by adradials). Like all Cnidaria[9] or Nematophora[10] (to which class the Scyphomedusae belong), they are equipped with tentacles; these contain the thread-cells or nematocysts with which they poison their prey.

197   Our text remarks that when the "round fish" is warmed or cooked on a slow fire it "begins to shine." In other words, the heat already present in it becomes visible as light. This suggests that the author of the recipe was influenced either by Pliny himself or by some one in the same tradition. Pliny describes a fish —the *stella marina*, 'star of the sea'—which, he says, has puzzled several great philosophers.[11] This fish was said to be hot and burning, and to consume as with fire everything it touched in the sea.[12] Pliny mentions the *stella marina*[13] in the same breath[14] as the *pulmo marinus*, which swims freely on the surface,[15] and attributes to the latter so fiery a nature that when you rub it with a stick, you can straightway use the stick as a torch.[16] From this we might conclude that our author did not take zoological distinctions too seriously, and may have confused the *stella marina* with the *pulmones*. However that may be, the Middle Ages with its passion for symbols eagerly seized on the legend of the "starfish." Nicholas Caussin regarded the "fish" as a starfish and describes it as such. This animal, he says, generates so much heat that it not only sets fire to everything it touches but also cooks its own food. Hence it signifies the "veri

---

[8] See du Cange, *Glossarium ad scriptores mediae et infimae latinitatis*, s.v. "cortex." [In the Swiss *Gesammelte Werke*, 11, p. 59, n. 27, "corticibus" in this same passage is translated as "scales."—EDITORS.]

[9] From κνίδη, *urtica*, 'nettle.' Hence Pliny's "sea-nettle" (*Hist. nat.*, XXXII, xi, 53).

[10] From νῆμα, 'thread, tentacle.'

[11] Caussin (*Polyhistor symbolicus*, 1618, s.v. "stella") cites Aristotle as a source.

[12] *Hist. nat.*, IX, 60. Cf. trans. by Rackham and Jones, III, pp. 346–48.

[13] This could be conceived as a starfish, since, as Pliny says, it has a hard exterior.

[14] *Hist. nat.*, XVIII, 35.   [15] IX, 47 (Rackham/Jones trans., III, p. 220).

[16] XXXII, 10.

amoris vis inextinguibilis" (the inextinguishable power of true love).[17]

98   Such an interpretation sounds very strange to modern ears. But for the Middle Ages "alles Vergängliche ist nur ein Gleichnis" was literally true: all ephemeral things were but a symbol of the divine drama, which to modern man has become almost meaningless. Picinellus interprets the fish in the same way, the only difference being that his amplification is much more elaborate. "This fish," he says, "glows forever in the midst of the waters, and whatsoever it touches grows hot and bursts into flames." This glow is a fire—the fire of the Holy Ghost. He cites as his authority Ecclesiasticus 48 : 1,[18] and refers also to the fiery tongues of the Pentecostal miracle. The miraculous fact that the fire of the *stella marina* does not go out in the water reminds him of the "divinae gratiae efficacitas" (action of divine grace), which sets on fire the hearts that are drowned in a "sea of sins." For the same reason the fish means charity and divine love, as the Song of Solomon 8 : 7 testifies: "Many waters cannot quench love, neither can the floods drown it." The fish, so our author supposes, spreads a radiance about itself from the first moment of its life and thus is an emblem of religion, by whose light the faithful live.

99   As the quotation from the Song of Solomon shows, the interpretation of the burning starfish brings out its connection with profane love. Picinellus even says that the starfish is the "hieroglyph of a lover's heart," whose passion not even the entire sea can extinguish, no matter whether his love be divine or profane. This fish, says our author inconsequently, burns but gives no light. He quotes St. Basil: "Then conceive in your mind a deep pit, impenetrable darkness, fire that has no brightness, having all fire's power of burning, but without any light. . . . Such a conception describes the fire of hell." [19] This fire is "concupiscentia," the "scintilla voluptatis" (spark of lechery).

200   It is curious how often the medieval symbolists give diametrically opposed interpretations of the same symbol, apparently without becoming aware of the far-reaching and

17 *Polyhistor symbolicus*, p. 414.
18 "And Elias the prophet stood up, as a fire; and his word burnt like a torch" (DV).
19 *Homilia in Ps.* 33, in Migne, *P.G.*, vol. 29, col. 371.

dangerous possibility that the unity of the symbol implies the identity of the opposites. Thus we can find certain views in alchemy which maintain that God himself "glows" in this subterranean or submarine [20] fire. The "Gloria mundi," for instance, says: [21]

Take fire or unslaked lime, which the Philosophers say grows on trees. In this fire God himself glows in divine love. . . . Likewise the Natural Master says regarding the art of fire, that Mercurius is to be decomposed . . . and fixed in the unquenchable or living fire, wherein God himself glows, together with the sun, in divine love, for the solace of all men; and without this fire can the art never be brought to perfection. It is also the fire of the Philosophers, which they keep hidden away and concealed. . . . It is also the noblest fire which God created upon earth, for it has a thousand virtues. To these things the teacher replies that God has bestowed upon it such virtue and efficacy . . . that with this fire is mingled the Godhead itself. And this fire purifies, as purgatory does in the lower regions.[22]

[20] This recalls the Vision of Arisleus, where the philosophers in the glass-house at the bottom of the sea suffer great torment on account of the extraordinary heat. (*Art. aurif.*, I, pp. 146ff., and Ruska, "Die Vision des Arisleus," pp. 22ff.)

[21] *Mus. herm.* (1678), pp. 246f. The "Gloria mundi" is an anonymous treatise, and it remains uncertain whether it was originally written in Latin or not. So far as is known, it was printed for the first time in 1620, in German. To the best of my knowledge it was first mentioned in the treatises of the 17th cent. It was highly esteemed and was considered especially dangerous. In the *Theatr. chem.* (1661), VI, pp. 513ff., there is a long extract from it, conjuring the reader to be discreet: "I will that all those who possess this book be admonished and besought for the love of Jesus Christ, that they conceal this art from all such as are puffed up, vainglorious, unjust oppressors of the poor, proud, worldly, scoffers, contemners, false accusers, and such unworthy folk, nor permit this writing to come into the hands of such, if they would escape the wrath of God and the punishments which he is wont to bring down upon those that are presumptuous and profane."

[22] "Recipito ignem, vel calcem vivam, de qua Philosophi loquuntur, quod in arboribus crescat, in quo (igne) Deus ipse ardet amore divino. . . . Item. Naturalis Magister ait ad artem hanc de igne, Mercurium putrefaciendum . . . et fixandum in igne indelebili, vel vivo, quo in Deus ipse ardeat, sed cum sole in amore divino, ad solatium omnium hominum; et absque isto igne ars numquam perfici poterit. Item, ignis Philosophorum quem occultatum occlusumque illi habent. . . . Item, ignis nobilissimus ignis est, quem Deus in terra creavit, millenas enim virtutes habet. Ad haec respondet didascalus quod Deus tantam virtutem efficaciamque tribuerit . . . ut divinitas ipsa cum hoc igne commixta siet. Et iste ignis purificat, tamquam purgatorium in inferno . . ."

The fire is "inextinguishable." "The Philosophers call this fire the fire of the Holy Ghost." [23] It unites Mercurius with the sun "so that all three make but one thing, which no man shall part asunder." [24] "Just as in these three God the Father, God the Son, and God the Holy Ghost are united, [i.e., as] the Holy Trinity in three Persons, and there yet remains the one single true God, so also the fire unites these three things: body, spirit, and soul, that is, Sun, Mercurius, and Soul." [25] "In this invisible fire the mystery of the Art is enclosed, as God the Father, Son, and Spirit in three Persons is verily included in one essence." [26] This fire is "fire and water at once." The Philosophers name it the "living fire" in honour of God, "who mingles himself with himself in the living water." [27]

Another treatise says of the water that it is the "hiding-place and dwelling-place of the whole treasure." [28] For in its midst is the "fire of Gehenna" which "contains this engine of the world in its own being." [29] The fire is caused by the "primum mobile" and is kindled by the influence of the stars. It never ceases its universal motion and is continually lit through the "influence of celestial forces." [30]

It is an "unnatural" fire, "contrary to nature." It puts bodies to the torture, it is itself the dragon that "burns furiously like hell-fire." [31] The life-spirit dwelling in nature, Phyton, has a double aspect: there is an infernal form of it, namely hell-fire, from which a hellish bath can be prepared. The treatise of Abraham Eleazar speaks of Phyton as a "god." [32]

23 "Philosophi hunc ignem Spiritus Sancti ignem appellant."

24 ". . . adeo ut omneis tres, una res fiant, quas nemo separaturus siet."

25 "Pari modo quo in hisce tribus sese uniunt, Deus pater, Deus filius et Deus spiritus sanctus, S. S. Trinitas in tres personas et tamen unicus verus Deus remanet; ita quoque ignis unit hasce tres res: utpote corpus, spiritum et animam, hoc est, Solem, Mercurium et Animam" (p. 247).

26 "In igni hoc invisibili artis mysterium inclusum est, quemadmodum tribus in personis Deus Pater, Filius et Spiritus S. in una essentia vere conclusus est" (p. 248).

27 ". . . qui seipsum sese in vivam aquam miscet" (p. 247). Presumably taken over from the "troubled" water of the pool of Bethesda (John 5 : 2).

28 "Occultatio et domicilium omnis thesauri."

29 "Continens hanc machinam mundi in suo esse."

30 Sendivogius, "Novi luminis chemici," *Mus. herm.,* p. 607.

31 Ripley, "Duodecim portarum," *Theatr. chem.,* II, p. 128.

32 *Uraltes Chymisches Werk* (1760), pp. 79 and 81.

203   According to Blaise de Vigenère, the fire has not two but four aspects: the intelligible, which is all light; the heavenly, partaking of heat and light; the elemental, pertaining to the lower world and compounded of light, heat, and glow (*ardor*); and finally the infernal, opposed to the intelligible, glowing and burning without any light.[33] Here again we encounter the quaternity which the ancients associated with fire, as we saw from the Egyptian conception of Set and the four sons of Horus,[34] and from Ezekiel's vision of the fiery region to the north. It is not at all likely that Vigenère was thinking of Ezekiel in this connection.[35]

204   In the "Introitus apertus" of Philalethes the arcane substance is named "chalybs" (steel). This, he says, is the "auri minera" (the *prima materia* of the gold), "the true key of our Work, without which no skill can kindle the fire of the lamp." Chalybs is a "spirit pre-eminently pure," a "secret, infernal, and yet most volatile fire,"[36] the "wonder of the world, the system of the higher powers in the lower. For this reason the Almighty has assigned to it a most glorious and rare heavenly conjunction, even that notable sign whose nativity is declared throughout the Philosophical East to the furthest horizon of its hemisphere. The wise Magi saw it at the [beginning of the] era, and were astonished, and straightway they knew that the most serene King was born in the world. Do you, when you see his star, follow it to the cradle, and there you shall behold the fair infant. Cast aside your defilements, honour the royal child, open your treasure, offer a gift of gold; and after death he will give you

---

[33] "De igne et sale," *Theatr. chem.*, VI, p. 39.

[34] They are also the sons of Set, in so far as Heru-ur and Set have one body with two heads. [For the association of fire and north, see pp. 99 and 124.]

[35] The quaternary symbols that appear spontaneously in dreams always point, so far as I can see, to totality or the self. Fire means passion, affects, desires, and the emotional driving-forces of human nature in general, that is, everything which is understood by the term "libido." (Cf. *Symbols of Transformation*, Part II, chs. 2 and 3.) When the alchemists attribute a quaternary nature to the fire, this amounts to saying that the self is the source of energy.

[36] Hell-fire is identical with the devil, who, on the authority of Artefius ("Clavis maioris sapientiae," *Theatr. chem.*, IV, p. 237), has an outer body made of air and an inner one of fire.

flesh and blood, the supreme Medicine in the three monarchies of the earth." [37]

05   This passage is particularly interesting because it allows us to look deep into the world of obscure archetypal ideas that fill the mind of the alchemist. The author goes on to say that the steel, which is at the same time the "infernal fire," the "key of our Work," is attracted by the magnet, for which reason "our magnet" is the true "minera" (raw material) of the steel. The magnet has a hidden centre which "with an archetic appetite [38] turns towards the Pole, where the virtue of the steel is exalted." The centre "abounds in salt"—evidently the *sal sapientiae*, for immediately afterwards the text says: "The wise man will rejoice, but the fool will pay small heed to these things, and will not learn wisdom, even though he see the outward-turned central Pole marked with the notable sign [39] of the Almighty."

06   In the Pole is found the heart of Mercurius, "which is the true fire wherein its Lord has his rest. He who journeys through this great and wide sea may touch at both Indies, may guide his course by the sight of the North Star, which our Magnet will cause to appear unto you." This is an allusion to the mystic journey, the "peregrinatio." As I have explained elsewhere, it leads to the four quarters, here indicated by the two Indies—

[37] Philalethes, "Introitus apertus," *Mus. herm.*, pp. 654f.: ". . . ignis infernalis, secretus . . . mundi miraculum, virtutum superiorum in inferioribus systema, quare signo illum notabili notavit Omnipotens cuius nativitas per Orientem in Horizonte Hemisphaerii sui philosophicum annunciatur. Viderunt Sapientes in Evo Magi, et obstupuerunt statimque agnoverunt Regem serenissimum in mundo natum. Tu cum ejus Astra conspexeris, sequere ad usque cunabula, ibi videbis infantem pulcrum, sordes semovendo, regium puellum honora, gazam aperi, auri donum offeras, sic tandem post mortem tibi carnem sanguinemque dabit, summam in tribus Terrae Monarchiis medicinam."

(Cf. Waite, trans., *The Hermetic Museum Restored and Enlarged*, II, pp. 166f.) Philalethes ("lover of truth") is a pseudonym. Waite (*The Works of Thomas Vaughan: Eugenius Philaletha*) conjectures the Hermetic philosopher Vaughan (1621–65), an hypothesis that is doubtful for several reasons. See also Waite, *Lives of Alchemystical Philosophers*, p. 187, and Ferguson, *Bibliotheca Chemica*, II, pp. 194 and 197.

[38] From the Paracelsan concept of the "Archeus." See my "Paracelsus the Physician," par. 39 n. 56. Ruland (*Lexicon of Alchemy*, p. 36) defines: "Archeus is a most high, exalted, and invisible spirit, which is separated from bodies, is exalted, and ascends; it is the occult virtue of Nature, universal in all things, the artificer, the healer . . . the dispenser and composer of all things."

[39] Probably magnetism is meant.

133

East, West—and by the turning of the compass to the north.[40] Together they form a cross, i.e., a quaternity, which characterizes the nature of the Pole. For from the Pole the four directions radiate out, and also the division of the hemispheres (east and west of the Greenwich meridian). Thus the northern hemisphere resembles the round body of the hydromedusa, whose spherical surface is divided by four (or multiples of four) radials, and therefore looks like a globe seen from the Pole.

207   In this connection I would like to mention the dream of a twenty-year-old student, who got into a state of confusion when he found that the philosophical faculty for which he had opted did not suit him. He could discover no reason for this. His disorientation reached the point where he simply did not know what profession he wanted to take up. Then a dream came to his help and showed him his goal in the fullest sense:

208   *He dreamt that he was walking in a wood. Gradually this grew more and more lonely and wild, and finally he realized that he was in a primeval forest. The trees were so high and the foliage so thick that it was almost dark on the ground. All trace of a path had long since disappeared, but, driven on by a vague sense of expectation and curiosity, he pressed forward and soon came to a circular pool, measuring ten to twelve feet across. It was a spring, and the crystal-clear water looked almost black in the dark shadows of the trees. In the middle of the pool there floated a pearly organism, about eighteen inches in diameter, that emitted a faint light. It was a jelly-fish.*[40a] Here the dreamer awoke with a violent emotion: he decided there and then to study science, and he kept to this decision. I must emphasize that the dreamer was not under any psychological influence that might have suggested such an interpretation. The conclusion he drew from the dream was undoubtedly the right one, but it does not by any means exhaust the meaning of the symbol. The dream is archetypal—a "big" dream. The wood that grows dusky and turns into a primeval forest means entry into the unconscious. The round pool with the jelly-fish in it represents a three-dimensional mandala, the self: wholeness as the goal to which the "archetic appetite" points, the magnetic north which gives the traveller his bearings on the "sea of the world."

40 Cf. *Psychology and Alchemy*, par. 457.
40a [Cf. *Memories, Dreams, Reflections*, p. 85 (Brit. edn., p. 91).]

Turning back to our text, I would emphasize, by way of recapitulation, that the infernal fire is nothing other than the *Deus absconditus* (hidden God) who dwells at the North Pole and reveals himself through magnetism. His other synonym is Mercurius, whose heart is to be found at the Pole, and who guides men on their perilous voyage over the sea of the world. The idea that the whole machinery of the world is driven by the infernal fire at the North Pole, that this is hell, and that hell is a system of upper powers reflected in the lower—this is a shattering thought. But the same note is struck by Meister Eckhart when he says that, on returning to his true self, he enters an abyss "deeper than hell itself." Scurrilous as it is, the alchemical idea cannot be denied a certain grandeur. What is particularly interesting, psychologically, is the nature of the image: it is the projection of an archetypal pattern of order,[41] the mandala, which represents the idea of totality. The centering of the image on hell, which at the same time is God, is grounded on the experience that highest and lowest both come from the depths of the soul, and either bring the frail vessel of consciousness to shipwreck or carry it safely to port, with little or no assistance from us. The experience of this "centre" is therefore a numinous one in its own right.

Picinellus feels that his *stella maris*, "this fish which burns in the midst of the water but gives no light," besides meaning the Holy Ghost, love, grace, and religion, also symbolizes something in man, namely his *tongue,* speech, and powers of expression, for it is in these faculties that all psychic life is manifest. He is evidently thinking of an instinctive, unreflecting psychic activity, because at this point he cites James 3 : 6: "And the tongue is a fire, a world of iniquity among our members, defiling the whole body, setting on fire the wheel of birth, and set on fire by hell."[42]

Hence the evil "fish" coincides with our untamed and apparently untameable propensities, which, like a "small fire that sets a great forest ablaze,"[43] defiles the whole body and

41 "The Psychology of Eastern Meditation," pars. 942ff.
42 Ecclesiasticus 9 : 18 (Vulg. 25): "A man full of tongue is terrible in his city" (DV). Conversely, the fiery tongue is an allegory (or symbol?) of the Holy Ghost: "cloven tongues, as of fire" (Acts 2 : 3).   43 James 3 : 5 (RSV).

even sets on fire the "wheel of birth." The τροχός τῆς γενέσεως (*rota nativitatis*) is a distinctly curious expression to use in this connection. The wheel, it is explained, symbolizes the circle or course or cycle of life. This interpretation presupposes ideas akin to Buddhism, if we are not to conceive the wheel merely as the banal statistical cycle of births and deaths. How the wheel could ever be set on fire is a difficult question that cannot be answered without further reflection. We must consider, rather, that it is meant as a parallel to the defilement of the whole body—in other words, a destruction of the *soul*.

212   Ever since the *Timaeus* it has been repeatedly stated that the soul is a sphere.[44] As the *anima mundi*, the soul revolves with the world wheel, whose hub is the Pole. That is why the "heart of Mercurius" is found there, for Mercurius is the *anima mundi*.[45] The *anima mundi* is really the motor of the heavens. The wheel of the starry universe is reflected in the horoscope, called the "thema" of birth. This is a division of the heavens into twelve houses, calculated at the moment of birth, the first house coinciding with the ascendent. Divided up in this way the firmament looks like a wheel turning, and the astronomer Nigidius[46] is said to have received the name Figulus ("potter") because the wheel of heaven turns like a potter's wheel.[47] The "thema" (that which is "set" or "ordained") is indeed a τροχός, 'wheel'. The basic meaning of the horoscope is that, by mapping out the positions of the planets and their relations to one another (aspects), together with the distribution of the signs of the zodiac at the cardinal points, it gives a picture first of the psychic and then of the physical constitution of the individual. It represents, in essence, a system of original and fundamental qualities in a person's character, and can therefore be regarded as an equivalent of the individual psyche. Priscillian (d. 385) evidently took the wheel in this sense. He says of Christ: "He alone has the power to join together the Pleiades and to loose the bands of Orion. Knowing the changes of the firmament and destroying the wheel of generation, he has overcome the day of

---

[44] *Psychology and Alchemy*, par. 109.
[45] "The Spirit Mercurius," par. 263. Cf. *Psychology and Alchemy*, fig. 208.
[46] P. Nigidius Figulus lived in the 1st cent. B.C.
[47] Hertz, *De P. Nigidii Figuli Studiis atque operibus*, p. 5.

our birth by the renewal of baptism."[48] From this it is plain
that in the fourth century the wheel of birth was in fact regarded as the horoscope. "Setting fire to the wheel" is therefore
a figurative expression for a catastrophic revolt of all the original components of the psyche, a conflagration resembling panic
or some other uncontrollable, and hence fatal outburst of emotion.[49] The total nature of the catastrophe is explained by the
central position of the so-called "tongue," the diabolical element whose destructiveness is an essential part of every psyche.
Seen in this light, the *stella maris* stands for the fiery centre in
us from which creative or destructive influences come.

2. *The Fish*

In our discussion of medieval fish symbolism we have so far
been concerned with a fish only in name, the jelly-fish, without
taking due account of the fact that this is not a fish at all in the
zoological sense, and—more important still—is not shaped like
one. It was simply the description of the "round fish" that
brought it to our attention. That, however, was not the case in
the Middle Ages, for we have the testimony of a sixteenth-
century adept, Theobald de Hoghelande, which shows that he
at least understood the fish to be a real fish. Listing the numerous synonyms for the tincture, he remarks: "Likewise they compared it to fishes. Hence Mundus says in the *Turba:* Take one
part fish-gall and one part calf's urine, etc. And in the 'Aenigmata sapientum' it says: There is in our sea a small round fish,
without bones or legs [*cruribus*]."[50] Since the gall mentioned in
the quotation can only come from a real fish, Hoghelande obviously took the "small round fish" to be a real one, and since one
can imagine a fish without bones, but hardly without skin or
some kind of integument, the incomprehensible "corticibus" of

48 Tract. I, 31, in *Opera.* For Christ as destroyer of Heimarmene see *Pistis
Sophia,* Mead trans., p. 17.
49 Fire in this sense often appears in dreams.
50 Hoghelande, "Liber de alchemiae difficultatibus," *Theatr. chem.,* I, p. 163.
The quotation from Mundus in the *Turba* (Ruska, p. 128) runs: "Take therefore one part white gum at an intense heat, and one part calf's urine, and
one part fish-gall, and one part substance of the gum, without which it cannot
be made free from error." "Mundus" is a corruption of "Parmenides," due to
Arabic transcription: (Bar)Mnds. See Ruska, p. 25.

the original version [51] had to be changed into "cruribus" (legs). Of course, fishes don't have legs either. But this passage from a sixteenth-century text proves that the "small round fish" of the "Aenigmata" was understood, in alchemical tradition, as a real fish and not as a jelly-fish. A round and transparent fish of a peculiar sort, without "cortices," is described in the *Cyranides:* the "cinedian fish" lives in the sea on the shores of Syria, Palestine, and Libya, is six fingers long, and is a "pisciculus rotundus." It has two stones in its head and another one in the third vertebra of the tail (*spondilo*), or notochord. This stone is especially potent and is used as a love-potion.[52] The cinedian stone is practically unknown, because it is very rare. It is also called "opsianus," [53] which is interpreted as "serotinus" (of late growth or origin) and "tardus" (slow, hesitant). It pertains to Saturn. "This stone is twin or twofold: the one is opaque and black, but the other though black is brilliant and shining like a mirror." [54] This is the stone which many seek, without finding it: for it is the dragon's stone (*dracontius lapis*).[55]

214   The only thing that can be elicited with certainty from this involved description is that the animal in question must be a vertebrate, and is therefore presumably a genuine fish. What exactly is the justification for calling it "round" is far from clear. It is obvious that the fish is mainly a mythologem, since it is said to contain the dragon's stone. This stone was known to Pliny [56] and also to the medieval alchemists, who named it *draconites, dracontias,* or *drachates*.[57] It was reputed to be a precious stone, which could be obtained by cutting off the head of a sleeping dragon. But it becomes a gem only when a bit of the dragon's soul remains inside,[58] and this is the "hate of the monster as it feels itself dying." The gem is of a *white* colour,

[51] "Ossibus et corticibus carens." [Cf. supra, p. 128 n. 8.]
[52] Du Cange, *Glossarium*, s.v. "ligaturae": "*Corrigia* or *ligatura* of Aphrodite. *Ligaturae, alligaturae* and *alligamenta* are amulets for dispelling diseases. *Suballigaturae* are magic draughts [poisons], precautionary measures [spells]," etc.
[53] *Opsianos lithos* = 'black stone,' obsidian.
[54] "Iste lapis est geminus vel duplex: unus quidem est obscurus et niger, alter autem niger quidem, lucidus et splendidus est sicut speculum."
[55] Delatte, *Textes latins et vieux français relatifs aux Cyranides,* Fasc. XCIII, p. 56.   [56] *Hist. nat.,* XXXVII, 10.   [57] Ruland, *Lexicon,* pp. 128–29.
[58] Ibid., p. 128: "But unless it is removed while they [the serpents] are alive, it will never become a precious stone."

and a powerful alexipharmic. Even though there are no dragons nowadays, the text says, these draconites are occasionally found in the heads of water-snakes. Ruland asserts that he has seen such stones, blue or black in colour.

5   The cinedian stone has a double nature, though, as the text shows, it is not at all clear.[59] One might almost conjecture that its double nature consisted originally in a white and a black variety, and that a copyist, puzzled by the contradiction, inserted "niger quidem" ('though black'). But Ruland distinctly emphasizes that "the colour of the Draconite is white." [60] Its affinity with Saturn may shed light on this dilemma. Saturn, in astrology the "star of the sun," is alchemically interpreted as black; it is even called "sol niger" and has a double nature as the arcane substance,[61] being black outside like lead, but white inside. Johannes Grasseus cites the opinion of the Augustinian monk Degenhardus concerning the lead: the lead of the Philosophers, named lead of the air (*Pb aeris*), contains the "shining white dove" which is called the "salt of the metals." [62] Vigenère assures us that lead, "than which nothing is more opaque," can be turned into "hyacinth" and back again to lead.[63] Quicksilver, says Mylius,[64] comes from the "heart of Saturn," in fact *is* Saturn, the bright silveriness of mercury contrasting with the "blackness" of lead. The "bright" water [65] that flows from the plant Saturnia is, according to Sir George Ripley, "the most perfect water and the bloom of the world." [66] How old this idea is can be seen from the remark of Hippolytus,[67] that Chronos (Saturn) is a "power of the colour of water, and all-destructive."

6   In view of all this, the double nature of the cinedian stone might signify the polarity and union of opposites, which is just what gives the *lapis philosophorum* its peculiar significance as

---

59 *Lucidus* (see above, n. 54), 'brilliant, shining,' can also mean 'white,' thus contrasting with black. But the description would also fit the obsidian.
60 *Lexicon*, p. 203.
61 "The sacred lead of the wise," from which are extracted mercury, sulphur, and salt. Cf. Chartier, "Scientia plumbi sacri sapientum," *Theatr. chem.*, VI, p. 571.
62 "Arca arcani," ibid., p. 314.
63 "De igne et sale," ibid., p. 131.
64 *Philosophia reformata*, p. 305.
65 Pantheus, *Ars transmutationis metallicae* (1519), fol. 9r.
66 *Opera omnia chemica* (1649), p. 317.
67 *Elenchos*, V, 16, 2 (Legge trans., I, p. 154).

a uniting symbol,[68] and hence its magical and divine properties. Our draconite, too, is endowed with extraordinary powers ("potentissimus valde"), which make it eminently suitable as the "ligature of Aphrodite," i.e., love-magic. Magic exercises a *compulsion* that prevails over the conscious mind and will of the victim: an alien will rises up in the bewitched and proves stronger than his ego. The only comparable effect capable of psychological verification is that exerted by unconscious contents, which by their compelling power demonstrate their affinity with or dependence on man's totality, that is, the self and its "karmic" functions.[69] We have already seen that the alchemical fish symbol points ultimately to an archetype of the order of magnitude of the self. So it should not surprise us to see that the principle of "outward uncomeliness," which applies to the lead and the *lapis,* is also applied to Christ. The same that is said of the *lapis* is said of Christ by Ephrem the Syrian (d. 373): "He is clothed in figures, he is the bearer of types. . . . His treasure is hidden and of small account, but when it is laid open, it is wonderful to look upon." [70]

217   In a treatise of the seventeenth century, by an anonymous French author,[71] our strange hybrid, the "round fish," finally becomes a verifiable vertebrate known to zoology: *Echeneis remora,* the common remora or sucking-fish. It belongs to the mackerel family, and is distinguished by a large, flat, oval-shaped sucker on the top of the head in place of the dorsal fin. By means of this it attaches itself either to a larger fish or to a ship's bottom and in this wise is transported about the world.

218   The text says of this fish:

For that which we take, in order to prepare from it the Philosophical Work, is naught else but that little fish the *Echeneis,* which has no blood or spiny bones, and is shut up in that deep mid region

---

68 *Psychology and Alchemy,* "The Lapis-Christ Parallel."

69 We could conceive these as hereditary influences, vestiges of ancestral life, although this idea does not suggest as much as *karma* does to the Indian.

70 *Hymni et sermones,* ed. Lamy, II, col. 770.

71 "Fidelissima et Jucunda Instructio ex manuscripto Gallico Philosophi Anonymi desumpta, per quam Pater filio suo omnia declarat, quae ad compositionem et praeparationem Lapidis Sapientum sunt necessaria, decem capitibus comprehensa." The abbreviated title of this treatise as printed in Vol. VI of *Theatr. chem.* is "Instructio de arbore solari."

of the great universal sea. This little fish is extremely small, alone, and unique in its shape, but the sea is great and vast, and hence it is impossible for those to catch it who do not know in what part of the world it dwells. Believe me verily, that he who, as Theophrastus says, does not well understand the art by which he can draw down the moon from the sky and bring it from heaven to earth, and change it into water and then into earth, will never find the material of the stone of the wise, for it is not more difficult to perform the one than to find the other. Yet none the less, when we speak somewhat in confidence in the ear of a trusted friend, we teach him that hidden secret of the wise, how he can naturally, speedily, and easily catch the little fish called Remora, which is able to hold back the proud vessels of the great Ocean sea (that is the spirit of the world). Those who are not sons of the art are altogether ignorant and know not those precious treasures which are concealed by nature in the precious and heavenly Aqua Vitae of our sea. But, that I may declare to you the clear light of our unique material, or our virgin soil, and teach you in what wise you may acquire the supreme art of the sons of wisdom, it is needful that I instruct you concerning the magnet of the wise, which has the power of attracting the little fish called Echeneis or Remora from out the centre and depth of the sea. If it is caught in accordance with nature, it changes in a natural way first into water and then into earth. And this, when properly prepared by the cunning secret of the wise, has the power of dissolving all solid bodies and making them volatile, and of purifying all bodies that are poisoned.[72]

72 "Quia illud quod accipimus ut opus Philosophicum ex eo praeparemus, nihil aliud est quam pisciculus Echen[e]is sanguine et ossibus spinosis carens, et in profunda parte centri magni maris mundi est inclusus. Hic pisc[ic]ulus valde est exiguus, solus et in sua forma unicus, mare autem magnum et vastum, unde illum capere impossibile est illis, qui qua in parte mundi moretur ignorant. Certam mihi fidem habe, illum qui ut Theophrastus loquitur, artem illam non callet, qua Lunam de firmamento trahat, et de coelo super terram adducat, et in aquam convertat, et postea in terram mutet, nunquam materiam lapidis sapientum inventurum, unum tamen non est difficilius facere, quam alterum invenire. Nihilominus tamen, cum fido amico aliquid in au[re]m fideliter dicimus, tunc ipsum occultum secretum sapientum docemus, quomodo pisc[ic]ulum Remora dictum naturaliter cito et facile capere possit, qui navigia magni maris Oceani (hoc est spiritus mundi), superba retinere potest, qui cum filii artis non sint, prorsus ignari sunt et preciosos thesauros, per naturam in preciosa et coelesti aqua vitae nostri maris delitescentes, non noverunt. Sed ut clarum lumen unicae nostrae materiae, seu terrae virgineae nostrae tibi tradam summam artem filiorum sapientiae, quomodo videlicet illam acquirere possis, te doceam, necesse est ut prius de magnete sapientum te instruam, qui potestatem habet, pisc[ic]ulum

219   We learn from this text that the fish is found, if it can be
found at all, in the centre of the ocean. But the ocean is the
"spirit of the world." Our text, as the above sample shows, derives from a time when alchemy had almost given up its laboratory work and was becoming more and more of a philosophy.
For an alchemist living in the early part of the seventeenth
century, the "spirit of the world" is a somewhat unusual term,
because the expression more commonly used was the "anima
mundi." The world-soul or, in this case, the world-spirit is a
projection of the unconscious, there being no method or apparatus which could provide an objective experience of this kind
and thus furnish objective proof of the world's animation. This
idea is nothing more than an analogy of the animating principle
in man which inspires his thoughts and acts of cognition. "Soul"
and "spirit," or psyche as such, is in itself totally unconscious.
If it is assumed to be somewhere "outside," it cannot be anything except a projection of the unconscious. This may mean a
lot or a little, according to the way you look at it. At any rate,
we know that in alchemy "our sea" is a symbol for the unconscious in general, just as it is in dreams. The extremely small fish
that dwells in the centre of the universal sea nevertheless has
the power to stop the largest ships. From the description of the
Echeneis it is evident that the author was acquainted with the
"pisciculus rotundus ossibus et corticibus carens" of the "Aenigmata." Our interpretation of the round fish as the self can,
accordingly, be extended to the Echeneis. The symbol of the
self appears here as an "extremely small" fish in the vast ocean
of the unconscious, like a man alone on the sea of the world. Its
symbolization as a fish characterizes the self, in this state, as an
unconscious content. There would be no hope whatever of
catching this insignificant creature if a "magnet of the wise" did
not exist in the conscious subject. This "magnet" is obviously
something a master can teach to his pupil; it is the "theoria,"
the one solid possession from which the adept can proceed. For
the *prima materia* always remains to be found, and the only

Echen[e]is vel Remora dictum ex centro et profunditate nostri maris attrahendi.
Qui si secundum naturam capitur, naturaliter primo in aquam deinde in terram
convertitur: Quae per artificiosum secretum sapientum debito modo praeparata
potestatem habet, omnia fixa corpora dissolvendi, et volatilia faciendi et omnia
corpora venenata purgandi etc."

thing that helps him is the "cunning secret of the wise," a theory that can be communicated.

20   This is affirmed by Bernardus Trevisanus (1406–1490) in his treatise "De secretissimo philosophorum opere chemico": it was the sermons of Parmenides in the *Turba* that first freed him from error and guided him into the right way.[73] But Parmenides says the same thing as Arisleus [74] in the *Turba:* "Nature is not improved save through its own nature," [75] and Bernardus adds by way of confirmation: "Thus our material cannot be improved save through itself." It was the *theory* of Parmenides that helped Bernardus on to the right track after much fruitless laboratory work, and there is a legend that he even succeeded in making the philosophers' stone. As to the theory, he is obviously of the opinion that its basic thought is expressed in the saying quoted above, that "nature" [76] can improve or free itself from error only in and through itself. The same idea is expressed in the repeated warning of other treatises not to mix anything from outside with the content of the Hermetic vessel, because the *lapis* "has everything it needs." [77]

1   It is not exactly probable that the alchemists always knew what they were writing, otherwise they would have dropped dead at their own enormities, and of this there is no sign in the literature. *Who* has everything he needs? Even the loneliest meteor circles round some distant sun, or hesitantly draws near to a cluster of brother meteors. Everything hangs together with everything else. By definition, only absolute totality contains everything in itself, and neither need nor compulsion attaches it to anything outside. This is undoubtedly the same as the idea of an absolute God who encompasses everything that exists. But which of us can pull himself out of the bog by his own pigtail? Which of us can improve himself in total isolation? Even the holy anchorite who lives three days' journey off in the desert not only needs to eat and drink but finds himself utterly and

---

73 "Liber de alchemia," *Theatr. chem.,* I, p. 795.

74 Arisleus is legendary. He was regarded as the author of the *Turba.*

75 "Natura non emendatur nisi in sua natura."

76 "Natura" and "naturae," in the language of the *Turba,* correspond to the φύσεις of the alchemist Democritus (1st cent.). See Berthelot, *Alch. grecs.* They are substances or states of substances.

77 "Omne quo indiget."

terribly dependent on the ceaseless presence of God.[78] Only absolute totality can renew itself out of itself and generate itself anew.

222   What is it, then, that one adept whispers into the ear of another, fearfully looking round lest any betray them, or even guess their secret? Nothing less than this: that through this teaching the One and All, the Greatest in the guise of the Smallest, God himself in his everlasting fires, may be caught like a fish in the deep sea. Further, that he may be "drawn from the deep" by a eucharistic act of integration (called *teoqualo,* 'God-eating,' by the Aztecs [79]), and incorporated in the human body.

223   This teaching is the secret and "cunning" magnet by virtue of which the remora ("little in length / mighty in strength") stops the proud frigates in the sea, an adventure which befell the quinquereme of the emperor Caligula "in our own day," as Pliny says in his interesting and edifying tale. The little fish, that was only half a foot long, had sucked fast to the rudder on the return journey from Stura to Entium, and had brought the ship to a standstill. On returning to Rome after this journey, Caligula was murdered by his soldiers. So the Echeneis turned out to be an omen, as Pliny points out. The fish played another such trick on Mark Antony before the naval engagement with Augustus, during which Antony was killed. Pliny cannot marvel enough at the mysterious powers of the Echeneis. His amazement obviously impressed the alchemists so much that they identified the "round fish in our sea" with the remora, and in this way the remora came to symbolize that extremely small thing in the vastness of the unconscious which is charged with such fateful significance: it is the self, the *atman,* "smaller than small, greater than great."

224   The alchemical fish symbol, the Echeneis, clearly derives from Pliny. But fishes also crop up in the writings of Sir George Ripley.[80] What is more, they appear in their "messianic" role: together with the birds, they bring the stone, just as in the Oxyrhynchus sayings of Jesus [81] it is the "fowls of the air and the fishes of the sea and whatsoever is upon or beneath the earth"

---

[78] "Who among us shall dwell with the devouring fire? who among us shall dwell with everlasting burnings?" Isaiah 33 : 14.

[79] [Cf. "Transformation Symbolism in the Mass," pars. 339ff.—EDITORS.]

[80] *Opera,* p. 10.   [81] Grenfell and Hunt, *New Sayings of Jesus,* p. 16.

that point the way to the kingdom of heaven (motif of the "helpful animals"). In Lambspringk's symbols [82] the zodiacal fishes
that move in opposite directions symbolize the arcane substance.
All this theriomorphism is simply a visualization of the unconscious self manifesting itself through "animal" impulses. Some
of these can be attributed to known instincts, but for the most
part they consist of feelings of certainty, beliefs, compulsions,
idiosyncrasies, and phobias that may run directly counter to the
so-called biological instincts without necessarily being pathological on that account. Wholeness is perforce paradoxical in its
manifestations, and the two fishes going in opposite directions,
or the co-operation of birds and fishes, are an instructive illustration of this.[83] The arcane substance, as its attributes show,
refers to the self, and so, in the Oxyrhynchus sayings, does the
"kingdom of heaven" or the conjectural "city."

3. *The Fish Symbol of the Cathars*

The use of fishes as symbols for the psychopompos and for
the antithetical nature of the self points to another tradition
that seems to run parallel with the Echeneis. And there is, in
fact, a very remarkable clue to be found, not in the literature
of alchemy, but in heresiology. The document in question
comes from the archives of the Inquisition at Carcassonne, published by Benoist in his *Histoire des Albigeois et des Vaudois*,
in 1691.[84] It concerns an alleged revelation which Christ's
favourite disciple John was vouchsafed as he "rested in the
Lord's bosom." John wished to know what Satan's state was before his fall, and the Lord answered: "He was in such splendour
that he ruled the powers of heaven." He wanted to be like God,
and to this end he descended through the elements of air and
water, and found that the earth was covered with water. Pene-
trating beneath the surface of the earth, "he found two fishes
lying upon the waters, and they were like oxen yoked for
ploughing the whole earth from sunset to sunrise [or, from West
to East] at the command of the invisible Father. And when he

82 *Mus. herm.*, p. 343.
83 Regarding the combination of fish and bird in ancient mythology, cf. Goodenough, V, pp. 58ff. and figs. 63, 66, 69.
84 Cited by Hahn, *Geschichte der Ketzer im Mittelalter*, II, pp. 815ff.

went down, he found hanging clouds which covered the broad sea. . . . And when he went down, he found set apart therefrom his 'Osob,' which is a kind of fire." On account of the flames he could not descend any further, so he went back to heaven and announced to the angels that he was going to set up his throne on the clouds and be like the All-highest. He then treated the angels as the unjust steward treated his master's debtors, whereupon he and the angels were cast out of heaven by God.[85] But God took pity on him and allowed him and his angels to do what they liked for a week. During this time Satan, using Genesis 1 as a model, created the world and mankind.

226   A prominent Cathar, John de Lugio, confesses to a similar belief.[86] This belief seems to have been known in Catharist circles during the eleventh and twelfth centuries, for the conviction that the world was created by the devil is found in many of the sects. The alchemist Johannes de Rupescissa was in all probability a member of the Poor Men of Lyons,[87] who were influenced by the Cathars. In any case, he could be considered as a connecting link with this tradition.

227   What strikes us most of all in this text is the fact that it contains the Old Bulgarian word *Osob*. Karl Meyer, in his Old Church Slavonic dictionary,[88] gives особь as κατ' ἰδίαν: особа (*osóba*) means in Russian, Polish, and Czech 'individual, personality.' "His osob" could therefore be translated as "that

---

[85] In contradiction to Luke 16 : 8, where "the lord commended the unjust steward, because he had done wisely."

[86] Despite the fact that the sect of this John condemned the Concorricci, with whom our Johannine revelation originated. In the *Summa Fratris Reineri* ("De propriis opinionibus Joh. de Lugio") we read: "He says this world is of the devil." Hahn, I, p. 580.

[87] Rupescissa, *La Vertu et la propriété de la quinte essence* (1581), p. 31: "Since it is our intention to comfort and strengthen the poor preachers of the gospel [*hommes evangelisans*] by means of our book, to the end that their prayers and supplications be not in vain and lost in this work, and that they be not greatly hindered in this pursuit, I will declare and give to them a secret drawn from the bosom of the secrets of the treasures of Nature, which is a thing truly worthy of wonderment, and is to be honoured."

In Rupescissa's treatise "De confectione veri lapidis" (in Gratarolus, *Verae alchemiae artisque metallicae*, 1561, II, p. 299) there is the following exhortation, very unusual in alchemical literature: "Credas, vir Evangelice." Presumably, this was originally an "homme evangelisant."

[88] *Altkirchenslavisch-griechisches Wörterbuch des Codex Suprasliensis.*

which is peculiar to him." [89] This, in the case of the devil, would naturally be fire.[90]

The idea of the two fishes lying on the waters, yoked like oxen for ploughing, is very strange and needs some elucidation. To this end I must recall to the reader St. Augustine's interpretation of the two fishes in the miraculous feeding of the five thousand: for him they represent the *kingly* and the *priestly* person or power,[91] because, like fishes surviving the tempests of the sea, they outlast the turbulence of the multitude. These two powers are united in Christ: he is the king and priest.[92]

Although the two fishes in the Cathar text certainly do not refer to the miraculous fishes, Augustine's interpretation tells us something of importance about the way people thought in those days: the fishes were regarded as *ruling powers*. Since the text is indubitably heretical and a Bogomil document at that, there can be no question of a uniform interpretation of the two fishes as Christ. It may be that they symbolize, as might easily be conjectured, two different persons or powers, from before the creation of the world: Satanaël the elder son of God, and Christ the younger. In the thirtieth heresy of his *Panarium*, Epiphanius reports that the Ebionites believed in a double sonship: "Two, they maintain, were begotten by God, one of them Christ, the other the devil." [93] This doctrine must obviously have spread throughout the Near and Middle East, for it was there that the Bogomil doctrine of Satanaël as the demiurge

89 Dragomanov ("Zabelezhki vrkhy slavyanskite religioznoeticheski Legendi," p. 7) merely remarks about "suum Osob" that, in a Gipsy legend, the devil was hampered by burning sand when creating the world.

90 Cf. supra, n. 36, on Artefius.

91 "But the two fishes . . . seem to signify those two persons by whom that people was governed . . . that is, the kingly and the priestly" (*De diversis quaestionibus*, LXI, 2; Migne, *P.L.*, vol. 40, col. 48). The derivation of the two fishes from II Esdras 6 : 49ff. (Soederberg, *La Religion de Cathares*, p. 97) seems to me questionable. The passage runs (Charles, *Apocryph. and Pseudepigrapha*, II, p. 579): "Then didst thou preserve two living creatures; the name of the one thou didst call Behemoth and the name of the other thou didst call Leviathan. And thou didst separate the one from the other. . . . " This image does not fit in at all with the two fishes mentioned in the Cathar text.

92 "So is our Lord Jesus Christ shown to be our king. He is also our priest for ever after the order of Melchisedek" (Augustine, *De diversis quaestionibus*, LXI, 1).

93 Cap. XVI (Oehler edn., I, p. 266).

arose among the Paulicians and Euchites.[94] Our document is nothing but a Latin version of the report in the *Panoplia* of Euthymios Zigabenos, which in its turn goes back to the confession of faith made before the emperor Alexius Comnenus by the Bogomil bishop Basilius in the year 1111.[95]

230   Note that Satan finds the two fishes *before* the creation, i.e., "in the beginning," when the spirit of God still brooded upon the dark face of the waters (Gen. 1 : 2). Had it been *one* fish only, we could interpret it as a prefiguration of the Redeemer, as the pre-existent Christ of St. John's gospel, the Logos that "was in the beginning with God." (Christ himself says in this document, with reference to John 1 : 2: "But I shall sit with my Father.") There are, however, two fishes, joined by a commissure (= the yoke), which can refer only to the zodiacal fishes. The zodia are important determinants in horoscopes, modifying the influence of the planets that have moved into them, or, even if there are no planets, giving the individual houses a special character. In the present instance the fishes would characterize the ascendent, the moment of the world's birth.[96] Now we know that cosmogonic myths are, at bottom, symbols for the coming of consciousness (though I cannot go into this here).[97] The dawn-state corresponds to the unconscious; in alchemical terms, it is the chaos, the *massa confusa* or *nigredo;* and by means of the *opus,* which the adept likens to the creation of the world, the *albedo* or *dealbatio* is produced, the whitening, which is compared sometimes to the full moon, sometimes to sunrise.[98] It also means illumination, the broadening of consciousness that goes hand in hand with the "work." Expressed psychologically, therefore, the two fishes which the devil found on the primeval waters would signify the newly arisen world of consciousness.

231   The comparison of the fishes with a yoke of oxen ploughing merits special attention. Oxen stand for the motive power of the plough. In the same way, the fishes represent the driving forces of the coming world of consciousness. Since olden times the plough has stood for man's mastery over the earth: wherever

---

[94] Psellus, "De daemonibus," in Ficinus, *Auctores Platonici* (1497), fol. N. Vᵛ.
[95] Migne, *P.G.,* vol. 130, cols. 1290ff.
[96] This interpretation accords with modern astrological speculations.
[97] Concerning such symbols, see Neumann, *The Origins and History of Consciousness.*   [98] Ripley, *Chymische Schrifften* (1624), p. 25.

man ploughs, he has wrested a patch of soil from the primal state and put it to his own use. That is to say: the fishes will rule this world and subdue it by working astrologically through man and moulding his consciousness. Oddly enough, the ploughing does not begin, like all other things, in the east, but in the west. This motif turns up again in alchemy. "Know," says Ripley, "that your beginning should be made towards sunset, and from there you should turn towards midnight, when the lights cease altogether to shine, and you should remain ninety nights in the dark fire of purgatory without light. Then turn your course towards the east, and you will pass through many different colours," etc.[99] The alchemical work starts with the descent into darkness (*nigredo*), i.e., the unconscious. The ploughing or mastery of the earth is undertaken "at the command of the Father." Thus God not only foresaw the enantiodromia that began in the year 1000, but also intended it. The Platonic month of the Fishes is to be ruled by two principles. The fishes in our text are parallel, like the oxen, and point to the same goal, although one is Christ and the other the Antichrist.

32   This, roughly, would be the early medieval line of reasoning (if we can speak of "reasoning" here). I do not know whether the argument we have outlined was ever discussed consciously. Yet it would be possible; the Talmudic prophecy concerning the year 530 (pars. 133ff.) leads one to conjecture astronomical calculations on the one hand and on the other an astrological allusion to the sign of Fishes favoured by the Jewish masters. As against this, it is possible that the fishes in our text are not a conscious reference to astrological ideas but rather a product of the unconscious. That the unconscious is quite capable of "reflections" of this kind we know well enough from dreams and the analysis of myths and fairytales.[100] The image of the fishes as such belonged to the common stock of conscious ideas and may—unconsciously—have expressed the meaning in symbolic form. For it was about this time (11th cent.) that the Jewish astrologers began calculating the birth of the Messiah in Pisces, and the universal feeling that a new age had commenced was given clear expression by Joachim of Flora.

99 Ibid., p. 33f.
100 Cf. Laiblin, "Vom mythischen Gehalt unserer Märchen."

233   The text of our Johannine revelation can hardly be earlier, or much later, than the eleventh century. With the beginning of this century, which is astrologically the middle of the Pisces aeon, heresies sprang up everywhere like mushrooms, and at the same time Christ's adversary, the second fish, alias the devil, appears as the demiurge. Historically speaking, this idea represents a kind of Gnostic Renaissance, since the Gnostic demiurge was regarded as an inferior being from whom all evil comes.[101] The significant thing about this phenomenon is its synchronicity, that is, its occurrence at a time that had been fixed astrologically.

234   That Catharist ideas found their way into alchemy is not altogether surprising. I have not, however, come across any texts which would prove that the Catharist fish symbol was assimilated into the alchemical tradition and so could be held responsible for Lambspringk's fish symbol, signifying the arcane substance and its inner antinomy. Lambspringk's symbol appeared not much earlier than the end of the sixteenth century and represented a revitalization of the archetype. It shows two reversed fishes swimming in the sea—*nostro mari*—by which was meant the *aqua permanens* or arcane substance. They are designated "spiritus et anima," and like the stag and unicorn, the two lions, the dog and wolf, and the two fighting birds, they indicate the double nature of Mercurius.[102]

235   If my reflections, which are based on some knowledge of the symbolic thinking of the Middle Ages, are justified, then we have here a remarkable confirmation of the views I expressed in an earlier chapter. With the year 1000 a new world begins, proclaiming its advent in a strange medley of religious movements such as the Bogomils, Cathari, Albigenses, Waldenses, Poor Men of Lyons, Brethren of the Free Spirit, Beguins, Beghards, etc., and in the Holy Ghost Movement of Joachim of Flora. These movements are also associated with the rise of alchemy, Protestantism, the Enlightenment, and natural science, leading ultimately to the increasingly devilish developments we have lived to experience in our own day, and to the evaporation of Christianity under the assaults of rationalism, intellectualism, materialism, and "realism."

[101] According to Irenaeus, the Gnostics held that the demiurge was the younger brother of Christ.   [102] *Mus. herm.*, p. 343.

36   In conclusion, I would like to give a concrete example of the way the symbol of the fish springs out of the unconscious autochthonously. The case in question is that of a young woman who had uncommonly lively and plastic dreams. She was very much under the influence of her father, who had a materialistic outlook and was not happily married. She shut herself off from these unfavourable surroundings by developing, at a very early age, an intense inner life of her own. As a small child, she replaced her parents by two trees in the garden. In her sixth or seventh year, she dreamt that God had promised her a golden fish. From this time forth she frequently dreamt of fishes. Later, a little while before starting psychological treatment on account of her manifold problems, she dreamt that she was *"standing on the bank of the Limmat and looking down into the water. A man threw a gold coin into the river, the water became transparent and I could see the bottom.*[103] *There was a coral reef and a lot of fishes. One of them had a shining silver belly and a golden back."* During treatment she had the following dream: *"I came to the bank of a broad, flowing river. I couldn't see much at first, only water, earth, and rock. I threw the pages with my notes on them into the water, with the feeling that I was giving something back to the river. Immediately afterwards I had a fishing-rod in my hand. I sat down on a rock and started fishing. Still I saw nothing but water, earth, and rock. Suddenly a big fish bit. He had a silver belly and a golden back. As I drew him to land, the whole landscape became alive: the rock emerged like the primeval foundation of the earth, grass and flowers sprang up, and the bushes expanded into a great forest. A gust of wind blew and set everything in motion. Then, suddenly, I heard behind me the voice of Mr. X [an older man whom she knew only from photographs and from hearsay, but who seems to have been some kind of authority for her]. He said, quietly but distinctly: 'The patient ones in the innermost realm are given the fish, the food of the deep.' At this moment a circle ran round me, part of it touching the water. Then I heard the voice again: 'The brave ones in the second realm may be given victory, for there the battle is fought.' Immediately*

103 The transparency of the water means that attention (value, gold) is given to the unconscious. It is an offering to the genius of the fountain. Cf. the vision of the Amitābha Land in my "Psychology of Eastern Meditation."

*another circle ran round me, this time touching the other bank.
At the same time I saw into the distance and a colourful landscape was revealed. The sun rose over the horizon. I heard the
voice, speaking as if out of the distance: 'The third and the
fourth realms come, similarly enlarged, out of the other two.
But the fourth realm'—and here the voice paused for a moment,
as if deliberating—'the fourth realm joins on to the first.*[104] *It is
the highest and the lowest at once, for the highest and the lowest come together. They are at bottom one.'* " Here the dreamer
awoke with a roaring in her ears.

237   This dream has all the marks of a "big" dream, and it also
has the quality of something "thought," which is characteristic
of the intuitive type. Even though the dreamer had acquired
some knowledge of psychology by this time, she had no knowledge whatever of the historical fish symbol. The details of the
dream may be commented on as follows: The bank of the river
represents the threshold, so to speak, to the unconscious. Fishing is an intuitive attempt to "catch" unconscious contents
(fishes). Silver and gold, in alchemical language, signify feminine
and masculine, the hermaphrodite aspect of the fish, indicating
that it is a *complexio oppositorum*.[105] It also brings about a
magical animation.[106] The older man is a personification of the
archetype of the "wise old man." We know already that the fish
is a "miraculous food," the eucharistic food of the τέλειοι. The
first circle that touches the water illustrates the partial integration of the unconscious. The battle is the conflict of opposites,
maybe between consciousness and the shadow. The second circle
touches the "other bank," where the union of opposites takes
place. In the Indian "quicksilver system" the arcane substance
is called *para-da*, 'leading to the other shore'; in the West it is
Mercurius.[107] The fourth realm, stressed by a weighty pause, is
the One that adds itself to the three and makes all four into a
unity.[108] The circles naturally produce a mandala, the outermost
circle paradoxically coinciding with the centre, and recalling

---

104 Cf. infra, pars. 395ff.   105 Cf. *Psychology and Alchemy*, s.v. "coniunctio."
106 The Ichthys (= Christ or Attis) is the food that bestows (immortal) life.
107 Deussen, *Allgemeine Geschichte der Philosophie*, I, pt. iii, pp. 336ff. and
"The Spirit Mercurius," pars. 282ff.
108 *Psychology and Alchemy*, pars. 26 and 209, and "A Psychological Approach to
the Dogma of the Trinity," pars. 184ff.

the old image for God. "God is a circle whose centre is everywhere and the circumference nowhere." [109] The motif of the first coinciding with the fourth was expressed long ago in the axiom of Maria: "One becomes two, two becomes three, and out of the third comes the One as the fourth."

38   The dream sums up in condensed form the whole symbolism of the individuation process in a person who was totally unacquainted with the literature of the subject. Cases of this kind are by no means rare and ought to make us think. They demonstrate the existence of an unconscious "knowledge" of the individuation process and its historical symbolism.

109 [For the source of this saying, see "A Psychological Approach to the Dogma of the Trinity," par. 229, n. 6.—EDITORS.]

XI

THE ALCHEMICAL INTERPRETATION
OF THE FISH

239 We shall now turn to the problem raised by the anonymous French author of the "Instructio de arbore solari," the problem of how the fish is caught. The Echeneis exercises an attraction on ships that could best be compared with the influence of a magnet on iron. The attraction, so the historical tradition says, emanates from the fish and brings the vessel, whether powered by sail or oarsmen, to a standstill.[1] I mention this seemingly unimportant feature because, as we shall see, in the alchemical view the attraction no longer proceeds from the fish but from a magnet which man possesses and which exerts the attraction that was once the mysterious property of the fish. If we bear in mind the significance of the fish, it is easy to understand why a powerful attraction should emanate from this arcane centre, which might aptly be compared with the magnetism of the North Pole.[2] As we shall see in a later chapter, the Gnostics said the same thing about the magnetic effect of their central figure

[1] "The Echenaïs is a small fish, half a foot in length [*semipedalis*], and takes its name from the fact that it holds back a ship by cleaving to it, so that though winds blow and storms rage, yet the ship seems to stand still as if rooted in the sea, and cannot be moved. . . . Hence the Latins call it *delay* (Remora)." (Du Cange, *Glossarium,* s.v. "Echenaïs." Cited from the ms. of a bestiary.) This passage is taken verbatim from the *Liber etymologiarum* (Lib. XII, cap. VI) of Isidore of Seville. There the name of the fish is "echinus," which strictly speaking is a sea-urchin. Because of its radial structure, this creature comes into the same class as the starfish and the jelly-fish. (For the "Instructio," see supra, p. 140, n. 71.)

[2] That the power of the Echeneis was understood to be magnetic is clear from the legend that if a salted Echeneis is let down into a mine it will attract the gold and bring it to the surface. Cf. Masenius, *Speculum imaginum veritatis occultae* (1714), s.v. "Echeneis." "Magnet" is also the name given to sal ammoniac, which, when added to metallic solutions, "instantly draws all that is good in them, be it gold or tincture, to the bottom of the glass." (*Lexicon medico-chymicum,* 1711, p. 156.)

(point, monad, son, etc.). It is therefore a remarkable innovation when the alchemists set out to manipulate an instrument that would exert the same powers as the Echeneis, but on the Echeneis itself. This reversal of direction is important for the psychology of alchemy because it offers a parallel to the adept's claim to be able to produce the *filius macrocosmi*, the equivalent of Christ—*Deo concedente*—through his art. In this way the artifex or his instrument comes to replace the Echeneis and everything it stood for as the arcane substance. He has, so to speak, inveigled the secret out of the fish and seeks to draw the arcane substance to the surface in order to prepare from it the *filius philosophorum*, the *lapis*.

40   The "magnet of the wise" which is to draw the wonder-working fish to the surface can, our text says, be *taught*. The content of this secret teaching is the real arcanum of alchemy: the discovery or production of the *prima materia*. The "doctrine" or "theory" is personified—or rather, concretized—as "Mercurius non vulgi," the philosophical mercury. This conception is as ambiguous as the antique Hermes; sometimes Mercurius is a substance like quicksilver, sometimes it is a philosophy. Dom Pernety formulates it somewhat drastically: "[La matière du mercure philosophique] a une vertu aimantive qui attire des rayons du Soleil et de la Lune le mercure des Sages." [3] Concerning the *prima materia* the adepts talk a great deal but say very little—so little that in most cases one can form no conception of it whatever.[4] This attitude is proof of serious intellectual difficulties—understandably so, because in the first place no such material existed from which the *lapis* could be prepared, nor did anyone ever succeed in making a *lapis* that would have come up to expectations. Secondly, the names given to the *prima materia* show that it was not a definite substance at all, but rather an intuitive concept for an *initial psychic situation*, symbolized by such terms as water of life, cloud, heaven, shadow, sea, mother, moon, dragon, Venus, chaos, *massa confusa*, Microcosmos, etc.

41   In the long lists of names one that frequently figures is "magnesia," though this should certainly not be understood as the

<hr>

3 *Dictionnaire mytho-hermétique* (1787), s.v. "Magnès."
4 Cf. *Psychology and Alchemy*, pars. 425ff.

magnesium oxide of the pharmacopoeia.[5] Magnesia is rather the "complete or conjoined mixture from which this moisture is extracted,[6] i.e., the root-matter of our stone."[7] The complicated procedure for producing the magnesia is described in the treatise "Aristoteles de perfecto Magisterio."[8] It is the whitened arcane substance.[9] Pandolfus says in the *Turba:* "I command you to take the hidden and venerable secret thing, which is the white magnesia."[10] In Khunrath, magnesia is synonymous with "chaos" and "Aes Hermetis." He calls it "A Catholic or Universal, that is, a Cosmic Ens or Entity, Three-in-One, naturally compounded of Body, Spirit, and Soul, the one and only true Subiectum Catholicon and true Universal Materia lapidis Philosophorum."[11] The magnesia is feminine,[12] just as the magnet is masculine by nature.[13] Hence it carries "in its belly the sal Armoniacum et vegetabile," meaning the arcane substance of the stone.[14] Even in Greek alchemy magnesia or "magnes" denoted the hermaphroditic transformative substance.[15] For the alchemists, magnesia is associated with "magnes" (magnet) not only phonetically, but also in meaning, as a recipe of Rosinus shows: "Take therefore this animate stone, the stone which has a soul in it, the mercurial,[16] which is sensible and sensitive to the presence and influence of the magnesia and the magnet, and

[5] Berthelot says of the "Magnésie": "Jusqu'au XVIIIe siècle, [le mot] n'a rien eu de commun avec la magnésie des chimistes d'aujourd'hui" (*Alch. grecs,* Introduction, p. 255). In Pliny and Dioscorides it meant the magnetic iron-stone.
[6] Mylius, *Phil. ref.,* p. 31.
[7] The *corpus Magnesiae* is the "root of the closed house," the "belly" in which Sol and Luna are united. ("Aurora consurgens," Part II, *Art. aurif.,* I, p. 191.)
[8] *Theatr. chem.,* III, pp. 88f.
[9] Mylius calls the tenth grade of the process "the exaltation, which is the ingenious ennobling of our whitened magnesia" (p. 129). Hence the *Rosarium philosophorum* (*Art. aurif.,* II, p. 231) says: "The magnesia is the full moon."
[10] Sermo XXI.
[11] *Von hylealischen Chaos,* pp. 5f.
[12] "Magnesia—the Woman." Ruland, *Lexicon,* p. 216.
[13] But in the region of Alexandria and in the Troad there was said to be a magnetic stone "of the feminine sex, and totally useless." (Ruland, p. 215.)
[14] "Duodecim tractatus," *Theatr. chem.,* IV, p. 499.
[15] Berthelot, Intro., p. 255.
[16] "Magnesia is further the mixed water congealed in air which offers resistance to the fire, the earth of the stone, our mercury, mixture of the substances. The whole therein is mercury." Ruland, p. 216.

[which is] the calaminary and the living Stone, yielding and repelling by local motion." [17]

This text shows clearly enough that the real alchemical procedure was not concerned at all with chemical processes, for if it were, the substance to be transformed would not need to be animate or endowed with sensitivity. But a psychic function was absolutely necessary to it when, as in the case of the magnesia, the adept was preoccupied with one of the innumerable expressions used for the unconscious, that is, for the hidden part of the psyche that had slipped into the unknown chemical compound by projection, and that bedevilled and befooled him in the guise of a hundred "arcane substances." Naturally only the most stupid and unobservant of the alchemists were hoodwinked in this way, for there were plenty of hints in the classical texts that could have put them on the right track. Unfortunately, we today are not so far removed from the Middle Ages: we still have to overcome considerable difficulties before we can begin to understand the real purpose of alchemy.

The "lapis animalis" of Rosinus, then, is a live thing, credited with the ability to *feel* or *perceive* the influence of the magnesia and the magnet. But the magnet, too, is a live thing. Thus, the jurisconsult and alchemist Chrysippus Fanianus, of Basel, says: "But if Thales of Miletus chose to call that stone of Hercules, the magnet, an animate thing, because we see it attract and move iron, why shall we not likewise call salt, which in wondrous wise penetrates, purges, contracts, expands, hinders, and reduces, a living thing?" [18] Dorn writes: "The magnetic stone teaches us, for in it the power of magnetizing and attracting iron is not seen [with the eyes]; it is a spirit hidden within, not perceptible to the sense." [19] The numinous effect which the

---

[17] "Rosinus ad Sarratantam" (*Art. aurif.*, I, p. 311): "Recipe ergo hunc lapidem animalem: id est animam in se habentem, scilicet Mercurialem sensibilem: id est, sentientem praesentiam et influentiam magnesiae et magnetis et calaminarem [et lapidem] per motum localem, prosequendo et fugando vegetabilem. . . ." Instead of "et lapidem" the text of 1593 has "ac apicem," which does not make sense. Rosinus is a corruption of Zosimos due to Arabic transcription.

[18] *De arte metallicae metamorphoseos ad Philoponum liber singularis* (1576). Reprinted in *Theatr. chem.*, I (1602), p. 44.

[19] "Philosophia chemica," *Theatr. chem.*, I, p. 497. Here Dorn discusses his view of the *anima rerum*: "The body . . . of every thing is a prison, wherein the powers of the soul of things are detained and held in fetters, so that their natural

incomprehensible power of magnetism had upon our fore-fathers is graphically described by St. Augustine: "We know that the lodestone draws iron strangely; the which, when I saw it for the first time, did send a cold shiver through me [*vehe-menter inhorrui*]." [20] Even the humanist Andrea Alciati (d. 1550) exclaims: "Wherefore he who first perceives and beholds the power of the magnet to attract iron cannot but be rapt in ad-miration. . . . And it is not enough for some to obtrude upon us that there is a certain secret power in these things, which is generally known. For how will they define that hidden force, of which they can tell us nothing but the name?" [21] The famous anatomist and astrologer Gabriel Fallopius (1490–1563) is said to have considered the magnet, together with quicksilver and purgatives, to be inexplicable marvels, "whose effect is to be wondered at with amazement," as Libavius relates in his "Ars prolatoria." [22] These utterances bear witness to the naïve reac-tion of intelligent and thoughtful people who took what they saw to be an inexplicable miracle. So it is quite understandable if they felt that such an astonishing object was *alive* (like the "lapis *animatus*," "calx *viva*," etc.). The magnet, too, had a soul, like the mysterious stone that could feel. In the "Duodecim tractatus" [23] the magnet appears as the symbol of the *aqua roris nostri* (water of our dew), "whose mother is the midpoint of the heavenly and earthly Sun and Moon." This water, the famed *aqua permanens,* is apostrophized by the anonymous author as follows: "O holy and wonderful nature, which permittest not the sons of the doctrine to err, as thou showest in man's daily life. Further in these . . . treatises I have put forward so many natural reasons, that . . . the reader may understand all those

---

spirits are not able freely to impress their powers and activities upon them. The spirit of such insensate things in relation to its subject is similar to and of the same efficacy as undoubting faith is in man." The divine powers imprisoned in bodies are nothing other than *Dionysus dispersed in matter.*

20 Cf. *City of God,* Healey trans., II, p. 322. Augustine finds quick-lime (*calx viva*) equally wonderful: "Quam mirum est quod cum extinguitur, tunc accendi-tur" (But the wonder is that when it is killed it is quickened).

21 *Emblemata* (1621), Embl. CLXXI, p. 715 a.

22 *Commentariorum alchymiae* (1606), Part II, p. 101.

23 *Theatr. chem.,* IV, p. 499.

things which, by God's blessing, I have seen with my own eyes." [24]

4   The underlying thought here is the idea of the doctrine, the "aqua doctrinae." As we have seen, the "magnet" or "heavenly dew" can be *taught*. Like the water, it symbolizes the doctrine itself. This is contrasted with the "animate stone" that "perceives" the influence of the magnetic pair, magnes and magnesia. The animate stone, like the magnet, is an arcane substance, and only such substances can enter into a combination finally leading to the goal of the *lapis philosophorum*. Dorn says: "The pagan Gentiles say that nature seeks after a nature like to itself, and rejoices in its own nature; if it is joined to another, the work of nature is destroyed." [25] This is an allusion to the axiom usually attributed to the alchemist Democritus: "Nature rejoices in nature; nature subdues nature; nature rules over nature." [26]

5   Just as magnes and magnesia form a pair, so the *lapis animatus sive vegetabilis* [27] is a Rebis or hermaphrodite that is born of the royal marriage. We have, then, two contrasting pairs, forming by mutual attraction a *quaternio,* the fourfold basis of wholeness.[28] As the symbolism shows, the pairs both signify the same thing: a *complexio oppositorum* or uniting symbol.[29] If our texts do not represent them as the same thing and as coinciding with the arcane substance, then there must be a reason for this, though it cannot be ascertained from the symbols used for the two substances to be combined. Sometimes the arcane

[24] The extraordinary importance of the water in alchemy goes back, in my view, to Gnostic sources: "And water is honoured, and they believe in it as if it were a god, going almost so far as to allege that life arises therefrom" (Epiphanius, *Panarium*, LXIII, cap. I).

[25] "Inquiunt enim, natura naturam sibi similem appetit, et congaudet suae naturae; si alienae iungatur, destruitur opus naturae" ("Ars chemistica," *Theatr. chem.*, I, p. 252).

[26] Δημοκρίτου φυσικὰ καὶ μυστικά.—Berthelot, *Alch. grecs,* II, i, 3. According to the story of Democritus, this axiom was revealed to him by his deceased teacher. Synesius, in the treatise addressed to Dioscorus, priest of Serapis (Berthelot, II, iii), says that the teacher of Democritus was Ostanes, and that the axiom came from him.

[27] *Vegetabilis* in our texts means 'living' when applied to Mercurius, 'vivifying' when applied to the Quinta Essentia.

[28] Cf. "Psychology of the Transference," pars. 433ff., and "Phenomenology of the Spirit in Fairytales," in Part I of vol. 9, pars. 429ff.

[29] *Psychological Types,* ch. V, 3.

substance is magnesia, sometimes the water, sometimes the magnet, sometimes the fish; and yet they all mean the *prima materia* from which the miraculous birth ensues. The distinction that the alchemists had in mind is made clear by a passage from a seventeenth-century treatise written by John Collesson, prior of the Benedictine Order: [30] "But as to that substance whereby common gold and silver are naturally and Philosophically dissolved, let no man imagine that it is any other than the general soul of the world, which by magnets and Philosophical means is attracted and drawn down from the higher bodies, and especially from the rays of the Sun and Moon. And hence it is clear that they have no knowledge whatever of Mercurius or of the Philosophical fluid who think to dissolve perfect metals by natural and physical means." [31]

246   Obviously a distinction must be made between two categories of symbols: first, those which refer to the extrapsychic chemical substance or its metaphysical equivalent, e.g., *serpens mercurialis, spiritus, anima mundi, veritas, sapientia,* etc.; second, those denoting the chemical preparations produced by the adept, such as solvents (*aqua, acetum, lac virginis*) or their "philosophical" equivalent, the *theoria* or *scientia,* which, when it is "right," has miraculous effects on matter, as Dorn explains in his philosophical treatises.[32]

247   These two categories continually overlap: sometimes the arcane substance is apparently nothing but a chemical body, sometimes an idea, which today we would call a psychic content. Pernety describes this confusion very clearly in his explanation of the magnet: "But it must not be supposed that this magnet is

---

[30] "Idea perfecta philosophiae hermeticae," *Theatr. chem.* (1661), VI, p. 152. The treatise was first published 1630. Of the author Collesson nothing appears to be known.

[31] "Quantum autem ad substantiam, qua naturaliter et Philosophice aurum et argentum vulgare solvuntur, attinet, nemo sibi imaginari debet, ullam aliam, quam animam mundi generalem, quae per magnetes et media Philosophica trahitur et attrahitur de corporibus superioribus, maxime vero de radiis Solis et Lunae. Unde liquet illos Mercurii seu menstrui Philosophici nullam habere cognitionem, qui naturaliter et physice metalla perfecta dissolvere cogitant."

[32] "There is a certain truth in natural things which is not seen with the outward eye, but is perceived by the mind alone, and of this the Philosophers have had experience, and have ascertained that its virtue is such that it performs miracles" ("Speculativa philosophia," *Theatr. chem.,* I, p. 298).

the common magnet. They [the alchemists] have given it this name only because of its natural sympathy with what they call their steel [*adamas*]. This is the ore [*prima materia*] of their gold, and the magnet is the ore of their steel. The centre of this magnet contains a hidden salt, a menstruum for calcining the philosophical gold. This prepared salt forms their Mercury, with which they perform the magistery of the Sages in white and in red. It becomes an ore of heavenly fire, which acts as a ferment for their stone." [33] In his view, therefore, the secret of the magnet's effect lies in a salt prepared by the adept. Whenever an alchemist speaks of "salt," he does not mean sodium chloride or any other salt, or only in a very limited sense. He could not get away from its symbolic significance, and therefore included the *sal sapientiae* in the chemical substance. That is the salt hidden in the magnet and prepared by the adept—on the one hand, a product of his art; on the other, already present in nature. This contradiction can be resolved very easily by taking it simply as the projection of a psychic content.

48   A similar state of affairs can be found in Dorn's writings. In his case it is not a question of the *sal sapientiae* but of the "veritas," which for him is hidden in natural things and at the same time is obviously a "moral" concept. This truth is the "medicine, improving and transforming that which *is no longer* into that which it *was before* its corruption, and that which *is not* into that which it *ought to be*." [34] It is a "metaphysical substance," hidden not only in things, but in the human body: "In the human body is concealed a certain metaphysical substance known to very few, which needeth no medicament, being itself an incorrupt medicament." [35] Therefore "it is the study of the Chemists to liberate that unsensual truth from its fetters in things of sense." [36] He that would acquire the chemical art must study the "true Philosophy" and not the "Aristotelian," adds

[33] Pernety, *Dictionnaire mytho-hermétique*, s.v. "Aimant."

[34] ". . . medicina, corrigens et transmutans id, quod non est amplius, in id quod fuit ante corruptionem, ac in melius, et id, quod non est, in id quod esse debet" (p. 267).

[35] "In corpore humano latet quaedam substantia methaphysica, paucissimis nota, quae nullo . . . indiget medicamento, sed ipsa medicamentum est incorruptum" (p. 265).

[36] ". . . Chemistarum studium, in sensualibus insensualem illam veritatem a suis compedibus liberare" (p. 271).

Dorn, because the true doctrine, in Collesson's words, is the magnet whereby the "centre of truth" is liberated from bodies and whereby the bodies are transformed. "The Philosophers, through a kind of divine inspiration, knew that this virtue and heavenly vigour can be freed from its fetters; not by its contrary . . . but by its like. Since therefore some such a thing is found, whether within man or outside him, which is conformable to this substance, the wise concluded that like things are to be fortified by like, by peace rather than by war." [37]

249   Thus the doctrine, which may be consciously acquired "through a kind of divine inspiration," is at the same time the instrument whereby the object of the doctrine or theory can be freed from its imprisonment in the body, because the symbol for the doctrine—the "magnet"—is at the same time the mysterious "truth" of which the doctrine speaks. The doctrine enters the consciousness of the adept as a gift of the Holy Ghost. It is a thesaurus of knowledge about the secret of the art, of the treasure hidden in the *prima materia,* which was thought to be outside man. The treasure of the doctrine and the precious secret concealed in the darkness of matter are one and the same thing. For us this is not a discovery, as we have known for some time that such secrets owe their existence to unconscious projections. Dorn was the first thinker to recognize with the utmost clarity the extraordinary dilemma of alchemy: *the arcane substance is one and the same, whether it is found within man or outside him.* The "alchymical" procedure takes place within and without. He who does not understand how to free the "truth" in his own soul from its fetters will never make a success of the physical opus, and he who knows how to make the stone can only do so on the basis of right doctrine, through which he himself is transformed, or which he creates through his own transformation.

250   Helped by these reflections, Dorn comes to realize the fundamental importance of self-knowledge: "See, therefore, that thou

[37] "Philosophi divino quodam afflatu cognoverunt hanc virtutem caelestemque vigorem a suis compedibus liberari posse: non contrario . . . sed suo simili. Cum igitur tale quid, sive in homine sive extra ipsum inveniatur, quod huic est conforme substantiae, concluserunt sapientes similia similibus esse corroboranda, pace potius quam bello." (P. 265.)

goest forth such as thou desirest the work to be which thou seekest." [38] In other words, the expectations you put into the work must be applied to your own ego. The production of the arcane substance, the "generatio Mercurii," is possible only for one who has full knowledge of the doctrine; but "we cannot be resolved of any doubt except by experiment, and there is no better way to make it than on ourselves." [39] The doctrine formulates our inner experience or is substantially dependent upon it: "Let him know that man's greatest treasure is to be found within man, and not outside him. From him it goes forth inwardly . . . whereby that is outwardly brought to pass which he sees with his own eyes. Therefore unless his mind be blinded, he will see, that is, understand, who and of what sort he is inwardly, and by the light of nature he will know himself through outward things." [40] The secret is first and foremost *in man;* it is his *true self,*[41] which he does not know but learns to know by experience of outward things. Therefore Dorn exhorts the alchemist: "Learn from within thyself to know all that is in heaven and on earth, that thou mayest be wise in all things. Knowest thou not that heaven and the elements were formerly one, and were separated by a divine act of creation from one another, that they might bring forth thee and all things?" [42]

251   Since knowledge of the world dwells in his own bosom, the adept should draw such knowledge out of his knowledge of himself, for the self he must seek to know is a part of that nature which was bodied forth by God's original oneness with the world. It is manifestly *not* a knowledge of the nature of the ego,

---

38 "Fac igitur ut talis evadas, quale tuum esse vis quod quaesieris opus" (p. 277).
39 ". . . non possumus de quovis dubio certiores fieri, quam experiendo, nec melius quam in nobis ipsis" ("Philosophia meditativa," *Theatr. chem.*, I, p. 467).
40 "Cognoscat hominis in homine thesaurum existere maximum, et non extra ipsum. Ab ipso procedit interius . . . per quod operatur extrinsecus id, quod oculariter videt. Ergo nisi mente caecus fuerit, videbit (id est) intelliget, quis et qualis sit intrinsecus, luceque naturae seipsum cognoscet per exteriora." ("Speculativae philosophiae," p. 307.)
41 The alchemist and mystic John Pordage (1607–81) called the inner "eternal" man an "extract and summary concept of the Macrocosm" (*Sophia*, 1699, p. 34).
42 "Disce ex te ipso, quicquid est et in caelo et in terra, cognoscere, ut sapiens fias in omnibus. Ignoras caelum et elementa prius unum fuisse, divino quoque ab invicem artificio separata, ut et te et omnia generare possent?" ("Speculativae philosophiae," p. 276.)

though this is far more convenient and is fondly confused with self-knowledge. For this reason anyone who seriously tries to know himself as an object is accused of selfishness and eccentricity. But such knowledge has nothing to do with the ego's subjective knowledge of itself. *That* is a dog chasing its own tail. The other, on the contrary, is a difficult and morally exacting study of which so-called psychology knows nothing and the educated public very little. The alchemist, however, had at the very least an indirect inkling of it: he knew definitely that as part of the whole he had an image of the whole in himself, the "firmament" or "Olympus," as Paracelsus calls it.[43] This interior microcosm was the unwitting object of alchemical research. Today we would call it the collective unconscious, and we would describe it as "objective" because it is identical in all individuals and is therefore *one*. Out of this universal One there is produced in every individual a *subjective* consciousness, i.e., the ego. This is, roughly, how we today would understand Dorn's "formerly one" and "separated by a divine act of creation."

252   This objective knowledge of the self is what the author means when he says: "No one can know himself unless he knows *what,* and not *who,* he is, on what he depends, or whose he is [or: to whom or what he belongs] and for what end he was made."[44] The distinction between "quis" and "quid" is crucial: whereas "quis" has an unmistakably personal aspect and refers to the ego, "quid" is neuter, predicating nothing except an object which is not endowed even with personality. Not the subjective ego-consciousness of the psyche is meant, but the psyche itself as the unknown, unprejudiced object that still has to be investigated. The difference between knowledge of the ego and knowledge of the self could hardly be formulated more trenchantly than in this distinction between "quis" and "quid."

---

[43] An idea that reached its full development 200 years later in Leibniz' monadology, and then fell into complete oblivion for another 200 years owing to the rise of the scientific trinity—space, time, causality. Herbert Silberer, who was also interested in alchemy, says: "I would almost prefer to surrender entirely to picture-language, and to call the deepest subconsciousness *our internal heaven of fixed stars.*" (*Der Zufall und die Koboldstreiche des Unbewussten*, p. 66.) Further material in "On the Nature of the Psyche," pars. 389ff.

[44] "Nemo vero potest cognoscere se, nisi sciat quid, et non quis ipse sit, a quo dependeat, vel cuius sit . . . et in quem finem factus sit" (p. 272).

An alchemist of the sixteenth century has here put his finger on something that certain psychologists (or those of them who allow themselves an opinion in psychological matters) still stumble over today. "What" refers to the neutral self, the objective fact of totality, since the ego is on the one hand causally "dependent on" or "belongs to" it, and on the other hand is directed towards it as to a goal. This recalls the impressive opening sentence of Ignatius Loyola's "Foundation": "Man was created to praise, do reverence to, and serve God our Lord, and thereby to save his soul." [45]

3   Man knows only a small part of his psyche, just as he has only a very limited knowledge of the physiology of his body. The causal factors determining his psychic existence reside largely in unconscious processes outside consciousness, and in the same way there are final factors at work in him which likewise originate in the unconscious. Freud's psychology gives elementary proof of the causal factors, Adler's of the final ones. Causes and ends thus transcend consciousness to a degree that ought not to be underestimated, and this implies that their nature and action are unalterable and irreversible so long as they have not become objects of consciousness. They can only be corrected through conscious insight and moral determination, which is why self-knowledge, being so necessary, is feared so much. Accordingly, if we divest the opening sentence of the "Foundation" of its theological terminology, it would run as follows: "Man's consciousness was created to the end that it may (1) recognize (*laudet*) its descent from a higher unity (*Deum*); (2) pay due and careful regard to this source (*reverentiam exhibeat*); (3) execute its commands intelligently and responsibly (*serviat*); and (4) thereby afford the psyche as a whole the optimum degree of life and development (*salvet animam suam*)."

4   This paraphrase not only sounds rationalistic but is meant to be so, for despite every effort the modern mind no longer understands our two-thousand-year-old theological language unless it "accords with reason." As a result, the danger that lack of understanding will be replaced by lip-service, affectation,

---

[45] *Exercitia spiritualia*, "Principio y Fundamento": "Homo creatus est (ad hunc finem), ut laudet Deum Dominum nostrum, ei reverentiam exhibeat, eique serviat, et per haec salvet animam suam." See trans. by Rickaby, p. 18.

and forced belief or else by resignation and indifference has long since come to pass.

255   The final factors at work in us are nothing other than those talents which "a certain nobleman" entrusted to his "servants," that they might trade with them (Luke 19 : 12ff.). It does not require much imagination to see what this involvement in the ways of the world means in the moral sense. Only an infantile person can pretend that evil is not at work everywhere, and the more unconscious he is, the more the devil drives him. It is just because of this inner connection with the black side of things that it is so incredibly easy for the mass man to commit the most appalling crimes without thinking. Only ruthless self-knowledge on the widest scale, which sees good and evil in correct perspective and can weigh up the motives of human action, offers some guarantee that the end-result will not turn out too badly.

256   We find the crucial importance of self-knowledge for the alchemical process of transformation expressed most clearly in Dorn, who lived in the second half of the sixteenth century. The idea itself is much older and goes back to Morienus Romanus (7th–8th cent.), in the saying which he wrote on the rim of the Hermetic vessel: "All those who have all things with them have no need of outside aid." [46] He is not referring to the possession of all the necessary chemical substances; it is far more a moral matter, as the text makes clear.[47] God, says Morienus, made the world out of four unequal elements and set man as the "greater ornament" between them: "This thing is extracted from thee, for thou art its ore; in thee they find it, and, to speak more plainly, from thee they take it; and when thou hast experienced this, the love and desire for it will be increased in thee." [48] This "thing" is the *lapis,* and Morienus says that it contains the four elements and is likened to the cosmos and its structure. The procedure for making the stone "cannot be performed with hands," [49] for it is a "human attitude" (*dispositio hominum*). This alone accomplishes the "changing of the natures." The

---

[46] "De transmutatione metallica," *Art. aurif.,* II, p. 11.

[47] "Not, that is, that I should require of them riches or gifts, but that I should diligently furnish them with spiritual gifts" (p. 10).

[48] "Haec enim res a te extrahitur: cuius etiam minera tu existis, apud te namque illam inveniunt, et ut verius confitear, a te accipiunt; quod quum probaveris, amor eius (rei) et dilectio in te augebitur" (p. 37).   [49] Pp. 40f.

transformation is brought about by the *coniunctio*, which forms the essence of the work.[50]

The "Rosinus ad Sarratantam Episcopum"—which, if not altogether Arabic in origin, is one of the oldest texts in Arabic style—cites Magus Philosophus: [51] "This stone is below thee, as to obedience; above thee, as to dominion; therefore from thee, as to knowledge; about thee, as to equals." [52] The passage is somewhat obscure. Nevertheless, it can be elicited that the stone stands in an undoubted psychic relationship to man: the adept can expect obedience from it, but on the other hand the stone exercises dominion over him. Since the stone is a matter of "knowledge" or science, it springs from man. But it is outside him, in his surroundings, among his "equals," i.e., those of like mind. This description fits the paradoxical situation of the self, as its symbolism shows. It is the smallest of the small, easily overlooked and pushed aside. Indeed, it is in need of help and must be perceived, protected, and as it were built up by the conscious mind, just as if it did not exist at all and were called into being only through man's care and devotion. As against this, we know from experience that it had long been there and is older than the ego, and that it is actually the secret *spiritus rector* of our fate. The self does not become conscious by itself, but has always been taught, if at all, through a tradition of knowing (the *purusha/atman* teaching, for instance). Since it stands for the essence of individuation, and individuation is impossible without a relationship to one's environment, it is found among those of like mind with whom individual relations can be established. The self, moreover, is an archetype that invariably expresses a situation within which the ego is contained. Therefore, like every archetype, the self cannot be localized in an individual

---

50 "The whole perfection of the magistery consists in the taking of conjoined and concordant bodies" (p. 43). The "Interpretatio cuiusdam epistolae Alexandri Macedonum regis" (*Art. aurif.*, I, p. 384) says: "And know that nothing is born without male and female." And in the "Tractatulus Avicennae" it is said: "Marriage is the mingling of the subtle with the dense." Cf. "Psychology of the Transference," index, s.v. "coniunctio."

51 The text has "Malus" (*Art. aurif.*, I, p. 310), probably a miswriting of Magus, who is a known author.

52 "Hic lapis est subtus te, quantum ad obedientiam; supra te, quoad dominium; ergo a te, quantum ad scientiam; circa te, quantum ad aequales" (*Art. aurif.*, I, p. 310).

ego-consciousness, but acts like a circumambient atmosphere to which no definite limits can be set, either in space or in time. (Hence the synchronistic phenomena so often associated with activated archetypes.)

258   The treatise of Rosinus contains a parallel to Morienus: [53] "This stone is something which is fixed more in thee [than elsewhere], created of God, and thou art its ore, and it is extracted from thee, and wheresoever thou art it remains inseparably with thee. . . . And as man is made up of four elements, so also is the stone, and so it is [dug] out of man, and thou art its ore, namely by working; and from thee it is extracted, that is by division; and in thee it remains inseparably, namely by knowledge. [To express it] otherwise, fixed in thee: namely in the Mercurius of the wise; thou art its ore: that is, it is enclosed in thee and thou holdest it [54] secretly; and from thee it is extracted when it is reduced [to its essence] by thee and dissolved; for without thee it cannot be fulfilled, and without it canst thou not live, and so the end looks to the beginning, and contrariwise." [55]

259   This looks like a commentary on Morienus. We learn from it that the stone is implanted in man by God, that the laborant is its *prima materia,* that the extraction corresponds to the so-called *divisio* or *separatio* of the alchemical procedure, and that through his knowledge of the stone man remains inseparably bound to the self. The procedure here described could easily be understood as the realization of an unconscious content. Fixation in the Mercurius of the wise would then correspond to the traditional Hermetic knowledge, since Mercurius symbolizes the Nous; [56] through this knowledge the self, as a content of the

53 The dating of these texts is very uncertain. Allowing for error, it seems to me that Morienus is the older.

54 The text has "ipsum." But the object here is "res."

55 "Hic lapis talis est res, quae in te magis fixa est, a Deo creata, et tu eius minera es ac a te extrahitur et ubicunque fueris, tecum inseparabiliter manet. . . . Et ut homo ex 4 elementis est compositus, ita et lapis, et ita est ex homine, et tu es eius minera, scil. per operationem; et de te extrahitur, scil. per divisionem; et in te inseparabiliter manet, scil. per scientiam. Aliter in te fixa, scil. in Mercurio sapientum; tu eius minera es; id est, in te est conclusa et ips[a]m occulte tenes, et ex te extrahitur, cum a te reducitur et solvitur; quia sine te compleri non potest, et tu sine ips[a] vivere non potes et sic finis respicit principium et contra." (*Art. aurif.,* I, pp. 311f.)

56 "The Spirit Mercurius," pars. 264ff.

unconscious, is made conscious and "fixed" in the mind. For without the existence of conscious concepts apperception is, as we know, impossible. This explains numerous neurotic disturbances which arise from the fact that certain contents are constellated in the unconscious but cannot be assimilated owing to the lack of apperceptive concepts that would "grasp" them. That is why it is so extremely important to tell children fairytales and legends, and to inculcate religious ideas (dogmas) into grown-ups, because these things are instrumental symbols with whose help unconscious contents can be canalized into consciousness, interpreted, and integrated. Failing this, their energy flows off into conscious contents which, normally, are not much emphasized, and intensifies them to pathological proportions. We then get apparently groundless phobias and obsessions—crazes, idiosyncrasies, hypochondriac ideas, and intellectual perversions suitably camouflaged in social, religious, or political garb.

60   The old master saw the alchemical *opus* as a kind of apocatastasis, the restoring of an initial state in an "eschatological" one ("the end looks to the beginning, and contrariwise"). This is exactly what happens in the individuation process, whether it take the form of a Christian transformation ("Except ye become as little children"), or a *satori* experience in Zen ("show me your original face"), or a psychological process of development in which the original propensity to wholeness becomes a conscious happening.

61   For the alchemist it was clear that the "centre," or what we would call the self, does not lie in the ego but is outside it, "in us" yet not "in our mind," being located rather in that which we unconsciously are, the "quid" which we still have to recognize. Today we would call it the unconscious, and we distinguish between a personal unconscious which enables us to recognize the shadow and an impersonal unconscious which enables us to recognize the archetypal symbol of the self. Such a point of view was inaccessible to the alchemist, and having no idea of the theory of knowledge, he had to exteriorize his archetype in the traditional way and lodge it in matter, even though he felt, as Dorn and others undoubtedly did, that the centre was paradoxically in man and yet at the same time outside him.

169

262 The "incorrupt medicament," the *lapis*, says Dorn, can be found nowhere save in heaven, for heaven "pervades all the elements with invisible rays meeting together from all parts at the centre of the earth, and generates and hatches forth all creatures." "No man can generate in himself, but [only] in that which is like him, which is from the same [heaven]." [57]

263 We see here how Dorn gets round his paradox: no one can produce anything without an object that is like him. But it is like him because it comes from the same source. If he wants to produce the incorrupt medicament, he can only do so in something that is akin to his own centre, and this is the centre in the earth and in all creatures. It comes, like his own, from the same fountainhead, which is God. Separation into apparently dissimilar things, such as heaven, the elements, man, etc., was necessary only for the work of generation. Everything separated must be united again in the production of the stone, so that the original state of unity shall be restored. But, says Dorn, "thou wilt never make from others the One which thou seekest, except first there be made one thing of thyself. . . . For so is the will of God, that the pious shall pursue the pious work which they seek, and the perfect shall perfect the other on which they were intent. . . . See therefore that thou goest forth such as thou desirest the work to be which thou seekest." [58]

264 The union of opposites in the stone is possible only when the adept has become One himself. The unity of the stone is the equivalent of individuation, by which man is made one; we would say that the stone is a projection of the unified self. This formulation is psychologically correct. It does not, however, take sufficient account of the fact that the stone is a *transcendent* unity. We must therefore emphasize that though the self can become a symbolic content of consciousness, it is, as a supraordinate totality, necessarily transcendental as well. Dorn recognized the identity of the stone with the transformed man when he exclaimed: "Transmute yourselves from dead stones into

---

[57] "Nemo in se ipso, sed in sui simili, quod etiam ex ipso sit, generare potest" ("Speculativae philosophiae," p. 276).

[58] ". . . ex aliis numquam unum facies quod quaeris, nisi prius ex te ipso fiat unum. . . . Nam talis est voluntas Dei, ut pii pium consequantur opus quod quaerunt, et perfecti perficiant aliud cui fuerint intenti. . . . Fac igitur ut talis evadas, quale tuum esse vis quod quaesieris opus" (p. 276f.).

living philosophical stones!" [59] But he lacked the concept of an unconscious existence which would have enabled him to express the identity of the subjective psychic centre and the objective alchemical centre in a satisfactory formula. Nevertheless, he succeeded in explaining the magnetic attraction between the imagined symbol—the "theoria"—and the "centre" hidden in matter, or in the interior of the earth or in the North Pole, as the identity of two extremes. That is why the theoria and the arcanum in matter are both called *veritas*. This truth "shines" in us, but it is not of us: it "is to be sought not in us, but in the image of God which is in us." [60]

5   Dorn thus equates the transcendent centre in man with the God-image. This identification makes it clear why the alchemical symbols for wholeness apply as much to the arcanum in man as to the Deity, and why substances like mercury and sulphur, or the elements fire and water, could refer to God, Christ, and the Holy Ghost. Indeed, Dorn goes even further and allows the predicate of *being* to this truth, and to this truth alone: "Further, that we may give a satisfactory definition of the truth, we say *it is*, but nothing can be added to it; for what, pray, can be added to the One, what is lacking to it, or on what can it be supported? For in truth nothing exists beside that One." [61] The only thing that truly exists for him is the transcendental self, which is identical with God.

56   Dorn was probably the first alchemist to sum up the results of all the symbolical terms and to state clearly what had been the impelling motive of alchemy from the very beginning. It is remarkable that this thinker, who is far more lucid in his formulations than his successor Jakob Böhme, has remained completely unknown to historians of philosophy until today. He thus shares the fate of Hermetic philosophy in general, which, for those unacquainted with modern psychology, remains a

---

[59] "Transmutemini de lapidibus mortuis in vivos lapides philosophicos!" (p. 267). This is an allusion to I Peter 2 : 4f: "Come to him, to that living stone, rejected by men but in God's sight chosen and precious; and like living stones be yourselves built [up] . . ." (RSV).

[60] "Non in nobis quaerenda [veritas], sed in imagine Dei, quae in nobis est" (p. 268).

[61] "Ulterius, ut definitioni veri faciamus satis, dicimus esse, vero nihil adesse, nam uni quid adest, quaeso, quid etiam deest, aut quid contra niti potest? cum nihil vere praeter illud unum existit" (p. 268).

closed book sealed with seven seals. But this book has to be opened sometime if we wish to understand the mentality of the present day; for alchemy is the mother of the essential substance as well as the concreteness of modern scientific thinking, and not scholasticism, which was responsible in the main only for the discipline and training of the intellect.

XII

BACKGROUND TO THE PSYCHOLOGY OF CHRISTIAN ALCHEMICAL SYMBOLISM

67 "Mater Alchimia" could serve as the name of a whole epoch. Beginning, roughly, with Christianity, it gave birth in the sixteenth and seventeenth centuries to the age of science, only to perish, unrecognized and misunderstood, and sink from sight in the stream of the centuries as an age that had been outlived. But, just as every mother was once a daughter, so too was alchemy. It owes its real beginnings to the Gnostic systems, which Hippolytus rightly regarded as philosophic, and which, with the help of Greek philosophy and the mythologies of the Near and Middle East, together with Christian dogmatics and Jewish cabalism, made extremely interesting attempts, from the modern point of view, to synthetize a unitary vision of the world in which the physical and the mystical aspects played equal parts. Had this attempt succeeded, we would not be witnessing today the curious spectacle of two parallel world-views neither of which knows, or wishes to know, anything about the other. Hippolytus was in the enviable position of being able to see Christian doctrine side by side with its pagan sisters, and similar comparisons had also been attempted by Justin Martyr. To the honour of Christian thinking it must be said that up till the time of Kepler there was no lack of praiseworthy attempts to interpret and understand Nature, in the broadest sense, on the basis of Christian dogma.

68 These attempts, however, inevitably came to grief for lack of any adequate knowledge of natural processes. Thus, in the course of the eighteenth century, there arose that notorious rift between faith and knowledge. Faith lacked experience and science missed out the soul. Instead, science believed fervently in absolute objectivity and assiduously overlooked the fundamental difficulty that the real vehicle and begetter of all knowledge is the *psyche*, the very thing that scientists knew the least about

for the longest time. It was regarded as a symptom of chemical reactions, an epiphenomenon of biological processes in the brain-cells—indeed, for some time it did not exist at all. Yet all the while scientists remained totally unaware of the fact that they were using for their observations a photographic apparatus of whose nature and structure they knew practically nothing, and whose very existence many of them were unwilling to admit. It is only quite recently that they have been obliged to take into their calculations the objective reality of this psychic factor. Significantly enough, it is microphysics that has come up against the psyche in the most tangible and unexpected way. Obviously, we must disregard the psychology of the unconscious in this connection, since its working hypothesis consists precisely in the reality of the psyche. What is significant here is the exact opposite, namely the psyche's collision with physics.[1]

269   Now for the Gnostics—and this is their real secret—the psyche existed as a source of knowledge just as much as it did for the alchemists. Aside from the psychology of the unconscious, contemporary science and philosophy know only of what is outside, while faith knows only of the inside, and then only in the Christian form imparted to it by the passage of the centuries, beginning with St. Paul and the gospel of St. John. Faith, quite as much as science with its traditional objectivity, is *absolute*, which is why faith and knowledge can no more agree than Christians can with one another.

270   Our Christian doctrine is a highly differentiated symbol that expresses the transcendent psychic—the God-image and its properties, to speak with Dorn. The Creed is a "symbolum." This comprises practically everything of importance that can be ascertained about the manifestations of the psyche in the field of inner experience, but it does not include Nature, at least not in any recognizable form. Consequently, at every period of Christianity there have been subsidiary currents or undercurrents that have sought to investigate the empirical aspect of Nature not only from the outside but also from the inside.

271   Although dogma, like mythology in general, expresses the quintessence of inner experience and thus formulates the operative principles of the objective psyche, i.e., the collective uncon-

[1] Cf. "On the Nature of the Psyche," pars. 417ff., 438ff.

scious, it does so by making use of a language and outlook that have become alien to our present way of thinking. The word "dogma" has even acquired a somewhat unpleasant sound and frequently serves merely to emphasize the rigidity of a prejudice. For most people living in the West, it has lost its meaning as a symbol for a virtually unknowable and yet "actual"—i.e., operative—fact. Even in theological circles any real discussion of dogma had as good as ceased until the recent papal declarations, a sign that the symbol has begun to fade, if it is not already withered. This is a dangerous development for our psychic health, as we know of no other symbol that better expresses the world of the unconscious. More and more people then begin looking round for exotic ideas in the hope of finding a substitute, for example in India. This hope is delusory, for though the Indian symbols formulate the unconscious just as well as the Christian ones do, they each exemplify their own spiritual past. The Indian teachings constitute the essence of several thousand years of experience of Indian life. Though we can learn a lot from Indian thought, it can never express the past that is stored up within us. The premise we start from is and remains Christianity, which covers anything from eleven to nineteen centuries of Western life. Before that, there was for most Western peoples a considerably longer period of polytheism and polydemonism. In certain parts of Europe Christianity goes back not much more than five hundred years—a mere sixteen generations. The last witch was burnt in Europe the year my grandfather was born, and barbarism with its degradation of human nature has broken out again in the twentieth century.

I mention these facts in order to illustrate how thin is the wall that separates us from pagan times. Besides that, the Germanic peoples never developed organically out of primitive polydemonism to polytheism and its philosophical subtleties, but in many places accepted Christian monotheism and its doctrine of redemption only at the sword's point of the Roman legions, as in Africa the machine-gun is the latent argument behind the Christian invasion.[2] Doubtless the spread of Christianity among barbarian peoples not only favoured, but actually necessitated, a certain inflexibility of dogma. Much the same thing

2 I was able to convince myself on the spot of the existence of this fear.

can be observed in the spread of Islam, which was likewise obliged to resort to fanaticism and rigidity. In India the symbol developed far more organically and pursued a less disturbed course. Even the great Hindu Reformation, Buddhism, is grounded, in true Indian fashion, on yoga, and, in India at least, it was almost completely reassimilated by Hinduism in less than a millennium, so that today the Buddha himself is enthroned in the Hindu pantheon as the avatar of Vishnu, along with Christ, Matsya (the fish), Kurma (the tortoise), Vamana (the dwarf), and a host of others.

273   The historical development of our Western mentality cannot be compared in any way with the Indian. Anyone who believes that he can simply take over Eastern forms of thought is uprooting himself, for they do not express our Western past, but remain bloodless intellectual concepts that strike no chord in our inmost being. We are rooted in Christian soil. This foundation does not go very deep, certainly, and, as we have seen, it has proved alarmingly thin in places, so that the original paganism, in altered guise, was able to regain possession of a large part of Europe and impose on it its characteristic economic pattern of slavery.

274   This modern development is in line with the pagan currents that were clearly present in alchemy and had remained alive beneath the Christian surface ever since the days of antiquity. Alchemy reached its greatest efflorescence in the sixteenth and seventeenth centuries, then to all appearances it began to die out. In reality it found its continuation in natural science, which led in the nineteenth century to materialism and in the twentieth century to so-called "realism," whose end is not yet in sight. Despite well-meaning assurances to the contrary, Christianity is a helpless bystander. The Church still has a little power left, but she pastures her sheep on the ruins of Europe. Her message works, *if* one knows how to combine her language, ideas, and customs with an understanding of the present. But for many she no longer speaks, as Paul did in the market-place of Athens, the language of the present, but wraps her message in sacrosanct words hallowed by age. What success would Paul have had with his preaching if he had had to use the language and myths of the Minoan age in order to announce the gospel to the Athenians? We overlook the unfortunate fact that far greater demands are

made on present-day man than were ever made on people living in the apostolic era: for them there was no difficulty at all in believing in the virgin birth of the hero and demigod, and Justin Martyr was still able to use this argument in his apology. Nor was the idea of a redeeming God-man anything unheard of, since practically all Asiatic potentates together with the Roman Emperor were of divine nature. But we have no further use even for the divine right of kings! The miraculous tales in the gospels, which easily convinced people in those days, would be a *petra scandali* in any modern biography and would evoke the very reverse of belief. The weird and wonderful nature of the gods was a self-evident fact in a hundred living myths and assumed a special significance in the no less credible philosophic refinements of those myths. "Hermes ter unus" (Hermes-Thrice-One) was not an intellectual absurdity but a philosophical truth. On these foundations the dogma of the Trinity could be built up convincingly. For modern man this dogma is either an impenetrable mystery or an historical curiosity, preferably the latter. For the man of antiquity the virtue of the consecrated water or the transmutation of substances was in no sense an enormity, because there were dozens of sacred springs whose workings were incomprehensible, and any amount of chemical changes whose nature appeared miraculous. Nowadays every schoolboy knows more, in principle, about the ways of Nature than all the volumes of Pliny's Natural History put together.

75   If Paul were alive today, and should undertake to reach the ear of intelligent Londoners in Hyde Park, he could no longer content himself with quotations from Greek literature and a smattering of Jewish history, but would have to accommodate his language to the intellectual faculties of the modern English public. If he failed to do this, he would have announced his message badly, for no one, except perhaps a classical philologist, would understand half of what he was saying. That, however, is the situation in which Christian kerygmatics[3] finds itself today. Not that it uses a dead foreign language in the literal sense, but it speaks in images that on the one hand are hoary with age and look deceptively familiar, while on the other hand they are miles away from a modern man's conscious understanding,

3 Kerygmatics = preaching, declaration of religious truth.

addressing themselves, at most, to his unconscious, and then only if the speaker's whole soul is in his work. The best that can happen, therefore, is that the effect remains stuck in the sphere of feeling, though in most cases it does not get even that far.

276   The bridge from dogma to the inner experience of the individual has broken down. Instead, dogma is "believed"; [4] it is hypostatized, as the Protestants hypostatize the Bible, illegitimately making it the supreme authority, regardless of its contradictions and controversial interpretations. (As we know, anything can be authorized out of the Bible.) Dogma no longer formulates anything, no longer expresses anything; it has become a tenet to be accepted in and for itself, with no basis in any experience that would demonstrate its truth.[5] Indeed, faith has itself become that experience. The faith of a man like Paul, who had never seen our Lord in the flesh, could still appeal to the overwhelming apparition on the road to Damascus and to the revelation of the gospel in a kind of ecstasy. Similarly, the faith of the man of antiquity and of the medieval Christian never ran counter to the *consensus omnium* but was on the contrary supported by it. All this has completely changed in the last three hundred years. But what comparable change has kept pace with this in theological circles?

277   The danger exists—and of this there can be no doubt—that the new wine will burst the old bottles, and that what we no longer understand will be thrown into the lumber-room, as happened once before at the time of the Reformation. Protestantism then discarded (except for a few pallid remnants) the ritual that every religion needs, and now relies solely on the *sola fides* standpoint. The content of faith, of the symbolum, is continually crumbling away. What is still left of it? The person of Jesus Christ? Even the most benighted layman knows that the

4 Father Victor White, O.P., has kindly drawn my attention to the concept of the *veritas prima* in St. Thomas Aquinas (*Summa theol.*, II, II, i, 1 and 2): This "first truth" is invisible and unknown. It is this, and not the dogma, that underlies belief.

5 This is not to contest the legitimacy and importance of dogma. The Church is not concerned only with people who have a religious life of their own, but also with those from whom no more can be expected than that they should hold a tenet to be true and confess themselves satisfied with this formula. Probably the great majority of "believers" do not get beyond this level. For them dogma retains its role as a magnet and can therefore claim to be the "final" truth.

personality of Jesus is, for the biographer, the obscurest item of all in the reports of the New Testament, and that, from a human and psychological point of view, his personality must remain an unfathomable enigma. As a Catholic writer pithily remarked, the gospels record the history of a man and a god at the same time. Or is only God left? In that case, what about the Incarnation, the most vital part of the symbolum? In my view one would be well advised to apply the papal dictum: "Let it be as it is, or not be at all," [6] to the Creed and leave it at that, because nobody really understands what it is all about. How else can one explain the notorious drift away from dogma?

78   It may strike my reader as strange that a physician and psychologist should be so insistent about dogma. But I *must* emphasize it, and for the same reasons that once moved the alchemist to attach special importance to his "theoria." His doctrine was the quintessence of the symbolism of unconscious processes, just as the dogmas are a condensation or distillation of "sacred history," of the myth of the divine being and his deeds. If we wish to understand what alchemical doctrine means, we must go back to the historical as well as the individual phenomenology of the symbols, and if we wish to gain a closer understanding of dogma, we must perforce consider first the myths of the Near and Middle East that underlie Christianity, and then the whole of mythology as the expression of a universal disposition in man. This disposition I have called the collective unconscious, the existence of which can be inferred only from individual phenomenology. In both cases the investigator comes back to the individual, for what he is all the time concerned with are certain complex thought-forms, the archetypes, which must be conjectured as the unconscious organizers of our ideas. The motive force that produces these configurations cannot be distinguished from the transconscious factor known as instinct. There is, therefore, no justification for visualizing the archetype as anything other than the image of instinct in man.[7]

79   From this one should not jump to the conclusion that the world of religious ideas can be reduced to "nothing but" a biological basis, and it would be equally erroneous to suppose that, when approached in this way, the religious phenomenon

6 "Sit, ut est, aut non sit."
7 "On the Nature of the Psyche," par. 415.

is "psychologized" and dissolved in smoke. No reasonable person would conclude that the reduction of man's morphology to a four-legged saurian amounts to a nullification of the human form, or, alternatively, that the latter somehow explains itself. For behind all this looms the vast and unsolved riddle of life itself and of evolution in general, and the question of overriding importance in the end is not the origin of evolution but its goal. Nevertheless, when a living organism is cut off from its roots, it loses the connections with the foundations of its existence and must necessarily perish. When that happens, anamnesis of the origins is a matter of life and death.

280   Myths and fairytales give expression to unconscious processes, and their retelling causes these processes to come alive again and be recollected, thereby re-establishing the connection between conscious and unconscious. What the separation of the two psychic halves means, the psychiatrist knows only too well. He knows it as dissociation of the personality, the root of all neuroses: the conscious goes to the right and the unconscious to the left. As opposites never unite at their own level (*tertium non datur!*), a supraordinate "third" is always required, in which the two parts can come together. And since the symbol derives as much from the conscious as from the unconscious, it is able to unite them both, reconciling their conceptual polarity through its form and their emotional polarity through its numinosity.

281   For this reason the ancients often compared the symbol to water, a case in point being *tao*, where *yang* and *yin* are united. *Tao* is the "valley spirit," the winding course of a river. The symbolum of the Church is the *aqua doctrinae*, corresponding to the wonder-working "divine" water of alchemy, whose double aspect is represented by Mercurius. The healing and renewing properties of this symbolical water—whether it be *tao*, the baptismal water, or the elixir—point to the therapeutic character of the mythological background from which this idea comes. Physicians who were versed in alchemy had long recognized that their arcanum healed, or was supposed to heal, not only the diseases of the body but also those of the mind. Similarly, modern psychotherapy knows that, though there are many interim solutions, there is, at the bottom of every neurosis, a moral problem of opposites that cannot be solved rationally, and can be answered only by a supraordinate third, by a symbol which ex-

presses both sides. This was the "veritas" (Dorn) or "theoria" (Paracelsus) for which the old physicians and alchemists strove, and they could do so only by incorporating the Christian revelation into their world of ideas. They continued the work of the Gnostics (who were, most of them, not so much heretics as theologians) and the Church Fathers in a new era, instinctively recognizing that new wine should not be put into old bottles, and that, like a snake changing its skin, the old myth needs to be clothed anew in every renewed age if it is not to lose its therapeutic effect.

282   The problems which the integration of the unconscious sets modern doctors and psychologists can only be solved along the lines traced out by history, and the upshot will be a new assimilation of the traditional myth. This, however, presupposes the continuity of historical development. Naturally the present tendency to destroy all tradition or render it unconscious could interrupt the normal process of development for several hundred years and substitute an interlude of barbarism. Wherever the Marxist utopia prevails, this has already happened. But a predominantly scientific and technological education, such as is the usual thing nowadays, can also bring about a spiritual regression and a considerable increase of psychic dissociation. With hygiene and prosperity alone a man is still far from health, otherwise the most enlightened and most comfortably off among us would be the healthiest. But in regard to neuroses that is not the case at all, quite the contrary. Loss of roots and lack of tradition neuroticize the masses and prepare them for collective hysteria. Collective hysteria calls for collective therapy, which consists in abolition of liberty and terrorization. Where rationalistic materialism holds sway, states tend to develop less into prisons than into lunatic asylums.

*

283   I have tried, in the foregoing, to indicate the kind of psychic matrix into which the Christ-figure was assimilated in the course of the centuries. Had there not been an affinity—magnet!—between the figure of the Redeemer and certain contents of the unconscious, the human mind would never have been able to perceive the light shining in Christ and seize upon it so passionately. The connecting link here is the archetype of the God-

man, which on the one hand became historical reality in Christ, and on the other, being eternally present, reigns over the soul in the form of a supraordinate totality, the self. The God-man, like the priest in the vision of Zosimos, is a Κύριος τῶν πνευμάτων, not only "Lord of the spirits," but "Lord over the (evil) spirits," which is one of the essential meanings of the Christian Kyrios.[8]

284   The noncanonical fish symbol led us into this psychic matrix and thus into a realm of experience where the unknowable archetypes become living things, changing their name and guise in never-ending succession and, as it were, disclosing their hidden nucleus by perpetually circumambulating round it. The *lapis* that signifies God become man or man become God "has a thousand names." It is not Christ; it is his parallel in the subjective realm, which dogma calls Christ. Alchemy gives us, in the *lapis,* a concrete idea of what Christ means in the realm of subjective experience, and under what delusive or illuminative disguises his actual presence may be experienced in its transcendent ineffability. One could demonstrate the same thing in the psychology of a modern individual, as I attempted to do in Part II of *Psychology and Alchemy.*[9] Only, this would be a much more exacting task, running into great detail and requiring a mass of personal biographical data with which one could fill volumes. Such an undertaking would exceed my powers. I must therefore rest content with having laid some of the historical and conceptual foundations for this work of the future.

285   In conclusion, I would like to emphasize once again that the fish symbol is a spontaneous assimilation of the Christ-figure of the gospels, and is thus a symptom which shows us in what manner and with what meaning the symbol was assimilated by the unconscious. In this respect the patristic allegory of the capture of Leviathan (with the Cross as the hook, and the Crucified as the bait) is highly characteristic: a content (fish) of the unconscious (sea) has been caught and has attached itself to the Christ-figure. Hence the expression used by St. Augustine: "de profundo levatus" (drawn from the deep). This is true enough of the fish; but of Christ? The image of the fish came out of the

[8] Like the Old Testament "Yahweh Zebaoth," Lord of Hosts. Cf. Maag, "Jahwäs Heerscharen."
[9] Also in "Psychology and Religion"; "Relations between the Ego and the Unconscious"; and my commentary on *The Secret of the Golden Flower.*

depths of the unconscious as an equivalent of the historical Christ figure, and if Christ was invoked as "Ichthys," this name referred to what had come up out of the depths. The fish symbol is thus the bridge between the historical Christ and the psychic nature of man, where the archetype of the Redeemer dwells. In this way Christ became an inner experience, the "Christ within."

As I have shown, the alchemical fish symbolism leads direct to the *lapis*, the *salvator, servator,* and *deus terrenus;* that is, psychologically, to the self. We now have a new symbol in place of the fish: a psychological concept of human wholeness. In as much or in as little as the fish is Christ does the self mean God. It is something that corresponds, an inner experience, an assimilation of Christ into the psychic matrix, a new realization of the divine Son, no longer in theriomorphic form, but expressed in a conceptual or "philosophic" symbol. This, compared with the mute and unconscious fish, marks a distinct increase in conscious development.[10]

10 For the significance of conscious development in relation to mythological symbolism, see Neumann, *The Origins and History of Consciousness.*

XIII

GNOSTIC SYMBOLS OF THE SELF

1

287   Since all cognition is akin to recognition, it should not come as a surprise to find that what I have described as a gradual process of development had already been anticipated, and more or less prefigured, at the beginning of our era. We meet these images and ideas in Gnosticism, to which we must now give our attention; for Gnosticism was, in the main, a product of cultural assimilation and is therefore of the greatest interest in elucidating and defining the contents constellated by prophecies about the Redeemer, or by his appearance in history, or by the synchronicity of the archetype.[1]

288   In the *Elenchos* of Hippolytus the attraction between the magnet and iron is mentioned, if I am not mistaken, three times. It first appears in the doctrine of the NAASSENES, who taught that the four rivers of Paradise correspond to the eye, the ear, the sense of smell, and the mouth. The mouth, through which prayers go out and food goes in, corresponds to the fourth river, the Euphrates. The well-known significance of the "fourth" helps to explain its connection with the "whole" man, for the fourth always makes a triad into a totality. The text says: "This is the water above the firmament,[2] of which, they say, the Saviour spoke: 'If you knew who it is that asks, you would have asked him, and he would have given you a spring of living water to drink.'[3] To this water comes every nature to choose its own

---

[1] Unfortunately it is not possible for me to elucidate or even to document this statement here. But, as Rhine's ESP (extrasensory perception) experiments show, any intense emotional interest or fascination is accompanied by phenomena which can only be explained by a psychic relativity of time, space, and causality. Since the archetypes usually have a certain numinosity, they can arouse just that fascination which is accompanied by synchronistic phenomena. These consist in the *meaningful* coincidence of two or more causally unrelated facts. For details I would refer the reader to my "Synchronicity: An Acausal Connecting Principle."
[2] Genesis 1 : 7.   [3] Non-verbatim quotation from John 4 : 10.

substances, and from this water goes forth to every nature that which is proper to it, more [certainly] than iron to the Heracleian stone," [4] etc.

89   As the reference to John 4 : 10 shows, the wonderful water of the Euphrates has the property of the *aqua doctrinae,* which perfects every nature in its individuality and thus makes man whole too. It does this by giving him a kind of magnetic power by which he can attract and integrate that which belongs to him. The Naassene doctrine is, plainly, a perfect parallel to the alchemical view already discussed: the doctrine is the magnet that makes possible the integration of man as well as the *lapis.*

90   In the PERATIC doctrine, so many ideas of this kind reappear that Hippolytus even uses the same metaphors, though the meaning is more subtle. No one, he says, can be saved without the Son:

But this is the serpent. For it is he who brought the signs of the Father down from above, and it is he who carries them back again after they have been awakened from sleep, transferring them thither from hence as substances proceeding from the Substanceless. This, they say, is [what is meant by] the saying, "I am the Door." [5] But they say he transfers them to those whose eyelids are closed, [6] as naphtha draws everywhere the fire to itself, [7] more than the Heracleian stone draws iron . . . [8] Thus, they say, the perfect race of men, made in the image [of the Father] and of the same substance [*homoousion*], is drawn from the world by the Serpent, even as it was sent down by him; but naught else [is so drawn]. [9]

291   Here the magnetic attraction does not come from the doctrine or the water but from the "Son," who is symbolized by the serpent, as in John 3 : 14. [10] Christ is the magnet that draws to

---

[4] *Elenchos,* V, 9, 18f. (Cf. Legge trans., I, pp. 143f.) "Heracleian stone" = magnet.

[5] John 10 : 9: "I am the door. By me, if any man enter in, he shall be saved."

[6] I use the reading: καμμύουσιν ὀφθαλμοῦ βλέφαρον. Does this mean those who close their eyes to the world?

[7] The naphtha analogy reappears in the teachings of the Basilidians (*Elenchos,* VII, 24, 6f.). There it refers to the son of the highest archon, who comprehends the νοήματα ἀπὸ τῆς μακαρίας υἱότητος (idea of the blessed sonship). Hippolytus' exposition seems to be a trifle confused at this point.

[8] Several more metaphors now follow, and it should be noted that they are the same as in the passage previously quoted (V, 9, 19).

[9] *Elenchos,* V, 17, 8ff. (Cf. Legge trans., I, pp. 158f.)

[10] "And as Moses lifted up the serpent in the wilderness, even so must the Son of man be lifted up."

itself those parts or substances in man that are of divine origin, the πατρικοὶ χαρακτῆρες (signs of the Father), and carries them back to their heavenly birthplace. The serpent is an equivalent of the fish. The consensus of opinion interpreted the Redeemer equally as a fish and a serpent; he is a fish because he rose from the unknown depths, and a serpent because he came mysteriously out of the darkness. Fishes and snakes are favourite symbols for describing psychic happenings or experiences that suddenly dart out of the unconscious and have a frightening or redeeming effect. That is why they are so often expressed by the motif of helpful animals. The comparison of Christ with the serpent is more authentic than that with the fish, but, for all that, it was not so popular in primitive Christianity. The Gnostics favoured it because it was an old-established symbol for the "good" *genius loci,* the Agathodaimon, and also for their beloved Nous. Both symbols are of inestimable value when it comes to the natural, instinctive interpretation of the Christ-figure. Theriomorphic symbols are very common in dreams and other manifestations of the unconscious. They express the psychic level of the content in question; that is to say, such contents are at a stage of unconsciousness that is as far from human consciousness as the psyche of an animal. Warm-blooded or cold-blooded vertebrates of all kinds, or even invertebrates, thus indicate the degree of unconsciousness. It is important for psychopathologists to know this, because these contents can produce, at all levels, symptoms that correspond to the physiological functions and are localized accordingly. For instance, the symptoms may be distinctly correlated with the cerebrospinal and the sympathetic nervous system. The Sethians may have guessed something of this sort, for Hippolytus mentions, in connection with the serpent, that they compared the "Father" with the cerebrum (ἐγκέφαλον) and the "Son" with the cerebellum and spinal cord (παρεγκεφαλὶς δρακοντοειδής). The snake does in fact symbolize "cold-blooded," inhuman contents and tendencies of an abstractly intellectual as well as a concretely animal nature: in a word, the extra-human quality in man.

292   The third reference to the magnet is to be found in Hippolytus' account of the SETHIAN doctrine. This has remarkable analogies with the alchemical doctrines of the Middle Ages,

though no direct transmission can be proved. It expounds, in Hippolytus' words, a theory of "composition and mixture": the ray of light from above mingles with the dark waters below in the form of a minute spark. At the death of the individual, and also at his figurative death as a mystical experience, the two substances unmix themselves. This mystical experience is the *divisio* and *separatio* of the composite (τὸ διχάσαι καὶ χωρίσαι τὰ συγκεκραμένα). I purposely give the Latin terms used in medieval alchemy, because they denote essentially the same thing as do the Gnostic concepts. The separation or unmixing enables the alchemist to extract the *anima* or *spiritus* from the *prima materia*. During this operation the helpful Mercurius appears with the dividing sword (used also by the adept!), which the Sethians refer to Matthew 10 : 34: "I came not to send peace, but a sword." The result of the unmixing is that what was previously mixed up with the "other" is now drawn to "its own place" and to that which is "proper" or "akin" to it, "like iron to the magnet" (ὡς σίδηρος [πρὸς] Ἡράκλειον λίθον).[11] In the same way, the spark or ray of light, "having received from the teaching and learning its proper place, hastens to the Logos, which comes from above in the form of a slave . . . more [quickly] than iron [flies] to the magnet."[12]

93   Here the magnetic attraction comes from the Logos. This denotes a thought or idea that has been formulated and articulated, hence a content and a product of consciousness. Consequently the Logos is very like the *aqua doctrinae*, but whereas the Logos has the advantage of being an autonomous personality, the latter is merely a passive object of human action. The Logos is nearer to the historical Christ-figure, just as the "water" is nearer to the magical water used in ritual (ablution, aspersion,

[11] Here, as in the previous passages about the magnet, mention is made of *electron* (amber) and the sea-hawk, emphasis being laid on the bird's *centre*.
[12] *Elenchos*, V, 21, 8 (Legge trans., I, p. 168). The ray of light (*radius*) plays an analogous role in alchemy. Dorn (*Theatr. chem.*, I, p. 276) speaks of the "invisible rays of heaven meeting together at the centre of the earth," and there, as Michael Maier says, shining with a "heavenly light like a carbuncle" (*Symbola aureae mensae*, 1617, p. 377). The arcane substance is extracted from the ray, and constitutes its "shadow" (*umbra*), as the "Tractatus aureus" says (*Ars chemica*, 1566, p. 15). The *aqua permanens* is extracted from the rays of the sun and moon by the magnet (Mylius, *Philosophia reformata*, p. 314), or the rays of the sun are united in the "silver water" (Beatus, "Aurelia occulta," *Theatr. chem.*, IV, p. 563).

baptism). Our three examples of magnetic action suggest three different forms of magnetic agent:

1. The agent is an inanimate and in itself passive substance, *water*. It is drawn from the depths of the well, handled by human hands, and used according to man's needs. It signifies the visible doctrine, the *aqua doctrinae* or the Logos, communicated to others by word of mouth and by ritual.

2. The agent is an animate, autonomous being, the *serpent*. It appears spontaneously or comes as a surprise; it fascinates; its glance is staring, fixed, unrelated; its blood cold, and it is a stranger to man: it crawls over the sleeper, he finds it in a shoe or in his pocket. It expresses his fear of everything inhuman and his awe of the sublime, of what is beyond human ken. It is the lowest (devil) and the highest (son of God, Logos, Nous, Agathodaimon). The snake's presence is frightening, one finds it in unexpected places at unexpected moments. Like the fish, it represents and personifies the dark and unfathomable, the watery deep, the forest, the night, the cave. When a primitive says "snake," he means an experience of something extrahuman. The snake is not an allegory or metaphor, for its own peculiar form is symbolic in itself, and it is essential to note that the "Son" has the form of a snake and not the other way round: the snake does not signify the "Son."

3. The agent is the *Logos*, a philosophical idea and abstraction of the bodily and personal son of God on the one hand, and on the other the dynamic power of thoughts and words.

294   It is clear that these three symbols seek to describe the unknowable essence of the incarnate God. But it is equally clear that they are hypostatized to a high degree: it is real water, and not figurative water, that is used in ritual. The Logos was in the beginning, and God was the Logos, long before the Incarnation. The emphasis falls so much on the "serpent" that the Ophites celebrated their eucharistic feast with a live snake, no less realistic than the Aesculapian snake at Epidaurus. Similarly, the "fish" is not just the secret language of the mystery, but, as the monuments show, it meant something in itself. Moreover, it acquired its meaning in primitive Christianity without any real support from the written tradition, whereas the serpent can at least be referred back to an authentic logion.

95   All three symbols are phenomena of assimilation that are in themselves of a numinous nature and therefore have a certain degree of autonomy. Indeed, had they never made their appearance, it would have meant that the annunciation of the Christ-figure was ineffective. These phenomena not only prove the effectiveness of the annunciation, but provide the necessary conditions in which the annunciation can take effect. In other words, the symbols represent the prototypes of the Christ-figure that were slumbering in man's unconscious and were then called awake by his actual appearance in history and, so to speak, magnetically attracted. That is why Meister Eckhart uses the same symbolism to describe Adam's relation to the Creator on the one hand and to the lower creatures on the other.[13]

296   This magnetic process revolutionizes the ego-oriented psyche by setting up, in contradistinction to the ego, another goal or centre which is characterized by all manner of names and symbols: fish, serpent, centre of the sea-hawk,[14] point, monad, cross, paradise, and so on. The myth of the ignorant demiurge who imagined he was the highest divinity illustrates the perplexity of the ego when it can no longer hide from itself the knowledge that it has been dethroned by a supraordinate authority. The "thousand names" of the *lapis philosophorum* correspond to the innumerable Gnostic designations for the Anthropos, which make it quite obvious what is meant: the greater, more comprehensive Man, that indescribable whole consisting of the sum of conscious and unconscious processes. This objective whole, the antithesis of the subjective ego-psyche, is what I have called the self, and this corresponds exactly to the idea of the Anthropos.

2

297   When, in treating a case of neurosis, we try to supplement the inadequate attitude (or adaptedness) of the conscious mind

---

13 "And therefore the highest power, seeing her stability in God, communicates it to the lowest, that they may discern good and evil. In this union Adam dwelt, and while this union lasted he had all the power of creatures in his highest power. As when a lodestone exerts its power upon a needle and draws it to itself, the needle receives sufficient power to pass on to all the needles beneath, which it raises and attaches to the lodestone." (Meister Eckhart, trans. by Evans, I, p. 274, slightly modified.)   14 [Cf. n. 11, supra.]

by adding to it contents of the unconscious, our aim is to create a wider personality whose centre of gravity does not necessarily coincide with the ego, but which, on the contrary, as the patient's insights increase, may even thwart his ego-tendencies. Like a magnet, the new centre attracts to itself that which is proper to it, the "signs of the Father," i.e., everything that pertains to the original and unalterable character of the individual ground-plan. All this is older than the ego and acts towards it as the "blessed, nonexistent God" of the Basilidians acted towards the archon of the Ogdoad, the demiurge, and—paradoxically enough—as the son of the demiurge acted towards his father. The son proves superior in that he has knowledge of the message from above and can therefore tell his father that he is not the highest God. This apparent contradiction resolves itself when we consider the underlying psychological experience. On the one hand, in the products of the unconscious the self appears as it were *a priori,* that is, in well-known circle and quaternity symbols which may already have occurred in the earliest dreams of childhood, long before there was any possibility of consciousness or understanding. On the other hand, only patient and painstaking work on the contents of the unconscious, and the resultant synthesis of conscious and unconscious data, can lead to a "totality," which once more uses circle and quaternity symbols for purposes of self-description.[15] In this phase, too, the original dreams of childhood are remembered and understood. The alchemists, who in their own way knew more about the nature of the individuation process than we moderns do, expressed this paradox through the symbol of the uroboros, the snake that bites its own tail.

298   The same knowledge, formulated differently to suit the age they lived in, was possessed by the Gnostics. The idea of an unconscious was not unknown to them. For instance, Epiphanius quotes an excerpt from one of the Valentinian letters, which says: "In the beginning the Autopator contained in himself everything that is, in a state of unconsciousness [lit., 'not-knowing': ἀγνωσία]."[16] It was Professor G. Quispel who kindly drew my

15 Cf. *Psychology and Alchemy,* pars. 127ff., and "A Study in the Process of Individuation," in Part I of vol. 9.

16 Ἐξ ἀρχῆς ὁ Αὐτοπάτωρ αὐτὸς ἐν ἑαυτῷ περιεῖχε τὰ πάντα ὄντα ἐν ἑαυτῷ ἐν ἀγνωσίᾳ κτλ. *Panarium,* XXXI, cap. V (Oehler edn., I, p. 314).

attention to this passage. He also points out the passage in Hippolytus: ὁ Πατὴρ . . . ὁ ἀνεννόητος καὶ ἀνούσιος, ὁ μήτε ἄρρεν μήτε θῆλυ, which he translates: "le Père . . . qui est dépourvu de conscience et de substance, celui qui est ni masculin, ni féminin." [17] So the "Father" is not only unconscious and without the quality of being, but also *nirdvandva*, without opposites, lacking all qualities and therefore unknowable. This describes the state of the unconscious. The Valentinian text gives the Autopator more positive qualities: "Some called him the ageless Aeon, eternally young, male and female, who contains everything in himself and is [himself] contained by nothing." In him was ἔννοια, consciousness, which "conveys the treasures of the greatness to those who come from the greatness." But the presence of ἔννοια does not prove that the Autopator himself is conscious, for the differentiation of consciousness results only from the syzygies and tetrads that follow afterwards, all of them symbolizing processes of conjunction and composition. Ἔννοια must be thought of here as the latent possibility of consciousness. Oehler translates it as *mens*, Cornarius as *intelligentia* and *notio*.

299   St. Paul's concept of ἄγνοια (*ignorantia*) may not be too far removed from ἀγνωσία, since both mean the initial, unconscious condition of man. When God "looked down" on the times of ignorance, the Greek word used here, ὑπεριδών (Vulgate: *despiciens*) has the connotation 'to disdain, despise.' [18] At all events, Gnostic tradition says that when the highest God saw what miserable, unconscious creatures these human beings were whom the demiurge had created, who were not even able to walk upright, he immediately got the work of redemption under way. [19] And in the same passage in the Acts, Paul reminds the Athenians that they were "God's offspring," [20] and that God, looking back disapprovingly on "the times of ignorance," had sent the message to mankind, commanding "all men every-

---

17 *Elenchos*, VI, 42, 4; Quispel, "Note sur 'Basilide,'" p. 115.

18 Acts 17 : 30.

19 Cf. Scott, *Hermetica* (I, pp. 150f.) where there is a description of the *krater* filled with Nous which God sent down to earth. Those whose hearts strive after consciousness (γνωρίζουσα ἐπὶ τὶ γέγονας) can "baptize" themselves in the *krater* and thereby obtain Nous. "God says that the man filled with Nous should know himself" (pp. 126f.).

20 Γένος οὖν ὑπάρχοντες τοῦ θεοῦ (Acts 17 : 29).

where to repent." Because that earlier condition seemed to be altogether too wretched, the μετάνοια (transformation of mind) took on the moral character of repentance of sins, with the result that the Vulgate could translate it as "poenitentiam agere." [21] The sin to be repented, of course, is ἄγνοια or ἀγνωσία, unconsciousness.[22] As we have seen, it is not only man who is in this condition, but also, according to the Gnostics, the ἀνεννόητος, the God without consciousness. This idea is more or less in line with the traditional Christian view that God was transformed during the passage from the Old Testament to the New, and, from being the God of wrath, changed into the God of Love—a thought that is expressed very clearly by Nicolaus Caussin in the seventeenth century.[23]

300   In this connection I must mention the results of Riwkah Schärf's examination of the figure of Satan in the Old Testament.[24] With the historical transformation of the concept of Satan the image of Yahweh changes too, so that one can well say that there was a differentiation of the God-image even in the Old Testament, not to speak of the New. The idea that the world-creating Deity is not conscious, but may be dreaming, is found also in Hindu literature:

> Who knows how it was, and who shall declare
> Whence it was born and whence it came?
> The gods are later than this creation;
> Who knows, then, whence it has sprung?

> Whence this created world came,
> And whether he made it or not,
> He alone who sees all in the highest heaven
> Knows—or does not know.[25]

---

[21] Likewise the μετανοεῖτε of the Baptist (Matt. 3 : 2).

[22] Cf. the τὸ τῆς ἀγνοίας ἁμάρτημα, 'sin of unconsciousness' in pseudo-Clement (*Homilies* XIX, cap. XXII), referring to the man who was born blind (John 9 : 1).

[23] *Polyhistor symbolicus*, p. 348: "God, formerly the God of vengeance, who with thunders and lightnings brought the world to disorder, took his rest in the lap of a Virgin, nay, in her womb, and was made captive by love."

[24] "Die Gestalt des Satans im Alten Testament."

[25] *Rig-Veda*, X, 129. (Cf. MacNicol trans., *Hindu Scriptures*, p. 37.)

Meister Eckhart's theology knows a "Godhead" of which no qualities, except unity and being,[26] can be predicated;[27] it "is becoming," it is not yet Lord of itself, and it represents an absolute coincidence of opposites: "But its simple nature is of forms formless; of becoming becomingless; of beings beingless; of things thingless," etc.[28] Union of opposites is equivalent to unconsciousness, so far as human logic goes, for consciousness presupposes a differentiation into subject and object and a relation between them. Where there is no "other," or it does not yet exist, all possibility of consciousness ceases. Only the Father, the God "welling" out of the Godhead, "notices himself," becomes "beknown to himself," and "confronts himself as a Person." So, from the Father, comes the Son, as the Father's thought of his own being. In his original unity "he knows nothing" except the "suprareal" One which he *is*. As the Godhead is essentially unconscious,[29] so too is the man who lives in God. In his sermon on "The Poor in Spirit" (Matt. 5 : 3), the Meister says: "The man who has this poverty has everything he was when he lived not in any wise, neither in himself, nor in truth, nor in God. He is so quit and empty of all knowing that no knowledge of God is alive in him; for while he stood in the eternal nature of God, there lived in him not another: what lived there was himself. And so we say this man is as empty of his own knowledge as he was when he was not anything; he lets God work what he will, and he stands empty as when he came from God."[30] Therefore he should love God in the following way: "Love him as he is: a not-God, a not-spirit, a not-person, a not-image; as a sheer, pure, clear One, which he is, sundered from all secondness; and in this One let us sink eternally, from nothing to nothing. So help us God. Amen."[31]

---

26 "Being" is controversial. The Master says: "God in the Godhead is a spiritual substance, so unfathomable that we can say nothing about it except that it is naught [*niht ensi*]. To say it is aught [*iht*] were more lying than true." (Cf. Evans trans., I, p. 354.)

27 "To this end there is no way, it is beyond all ways." (Cf. ibid., p. 211.)

28 ". . . von formen formelôs, von werdenne werdelôs, von wesenne weselôs und ist von sachen sachelôs." (Cf. ibid., p. 352.)

29 "[The will] is the nobler in that it plunges into unknowing, which is God." Cf. ibid., p. 351. Cf. also n. 16, supra: ἀγνωσία.

30 Evans, I, p. 219.

31 End of the sermon "Renovamini spiritu" (Eph. 4 : 23). Ibid., pp. 247f.

302   The world-embracing spirit of Meister Eckhart knew, without discursive knowledge, the primordial mystical experience of India as well as of the Gnostics, and was itself the finest flower on the tree of the "Free Spirit" that flourished at the beginning of the eleventh century. Well might the writings of this Master lie buried for six hundred years, for "his time was not yet come." Only in the nineteenth century did he find a public at all capable of appreciating the grandeur of his mind.

303   These utterances on the nature of the Deity express transformations of the God-image which run parallel with changes in human consciousness, though one would be at a loss to say which is the cause of the other. The God-image is not something *invented*, it is an *experience* that comes upon man spontaneously —as anyone can see for himself unless he is blinded to the truth by theories and prejudices. The unconscious God-image can therefore alter the state of consciousness, just as the latter can modify the God-image once it has become conscious. This, obviously, has nothing to do with the "prime truth," the unknown God—at least, nothing that could be verified. Psychologically, however, the idea of God's ἀγνωσία, or of the ἀνεννόητος θεός, is of the utmost importance, because it identifies the Deity with the numinosity of the unconscious. The *atman/purusha* philosophy of the East and, as we have seen, Meister Eckhart in the West both bear witness to this.

304   Now if psychology is to lay hold of this phenomenon, it can only do so if it expressly refrains from passing metaphysical judgments, and if it does not presume to profess convictions to which it is ostensibly entitled on the ground of scientific experience. But of this there can be no question whatever. The one and only thing that psychology can establish is the presence of pictorial symbols, whose interpretation is in no sense fixed beforehand. It can make out, with some certainty, that these symbols have the character of "wholeness" and therefore presumably *mean* wholeness. As a rule they are "uniting" symbols, representing the conjunction of a single or double pair of opposites, the result being either a dyad or a quaternion. They arise from the collision between the conscious and the unconscious and from the confusion which this causes (known in alchemy as "chaos" or "nigredo"). Empirically, this confusion takes the form of restlessness and disorientation. The circle and qua-

ternity symbolism appears at this point as a compensating principle of order, which depicts the union of warring opposites as already accomplished, and thus eases the way to a healthier and quieter state ("salvation"). For the present, it is not possible for psychology to establish more than that the symbols of wholeness mean the wholeness of the individual.[32] On the other hand, it has to admit, most emphatically, that this symbolism uses images or schemata which have always, in all the religions, expressed the universal "Ground," the Deity itself. Thus the circle is a well-known symbol for God; and so (in a certain sense) is the cross, the quaternity in all its forms, e.g., Ezekiel's vision, the *Rex gloriae* with the four evangelists, the Gnostic Barbelo ("God in four") and Kolorbas ("all four"); the duality (*tao,* hermaphrodite, father-mother); and finally, the human form (child, son, anthropos) and the individual personality (Christ and Buddha), to name only the most important of the motifs here used.

5   All these images are found, empirically, to be expressions for the unified wholeness of man. The fact that this goal goes by the name of "God" proves that it has a numinous character; and indeed, experiences, dreams, and visions of this kind do have a fascinating and impressive quality which can be spontaneously felt even by people who are not prejudiced in their favour by prior psychological knowledge. So it is no wonder that naïve minds make no distinction between God and the image they have experienced. Wherever, therefore, we find symbols indicative of psychic wholeness, we encounter the naïve idea that they stand for God. In the case of those quite common Romanesque pictures of the Son of Man accompanied by three angels with animal heads and one with a human head, for example, it would be simpler to assume that the Son of Man meant the ordinary man and that the problem of one against three referred to the well-known psychological schema of one differentiated and three undifferentiated functions. But this interpretation would, according to the traditional view, devalue the symbol, for it

---

32 There are people who, oddly enough, think it a weakness in me that I refrain from metaphysical judgments. A scientist's conscience does not permit him to assert things he cannot prove or at least show to be probable. No assertion has ever yet brought anything corresponding to it into existence. "What he says, is" is a prerogative exclusive to God.

means the second Person of the Godhead in its universal, four-fold aspect. Psychology cannot of course adopt this view as its own; it can only establish the existence of such statements and point out, by way of comparison, that essentially the same symbols, in particular the dilemma of one and three, often appear in the spontaneous products of the unconscious, where they demonstrably refer to the psychic totality of the individual. They indicate the presence of an archetype of like nature, one of whose derivates would seem to be the quaternity of functions that orient consciousness. But, since this totality exceeds the individual's consciousness to an indefinite and indeterminable extent, it invariably includes the unconscious in its orbit and hence the totality of all archetypes. But the archetypes are complementary equivalents of the "outside world" and therefore possess a "cosmic" character. This explains their numinosity and "godlikeness."

3

306   To make my exposition more complete, I would like to mention some of the Gnostic symbols for the universal "Ground" or arcanum, and especially those synonyms which signify the "Ground." Psychology takes this idea as an image of the unconscious background and begetter of consciousness. The most important of these images is the figure of the demiurge. The Gnostics have a vast number of symbols for the source or origin, the centre of being, the Creator, and the divine substance hidden in the creature. Lest the reader be confused by this wealth of images, he should always remember that each new image is simply another aspect of the divine mystery immanent in all creatures. My list of Gnostic symbols is no more than an amplification of a single transcendental idea, which is so comprehensive and so difficult to visualize in itself that a great many different expressions are required in order to bring out its various aspects.

307   According to Irenaeus, the Gnostics held that Sophia represents the world of the Ogdoad,[33] which is a double quaternity.

33 *Adversus haereses*, I, 30, 3. In the system of Barbelo-Gnosis (ibid., 29, 4) the equivalent of Sophia is Προύνικος, who "sinks into the lower regions." The name Prunicus (προύνεικος) means both 'carrying a burden' and 'lewd.' The latter connotation is more probable, because this Gnostic sect believed that, through the

In the form of a dove, she descended into the water and begot Saturn, who is identical with Yahweh. Saturn, as we have already mentioned, is the "other sun," the *sol niger* of alchemy. Here he is the "primus Anthropus." He created the first man, who could only crawl like a worm.[34] Among the Naassenes, the demiurge Esaldaios, "a fiery god, the fourth by number," is set up against the Trinity of Father, Mother, and Son. The highest is the Father, the Archanthropos, who is without qualities and is called the higher Adam. In various systems Sophia takes the place of the Protanthropos.[35] Epiphanius mentions the Ebionite teaching that Adam, the original man, is identical with Christ.[36] In Theodor Bar-Kuni the original man is the five elements (i.e., $4 + 1$).[37] In the Acts of Thomas, the dragon says of itself: "I am the son . . . of him that hurt and smote the four brethren which stood upright." [38]

08   The primordial image of the quaternity coalesces, for the Gnostics, with the figure of the demiurge or Anthropos. He is, as it were, the victim of his own creative act, for, when he

---

sexual act, they could recharge Barbelo with the pneuma that was lost in the world. In Simon Magus it is Helen, the μήτηρ and ἔννοια, who "descended to the lower regions . . . and generated the inferior powers, angels, and firmaments." She was forcibly held captive by the lower powers (Irenaeus, I, 27, 1–4). She corresponds to the much later alchemical idea of the "soul in fetters" (cf. Dorn, *Theatr. chem.*, I, pp. 298, 497; Mylius, *Phil. ref.*, p. 262; *Rosarium philosophorum* in *Art. aurif.*, II, p. 284; "Platonis liber quartorum," *Theatr. chem.*, V, pp. 185f.; Vigenère, *Theatr. chem.*, VI, p. 19). The idea derives from Greek alchemy and can be found in Zosimos (Berthelot, *Alch. grecs*, III, xlix, 7; trans. in *Psychology and Alchemy*, pars. 456ff.). In the "Liber quartorum" it is of Sabaean origin. See Chwolsohn, *Die Ssabier und der Ssabismus* (II, p. 494): "The soul once turned towards matter, fell in love with it, and, burning with desire to experience bodily pleasures, was no longer willing to tear herself away from it. So was the world born." Among the Valentinians, Sophia Achamoth is the Ogdoad. In *Pistis Sophia* (trans. by Mead, p. 362) she is the daughter of Barbelo. Deluded by the false light of the demon Authades, she falls into imprisonment in chaos. Irenaeus (I, 5, 2) calls the demiurge the Heptad, but Achamoth the Ogdoad. In I, 7, 2 he says that the Saviour is compounded of four things in repetition of the first Tetrad. A copy of the Four is the quaternity of elements (I, 17, 1), and so are the four lights that stand round the Autogenes of Barbelo-Gnosis (I, 29, 2).   34 *Adv. haer.*, I, 24, 1.

35 Bousset, *Hauptprobleme der Gnosis*, p. 170.   36 *Panarium*, XXX, 3.

37 Theodor Bar-Kuni, *Inscriptiones mandaïtes des coupes de Khouabir*, Part 2, p. 185.

38 *The Apocryphal New Testament*, ed. James, p. 379.

descended into Physis, he was caught in her embrace.[39] The image of the *anima mundi* or Original Man latent in the dark of matter expresses the presence of a transconscious centre which, because of its quaternary character and its roundness, must be regarded as a symbol of wholeness. We may assume, with due caution, that some kind of psychic wholeness is meant (for instance, conscious + unconscious), though the history of the symbol shows that it was always used as a God-image. Psychology, as I have said, is not in a position to make metaphysical statements. It can only establish that the symbolism of psychic wholeness coincides with the God-image, but it can never prove that the God-image is God himself, or that the self takes the place of God.

309   This coincidence comes out very clearly in the ancient Egyptian Heb-Sed festival, of which Colin Campbell gives the following description: "The king comes out of an apartment called the sanctuary, then he ascends into a pavilion open at the four sides, with four staircases leading up to it. Carrying the emblems of Osiris, he takes his seat on a throne, and turns to the four cardinal points in succession. . . . It is a kind of second enthronement . . . and sometimes the king acts as a priest, making offerings to himself. This last act may be regarded as the climax of the deification of the king." [40]

310   All kingship is rooted in this psychology, and therefore, for the anonymous individual of the populace, every king carries the symbol of the self. All his insignia—crown, mantle, orb, sceptre, starry orders, etc.—show him as the cosmic Anthropos, who not only begets, but himself is, the world. He is the *homo maximus,* whom we meet again in Swedenborg's speculations. The Gnostics, too, constantly endeavoured to give visible form and a suitable conceptual dress to this being, suspecting that he was the matrix and organizing principle of consciousness. As the "Phrygians" (Naassenes) say in Hippolytus,[41] he is the "undivided point," the "grain of mustard seed" that grows into the kingdom of God. This point is "present in the body." But this is known only to the πνευματικοί the "spiritual" men as opposed to the ψυχικοί and the ὑλικοί ("material" men). He is τὸ ῥῆμα τοῦ

39 Bousset, pp. 114ff.
40 *The Miraculous Birth of King Amon-Hotep III,* p. 81.
41 *Elenchos,* V, 9, 5f. (Legge trans., I, pp. 140f.).

θεοῦ, the utterance of God (*sermo Dei*), and the "matrix of the Aeons, Powers, Intelligences, Gods, Angels, and Emissary Spirits, of Being and Non-Being, of Begotten and Unbegotten, of the Non-Intelligible Intelligible, of the Years, Moons, Days, Hours. . . ." This point, "being nothing and consisting of nothing," becomes a "certain magnitude incomprehensible by thought." Hippolytus accuses the Naassenes of bundling everything into their thought like the syncretists, for he obviously cannot quite understand how the point, the "utterance of God," can have a human form. The Naassenes, he complains, also call him the "polymorphous Attis," the young dying son of the Great Mother, or, as the hymn cited by Hippolytus says, τὸ κατέφες ἄκουσμα 'Ρέας, the 'dark rumour of Rhea.' In the hymn he has the synonyms Adonis, Osiris, Adam, Korybas, Pan, Bacchus, and ποιμὴν λευκῶν ἀστρῶν, 'shepherd of white stars.'

11   The Naassenes themselves considered Naas, the serpent, to be their central deity, and they explained it as the "moist substance," in agreement with Thales of Miletus, who said water was the prime substance on which all life depended. Similarly, all living things depend on the Naas; "it contains within itself, like the horn of the one-horned bull, the beauty of all things." It "pervades everything, like the water that flows out of Eden and divides into four sources" (ἄρχας). "This Eden, they say, is the brain." Three of the rivers of Paradise are sensory functions (Pison = sight, Gihon = hearing, Tigris = smell), but the fourth, the Euphrates, is the mouth, "the seat of prayer and the entrance of food." As the fourth function it has a double significance,[42] denoting on the one hand the purely material activity of bodily nourishment, while on the other hand it "gladdens,[43] feeds, and forms [χαρακτηρίζει] the spiritual, perfect [τέλειον] man." [44] The "fourth" is something special, ambivalent—a daimonion. A good example of this is in Daniel 3 : 24f., where the three men in the burning fiery furnace are joined by a fourth, whose form was "like a son of God."

12   The water of the Euphrates is the "water above the firmament," the "living water of which the Saviour spoke," [45] and

---

42 *Psychology and Alchemy*, index, s.v. "Axiom of Maria." Cf. infra, pars. 395ff.

43 εὐφραίνει, a play on the word εὐφραθής, 'well-speaking.'

44 *Elenchos*, V, 9, 15ff. [Cf. Legge, I, p. 143.]

45 An allusion to John 4 : 10.

possessing, as we have seen, magnetic properties. It is that miraculous water from which the olive draws its oil and the grape the wine. "That man," continues Hippolytus, as though still speaking of the water of the Euphrates, "is without honour in the world." [46] This is an allusion to the τέλειος ἄνθρωπος. Indeed, this water *is* the "perfect man," the ῥῆμα θεοῦ, the Word sent by God. "From the living water we spiritual men choose that which is ours," [47] for every nature, when dipped in this water, "chooses its own substances . . . and from this water goes forth to every nature that which is proper to it." [48] The water or, as we could say, this Christ is a sort of panspermia, a matrix of all possibilities, from which the πνευματικός chooses "his Osob," his idiosyncrasy,[49] that "flies to him more [quickly] than iron to the magnet." But the "spiritual men" attain their proper nature by entering in through the "true door," Jesus Makarios (the blessed), and thus obtaining knowledge of their own wholeness, i.e., of the complete man. This man, unhonoured in the world, is obviously the inner, spiritual man, who becomes conscious for those who enter in through Christ, the door to life, and are illuminated by him. Two images are blended here: the image of the "strait gate," [50] and that of John 14 : 6: "I am the way, and the truth, and the life. No one comes to the Father but through me." [51] They represent an integration process that is characteristic of psychological individuation. As formulated, the water symbol continually coalesces with Christ and Christ with the inner man. This, it seems to me, is not a confusion of thought but a psychologically correct formulation of the facts, since Christ as the "Word" is indeed the "living water" and at the same time the symbol of the inner "complete" man, the self.

313   For the Naassenes, the universal "Ground" is the Original Man, Adam, and knowledge of him is regarded as the begin-

---

[46] Legge, I, p. 144.   [47] *Elenchos*, V, 9, 21.

[48] V, 9, 19 (Legge trans., p. 144).

[49] This means the integration of the self, which is also referred to in very similar words in the Bogomil document discussed above (pars. 225ff.), concerning the devil as world creator. He too finds what is "proper" (ἴδιον) to him.

[50] Matt. 7 : 14: "Strait is the gate, and narrow is the way, which leadeth unto life."

[51] The passage discussed here is in *Elenchos*, V, 9, 4ff. (Legge trans., I, p. 140).

ning of perfection and the bridge to knowledge of God.[52] He is male/female; from him come "father and mother"; [53] he consists of three parts: the rational (νοερόν), the psychic, and the earthly (χοικόν). These three "came down together into one man, Jesus," and "these three men spoke together, each of them from his own substance to his own," i.e., from the rational to the rational, etc. Through this doctrine Jesus is related to the Original Man (Christ as second Adam). His soul is "of three parts and (yet) one"—a Trinity.[54] As examples of the Original Man the text mentions the Cabiros [55] and Oannes. The latter had a soul capable of suffering, so that the "figure (πλάσμα) of the great, most beautiful and perfect man, humbled to a slave," might suffer punishment. He is the "blessed nature, at once hidden and revealed, of everything that has come to be and will be," "the kingdom of heaven which is to be sought within man" (ἐντός ἀνθρώπου), even "in children of seven years." [56] For the Naassenes, says Hippolytus, place the "procreative nature of the Whole in the procreative seed." [57] On the face of it, this looks like the beginnings of a "sexual theory" concerning the underlying psychic substance, reminiscent of certain modern attempts in the same vein. But one should not overlook the fact that in reality man's procreative power is only a special instance of the "procreative nature of the Whole." "This, for them, is the hidden and mystical Logos," which, in the text that follows, is likened to the phallus of Osiris—"and they say Osiris is water." Although the substance of this seed is the cause of all things, it does not partake of their nature. They say therefore: "I become what I will, and I am what I am." For he who moves everything is himself unmoved. "He, they say, is alone good." [58] A further synonym is the ithyphallic Hermes Kyllenios. "For they say Hermes is the Logos, the interpreter and fashioner of what has

---

52 Elenchos, V, 6, 6: Θεοῦ δὲ γνῶσις ἀπηρτισμένη τελείωσις ("Knowledge of God is perfect wholeness").

53 V, 6, 5 (Legge trans., I, p. 120).   54 V, 6, 6f. (p. 121).

55 Nicknamed καλλίπαις, 'with beautiful children' or 'the beautiful child.' (Elenchos, V, 7, 4.)

56 According to Hippocrates, a boy at seven years old is half a father. (Elenchos, V, 7, 21.)

57 τὴν ἀρχέγονων φύσιν τῶν ὅλων ἐν ἀρχέγονῳ σπέρματι. Archegonos is the tribal father.

58 With express reference to Matt. 19:17: "One is good, God."

been, is, and will be." That is why he is worshipped as the phallus, because he, like the male organ, "has an urge [ὁρμήν] from below upwards."[59]

4

314   The fact that not only the Gnostic Logos but Christ himself was drawn into the orbit of sexual symbolism is corroborated by the fragment from the *Interrogationes maiores Mariae*, quoted by Epiphanius.[60] It is related there that Christ took this Mary with him on to a mountain, where he produced a woman from his side and began to have intercourse with her: ". . . seminis sui defluxum assumpsisset, indicasse illi, quod oportet sic facere, ut vivamus."[61] It is understandable that this crude symbolism should offend our modern feelings. But it also appeared shocking to Christians of the third and fourth centuries; and when, in addition, the symbolism became associated with a concretistic misunderstanding, as appeared to be the case in certain sects, it could only be rejected. That the author of the *Interrogationes* was by no means ignorant of some such reaction is evident from the text itself. It says that Mary received such a shock that she fell to the ground. Christ then said to her: "Wherefore do you doubt me, O you of little faith?" This was meant as a reference to John 3 : 12: "If I have told you earthly things and you do not believe, how can you believe if I tell you heavenly things?" and also to John 6 : 53: "Unless you eat the flesh of the Son of man and drink his blood, you have no life in you" (RSV).

315   This symbolism may well have been based, originally, on some visionary experience, such as happens not uncommonly today during psychological treatment. For the medical psychologist there is nothing very lurid about it. The context itself points the way to the right interpretation. The image expresses a psychologem that can hardly be formulated in rational terms and has, therefore, to make use of a concrete symbol, just as a dream must when a more or less "abstract" thought comes up during the *abaissement du niveau mental* that occurs in sleep. These "shocking" surprises, of which there is certainly no lack

59 Cf. Legge trans., p. 128.   60 *Panarium*, XXVI, cap. VIII.
61 ". . . partaking of his flowing semen, showed that this was to be done, that we might have life."

in dreams, should always be taken "as-if," even though they clothe themselves in sensual imagery that stops at no scurrility and no obscenity. They are unconcerned with offensiveness, because they do not really mean it. It is as if they were stammering in their efforts to express the elusive meaning that grips the dreamer's attention.[62]

6   The context of the vision (John 3 : 12) makes it clear that the image should be taken not concretistically but symbolically; for Christ speaks not of earthly things but of a heavenly or spiritual mystery—a "mystery" not because he is hiding something or making a secret of it (indeed, nothing could be more blatant than the naked obscenity of the vision!) but because its meaning is still hidden from consciousness. The modern method of dream-analysis and interpretation follows this heuristic rule.[63] If we apply it to the vision, we arrive at the following result:

7   1. The MOUNTAIN means ascent, particularly the mystical, spiritual ascent to the heights, to the place of revelation where the spirit is present. This motif is so well known that there is no need to document it.[64]

18   2. The central significance of the CHRIST-FIGURE for that epoch has been abundantly proved. In Christian Gnosticism it was a visualization of God as the Archanthropos (Original Man = Adam), and therefore the epitome of man as such: "Man and the Son of Man." Christ is the inner man who is reached by the path of self-knowledge, "the kingdom of heaven within

---

62 On the other hand, I cannot rid myself of the impression that dreams do occasionally twist things in a scurrilous way. This may have led Freud to the singular assumption that they disguise and distort for so-called "moral" reasons. However, this view is contradicted by the fact that dreams just as often do the exact opposite. I therefore incline to the alchemical view that Mercurius—the unconscious Nous—is a "trickster." [Cf. "The Spirit Mercurius" and "The Psychology of the Trickster Figure."—EDITORS.]

63 But not the Freudian, "psychoanalytical" method, which dismisses the manifest dream-content as a mere "façade," on the ground that the psychopathology of hysteria leads one to suspect incompatible wishes as dream-motifs. The fact that the dream as well as consciousness rest on an instinctual foundation has nothing to do either with the meaning of the dream-figures or with that of the conscious contents, for the essential thing in both cases is *what the psyche has made of the instinctual impulse.* The remarkable thing about the Parthenon is not that it consists of stone and was built to gratify the ambitions of the Athenians, but that it is—the Parthenon.

64 Cf. "Phenomenology of the Spirit in Fairytales," par. 403.

you." As the Anthropos he corresponds to what is empirically the most important archetype and, as judge of the living and the dead and king of glory, to the real organizing principle of the unconscious, the quaternity, or squared circle of the self.[65] In saying this I have not done violence to anything; my views are based on the experience that mandala structures have the meaning and function of a centre of the unconscious personality.[66] The quaternity of Christ, which must be borne in mind in this vision, is exemplified by the cross symbol, the *rex gloriae*, and Christ as the year.

319   3. The production of the WOMAN from his side suggests that he is interpreted as the second Adam. Bringing forth a woman means that he is playing the role of the Creator-god in Genesis.[67] Just as Adam, before the creation of Eve, was supposed by various traditions to be male/female,[68] so Christ here demonstrates his androgyny in a drastic way.[69] The Original Man is usually hermaphroditic; in Vedic tradition too he produces his own feminine half and unites with her. In Christian allegory the woman sprung from Christ's side signifies the Church as the Bride of the Lamb.

320   The splitting of the Original Man into husband and wife expresses an act of nascent consciousness; it gives birth to a pair of opposites, thereby making consciousness possible. For the beholder of the miracle, Mary, the vision was the spontaneous visualization or projection of an unconscious process in herself. Experience shows that unconscious processes are compensatory to a definite conscious situation. The splitting in the vision would therefore suggest that it is compensating a conscious condition of unity. This unity probably refers in the first place to the figure of the Anthropos, the incarnate God, who was then in the forefront of religious interest. He was, in Origen's words,

---

[65] Cf. "The Psychology of Eastern Meditation," pars. 942f.
[66] Cf. "A Study in the Process of Individuation."
[67] This is consistent with his nature as the Logos and second Person of the Trinity.
[68] Naturally this view is rejected by the Church.
[69] Three different interpretations of Christ are combined here. Such contaminations are characteristic not only of Gnostic thinking but of all unconscious image-formation.

the "Vir Unus," [70] the One Man. It was with this figure that Mary was confronted in her vision. If we assume that the recipient of the vision was in reality a woman—an assumption that is not altogether without grounds—then what she had been missing in the pure, deified masculinity of Christ was the counterbalancing femininity. Therefore it was revealed to her: "I am both, man and woman." This psychologem is still incorporated today in the Catholic conception of Christ's androgyny as the "Virgo de Virgine," though this is more a *sententia communis* than a *conclusio*. Medieval iconography sometimes shows Christ with breasts, in accordance with Song of Solomon 1 : 1: "For thy breasts are better than wine" (DV). In Mechthild of Magdeburg, the soul remarks that when the Lord kissed her,[71] he had, contrary to expectation, no beard. The tokens of masculinity were lacking. Mechthild had a vision similar to Mary's, dealing with the same problem from a different angle: she saw herself transported to a "rocky mountain" where the Blessed Virgin sat, awaiting the birth of the divine child. When it was born, she embraced it and kissed it three times. As the text points out, the mountain is an allegory of the "spiritualis habitus," or spiritual attitude. "Through divine inspiration she knew how the Son is the innermost core [*medulla*] of the Father's heart." This *medulla* is "strengthening, healing, and most sweet"; God's "strength and greatest sweetness" are given to us through the Son, the "Saviour and strongest, sweetest Comforter," but "the innermost [core] of the soul is that sweetest thing." [72] From this it is clear that Mechthild equates the "medulla" with the Father's heart, the Son, and the inner man. Psychologically speaking, "that sweetest thing" corresponds to the self, which is indistinguishable from the God-image.

There is a significant difference between the two visions. The antique revelation depicts the birth of Eve from Adam on

---

[70] Gregory the Great, *Expositiones in librum I Regum,* Lib. I, cap. I (Migne, *P.L.*, vol. 79, col. 23): "For God and man is one Christ. Therefore in that he is called one, he is shown to be incomparable." In accordance with the spirit of the age, his incomparability or uniqueness is explained by the "excellence of his virtue." It is, however, significant in itself.

[71] "He offered her his rosy [sic!] mouth to kiss" (*Liber gratiae spiritualis,* fol. J iv^v).

[72] "Medulla vero animae est illud dulcissimum." Ibid., fol. B.

the spiritual level of the second Adam (Christ), from whose side the feminine pneuma, or second Eve, i.e., the soul, appears as Christ's daughter. As already mentioned, in the Christian view the soul is interpreted as the Church: she is the woman who "embraces the man" [73] and anoints the Lord's feet. Mechthild's vision is a continuation of the sacred myth: the daughter-bride has become a mother and bears the Father in the shape of the Son. That the Son is closely akin to the self is evident from the emphasis laid on the quaternary nature of Christ: he has a "fourfold voice" (*quadruplex vox*),[74] his heart has four kinds of pulse,[75] and from his countenance go forth four rays of light.[76] In this image a new millennium is speaking. Meister Eckhart, using a different formulation, says that "God is born from the soul," and when we come to the *Cherubinic Wanderer* [77] of Angelus Silesius, God and the self coincide absolutely. The times have undergone a profound change: the procreative power no longer proceeds from God, rather is God born from the soul. The mythologem of the young dying god has taken on psychological form—a sign of further assimilation and conscious realization.

322   4. But to turn back to the first vision: the bringing forth of the woman is followed by COPULATION. The *hieros gamos* on the mountain is a well-known motif,[78] just as, in the old alchemical pictures, the hermaphrodite has a fondness for elevated places. The alchemists likewise speak of an Adam who always carries his Eve around with him. Their *coniunctio* is an incestuous act, performed not by father and daughter but, in accordance with the changed times, by brother and sister or mother and son. The latter variant corresponds to the ancient Egyptian mythologem of Amen as Ka-mutef, which means 'husband of his mother,' or of Mut, who is the "mother of her father and daughter of her

---

[73] Gregory the Great; Migne, *P.L.*, vol. 79, col. 23. Cf. Jerem. 31 : 22: "A woman shall compass a man" (AV).
[74] *Liber gratiae spiritualis*, fol. A viiʳ. The quaternity refers to the four gospels.
[75] Ibid., fol. B iiᵛ.
[76] Ibid., fol. B viiᵛ.
[77] Cf. Flitch, *Angelus Silesius*, pp. 128ff.
[78] For instance, the *hieros gamos* of Zeus and Hera on "the heights of Gargaros," *Iliad*, XIV, 246ff. (Cf. Rieu trans., p. 266.)

son." [79] The idea of self-copulation is a recurrent theme in descriptions of the world creator: for instance, God splits into his masculine and feminine halves,[80] or he fertilizes himself in a manner that could easily have served as a model for the *Interrogationes* vision, if literary antecedents must be conjectured. Thus the relevant passage in the Heliopolitan story of the Creation runs: "I, even I, had union with my clenched hand, I joined myself in an embrace with my shadow, I poured seed into my mouth, my own, I sent forth issue in the form of Shu, I sent forth moisture in the form of Tefnut." [81]

Although the idea of self-fertilization is not touched on in our vision, there can be no doubt that there is a close connection between this and the idea of the cosmogonic self-creator. Here, however, world creation gives place to spiritual renewal. That is why no visible creature arises from the taking in of seed; it means a nourishing of life, "that we may live." And because, as the text itself shows, the vision should be understood on the "heavenly" or spiritual plane, the pouring out (ἀπόρροια) refers to a λόγος σπερματικός, which in the language of the gospels means a living water "springing up into eternal life." The whole vision reminds one very much of the related alchemical symbolisms. Its drastic naturalism, unpleasantly obtrusive in comparison with the reticence of ecclesiastical language, points back on the one hand to archaic forms of religion whose ideas and modes of expression had long since been superseded, but forwards, on the other, to a still crude observation of Nature that was just beginning to assimilate the archetype of man. This attempt continued right up to the seventeenth century, when Johannes Kepler recognized the Trinity as underlying the structure of the universe—in other words, when he assimilated this archetype into the astronomer's picture of the world.[82]

[79] Brugsch, *Religion und Mythologie der alten Ägypter*, p. 94.
[80] In the ancient Egyptian view God is "Father and Mother," and "begets and gives birth to himself" (Brugsch, p. 97). The Indian Prajapati has intercourse with his own split-off feminine half.
[81] Budge, *Gods of the Egyptians*, I, pp. 310f.
[82] I owe this idea to a lecture delivered by Professor W. Pauli, in Zurich, on the archetypal foundations of Kepler's astronomy. Cf. his "The Influence of Archetypal Ideas" etc.

³²⁴ After this digression on the phallic synonyms for the Original Man, we will turn back to Hippolytus' account of the central symbols of the Naassenes and continue with a list of statements about Hermes.

³²⁵ Hermes is a conjurer of spirits (ψυχαγωγός), a guide of souls (ψυχοπομπός), and a begetter of souls (ψυχῶν αἴτιος). But the souls were "brought down from the blessed Man on high, the arch-man Adamas, . . . into the form of clay, that they might serve the demiurge of this creation, Esaldaios, a fiery god, the fourth by number." ⁸³ Esaldaios corresponds to Ialdabaoth, the highest archon, and also to Saturn.⁸⁴ The "fourth" refers to the fourth Person—the devil—who is opposed to the Trinity. Ialdabaoth means "child of chaos"; hence when Goethe, borrowing from alchemical terminology, calls the devil the "strange son of chaos," the name is a very apt one.

³²⁶ Hermes is equipped with the golden wand.⁸⁵ With it he "drops sleep on the eyes of the dead and wakes up the sleepers." The Naassenes referred this to Ephesians 5 : 14: "Awake, O sleeper, and arise from the dead, and Christ shall give you light." Just as the alchemists took the well-known allegory of Christ, the *lapis angularis* or cornerstone, for their *lapis philosophorum,* so the Naassenes took it as symbolizing their Protanthropos Adam, or more precisely, the "inner man," who is a rock or stone, since he came from the πέτρη τοῦ Ἀδάμαντος, "fallen from Adamas the arch-man on high." ⁸⁶ The alchemists said their stone was "cut from the mountain without hands," ⁸⁷ and the Naassenes say the same thing of the inner man, who was brought down "into the form of oblivion." ⁸⁸ In Epiphanius the

---

⁸³ *Elenchos,* V, 7, 30f. (Cf. Legge trans., I, p. 128.)

⁸⁴ Bousset, *Hauptprobleme der Gnosis,* pp. 352f.

⁸⁵ Here Hippolytus cites the text of *Odyssey,* XXIV, 2.

⁸⁶ *Elenchos,* V, 7, 36 (Legge trans., I, pp. 129f.).

⁸⁷ Daniel 2 : 34: "Thus thou sawest, till a stone was cut out of a mountain without hands" (DV). This was the stone that broke in pieces the clay and iron feet of the statue.

⁸⁸ Εἰς τὸ πλάσμα τῆς λήθης, i.e., *lethargia,* the state of forgetfulness and sleep resembling that of the dead. The "inner man" is as if buried in the somatic man. He is the "soul in fetters" or "in the prison of the body," as the alchemists say. *Lēthē* corresponds to the modern concept of the unconscious.

mountain is the Archanthropos Christ, from whom the stone or inner man was cut. As Epiphanius interprets it, this means that the inner man is begotten "without human seed," "a small stone that becomes a great mountain." [89]

7   The Archanthropos is the Logos, whom the souls follow "twittering," as the bats follow Hermes in the *nekyia*. He leads them to Oceanus and—in the immortal words of Homer—to "the doors of Helios and the land of dreams." "He [Hermes] is Oceanus, the begetter of gods and men, ever ebbing and flowing, now forth, now back." Men are born from the ebb, and gods from the flow. "It is this, they say, that stands written: 'I have said, you are gods, and all of you the sons of the most High.' " [90] Here the affinity or identity of God and man is explicit, in the Holy Scriptures no less than in the Naassene teachings.

6

8   The Naassenes, as Hippolytus says,[91] derived all things from a triad, which consists firstly of the "blessed nature of the blessed Man on high, Adamas," secondly of the mortal nature of the lower man, and thirdly of the "kingless race begotten from above," to which belong "Mariam the sought-for one, and Jothor [92] the great wise one, and Sephora [93] the seer, and Moses whose generation was not in Egypt." [94] Together these four form a marriage *quaternio* [95] of the classic type:

HUSBAND — WIFE

SISTER — BROTHER

89 *Ancoratus*, 40. Cf. Daniel 2 : 35: "But the stone that struck the statue became a great mountain and filled the whole earth" (DV).

90 *Elenchos*, V, 7, 37 (Legge trans., I, p. 130). Cf. Psalm 82 (Vulg. 81) : 6, to which reference is made in Luke 6 : 35 and John 10 : 34.

91 V, 8, 2 (ibid., p. 131).

92 'Ιοθώρ = Jethro, the priest-king of Midian and the father-in-law of Moses.

93 Zipporah, the wife of Moses.

94 This is probably an allusion to the pneumatic nature of the "generation" produced by Moses, for, according to *Elenchos*, V, 7, 41, "Egypt is the body" (Legge trans., I, p. 130).

95 The marriage *quaternio* is the archetype to which the cross-cousin marriage corresponds on a primitive level. I have given a detailed account of it in "The Psychology of the Transference," pars. 425ff.

Their synonyms are:

MOTHER	—	FATHER
QUEEN	—	KING
THE UNKNOWN WOMAN	—	THE DISTANT LOVER
ANIMA	—	ANIMUS

329   Moses corresponds to the husband, Sephora to the wife; Mariam (Miriam) is the sister of Moses; Jothor (Jethro) is the archetype of the wise old man and corresponds to the father-animus, if the *quaternio* is that of a woman. But the fact that Jothor is called "the great wise one" suggests that the *quaternio* is a man's. In the case of a woman the accent that falls here on the wise man would fall on Mariam, who would then have the significance of the Great Mother. At all events our *quaternio* lacks the incestuous brother-sister relationship, otherwise very common. Instead, Miriam has something of a mother significance for Moses (cf. Exodus 2 : 4ff.). As a prophetess (Exodus 15 : 20f.) she is a "magical" personality. When Moses took a Moor to wife—the "Ethiopian woman"—this incensed Miriam so much that she was smitten with leprosy and became "as white as snow" (Numbers 12 : 10). Miriam is therefore not altogether unsuited to play the role of the anima. The best-known anima-figure in the Old Testament, the Shulamite, says: "I am black, but comely" (Song of Songs 1 : 5). In the *Chymical Wedding* of Christian Rosenkreutz, the royal bride is the concubine of the Moorish king. Negroes, and especially Ethiopians, play a considerable role in alchemy as synonyms of the *caput corvi* and the *nigredo*.[96] They appear in the Passion of St. Perpetua [97] as representatives of the sinful pagan world.

330   The triad is characterized by various names that may be onomatopoetic: Kaulakau, Saulasau, Zeesar.[98] Kaulakau means the higher Adam, Saulasau the lower, mortal man, and Zeesar is named the "upwards-flowing Jordan." The Jordan was caused

---

[96] Cf. *Psychology and Alchemy*, par. 484.

[97] See the study by Marie-Louise von Franz.

[98] These words occur in the Hebrew of Isaiah 28 : 10, where they describe what "men with stammering lips and alien tongue" speak to the people. [The Hebrew runs: "tsaw latsaw, tsaw latsaw, kaw lakaw, kaw lakaw, zeer sham, zeer sham."—EDITORS.] AV: "For precept must be upon precept, precept upon precept, line upon line, line upon line; here a little and there a little."

by Jesus to flow up-stream; it is the rising flood and this, as already mentioned, is the begetter of gods. "This, they say, is the human hermaphrodite in all creatures, whom the ignorant call 'Geryon of the threefold body' [that is, ὡς ἐκ γῆς ῥέοντα, 'flowing from the earth']; but the Greeks name it the celestial horn of the moon." The text defines the above-mentioned *quaternio,* which is identical with Zeesar, the upwards-flowing Jordan, the hermaphrodite, Geryon of the threefold body, and the horn of the moon, as the cosmogonic Logos (John 1 : 1ff.), and the "life that was in him" (John 1 : 4) as a "generation of perfect men" (τέλειοι ἀνθρώποι).[99]

31   This Logos or quaternity is "the cup from which the king, drinking, draws his omens," [100] or the beaker of Anacreon. The cup leads Hippolytus on to the wine miracle at Cana, which, he says, "showed forth the kingdom of heaven"; for the kingdom of heaven lies within us, like the wine in the cup. Further parallels of the cup are the ithyphallic gods of Samothrace and the Kyllenic Hermes, who signify the Original Man as well as the spiritual man who is reborn. This last is "in every respect consubstantial" with the Original Man symbolized by Hermes. For this reason, says Hippolytus, Christ said that one must eat of his flesh and drink of his blood, for he was conscious of the *individual nature* of each of his disciples, and also of the need of each "to come to his own special nature." [101]

32   Another synonym is Korybas, who was descended from the crown of the head and from the unformed (ἀχαρακτήριστον) brain, like the Euphrates from Eden, and permeates all things. His image exists—unrecognized—"in earthly form." He is the god who *dwells in the flood.* I need not describe this symbol here, as I have already discussed it at some length in one of my Paracelsus studies.[102] So far as Korybas is concerned, the parallel between him and the Protanthropos is explained by the ancient view that the corybants were the original men.[103] The name "Korybas" does not denote a particular personality, but rather the anonymous member of a collectivity, such as the Curetes,

99 Cf. *Psychology and Alchemy,* pars. 550f. [Cf. Legge trans., I, p. 131.]
100 Cf. Genesis 44 : 5.
101 *Elenchos,* V, 8, 12 (Legge trans., I, p. 133).
102 "Paracelsus as a Spiritual Phenomenon," pars. 181ff.
103 Roscher, *Lexikon,* II, part 1, col. 1608, s.v. "Kuretes."

Cabiri, Dactyls, etc. Etymologically, it has been brought into connection with κορυφή (crown of the head), though this is not certain.[104] Korybas seems in our text to be the name of a single personality—the Kyllenian Hermes, who appears here as synonymous with the Cabiri of Samothrace. With reference to this Hermes the text says: "Him the Thracians . . . call Korybas."[105] I have suggested in an earlier publication[106] that this unusual single personality may perhaps be a product of contamination with Korybas, known to us from the Dionysus legend, because he too seems to have been a phallic being, as we learn from a scholium to Lucian's *De dea Syria*.[107]

333   From the centre of the "perfect man" flows the ocean (where, as we have said, the god dwells). The "perfect" man is, as Jesus says, the "true door," through which the "perfect" man must go in order to be reborn. Here the problem of how to translate "teleios" becomes crucial; for—we must ask—why should anyone who is "perfect" need renewal through rebirth?[108] One can only conclude that the perfect man was not so perfected that no further improvement was possible. We encounter a similar difficulty in Philippians 3 : 12, where Paul says: "Not that I . . . am already perfect" (τετελείωμαι). But three verses further on he writes: "Let us then, as many as are perfect (τέλειοι) be of this mind." The Gnostic use of τέλειος obviously agrees with Paul's. The word has only an approximate meaning and amounts to much the same thing as πνευματικός, 'spiritual,'[109] which is not connected with any conception of a definite degree of perfection or spirituality. The word "perfect" gives the sense of the Greek τέλειος correctly only when it refers to God. But when it applies to a man, who in addition is in need of rebirth, it can at most mean "whole" or "complete," especially if, as our text says, the

---

[104] Ibid., col. 1607. The descent from the brain may be an allusion to the ancient idea that the sperm was conducted down from the head to the genitals, through the spinal cord. [Cf. Onians, *The Origins of European Thought*, p. 234.—EDITORS.]

[105] *Elenchos*, V, 8, 13 (Legge trans., I, p. 133).

[106] "The Spirit Mercurius," par. 278.

[107] Roscher, col. 1392, s.v. "Korybos," where the text is given in full.

[108] The alchemists say very aptly: "Perfectum non perficitur" (that which is perfect is not perfected).

[109] *Elenchos*, V, 8, 22, describes the πνευματικοί as "perfect men endowed with reason," from which it is clear that the possession of an *anima rationalis* is what makes the "spiritual" man.

complete man cannot even be saved unless he passes through this door.[110]

34   The father of the "perfectus" is the higher man or Protanthropos, who is "not clearly formed" and "without qualities." Hippolytus goes on to say that he is called Papa (Attis) by the Phrygians. He is a bringer of peace and quells "the war of the elements" in the human body,[111] a statement we meet again word for word in medieval alchemy, where the *filius philosophorum* "makes peace between enemies or the elements." [112] This "Papa" is also called νέκυς (cadaver), because he is buried in the body like a mummy in a tomb. A similar idea is found in Paracelsus; his treatise *De vita longa* opens with the words: "Life, verily, is naught but a kind of embalmed mummy, which preserves the mortal body from the mortal worms." [113] The body lives only from the "Mumia," through which the "peregrinus microcosmus," the wandering microcosm (corresponding to the macrocosm), rules the physical body.[114] His synonyms are the Adech, Archeus, Protothoma, Ides, Idechtrum, etc. He is the

---

110 *Elenchos*, V, 8, 21 (Legge trans., I, p. 134). Cramer (*Bibl.-theol. Wörterbuch der Neutestamentlichen Gräzität*) gives as the meaning of τέλειος 'complete, perfect, lacking nothing, having reached the destined goal.' Bauer (*Griech.-deutsch. Wörterbuch zu den Schriften des Neuen Testaments*, col. 1344) has, with reference to age, 'mature, full-grown,' and with reference to the mysteries, 'initiated.' Lightfoot (*Notes on the Epistles of St Paul*, p. 173) says: "Τέλειος is properly that of which the parts are fully developed, as distinguished from ὁλόκληρος, that in which none of the parts are wanting, 'full-grown,' as opposed to νήπιος, 'childish,' or παιδία, 'childhood.'" *Teleios* is the man who has received Nous: he has gnosis (knowledge). Cf. Guignebert, "Quelques remarques sur la perfection (τελείωσις) et ses voies dans le mystère paulinien," p. 419. Weiss (*The History of Primitive Christianity*, II, p. 576) declares that it is just the "consciousness of imperfection and the will to progress that is the sign of perfection." He bases this on Epictetus (*Enchiridion*, 51, 1f.), where it says that he who has resolved to progress (προκόπτειν) is, by anticipation, already "perfect."
111 First mentioned at V, 8, 19. [Cf. Legge, I, p. 134.]
112 *Hermetis Trismegisti Tractatus vere Aureus cum scholiis* (1610), p. 44.
113 Published 1562 by Adam von Bodenstein. In *Paracelsus Sämtliche Werke*, ed. Sudhoff, III, p. 249. [Cf. "Paracelsus the Physician," par. 21.]
114 *De origine Morborum invisibilium*, beginning of Book IV, says of the Mumia: "All the power of herbs and of trees is found in the Mumia; not only the power of the plants grown of earth, but also of water, all the properties of metals, all the qualities of marcasites, all the essence of precious stones. How should I count all these things, and name them? They are all within man, no fewer and no less, as strong and as powerful, in the Mumia." (*Volumen Paramirum*, pp. 291ff.)

"Protoplast" (the first-created), and, as Ides, "the door whence all created things have come." [115] (Cf. the "true door" above!) The Mumia is born together with the body and sustains it,[116] though not to the degree that the "supercelestial Mumia" does.[117] The latter would correspond to the higher Adam of the Naassenes. Of the Ideus or Ides Paracelsus says that in it "there is but One Man . . . and he is the Protoplast." [118]

335 The Paracelsian Mumia therefore corresponds in every way to the Original Man, who forms the microcosm in the mortal man and, as such, shares all the powers of the macrocosm. Since it is often a question of cabalistic influences in Paracelsus, it may not be superfluous in this connection to recall the figure of the cabalistic *Metatron*. In the *Zohar* the Messiah is described as the "central column" (i.e., of the Sephiroth system), and of this column it is said: "The column of the centre is Metatron, whose name is like that of the Lord. It is created and constituted to be his image and likeness, and it includes all gradations from Above to Below and from Below to Above, and binds [them] together in the centre." [119]

336 The dead man, Hippolytus continues, will rise again by passing through the "door of heaven." Jacob saw the gate of heaven on his way to Mesopotamia, "but they say Mesopotamia is the stream of the great ocean that flows from the midst of the perfect man." This is the gate of heaven of which Jacob said: "How terrible is this place! This is no other but the house of God, and the gate of heaven." [120] The stream that flows out of the Original Man (the gate of heaven) is interpreted here as the flood-tide of Oceanus, which, as we have seen, generates the gods. The passage quoted by Hippolytus probably refers to John 7 : 38 or to an apocryphal source common to both. The passage in John—"He who believes in me, as the scripture has said, Out of his belly shall flow rivers of living water"—refers to a nonbiblical source, which, however, seemed scriptural to the author. Whoever drinks of this water, in him it shall be a foun-

---

[115] *Fragmentarische Ausarbeitungen zur Anatomie* (Sudhoff, III, p. 462).
[116] The Mumia is, accordingly, an alexipharmic. (*De mumia libellus;* ibid., p. 375.)
[117] *De vita longa,* Lib. IV, cap. VII (ibid., p. 284).
[118] "Paracelsus as a Spiritual Phenomenon," par. 168.
[119] *Zohar,* cited in Schoettgen, *Horae Hebraicae et Talmudicae,* II, p. 16.
[120] Gen. 28 : 17 (DV).

tain of water springing up into eternal life, says Origen.[121] This water is the "higher" water, the *aqua doctrinae*, the rivers from the belly of Christ, and the divine life as contrasted with the "lower" water, the *aqua abyssi*, where the darknesses are, and where dwell the Prince of this world and the deceiving dragon and his angels.[122] The river of water is the "Saviour" himself.[123] Christ is the river that pours into the world through the four gospels,[124] like the rivers of Paradise. I have purposely cited the ecclesiastical allegories in greater detail here, so that the reader can see how saturated Gnostic symbolism is in the language of the Church, and how, on the other hand, particularly in Origen, the liveliness of his amplifications and interpretations has much in common with Gnostic views. Thus, to him as to many of his contemporaries and successors, the idea of the cosmic correspondence of the "spiritual inner man" was something quite familiar: in his first Homily on Genesis he says that God first created heaven, the whole spiritual substance, and that the counterpart of this is "our mind, which is itself a spirit, that is, it is our spiritual inner man which sees and knows God." [125]

37   These examples of Christian parallels to the partly pagan views of the Gnostics may suffice to give the reader a picture of the mentality of the first two centuries of our era, and to show how closely the religious teachings of that age were connected with psychic facts.

121 *In Genesim hom.* XI, 3 (Migne, *P.G.*, vol. 12, col. 224): "And that ye may see the well of vision, and take from it the living water, which shall be in you a fountain of water springing up unto eternal life."
122 Ibid., I, 2 (col. 148).
123 *In Numeros hom.* XVII, 4 (Migne, *P.G.*, vol. 12, cols. 707f.): "For these paradises upon the waters are like and akin to that paradise in which is the tree of life. And the waters we may take to be either the writings of the apostles and evangelists, or the aid given by the angels and celestial powers to such souls; for by these they are watered and inundated, and nourished unto all knowledge and understanding of heavenly things; although our Saviour also is the river which maketh glad the city of God; and the Holy Spirit not only is himself that river, but out of those to whom he is given, rivers proceed from their belly."
124 See the valuable compilation of patristic allegories in Rahner, "Flumina de ventre Christi," pp. 269ff. The above reference is on p. 370 and comes from Hippolytus' *Commentary on Daniel*, I, 17 (*Werke*, I, pp. 28f.).
125 *In Genesim hom.* I, 2 (Migne, *P.G.*, vol. 12, col. 147).

7

338   Now let us come back to the symbols listed by Hippolytus. The Original Man in his *latent state*—so we could interpret the term ἀχαρακτηριστός—is named *Aipolos,* "not because he feeds he-goats and she-goats," but because he is ἀειπόλος, the Pole that turns the cosmos round.¹²⁶ This recalls the parallel ideas of the alchemists, previously mentioned, about Mercurius, who is found at the North Pole. Similarly the Naassenes named Aipolos —in the language of the Odyssey—*Proteus.* Hippolytus quotes Homer as follows: "This place is frequented by the Old Man of the Sea, immortal Proteus the Egyptian . . . who always tells the truth . . ."¹²⁷ Homer then continues: ". . . who owes allegiance to Poseidon and knows the sea in all its depths."¹²⁸ Proteus is evidently a personification of the unconscious:¹²⁹ it is difficult to "catch this mysterious old being . . . he might see me first, or know I am there and keep away." One must seize him quickly and hold him fast, in order to force him to speak. Though he lives in the sea, he comes to the lonely shore at the sacred noon-tide hour, like an amphibian, and lies down to sleep among his seals. These, it must be remembered, are warm-blooded—that is to say, they can be thought of as contents of the unconscious that are capable of becoming conscious, and at certain times they appear spontaneously in the light and airy world of consciousness. From Proteus the wandering hero learns how he may make his way homewards "over the fish-giving sea," and thus the Old Man proves to be a psychopomp.¹³⁰ Οὐ πιπρασκέται, Hippolytus says of him, which can best be translated by the French colloquialism "il ne se laisse pas rouler." "But," the text goes on, "he spins round himself and changes his shape." He behaves, therefore, like a revolving image that cannot be grasped. What he says is νημερτής, 'in sooth,' infallible; he is a

---

¹²⁶ *Elenchos,* V, 8, 34 (Legge, I, p. 137). This is a play on the words αἰπόλος (from αἰγοπόλος), 'goat-herd,' and ἀειπόλος (from ἀεὶ πολεῖν, 'ever turning'). Hence πόλος = the earth's axis, the Pole.

¹²⁷ *Odyssey,* trans. by Rouse, p. 65.   ¹²⁸ Ibid., trans. by Rieu, p. 74.

¹²⁹ He has something of the character of the "trickster" (cf. n. 62, supra).

¹³⁰ Proteus has much in common with Hermes: above all, the gift of second sight and the power of shape-shifting. In *Faust* (Part II, Act 5) he tells the Homunculus how and where to begin his labours.

"soothsayer." So it is not for nothing that the Naassenes say that "knowledge of the complete man is deep indeed and hard to comprehend."

39   Subsequently, Proteus is likened to the green ear of corn in the Eleusinian mysteries. To him is addressed the cry of the celebrants: "The Mistress has borne the divine boy, Brimo has borne Brimos!" A "lower" correspondence to the high Eleusinian initiations, says Hippolytus, is the dark path of Persephone, who was abducted by the god of the underworld; it leads "to the grove of adored Aphrodite, who rouses the sickness of love." Men should keep to this lower path in order to be initiated "into the great and heavenly" mysteries.[131] For this mystery is "the gate of heaven" and the "house of God," where alone the good God dwells, who is destined only for the spiritual men. They should put off their garments and all become νυμφίοι, 'bridegrooms,' "robbed of their virility by the virgin spirit." [132] This is an allusion to Revelation 14 : 4: ". . . for they are virgins. These . . . follow the Lamb whithersoever he goeth." [133]

[131] When I visited the ancient pagoda at Turukalukundram, southern India, a local pundit explained to me that the old temples were purposely covered on the outside, from top to bottom, with obscene sculptures, in order to remind ordinary people of their sexuality. The spirit, he said, was a great danger, because Yama, the god of death, would instantly carry off these people (the "imperfecti") if they trod the spiritual path directly, without preparation. The erotic sculptures were meant to remind them of their *dharma* (law), which bids them fulfil their ordinary lives. Only when they have fulfilled their *dharma* can they tread the spiritual path. The obscenities were intended to arouse the erotic curiosity of visitors to the temples, so that they should not forget their *dharma;* otherwise they would not fulfil it. Only the man who was qualified by his *karma* (the fate earned through works in previous existences), and who was destined for the life of the spirit, could ignore this injunction with impunity, for to him these obscenities mean nothing. That was also why the two seductresses stood at the entrance of the temple, luring the people to fulfil their *dharma,* because only in this way could the ordinary man attain to higher spiritual development. And since the temple represented the whole world, all human activities were portrayed in it; and because most people are always thinking of sex anyway, the great majority of the temple sculptures were of an erotic nature. For this reason too, he said, the *lingam* (phallus) stands in the sacred cavity of the adyton (Holy of Holies), in the *garbha griha* (house of the womb). This pundit was a Tantrist (scholastic; *tantra* = 'book').

[132] Their prototypes are the emasculated Attis and the priests of Eleusis, who, before celebrating the *hieros gamos,* were made impotent with a draught of hemlock.

[133] Cf. Matt. 5 : 8: "Blessed are the pure in heart, for they shall see God."

8

340   Among the objective symbols of the self I have already mentioned the Naassene conception of the ἀμέριστος στιγμή, the indivisible point. This conception fully accords with that of the
"Monad" and "Son of Man" in Monoïmos. Hippolytus says:

Monoïmos . . . thinks that there is some such Man as Oceanus, of
whom the poet speaks somewhat as follows: Oceanus, the origin
of gods and of men.[134] Putting this into other words, he says that
the Man is All, the source of the universe, unbegotten, incor-
ruptible, everlasting; and that there is a Son of the aforesaid Man,
who is begotten and capable of suffering, and whose birth is outside
time, neither willed nor predetermined . . . This Man is a single
Monad, uncompounded [and] indivisible, [yet] compounded [and]
divisible; loving and at peace with all things [yet] warring with all
things and at war with itself in all things; unlike and like [itself],
as it were a musical harmony containing all things . . . showing
forth all things and giving birth to all things. It is its own mother,
its own father, the two immortal names. The emblem of the perfect Man, says Monoïmos, is the jot or tittle.[135] This one tittle is
the uncompounded, simple, unmixed Monad, having its composition from nothing whatsoever, yet composed of many forms, of
many parts. That single, indivisible jot is the many-faced, thousand-
eyed and thousand-named, the jot of the iota. This is the emblem
of that perfect and indivisible Man. . . . The Son of the Man is
the one iota, the one jot flowing from on high, full and filling all
things, containing in himself everything that is in the Man, the
Father of the Son of Man.[136]

[134] A condensation of *Iliad*, XIV, 200f. and 246: "I am going to the ends of the
fruitful earth to visit Ocean, the forbear of the gods, and Mother Tethys . . .
even Ocean Stream himself, who is the forbear of them all." (Rieu trans., pp. 262f.)
[135] The iota (τὴν μίαν κεραίαν), the smallest Greek character, corresponding to our
"dot" (which did not exist in Greek). Cf. Luke 16 : 17: "And it is easier for
heaven and earth to pass than one tittle of the law to fall." Also Matt. 5 : 18.
This may well be the origin of the iota symbolism, as Irenaeus (*Adv. haer.*, I,
3, 2) suggests.
[136] *Elenchos*, VIII, 12, 5ff. (Legge, pp. 107ff.). All this is a Gnostic paraphrase of
John 1 and at the same time a meaningful exposition of the psychological self.
The relationship of the ι to the self is the same as that of the Hebrew letter
Yod (י) to the *lapis* in the cabala. The Original Man, Adam, signifies the small
hook at the top of the letter Yod. (*Shaare Kedusha*, III, 1.)

41   This paradoxical idea of the Monad in Monoïmos describes the psychological nature of the self as conceived by a thinker of the second century under the influence of the Christian message.

42   A parallel conception is to be found in Plotinus, who lived a little later (c. 205–70). He says in the *Enneads:* "Self-knowledge reveals the fact that the soul's natural movement is not in a straight line, unless indeed it have undergone some deviation. On the contrary, it circles around something interior, around a centre. Now the centre is that from which proceeds the circle, that is, the soul. The soul will therefore move around the centre, that is, around the principle from which she proceeds; and, trending towards it, she will attach herself to it, as indeed all souls should do. The souls of the divinities ever direct themselves towards it, and that is the secret of their divinity; for divinity consists in being attached to the centre. . . . Anyone who withdraws from it is a man who has remained un-unified, or who is a brute." [137]

343   Here the point is the centre of a circle that is created, so to speak, by the circumambulation of the soul. But this point is the "centre of all things," a God-image. This is an idea that still underlies the mandala-symbols in modern dreams.[138]

344   Of equal significance is the idea, also common among the Gnostics, of the σπινθήρ or spark.[139] It corresponds to the *scintilla vitae,* the "little spark of the soul" in Meister Eckhart,[140] which we meet with rather early in the teachings of Saturninus.[141] Similarly Heraclitus, "the physicist," is said to have conceived the soul as a "spark of stellar essence." [142] Hippolytus says that in the doctrine of the Sethians the darkness held "the bright-

137 Ennead, VI, 9, 8 (Guthrie trans., p. 163, slightly mod.).
138 See "A Study in the Process of Individuation" and "Concerning Mandala Symbolism."
139 Bousset, *Hauptprobleme der Gnosis,* p. 321, says: "[The Gnostics believed] that human beings, or at any rate some human beings, carry within them from the beginning a higher element [the *spinther*] deriving from the world of light, which enables them to rise above the world of the Seven into the upper world of light, where dwell the unknown Father and the heavenly Mother."
140 Meerpohl, "Meister Eckharts Lehre vom Seelenfünklein."
141 Irenaeus, *Adv. haer.,* I, 24. The *pneumatikoi* contain a small part of the Pleroma (II, 29). Cf. the doctrine of Satorneilos in Hippolytus, *Elenchos,* VII, 28, 3 (Legge trans., II, pp. 8of.).
142 Macrobius, *Commentarium in Somnium Scipionis,* XIV, 19.

ness and the spark of light in thrall," [143] and that this "very small spark" was finely mingled in the dark waters [144] below.[145] Simon Magus [146] likewise teaches that in semen and milk there is a very small spark which "increases and becomes a power boundless and immutable." [147]

345   The symbol of the point is found also in alchemy, where it stands for the arcane substance; in Michael Maier [148] it signifies "the purity or homogeneity of the essence." It is the "punctum solis" [149] in the egg-yolk, which grows into a chick. In Khunrath it represents Sapientia in the form of the "salt-point"; [150] in Maier it symbolizes gold.[151] To the scholiast of the "Tractatus aureus" it is the midpoint, the "circulus exiguus" and "mediator" which reconciles the hostile elements and "by persistent rotation changes the angular form of the square into a circular one like itself." [152] For Dorn the "punctum vix intelligibile" is

[143] Elenchos, V, 19, 7: ῞Ινα ἔχη τὸν σπινθῆρα δουλεύοντα.
[144] This idea reappears in alchemy in numerous variations. Cf. Michael Maier, Symbola aureae mensae, p. 380, and Scrutinium chymicum, Emblema XXXI: "The King swimming in the sea, and crying with a loud voice: Whosoever shall bring me out, shall have a great reward." Also Aurora Consurgens (ed. von Franz), p. 57: "For this cause have I laboured night by night with crying, my jaws become hoarse; who is the man that liveth, knowing and understanding, delivering my soul from the hand of hell?"
[145] Elenchos, V, 21, 1: Τὸν σπινθῆρα τὸν ἐλάχιστον ἐν τοῖς σκοτεινοῖς ὕδασι κάτω καταμεμίχθαι λεπτῶς.
[146] Elenchos, VI, 17, 7. Cf. "Transformation Symbolism in the Mass," par. 359.
[147] Cf. the vision reported by Wickes, The Inner World of Man, p. 245. It is a typical piece of individuation symbolism: "Then I saw that on the shaft there hung a human figure that held within itself all the loneliness of the world and of the spaces. Alone, and hoping for nothing, the One hung and gazed down into the void. For long the One gazed, drawing all solitude unto itself. Then deep in the fathomless dark was born an infinitesimal spark. Slowly it rose from the bottomless depth, and as it rose it grew until it became a star. And the star hung in space just opposite the figure, and the white light streamed upon the Lonely One." Conversely, it is related of Zoroaster that he drew down sparks from a star, which scorched him. (Bousset, p. 146.)
[148] Maier, De circulo physico quadrato (1616), p. 27.
[149] Or punctus solis. "In the egg therefore are four things: earth, water, air, and fire; but the 'punctum solis' is apart from these four, in the midst of the yolk (which) is the chick." (Turba, Sermo IV.) Ruska (Turba philosophorum, p. 51) puts "saliens" instead of "solis" ("springing point" instead of "sun-point"), in the belief that all the copyists repeated the same error. I am not so sure of this.
[150] Von hylealischen Chaos, p. 194.   [151] De circulo quadrato, p. 27.
[152] Theatr. chem., IV, p. 691.

the starting point of creation.[153] Similarly John Dee says that all things originated from the point and the monad.[154] Indeed, God himself is simultaneously both the centre and the circumference. In Mylius the point is called the bird of Hermes.[155] In the "Novum lumen" it is spirit and fire, the life of the arcane substance, similar to the spark.[156] This conception of the point is more or less the same as that of the Gnostics.

46   From these citations we can see how Christ was assimilated to symbols that also meant the kingdom of God, for instance the grain of mustard-seed, the hidden treasure, and the pearl of great price. He and his kingdom have the same meaning. Objections have always been made to this dissolution of Christ's personality, but what has not been realized is that it represents at the same time an assimilation and integration of Christ into the human psyche.[157] The result is seen in the growth of the human personality and in the development of consciousness. These specific attainments are now gravely threatened in our antichristian age, not only by the sociopolitical delusional systems, but above all by the rationalistic hybris which is tearing our consciousness from its transcendent roots and holding before it immanent goals.

153 "Physica genesis," *Theatr. chem.*, I, p. 382.
154 *Monas hieroglyphica* (first edn., 1564). Also in *Theatr. chem.* (1602), II, p. 218.
155 *Phil. ref.*, p. 131.   156 *Mus. herm.*, p. 559.
157 Here I would like to cite a theological opinion: "Jesus is a synthesis and a growth, and the resultant form is one which tells of a hundred forces which went to its making. But the interesting thing is that the process did not end with the closing of the canon. Jesus is still in the making." Roberts, "Jesus or Christ?— A Reply," p. 124.

XIV

THE STRUCTURE AND
DYNAMICS OF THE SELF

1

347   The examples given in the previous chapter should be sufficient to describe the progressive assimilation and amplification of the archetype that underlies ego-consciousness. Rather than add to their number unnecessarily, I will try to summarize them so that an over-all picture results. From various hints dropped by Hippolytus, it is clear beyond a doubt that many of the Gnostics were nothing other than psychologists. Thus he reports them as saying that "the soul is very hard to find and to comprehend," [1] and that knowledge of the whole man is just as difficult. "For knowledge of man is the beginning of wholeness (τελείωσις), but knowledge of God is perfect wholeness (ἀπηρτισμένη τελείωσις)." Clement of Alexandria says in the *Paedagogus* (III, 1): "Therefore, as it seems, it is the greatest of all disciplines to know oneself; for when a man knows himself, he knows God." And Monoïmos, in his letter to Theophrastus, writes: "Seek him from out thyself, and learn who it is that taketh possession of everything in thee, saying: *my* god, *my* spirit, *my* understanding, *my* soul, *my* body; and learn whence is sorrow and joy, and love and hate, and waking though one would not, and sleeping though one would not, and getting angry though one would not, and falling in love though one would not. And if thou shouldst closely investigate these things, thou wilt find Him in thyself, the One and the Many, like to that little point [κεραία], for it is in thee that he hath his origin and his deliverance." [2]

348   One cannot help being reminded, in reading this text, of the Indian idea of the Self as brahman and atman, for instance in

---

[1] *Elenchos*, V, 7, 8 (Legge trans., I, p. 123).
[2] *Elenchos*, VIII, 15, 1ff. Cf. Legge trans., II, p. 10.

the Kena Upanishad: "By whom willed and directed does the mind fly forth? By whom commanded does the first breath move? Who sends forth the speech we utter here? What god is it that stirs the eye and ear? The hearing of the ear, the thinking of the mind, the speaking of the speech . . . That which speech cannot express, by which speech is expressed . . . which the mind cannot think, by which the mind thinks, know that as Brahman." [3]

349   Yajñyavalkya defines it in indirect form in the Brihadāranyaka Upanishad: "He who dwells in all beings, yet is apart from all beings, whom no beings know, whose body is all beings, who controls all beings from within, he is your Self, the inner controller, the immortal. . . . There is no other seer but he, no other hearer but he, no other perceiver but he, no other knower but he. He is your Self, the inner controller, the immortal. All else is of sorrow." [4]

350   In Monoïmos, who was called "the Arab," Indian influences are not impossible. His statement is significant because it shows that even in the second century [5] the ego was considered the exponent of an all-embracing totality, the self—a thought that by no means all psychologists are familiar with even today. These insights, in the Near East as in India, are the product of intense introspective observation that can only be psychological. *Gnosis is undoubtedly a psychological knowledge whose contents derive from the unconscious.* It reached its insights by concentrating on the "subjective factor," [6] which consists empirically in the demonstrable influence that the collective unconscious exerts on the conscious mind. This would explain the astonishing parallelism between Gnostic symbolism and the findings of the psychology of the unconscious.

351   I would like to illustrate this parallelism by summarizing the symbols previously discussed. For this purpose we must first of all review the facts that led psychologists to conjecture an archetype of wholeness, i.e., the self. These are in the first place dreams and visions; in the second place, products of active imagination in which symbols of wholeness appear. The most

---

[3] Based on Radhakrishnan, *The Principal Upanishads*, pp. 581f.
[4] Ibid., pp. 228f.
[5] Hippolytus lived c. A.D. 230. Monoïmos must therefore antedate him.
[6] *Psychological Types*, pars. 620ff.

important of these are geometrical structures containing elements of the circle and quaternity; [7] namely, circular and spherical forms on the one hand, which can be represented either purely geometrically or as objects; and, on the other hand, quadratic figures divided into four or in the form of a cross. They can also be four objects or persons related to one another in meaning or by the way they are arranged. Eight, as a multiple of four, has the same significance. A special variant of the quaternity motif is the dilemma of $3 + 1$. Twelve (3×4) seems to belong here as a solution of the dilemma and as a symbol of wholeness (zodiac, year). Three can be regarded as a relative totality, since it usually represents either a spiritual totality that is a product of thought, like the Trinity,[8] or else an instinctual, chthonic one, like the triadic nature of the gods of the underworld—the "lower triad." Psychologically, however, three—if the context indicates that it refers to the self—should be understood as a defective quaternity or as a stepping-stone towards it.[9] Empirically, a triad has a trinity opposed to it as its complement. The complement of the quaternity is unity.[10]

352 From the circle and quaternity motif is derived the symbol of the geometrically formed crystal and the wonder-working stone. From here analogy formation leads on to the city,[11] castle, church,[12] house,[13] and vessel.[14] Another variant is the wheel (*rota*). The former motif emphasizes the ego's containment in the greater dimension of the self; the latter emphasizes the rotation which also appears as a ritual circumambulation. Psychologically, it denotes concentration on and preoccupation with a centre, conceived as the centre of a circle and thus formulated as a point. This leads easily enough to a relationship to the heavenly Pole and the starry bowl of heaven rotating round it. A parallel is the horoscope as the "wheel of birth."

[7] The circle has the character of wholeness because of its "perfect" form; the quaternity, because four is the minimum number of parts into which the circle may naturally be divided.

[8] Cf. "A Psychological Approach to the Dogma of the Trinity," pars. 182ff.

[9] Cf. "Spirit in Fairytales" pars. 425f., 436ff., and "Trinity," pars. 243ff.

[10] *Five* corresponds to the indistinguishability of quaternity and unity.

[11] [*Psychology and Alchemy*, pars. 138f., fig. 31.]

[12] Church built of living stones in the *Shepherd* of Hermas. [*Psychological Types*, ch. V, 4a.]

[13] *Golden Flower* (1962 edn.), pp. 22, 36.   [14] *Psychology and Alchemy*, par. 338.

53   The image of the city, house, and vessel brings us to their content—the inhabitant of the city or house, and the water contained in the vessel. The inhabitant, in his turn, has a relationship to the quaternity, and to the fifth as the unity of the four. The water appears in modern dreams and visions as a blue expanse reflecting the sky, as a lake, as four rivers (e.g., Switzerland as the heart of Europe with the Rhine, Ticino, Rhone, and Inn, or the Garden of Eden with the Gihon, Pison, Hiddekel, and Euphrates), as healing water and consecrated water, etc. Sometimes the water is associated with fire, or even combined with it as fire-water (wine, alcohol).

54   The inhabitant of the quadratic space leads to the human figure. Apart from the geometrical and arithmetical symbols, this is the commonest symbol of the self. It is either a god or a godlike human being, a prince, a priest, a great man, an historical personality, a dearly loved father, an admired example, the successful elder brother—in short, a figure that transcends the ego personality of the dreamer. There are corresponding feminine figures in a woman's psychology.

55   Just as the circle is contrasted with the square, so the quaternity is contrasted with the $3 + 1$ motif, and the positive, beautiful, good, admirable, and lovable human figure with a daemonic, misbegotten creature who is negative, ugly, evil, despicable and an object of fear. Like all archetypes, the self has a paradoxical, antinomial character. It is male and female, old man and child, powerful and helpless, large and small. The self is a true "complexio oppositorum," [15] though this does not mean that it is anything like as contradictory in itself. It is quite possible that the seeming paradox is nothing but a reflection of the enantiodromian changes of the conscious attitude which can have a favourable or an unfavourable effect on the whole. The same is true of the unconscious in general, for its frightening figures may be called forth by the fear which the conscious mind has of the unconscious. The importance of consciousness should not be underrated; hence it is advisable to relate the contradictory manifestations of the unconscious causally to the conscious attitude, at least in some degree. But consciousness should not be overrated either, for experience provides too

[15] A definition of God in Nicholas of Cusa. Cf. "The Psychology of the Transference," par. 537.

many incontrovertible proofs of the autonomy of unconscious compensatory processes for us to seek the origin of these antinomies only in the conscious mind. Between the conscious and the unconscious there is a kind of "uncertainty relationship," because the observer is inseparable from the observed and always disturbs it by the act of observation. In other words, exact observation of the unconscious prejudices observation of the conscious and vice versa.

356   Thus the self can appear in all shapes from the highest to the lowest, inasmuch as these transcend the scope of the ego personality in the manner of a daimonion. It goes without saying that the self also has its theriomorphic symbolism. The commonest of these images in modern dreams are, in my experience, the elephant, horse, bull, bear, white and black birds, fishes, and snakes. Occasionally one comes across tortoises, snails, spiders, and beetles. The principal plant symbols are the flower and the tree. Of the inorganic products, the commonest are the mountain and lake.

357   Where there is an undervaluation of sexuality the self is symbolized as a phallus. Undervaluation can consist in an ordinary repression or in overt devaluation. In certain differentiated persons a purely biological interpretation and evaluation of sexuality can also have this effect. Any such conception overlooks the spiritual and "mystical" implications of the sexual instinct.[16] These have existed from time immemorial as psychic facts, but are devalued and repressed on rationalistic and philosophical grounds. In all such cases one can expect an unconscious phallicism by way of compensation. A good example of this is the mainly sexualistic approach to the psyche that is to be found in Freud.

2

358   Coming now to the Gnostic symbols of the self, we find that the Naassenes of Hippolytus lay most emphasis on the human images; of the geometrical and arithmetical symbols the most important are the quaternity, the ogdoad, the trinity, and unity. Here we shall give our attention mainly to the totality symbol of the quaternity, and above all to the symbol mentioned in

16 Cf. Hurwitz, "Archetypische Motive in der chassidischen Mystik," ch. VI.

section 6 of the last chapter, which I would like to call, for short, the Moses Quaternio. We shall then consider the second Naassene Quaternio, the one with the four rivers of Paradise, which I shall call the Paradise Quaternio. Though differently constituted, the two quaternios express roughly the same idea, and in what follows I shall try not only to relate them to one another psychologically, but also to bring out their connection with later (alchemical) quaternary structures. In the course of these investigations, we shall see how far the two quaternios are characteristic of the Gnostic age, and how far they can be correlated with the archetypal history of the mind in the Christian aeon.

59   The quaternity in the Moses Quaternio [17] is evidently constructed according to the following schema:

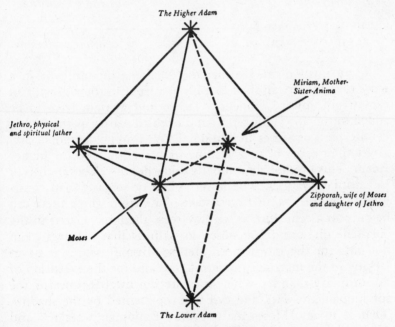

The Moses Quaternio

360   The "lower Adam" corresponds to the ordinary mortal man, Moses to the culture-hero and lawgiver, and thus, on a personalistic level, to the "father"; Zipporah, as the daughter of a king

17 *Elenchos*, V, 8, 2.

and priest, to the "higher mother." For the ordinary man, these two represent the "royal pair," [18] which for Moses corresponds on the one hand to his "higher man," and on the other hand to his anima, Miriam. The "higher" man is synonymous with the "spiritual, inner" man, who is represented in the quaternio by Jethro. Such is the meaning of the quaternio when seen from the standpoint of Moses. But since Moses is related to Jethro as the lower Adam, or ordinary man, is to Moses, the quaternio cannot be understood merely as the structure of Moses' personality, but must be looked at from the standpoint of the lower Adam as well. We then get the following quaternio:

MOSES ———————————————— ZIPPORAH
as culture-hero   *as higher mother*

THE LOWER ADAM ———————————————— EVE
as ordinary man   *as ordinary woman*

361   From this we can see that the Naassene quaternio is in a sense unsymmetrical, since it leads to a senarius (hexad) with an exclusively upward tendency: Jethro and Miriam have to be added to the above four as a kind of third storey, as the higher counterparts of Moses and Zipporah. We thus get a gradual progression, or series of steps leading from the lower to the higher Adam. This psychology evidently underlies the elaborate lists of Valentinian syzygies. The lower Adam or somatic man consequently appears as the lowest stage of all, from which there can be only an ascent. But, as we have seen, the four persons in the Naassene quaternio are chosen so skilfully that it leaves room not only for the incest motif [Jethro-Miriam], which is never lacking in the marriage quaternio, but also for the extension of the ordinary man's psychic structure downwards, towards the sub-human, the dark and evil side represented by the shadow. That is to say, Moses marries the "Ethiopian woman," and Miriam, the prophetess and mother-sister, becomes "leprous," which is clear proof that her relation to Moses has taken a negative turn. This is further confirmed by the fact that Miriam "spoke against" Moses and even stirred up his brother Aaron against him. Accordingly, we get the following senarius:

18 Cf. "The Psychology of the Transference," pars. 410ff.

THE LOWER ADAM	EVE
MOSES	ETHIOPIAN WOMAN
JETHRO, *the heathen priest*	MIRIAM, *the "white" leper*

52   Though nothing is said against Jethro, "the great wise one," in the Bible story, yet as a Midianite priest he did not serve Yahweh and did not belong to the chosen people, but departs from them to his own country.[19] He seems also to have borne the name Reguel ("friend of God") and to have helped Moses with his superior wisdom. He is, accordingly, a numinous personality, the embodiment of an archetype, obviously that of the "wise old man" who personifies the spirit in myth and folklore. The spirit, as I have shown elsewhere,[20] has a dichotomous nature. Just as Moses in this case represents his own shadow by taking to wife the black daughter of the earth, so Jethro, in his capacity as heathen priest and stranger, has to be included in the quaternio as the "lower" aspect of himself, with a magical and nefarious significance (though this is not vouched for in the text).[21]

53   As I have already explained, the Moses Quaternio is an individual variant of the common marriage quaternio found in folklore.[22] It could therefore be designated just as well with other mythical names. The basic schema of the cross-cousin marriage:

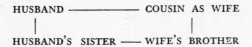

HUSBAND ——————— COUSIN AS WIFE

HUSBAND'S SISTER —— WIFE'S BROTHER

has numerous variants; for instance the sister can be replaced by the mother or the wife's brother by a fatherlike figure. But the incest motif remains a characteristic feature. Since the schema is a primary one characterizing the psychology of love relationships and also of the transference, it will, like all characterological schemata, obviously manifest itself in a "favourable" and an "unfavourable" form, for the relationships in question also exhibit the same ambivalence: everything a man does has a positive and a negative aspect.

19 Exodus 18 : 27.
20 "Phenomenology of the Spirit in Fairytales," pars. 400ff.
21 Since the whole Shadow Quaternio is a symmetrical construction, the "good Wise Man" must here be contrasted with a correspondingly dark, chthonic figure.
22 Cf. "Psychology of the Transference," pars. 425ff.

364   The reader, therefore, should not let himself be put off by the somewhat scurrilous Gnostic nomenclature. The names are accidental, whereas the schema itself is universally valid. The same is true of the "Shadow Quaternio," for which I have kept the same names because the biography of Moses offers certain features that are well suited to illustrate the shadow.

365   The lower senarius reaches its nadir not in the "lower Adam" but in his dark, theriomorphic prefiguration—the *serpent* who was created before man, or the Gnostic *Naas*. Accordingly we have the structures shown on the facing page.

366   This schema is no idle parlour game, because the texts make it abundantly clear that the Gnostics were quite familiar with the dark aspect of their metaphysical figures, so much so that they caused the greatest offence on that account. (One has only to think of the identification of the good God with Priapus,[23] or of the Anthropos with the ithyphallic Hermes.) It was, moreover, the Gnostics—e.g., Basilides—who exhaustively discussed the problem of evil (πόθεν τὸ κακόν;—'whence comes evil?'). The serpentine form of the Nous and the Agathodaimon does not mean that the serpent has only a good aspect. Just as the Apophis-serpent was the traditional enemy of the Egyptian sun-god, so the devil, "that ancient serpent,"[24] is the enemy of Christ, the "novus Sol." The good, perfect, spiritual God was opposed by an imperfect, vain, ignorant, and incompetent demiurge. There were archontic Powers that gave to mankind a corrupt "chirographum" (handwriting) from which Christ had to redeem them.[25]

367   With the dawn of the second millennium the accent shifted

---

[23] In the gnosis of Justin. See Hippolytus, *Elenchos*, V, 26, 32 (Legge trans., I, p. 178): ὁ δὲ ἀγαθός ἐστι Πρίαπος (But the Good One is Priapus).

[24] Rev. 12 : 9.

[25] Coloss. 2 : 14: "Blotting out the handwriting of the decree that was against us, which was contrary to us. And he hath taken the same out of the way, fastening it to the cross" (DV). The handwriting is imprinted on the *body*. This view is confirmed by Orosius ("Ad Aurelium Augustum commonitorium de errore Priscillianistarum et Origenistarum," p. 153), who says that in the opinion of Priscillian the soul, on descending through the spheres into birth, was caught by the powers of evil, and at the behest of the victor ("victoris principis") was cast into separate bodies, upon which a "handwriting" was written. The parts of the soul receive a divine *chirographum*, but the parts of the body are imprinted with the signs of the zodiac (*caeli signa*).

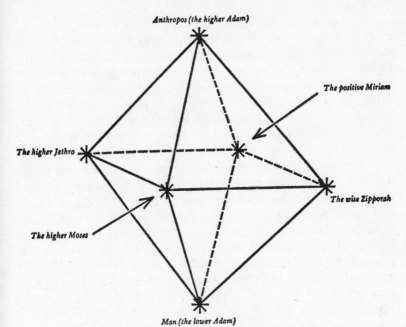

Anthropos (the higher Adam)

The positive Miriam

The higher Jethro

The wise Zipporah

The higher Moses

Man (the lower Adam)

A. The Anthropos Quaternio

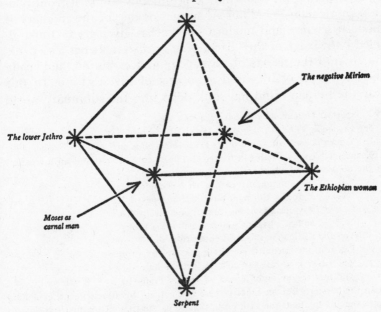

The negative Miriam

The lower Jethro

The Ethiopian woman

Moses as carnal man

Serpent

B. The Shadow Quaternio

231

more and more towards the dark side. The demiurge became the devil who had created the world, and, a little later, alchemy began to develop its conception of Mercurius as the partly material, partly immaterial spirit that penetrates and sustains all things, from stones and metals to the highest living organisms. In the form of a snake he dwells inside the earth, has a body, soul, and spirit, was believed to have a human shape as the homunculus or *homo altus,* and was regarded as the chthonic God.[26] From this we can see clearly that the serpent was either a forerunner of man or a distant copy of the Anthropos, and how justified is the equation Naas = Nous = Logos = Christ = Higher Adam. The medieval extension of this equation towards the dark side had, as I have said, already been prepared by Gnostic phallicism. This appears as early as the fifteenth century in the alchemical Codex Ashburnham 1166,[27] and in the sixteenth century Mercurius was identified with Hermes Kyllenios.[28]

3

368   It is significant that Gnostic philosophy found its continuation in alchemy.[29] "Mater Alchimia" is one of the mothers of modern science, and modern science has given us an unparalleled knowledge of the "dark" side of matter. It has also penetrated into the secrets of physiology and evolution, and made the very roots of life itself an object of investigation. In this way the human mind has sunk deep into the sublunary world

---

[26] "The Spirit Mercurius," esp. pars. 271, 282, 289.

[27] See *Psychology and Alchemy,* fig. 131.

[28] In "Chrysopoeia" (in Gratarolus, *Verae alchemiae artisque metallicae,* 1561, pp. 269ff.), which Augurellus dedicated to Pope Leo X. It contains an invocation of the *alma soror* of Phoebus:

> "Tu quoque, nec coeptis *Cylleni* audacibus usquam
> Defueris, tibi nam puro de fonte perennis
> Rivulus argentum, vulgo quod vivere dicunt,
> Sufficit, et tantis praestat primordia rebus."

(You too, Cyllenian, this bold enterprise
Fail not, the stream from whose pure spring supplies
The silver men call "quick," the primal state
And first beginning of a work so great. [Trans. by A. S. B. Glover.])

[29] In the Western Roman Empire there is a gap in this development, extending from the 3rd to about the 11th cent., that is, to the time of the first translations from the Arabic.

of matter, thus repeating the Gnostic myth of the Nous, who, beholding his reflection in the depths below, plunged down and was swallowed in the embrace of Physis. The climax of this development was marked in the eighteenth century by the French Revolution, in the nineteenth century by scientific materialism, and in the twentieth century by political and social "realism," which has turned the wheel of history back a full two thousand years and seen the recrudescence of the despotism, the lack of individual rights, the cruelty, indignity, and slavery of the pre-Christian world, whose "labour problem" was solved by the "ergastulum" (convict-camp). The "transvaluation of all values" is being enacted before our eyes.

⁹ The development briefly outlined here seems to have been anticipated in medieval and Gnostic symbolism, just as the Antichrist was in the New Testament. How this occurred I will endeavour to describe in what follows. We have seen that, as the higher Adam corresponds to the lower, so the lower Adam corresponds to the serpent. For the mentality of the Middle Ages and of late antiquity, the first of the two double pyramids, the *Anthropos Quaternio,* represents the world of the spirit, or metaphysics, while the second, the *Shadow Quaternio,* represents sublunary nature and in particular man's instinctual disposition, the "flesh"—to use a Gnostic-Christian term—which has its roots in the animal kingdom or, to be more precise, in the realm of warm-blooded animals. The nadir of this system is the cold-blooded vertebrate, the snake,[30] for with the snake the psychic rapport that can be established with practically all warm-blooded animals comes to an end. That the snake, contrary to expectation, should be a counterpart of the Anthropos is corroborated by the fact—of especial significance for the Middle Ages—that it is on the one hand a well-known allegory of Christ, and on the other hand appears to be equipped with the gift of wisdom and of supreme spirituality.[31] As Hippolytus says, the Gnostics identified the serpent with the spinal cord and the medulla. These are synonymous with the reflex functions.

⁷⁰ The second of these quaternios is the negative of the first; it is its shadow. By "shadow" I mean the inferior personality, the lowest levels of which are indistinguishable from the instinctu-

[30] Synonymous with the dragon, since *draco* also means snake.

[31] ζῷον πνευματικώτατόν, 'the most spiritual animal.'

ality of an animal. This is a view that can be found at a very early date, in the idea of the προσφύης ψυχή, the 'excrescent soul'[32] of Isidorus.[33] We also meet it in Origen, who speaks of the animals contained in man.[34] Since the shadow, in itself, is unconscious for most people, the snake would correspond to what is totally unconscious and incapable of becoming conscious, but which, as the collective unconscious and as instinct, seems to possess a peculiar wisdom of its own and a knowledge that is often felt to be supernatural. This is the treasure which the snake (or dragon) guards, and also the reason why the snake signifies evil and darkness on the one hand and wisdom on the other. Its unrelatedness, coldness, and dangerousness express the instinctuality that with ruthless cruelty rides roughshod over all moral and any other human wishes and considerations and is therefore just as terrifying and fascinating in its effects as the sudden glance of a poisonous snake.

371   In alchemy the snake is the symbol of *Mercurius non vulgi*, who was bracketed with the god of revelation, Hermes. Both have a pneumatic nature. The *serpens Mercurii* is a chthonic spirit who dwells in matter, more especially in the bit of original chaos hidden in creation, the *massa confusa* or *globosa*. The snake-symbol in alchemy points back to historically earlier images. Since the *opus* was understood by the alchemists as a recapitulation or imitation of the creation of the world, the serpent of Mercurius, that crafty and deceitful god, reminded them of the serpent in the Garden of Eden, and therefore of the devil, the tempter, who on their own admission played all sorts of tricks on them during their work. Mephistopheles, whose "aunt is the snake," is Goethe's version of the alchemical familiar, Mercurius. Like the dragon, Mercurius is the slippery, evasive, poisonous, dangerous forerunner of the hermaphrodite, and for that reason he has to be overcome.

372   For the Naassenes Paradise was a quaternity parallel with

[32] In Valentinus the "appendages" are spirits indwelling in man. Clement of Alexandria, *Stromata*, II, 20, 112 and 114 (trans. Wilson, II, pp. 64f.).

[33] Isidorus was the son of Basilides. See Clement of Alexandria, ibid., II, 20, 113 (Wilson, II, p. 65). The "outgrowths" are animal souls, as of wolves, monkeys, lions, etc.

[34] *In Levit. hom.* V, 2 (Migne, *P.G.*, vol. 12, col. 450): "So when thou seest that thou hast all the things the world has, doubt not that thou hast within thee even the animals which are offered in sacrifice."

the Moses quaternio and of similar meaning. Its fourfold nature consisted in the four rivers, Pison, Gihon, Hiddekel, and Phrat.[85] The serpent in Genesis is an illustration of the personified tree-numen; hence it is traditionally represented in or coiled round the tree. It is the tree's voice, which persuades Eve—in Luther's version—that "it would be good to eat of the tree, and pleasant to behold that it is a lusty tree." In the fairytale of "The Spirit in the Bottle," Mercurius can likewise be interpreted as a tree-numen.[36] In the Ripley "Scrowle" Mercurius appears as a snake in the shape of a Melusina descending from the top of the Philosophical Tree ("tree of knowledge").[37] The tree stands for the development and phases of the transformation process,[38] and its fruits or flowers signify the consummation of the work.[39] In the fairytale Mercurius is hidden in the roots of a great oak-tree, i.e., in the earth. For it is in the interior of the earth that the Mercurial serpent dwells.

For the alchemists Paradise was a favourite symbol of the *albedo*,[40] the regained state of innocence, and the source of its rivers is a symbol of the *aqua permanens*.[41] For the Church Fathers Christ is this source,[42] and Paradise means the ground of the soul from which the fourfold river of the Logos bubbles forth.[43] We find the same symbol in the alchemist and mystic John Pordage: divine Wisdom is a "New Earth, the heavenly Land. . . . For from this Earth grew all the Trees of Life. . . . Thus did Paradise . . . rise up from the Heart and Centre of this New Earth, and thus did the lost Garden of Eden flourish in greenness." [44]

---

85 Euphrates.   36 "The Spirit Mercurius," Part I.

87 See *Psychology and Alchemy*, fig. 257.   38 Ibid., par. 357.

89 Ibid., fig. 122, and "The Philosophical Tree," pars. 402ff.

40 Ripley, *Cantilena*, verse 28 [cf. *Mysterium Coniunctionis*, p. 317], and *Chymische Schrifften*, p. 51; also Mylius, *Phil. ref.*, p. 124.

41 "A land to be watered with the clear water of paradise" (Hollandus, "Fragmentum de lapide," *Theatr. chem.*, II, p. 142). The "Tractatus Aristotelis ad Alexandrum Magnum (conscriptus et collectus a quodam Christiano Philosopho)," *Theatr. chem.*, V, p. 885, compares the "practica Aristotelis" with the water of paradise, which makes man "whole" (*incolumem*) and immortal: "From this water all true Philosophers have had life and infinite riches."

42 Didymus of Alexandria, *De trinitate* (Migne, *P.G.*, vol. 39, col. 456).

43 St Ambrose, *Explanationes in Psalmos*, Ps. 45, 12 (*Corp. Script. Eccl. Lat.*, LXIV, p. 337). Cf. Rahner, "Flumina de ventre Christi," pp. 269ff.

44 *Sophia* (1699), p. 9.

4

374   The snake symbol brings us to the images of Paradise, tree, and earth. This amounts to an evolutionary regression from the animal kingdom back to plants and inorganic nature, epitomized in alchemy by the secret of matter, the *lapis*. Here the *lapis* is not to be understood as the end product of the *opus* but rather as its initial material. This arcane substance was also called *lapis* by the alchemists. The symbolism here described can be represented diagrammatically as another quaternio or double pyramid:

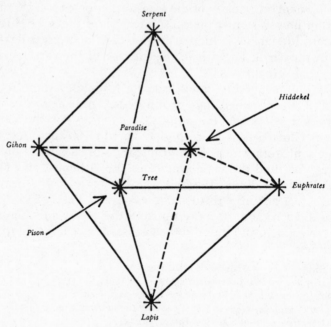

C. The Paradise Quaternio

375   The *lapis* was thought of as a unity and therefore often stands for the *prima materia* in general. But just as the latter is a bit of the original chaos which was believed to be hidden somewhere in metals, particularly in mercury, or in other substances, and is not in itself a simple thing (as the name "massa confusa" shows), so too the *lapis* consists of the four elements or

has to be put together from them.[45] In the chaos the elements are not united, they are merely coexistent and have to be combined through the alchemical procedure. They are even hostile to one another and will not unite of their own accord. They represent, therefore, an original state of conflict and mutual repulsion. This image serves to illustrate the splitting up or unfolding of the original unity into the multiplicity of the visible world. Out of the split-up quaternity the *opus* puts together the unity of the *lapis* in the realm of the inorganic. As the *filius macrocosmi* and a living being, the *lapis* is not just an allegory but is a direct parallel of Christ [46] and the higher Adam, of the heavenly Original Man, of the second Adam (Christ), and of the serpent. The nadir of this third quaternio is therefore a further counterpart of the Anthropos.

6   As already mentioned, the constitution of the *lapis* rests on the union of the four elements,[47] which in their turn represent an unfolding of the unknowable inchoate state, or chaos. This is the *prima materia,* the arcanum, the primary substance, which in Paracelsus and his followers is called the *increatum* and is regarded as coeternal with God—a correct interpretation of the Tehom in Genesis 1 : 2: "And the [uncreated] earth was without form and void, and darkness was upon the face of the deep; and the Spirit of God [brooded] over the face of the waters." This primary substance is round (*massa globosa, rotundum, στοιχεῖον στρογγύλον*), like the world and the world-soul; it is in fact the world-soul and the world-substance in one. It is the "stone that has a spirit," [48] in modern parlance the most elementary building-stone in the architecture of matter, the atom, which is an intellectual model. The alchemists describe the

45 The *lapis* is made of the four elements, like Adam. The centre of the squared circle is the "mediator, making peace between the enemies or elements, so that they may love one another in a meet embrace" ("Tractatus aureus," *Theatr. chem.,* IV, p. 691).

46 Cf. the evidence for this in *Psychology and Alchemy,* "The Lapis-Christ Parallel."

47 Mylius (*Phil. ref.,* p. 15) identifies the elements that constitute the *lapis* with *corpus, spiritus,* and *anima: corpus* is matter, earth, and *spiritus* is the *nodus* (bond) *animae et corporis,* and therefore corresponds to fire. Water and air, which would properly characterize the *anima,* are also "spirit." Three of the elements are "moving," one (earth) "unmoving." Cf. n. 89, infra.

48 Quotation from Ostanes in Zosimos, "Sur l'art" (Berthelot, *Alch. grecs,* III, vi, 5).

"round element" now as primal water, now as primal fire, or as pneuma, primal earth, or "corpusculum nostrae sapientiae," the little body of our wisdom.[49] As water or fire it is the universal solvent; as stone and metal it is something that has to be dissolved and changed into air (pneuma, spirit).

377   This *lapis* symbolism can once more be visualized diagrammatically as a double pyramid:

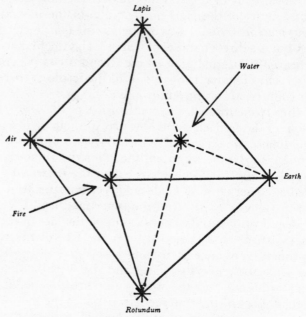

D. The Lapis Quaternio

Zosimos calls the *rotundum* the omega element (Ω), which probably signifies the head.[50] The skull is mentioned as the vessel of transformation in the Sabaean treatise "Platonis liber quartorum," [51] and the "Philosophers" styled themselves "children of the golden head," [52] which is probably synonymous with "filii sapientiae." The *vas* is often synonymous with the *lapis*, so that there is no difference between the vessel and its content;

[49] "Aurora consurgens," *Art. aurif.*, I, p. 208.
[50] Cf. my remarks on the significance of the head in "Transformation Symbolism in the Mass," pars. 365ff. "Head" also means "beginning," e.g., "head of the Nile," etc.   [51] *Theatr. chem.*, V, p. 151.   [52] Berthelot, III, x, 1.

in other words, it is the same arcanum.[53] According to the old view the soul is round [54] and the vessel must be round too, like the heavens or the world.[55] The form of the Original Man is round. Accordingly Dorn says that the vessel "should be made from a kind of squaring of the circle, so that the spirit and the soul of our material, separated from its body, may raise the body with them to the height of their own heaven." [56] The anonymous author of the scholia to the "Tractatus aureus" also writes about the squaring of the circle and shows a square whose corners are formed by the four elements. In the centre there is a small circle. The author says: "Reduce your stone to the four elements, rectify and combine them into one, and you will have the whole magistery. This One, to which the elements must be reduced, is that little circle in the centre of this squared figure. It is the mediator, making peace between the enemies or elements." [57] In a later chapter he depicts the vessel, "the true philosophical Pelican," [58] as shown on the next page.[59]

---

53 "There is one stone, one medicine, one vessel, one method, one disposition" (*Rosarium philosophorum*, *Art. aurif.*, II, 206). "In our water all modes of things are brought about. . . . In the said water they are made as in an artificial vessel, which is a mighty secret" (Mylius, *Phil. ref.*, p. 245). "The Philosophical vessel is their water" (ibid., p. 33). This saying comes from de Hoghelande's treatise in *Theatr. chem.*, I, p. 199. There we find: "Sulphur also is called by Lully the vessel of Nature," and Haly's description of the vessel as "ovum." The egg is content and container at once. The *vas naturale* is the *aqua permanens* and the "vinegar" of the Philosophers. ("Aurora consurgens," Part II, *Art. aurif.*, I, p. 203.)

54 Caesarius of Heisterbach, *Dialogue on Miracles,* trans. Scott and Bland, Dist. I, chs. XXXII and XXXIV.

55 In Olympiodorus the transforming vessel is the "spherical phial" or ὄργανον κυκλικόν (circular apparatus). (Berthelot, II, iv, 44.) "The spagiric vessel is to be made after the likeness of the natural vessel. For we see that all heaven and the elements have the likeness of a spherical body" (Dorn, *Theatr. chem.*, I, p. 430). "The end of all this master-work is, that the Philosophic Mercury be placed in the heavenly sphere" (ibid, p. 499). Trevisanus calls the vessel the *rotundum cubile,* "round bridal bed" ("Liber de alchemia," *Theatr. chem.*, I, p. 790).

56 "Congeries," *Theatr. chem.*, I, pp. 574f.   57 Ibid., IV, p. 691.

58 "Nor is any other to be sought after in all the world." The Pelican is a distilling vessel, but the distillate, instead of dripping into the receiver, runs back into the belly of the retort. We could take this as illustrating the process of conscious realization and the reapplication of conscious insights to the unconscious. "It restored their former security of life to those once near to death," the author says of the Pelican, which, as we know, is an allegory of Christ.

59 Cf. *Psychology and Alchemy*, par. 167, n. 44. [Also "Paracelsus as a Spiritual Phenomenon," fig. B7.]

378   He comments: "A is the inside, as it were the origin and source from which the other letters flow, and likewise the final goal to which all the others flow back, as rivers flow into the ocean or into the great sea." This explanation is enough to show that the vessel is nothing else but a mandala, symbolizing the self or the higher Adam with his four emanations (like Horus with his four sons). The author calls it the "Septenarius magicus occultus" (the hidden magic number, seven).[60] Likewise Maria

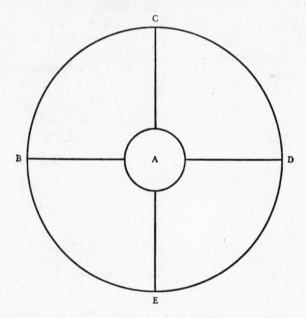

the Prophetess says: "The Philosophers teach everything except the Hermetic vessel, because that is divine and is hidden from the Gentiles by the Lord's wisdom; and they who know it not, know not the true method, because of their ignorance of the vessel of Hermes." Theobald de Hoghelande adds: "Senior says that the vision thereof is more to be sought after than [knowledge of] the Scriptures." Maria the Prophetess says: "This is the vessel of Hermes, which the Stoics hid, and it is no nigromantic vessel, but is the measure of thy fire [*mensura ignis tui*]."[61]

60 That is, counting the letters *F* and *G* (not included in the diagram), which signify Above and Below.

61 *Art. aurif.*, I, p. 324; *Theatr. chem.*, I, p. 199; *Art. aurif.*, I, p. 323.

79   It is clear from these quotations that the vessel had a great and unusual significance.[62] Philalethes, summing up the innumerable synonyms for Mercurius, says that Mercurius is not only the key to the alchemical art, and "that two-edged sword in the hand of the cherub who guards the way to the tree of life," but also "our true, hidden vessel, the Philosophic garden, wherein our Sun rises and sets." [63] This helps us to understand, more or less, the strange advice given by Johannes de Rupescissa: "Have a vessel made after the manner of a cherub, which is the figure of God, and have six wings, after the fashion of six arms, turning back on themselves; and above, a round head . . . and put within this vessel the said burning water," etc.[64] The definition of the cherub as "the figure of God" suggests that Rupescissa is referring here to the vision of Ezekiel, which was arranged in such a way that a horizontal section through it would produce a mandala divided into four parts. This, as I have already mentioned, is equivalent to the squaring of the circle, from which, according to one alchemical recipe, the vessel should be constructed. The mandala signifies the human or divine self, the totality or vision of God, as in this case is quite clear. Naturally a recipe of this sort can only be understood "philosophically," that is psychologically. It then reads: make the Hermetic vessel out of your psychic wholeness and pour into it the *aqua permanens,* or *aqua doctrinae,* one of whose synonyms is the *vinum ardens* (cf. Rupescissa's "burning water"). This would be a hint that the adept should "inwardly digest" and transform himself through the alchemical doctrine.

80   In this connection we can also understand what the *Aurora consurgens* (Part II) means when it speaks of the *vas naturale* as the *matrix:* it is the "One in which there are three things, namely water, air, and fire. They are three glass alembics, in which the son of the Philosophers is begotten. Therefore they have named it tincture, blood, and egg." [65] The three alembics are an allusion to the Trinity. That this is in fact so can be seen from the illustration on page 249 of the 1588 edition of *Pandora,* where, beside the three alembics immersed in a great cooking-pot, there stands the figure of Christ, with blood pouring from

62 Cf. *Psychology and Alchemy,* par. 338.   63 *Mus. herm.,* p. 770.
64 *La Vertu et la propriété de la quinte essence* (1581), p. 26.
65 *Art. aurif.,* I, p. 203.

the lance wound in his breast ("flumina de ventre Christi"!).[66]
The round Hermetic vessel in which the mysterious transformation is accomplished is God himself, the (Platonic) world-soul and man's own wholeness. It is, therefore, another counterpart of the Anthropos, and at the same time the universe in its smallest and most material form. So it is easy to see why the first attempts to construct a model of the atom took the planetary system as a prototype.

5

381   The quaternity is an organizing schema par excellence, something like the crossed threads in a telescope. It is a system of co-ordinates that is used almost instinctively for dividing up and arranging a chaotic multiplicity, as when we divide up the visible surface of the earth, the course of the year, or a collection of individuals into groups,[67] the phases of the moon, the temperaments, elements, alchemical colours, and so on. Thus, when we come upon a quaternio among the Gnostics, we find in it an attempt, more or less conscious, to organize the chaotic medley of numinous images that poured in upon them. As we have seen, the arrangement took a form that derives from the primitive cross-cousin marriage, namely the marriage quaternio.[68] This differs from the primitive form in that the sister-exchange marriage has sloughed off its biological character, the sister's husband no longer being the wife's brother but another close relative (such as the wife's father in the Moses Quaternio), or even a stranger. The loss of the cousin- and brother-attribute is compensated as a rule by magical qualities, such as more exalted rank, magical powers, and the like, both in the case of the husband's sister and the wife's brother. That is to say, an anima-animus projection takes place. This modification brings with it a great cultural advance, for the very fact of projection points to a constellation of the unconscious in the husband-wife relationship, which means that the marriage has become *psychologically* complicated. It is no longer a state of mere bio-

66 "Paracelsus as a Spiritual Phenomenon," fig. B4.
67 Marriage classes and settlements.
68 "Psychology of the Transference," pars. 433ff. [Cf. Layard, *Stone Men of Malekula*, chs. 5 and 6, and "The Incest Taboo and the Virgin Archetype," pp. 266ff.—EDITORS.]

logical and social coexistence, but is beginning to turn into a conscious relationship. This happens when the original cross-cousin marriage becomes obsolete as a result of the further differentiation of marriage classes into a six-, eight-, or twelve-class system. The cause of the activation of the unconscious that goes hand in hand with this development is the regression of the endogamous tendency—the "kinship libido"—which can no longer find adequate satisfaction owing to the increasing strangeness of the marriage partner.[69]

82   Besides the marriage quaternio, the Gnostics also used the quaternity of the rivers of Paradise as a means of organizing their numerous symbols. There are thus two (compensatory) attempts, in the symbols we have listed, to organize the apparently disconnected images. This accords with our experience of the series of pictures produced during active imagination and in chaotic psychic states. In both cases quaternity symbols appear from time to time.[70] They signify stabilization through order as opposed to the instability caused by chaos, and have a compensatory meaning.

83   The four quaternios depicted above are first and foremost an attempt to arrange systematically the almost limitless wealth of symbols in Gnosticism and its continuation, alchemy. But such an arrangement of principles also proves useful for understanding the individual symbolism of modern dreams. The images we encounter in this field are even more varied, and so confusing in their complexity that some kind of organizing schema is absolutely essential. As it is advisable to proceed historically, I have taken the Moses Quaternio as a starting point, because it derives directly from the primitive schema of the cross-cousin marriage. Naturally this quaternio has only a paradigmatic significance. One could base the system just as easily on any other marriage quaternio, but not on any other quaternity, such as, for instance, Horus and his four sons. This quaternity is not aboriginal enough, for it misses out the antagonistic, feminine element.[71]

69 "Psychology of the Transference," par. 438.

70 Case material in *Psychology and Alchemy*, part II. Triadic symbols also occur, but they are rarer.

71 The Gnostic quaternio is naturally later than the Horus quaternity in point of time, but psychologically it is older, because in it the feminine element reassumes its rightful place, as is not the case with the patriarchal Horus quaternio.

It is most important that just the extreme opposites, masculine-feminine and so on, should appear linked together. That is why the alchemical pairs of opposites are linked together in quaternities, e.g., warm-cold, dry-moist. Applied to the Moses Quaternio, the following schema of relationships would result:

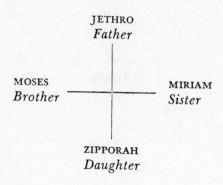

JETHRO
Father

MOSES   MIRIAM
Brother   *Sister*

ZIPPORAH
Daughter

384 Whereas the first double pyramid, the Anthropos Quaternio, corresponds to the Gnostic model, the second one is a construction derived psychologically from the first, but based on the data contained in the Biblical text used by the Gnostics. The psychological reasons for constructing a second quaternio have already been discussed. That the second must be the "shadow" of the first is due to the fact that the lower Adam, the mortal man, possesses a chthonic psyche and is therefore not adequately expressed by a quaternity supraordinate to him. If he were, he would be an unsymmetrical figure, just as the higher Adam is unsymmetrical and has to be complemented by a subordinate quaternity related to him like his shadow or his darker reflection.

385 Now just as the Anthropos Quaternio finds its symmetrical complement in the lower Adam, so the lower Adam is balanced by the subordinate Shadow Quaternio, constructed after the pattern of the upper one. The symmetrical complement of the lower Adam is the *serpent*. The choice of this symbol is justified firstly by the well-known association of Adam with the snake: it is his chthonic daemon, his familiar spirit. Secondly, the snake is the commonest symbol for the dark, chthonic world of instinct. It may—as frequently happens—be replaced by an equivalent cold-blooded animal, such as a dragon, crocodile, or fish.

But the snake is not just a nefarious, chthonic being; it is also, as we have already mentioned, a symbol of wisdom, and hence of light, goodness, and healing.[72] Even in the New Testament it is simultaneously an allegory of Christ and of the devil, just as we have seen that the fish was. Similarly the dragon, which for us has only a negative meaning, has a positive significance in China, and sometimes in Western alchemy too. The inner polarity of the snake-symbol far exceeds that of man. It is overt, whereas man's is partly latent or potential. The serpent surpasses Adam in cleverness and knowledge and can outwit him. She is older than he, and is evidently equipped by God with a superhuman intelligence, like that son of God who took over the role of Satan.[73]

86   Just as man culminates above in the idea of a "light" and good God, so he rests below on a dark and evil principle, traditionally described as the devil or as the serpent that personifies Adam's disobedience. And just as we symmetrized man by the serpent, so the serpent has its complement in the second Naassene quaternio, or Paradise Quaternio. Paradise takes us into the world of plants and animals. It is, in fact, a plantation or garden enlivened by animals, the epitome of all the growing things that sprout out of the earth. As *serpens mercurialis,* the snake is not only related to the god of revelation, Hermes, but, as a vegetation numen, calls forth the "blessed greenness," all the budding and blossoming of plant life.[74] Indeed, this serpent actually dwells in the interior of the earth and is the pneuma that lies hidden in the *stone.*[75]

87   The symmetrical complement of the serpent, then, is the *stone* as representative of the earth. Here we enter a later developmental stage of the symbolism, the alchemical stage, whose central idea is the *lapis.* Just as the serpent forms the lower opposite of man, so the *lapis* complements the serpent. It corresponds, on the other hand, to man, for it is not only represented

---

[72] Like, for instance, the Aesculapian and Agathodaimon serpent.

[73] Schärf, "Die Gestalt des Satans im Alten Testament," p. 151.

[74] "O blessed greenness, which givest birth to all things, whence know that no vegetable and no fruit appears in the bud but that it hath a green colour. Likewise know that the generation of this thing is green, for which reason the Philosophers have called it a bud." (*Ros. phil., Art. aurif.,* II, p. 220.)

[75] Cf. the Ostanes quotation in Zosimos, *Psychology and Alchemy,* par. 405.

in human form but even has "body, soul, and spirit," is an homunculus and, as the texts show, a symbol of the self. It is, however, not a human ego but a collective entity, a collective soul, like the Indian *hiranyagarbha,* 'golden seed.' The stone is the "father-mother" of the metals, an hermaphrodite. Though it is an ultimate unity, it is not an elementary but a composite unity that has evolved. For the stone we could substitute all those "thousand names" which the alchemists devised for their central symbol, but nothing different or more fitting would have been said.

388   This choice of symbol, too, is not arbitrary, but is documented by alchemical literature from the first to the eighteenth century. The *lapis* is produced, as we have already seen, from the splitting and putting together of the four elements, from the *rotundum.* The *rotundum* is a highly abstract, transcendent idea, which by reason of its roundness [76] and wholeness refers to the Original Man, the Anthropos.

389   Accordingly our four double pyramids would arrange themselves in a *circle* and form the well-known *uroboros.* As the fifth stage, the *rotundum* would then be identical with the first; that is to say, the heavy darkness of the earth, *metal,* has a secret relationship to the Anthropos. That is obvious in alchemy, but occurs also in the history of religion, where the metals grow from Gayomart's blood.[77] This curious relationship is explained by the identity of the lowest, most material thing with the highest and most spiritual, which we have already met in the interpretation of the serpent as a chthonic and at the same time the "most spiritual" animal. In Plato the *rotundum* is the world-soul and a "blessed God."[78]

---

[76] A hint that rotation may be a principle of matter.

[77] According to the report of the Damdad-Nashk (Reitzenstein and Schäder, *Studien zum antiken Syncretismus aus Iran und Griechenland,* p. 18). Gayomart is the Original Man in the theosophical version of Zarathustra's system. Yima, on the other hand, is the Original Man of ancient Aryan legend. His name is *Yimô kshaêtô,* 'the shining Yima.' According to the Mainyo-i-Khard, the metals were created from his body. (Kohut, "Die talmudisch-midraschische Adamssage," pp. 68, 70.) In the *Bundahish,* Gayomart's body consisted of metals. (Christensen, "Le Premier Homme et le premier roi dans l'histoire légendaire des Iraniens," p. 21.)

[78] [Cf. "A Psychological Approach to the Dogma of the Trinity," par. 185.— Editors.]

6

390   We shall now try to condense the argument of the previous chapter and represent it graphically. Vertically arranged, our schema looks like this:

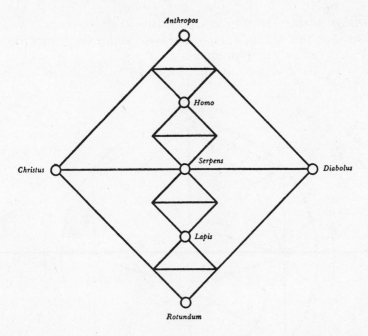

In the diagram I have emphasized the point of greatest tension between the opposites, namely the double significance of the serpent, which occupies the centre of the system. Being an allegory of Christ as well as of the devil, it contains and symbolizes the strongest polarity into which the Anthropos falls when he descends into Physis. The ordinary man has not reached this point of tension: he has it merely in the unconscious, i.e., in the serpent.[79] In the *lapis,* the counterpart of man,

---

[79] Most people do not have sufficient range of consciousness to become aware of the opposites inherent in human nature. The tensions they generate remain for the most part unconscious, but can appear in dreams. Traditionally, the snake stands for the vulnerable spot in man: it personifies his shadow, i.e., his weakness and unconsciousness. The greatest danger about unconsciousness is proneness to suggestion. The effect of suggestion is due to the release of an unconscious

the opposites are so to speak united, but with a visible seam or suture as in the symbol of the hermaphrodite. This mars the idea of the *lapis* just as much as the all-too-human element mars *Homo sapiens*. In the higher Adam and in the *rotundum* the opposition is invisible. But presumably the one stands in absolute opposition to the other, and if both are identical as indistinguishable transcendental entities, this is one of those paradoxes that are the rule: a statement about something metaphysical can only be antinomial.

391   The arrangement in the uroboros gives the following picture:

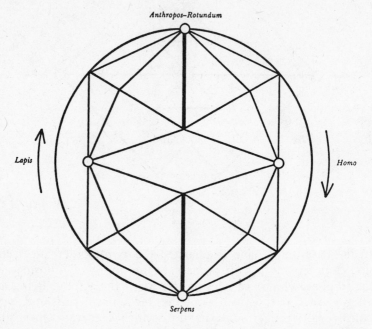

This arrangement shows the stronger tension between *anthropos-rotundum* and *serpens* on the one hand, and the lesser

dynamic, and the more unconscious this is, the more effective it will be. Hence the ever-widening split between conscious and unconscious increases the danger of psychic infection and mass psychosis. With the loss of symbolic ideas the bridge to the unconscious has broken down. Instinct no longer affords protection against unsound ideas and empty slogans. Rationality without tradition and without a basis in instinct is proof against no absurdity.

tension between *homo* and *lapis* on the other, expressed by the distance of the points in question from one another. The arrows indicate the descent into Physis and the ascent towards the spiritual. The lowest point is the serpent. The *lapis,* however, though of decidedly material nature, is also a spiritual symbol, while the *rotundum* connotes a transcendent entity symbolized by the secret of matter and thus comparable to the concept of the atom. The antinomial development of the concepts is in keeping with the paradoxical nature of alchemy.

The *lapis* quaternity, which is a product of alchemical gnosis, brings us to the interesting physical speculations of alchemy. In the *Scrutinium chymicum* (1687) of Michael Maier (1568–1622), there is a picture [30] of the four elements as four different stages of fire (Plate I).

As the picture shows, the four spheres are filled with fire. The author comments with the following verses:

> Naturae qui imitaris opus, tibi quattuor orbes
> Quaerendi, interius quos levis ignis agat.
> Imus Vulcanum referat, bene monstret at alter
> Mercurium, Lunam tertius orbis habet:
> Quartus, Apollo, tuus, naturae auditur et ignis,
> Ducat in arte manus illa catena tuas.

From this we learn that the lowest sphere corresponds to Vulcan, the earthly (?) fire; the second to Mercurius, the vegetative life-spirit; the third to the moon, the female, psychic principle; and the fourth to the sun, the male, spiritual principle. It is evident from Maier's commentary that he is concerned on the one hand with the four *elements* and on the other with the four kinds of *fire* which are responsible for producing different states of aggregation. His *ignis elementalis re et nomine* would, according to its place in the sequence, correspond to Vulcan; the fire of Mercurius to air; the third fire to water and the moon; and the fourth, which would correspond to the sun, he calls "terreus" (earthly). According to Ripley, whom Maier quotes, the *ignis elementalis* is the fire "which lights wood"; it must therefore be the ordinary fire. The sun-fire, on the other hand, seems to be the fire in the earth, which today we would

[80] Emblema XVII, p. 49.

call "volcanic," and corresponds to the solid state of aggregation ("terreus"). We thus get the following series:

VIGENÈRE SERIES[81]	RIPLEY SERIES	
ignis mundi intelligibilis	= *ignis naturalis*[82]	=
ignis caelestis	= *ignis innaturalis*[83]	=
ignis elementaris	= *ignis contra naturam*[84]	=
ignis infernalis[81]	= *ignis elementalis*	=

	MAIER SERIES		
ignis terreus	= *Sulfura et Mercurii*	= Sun (Apollo)	= earth
ignis aqueus	= *aquae*	= Moon (Luna)	= water
ignis aerius	= *dracones*	= Mercurius	= air
ignis elementalis	= *ignis elementalis re et nomine*	= Ordinary fire (Vulcan)	= fire

STATES OF AGGREGATION
= *solid*
= *liquid*
= *gas*
= *flame*

394   The remarkable thing about this paralleling of states of aggregation with different kinds of fire is that it amounts to a kind of *phlogiston theory*—not, of course, explicit, but clearly hinted at: fire is peculiar to all the states of aggregation and is therefore responsible for their constitution. This idea is old [85] and can be found as early as the *Turba,* where Dardaris says: "The sulphurs are four souls [*animae*] which were hidden in the four elements." [86] Here the active principle (*anima*) is not fire, but sulphur. The idea, however, is the same, namely that the elements or states of aggregation can be reduced to a common denominator. Today we know that the factor common to antagonistic elements is *molecular movement,* and that the states

---

[81] Vigenère comments: "The intelligible fire of the world: is all light. The heavenly fire: partakes of heat and light. The elemental fire: less in light, heat, and glow. The infernal fire: opposed to the intelligible, of heat and burning without any light." ("De igne et sale," *Theatr. chem.,* VI, p. 39.) [Cf. supra, par. 203.]
[82] "Is present in everything."   [83] "The heat of ashes and baths."
[84] "Tortures bodies, is the dragon."   [85] The oldest source is Heraclitus.
[86] *Turba,* ed. by Ruska, Sermo XLIII, p. 149.

I. The Four Elements

From Michael Maier, *Scrutinium chymicum* (1687)

of aggregation correspond to different degrees of this movement. Molecular movement in its turn corresponds to a certain quantum of energy, so that the common denominator of the elements is energy. One of the stepping-stones to the modern concept of energy is Stahl's phlogiston theory,[87] which is based on the alchemical premises discussed above. We can see in them, therefore, the earliest beginnings of a theory of energy.[88]

395   The phlogiston theory adumbrated by the alchemists did not get as far as that, but it points unmistakably in that direction. Moreover, all the mathematical and physical elements from which a theory of energy could have been constructed were known in the seventeenth century. Energy is an abstract concept which is indispensable for exact description of the behaviour of bodies in motion. In the same way bodies in motion can only be apprehended with the help of the system of space-time co-ordinates. Wherever movement is established, it is done by means of the space-time quaternio, which can be expressed either by the axiom of Maria, $3 + 1$, or by the sesquitertian proportion, $3 : 4$. This quaternio could therefore replace that of the four elements, where the unit that corresponds to the time-co-ordinate, or the fourth in the alchemical series of elements, is characterized by the fact that *one* element has an exceptional position, like fire or earth.[89]

396   The exceptional position of one of the factors in a quaternity can also be expressed by its *duplex nature*. For instance, the fourth of the rivers of Paradise, the Euphrates, signifies the mouth through which food goes in and prayers go out, as well as the Logos. In the Moses Quaternio, the wife of Moses plays the double role of Zipporah and of the Ethiopian woman. If we construct a quaternity from the divine equivalents of Maier's

---

[87] G. E. Stahl (1660–1734) supposed that all combustible (i.e., oxidizable) substances contain an igneous principle. It was assumed to be weightless, or even to possess a negative weight. Cf. H. E. Fierz-David, *Die Entwicklungsgeschichte der Chemie*, pp. 148f.

[88] Psychologically, of course, the primitive idea of mana is very much older, but here we are talking of *scientific* concepts. The *sulphur = anima* equation still contains a trace of the original mana theory. Earlier, mana was characteristically misunderstood as *animism*.

[89] Fire as spiritual, the other elements material; earth unmoving, the others moving.

four elements—Apollo, Luna, Mercurius, Vulcan—we get a marriage quaternio with a brother-sister relationship:

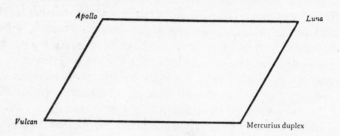

In alchemy Mercurius is male-female and frequently appears as a virgin too. This characteristic (3 + 1, or 3 : 4) is also apparent in the space-time quaternio:

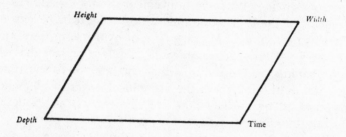

397   If we look at this quaternio from the standpoint of the three-dimensionality of space, then time can be conceived as a fourth dimension. But if we look at it in terms of the three qualities of time—past, present, future—then static space, in which changes of state occur, must be added as a fourth term. In both cases, the fourth represents an incommensurable Other that is needed for their mutual determination. Thus we measure space by time and time by space. The Other, the fourth, corresponds in the Gnostic quaternities to the fiery god, "the fourth by number," to the dual wife of Moses (Zipporah and the Ethiopian woman), to the dual Euphrates (river and Logos), to the fire [90] in the alchemical quaternio of elements, to Mercurius duplex in Maier's quaternio of gods, and in the "Christian

[90] Böhme calls the "fire of Nature" the "fourth form." "Tabula principiorum," *De signatura rerum* (1682), p. 279.

Quaternity"—if such an expression be permitted [91]—to Mary or the devil. These two incompatible figures are united in the Mercurius duplex of alchemy.[92]

98   The space-time quaternio is the archetypal *sine qua non* for any apprehension of the physical world—indeed, the very possibility of apprehending it. It is the organizing schema par excellence among the psychic quaternities. In its structure it corresponds to the psychological schema of the functions.[93] The 3 : 1 proportion frequently occurs in dreams and in spontaneous mandala-drawings.

99   A modern parallel to the diagram of quaternities arranged on top of one another (cf. par. 390), coupled with the idea of ascent and descent, can be found among the illustrations to my paper on mandala pictures.[94] The same idea also appears in the pictures relating to a case described there at some length, and dealing with vibrations that formed "nodes." [95] Each of these nodes signified an outstanding personality, as was true also of the picture in the first case. A similar motif may well underlie the representation of the Trinity here appended (Plate II), from the manuscript of a treatise by Joachim of Flora.[96]

[91] The doctrine of Sabellius (beginning of the 2nd cent.) concerning the preworldly Monad, the "silent and unacting God" and its three *prosopa* (modes of manifestation), calls for further investigation, as it bequeathed to posterity the first beginnings of a quaternary view of the Deity. Thus Joachim of Flora makes the following accusation against Peter Lombard: "Quod in suis dixit Sententiis, quoniam quaedam summa res est Pater et Filius et Spiritus Sanctus et illa non est generans, neque genita, neque procedens: unde asserit quod ille non tam Trinitatem, quam *quaternitatem* astruebat in Deo, videlicet tres personas, et illam communem essentiam quasi quartam." (As he [Peter] says in his Book of Sentences, For a certain supreme Something is Father, Son, and Holy Ghost, and It neither begets, nor is begotten, nor proceeds. On this basis Joachim asserts that the Lombard ascribed not Trinity, but Quaternity to God, that is to say, three Persons, and that common Something as a fourth). (Fourth Lateran Council, 1215. Decrees, Cap. 2; Denzinger and Bannwart, *Enchiridion*, p. 190.) Cf. "A Psychological Approach to the Dogma of the Trinity," pars. 243ff.

[92] Cf. "The Spirit Mercurius," pars. 267ff.

[93] The three relatively differentiated functions and one undifferentiated, "inferior" function. Cf. *Psychological Types*, and the diagrams in Jacobi, *The Psychology of C. G. Jung*.

[94] "A Study in the Process of Individuation," fig. 2, p. 309.

[95] Ibid., Picture 3 and accompanying text.

[96] Zurich Central Library, Graphics Collection, B x 606.

400 　　I would like, in conclusion, to mention the peculiar theory of world creation in the Clementine Homilies. In God, pneuma and soma are one. When they separate, pneuma appears as the Son and "archon of the future Aeon," but soma, actual substance (οὐσία) or matter (ὕλη), divides into four, corresponding to the four elements (which were always solemnly invoked at initiations). From the mixing of the four parts there arose the devil, the "archon of this Aeon," and the *psyche* of this world. Soma had become psychized (ἐμψῦχον): "God rules this world as much through the devil as through the Son, for both are in his hands." [97] God unfolds himself in the world in the form of syzygies (paired opposites), such as heaven/earth, day/night, male/female, etc. The last term of the first series is the Adam/Eve syzygy. At the end of this fragmentation process there follows the return to the beginning, the consummation of the universe (τελευτὴ τῶν πάντων) through purification and annihilation. [98]

401 　　Anyone who knows alchemy can hardly avoid being struck by the likeness which pseudo-Clement's theory bears to the basic conceptions of the alchemists, if we disregard its moral aspects. Thus we have the "hostile brothers," Christ and the devil, who were regarded as brothers in the Jewish-Christian tradition; the tetrameria into four parts or elements; the paired opposites and their ultimate unity; the parallel of the *lapis* and Mercurius with Christ and, because of the snake or dragon symbolism, also with the devil; and finally, the figure of Mercurius duplex and of the *lapis*, which unites the opposites indivisibly in itself.

*

402 　　If we look back over the course our argument has taken, we see at the beginning of it two Gnostic quaternities, one of which is supraordinate, and the other subordinate, to man, namely the "Positive Moses" or Anthropos Quaternio, and the Paradise Quaternio. [99] It is probably no accident that Hippolytus men-

---

[97] Harnack, *Dogmengeschichte*, I, p. 334.

[98] Condensed from the reconstruction by Uhlhorn, in *Realencyklopädie für Protestantische Theologie und Kirche,* ed. by Hauck, IV, pp. 173ff.

[99] To avoid misunderstandings I would like to emphasize that "Paradise" is used here not in the metaphorical sense, as "future heaven" or the Abode of the Blessed, but in the sense of the earthly Garden of Eden.

II. The Trinity

From a manuscript by Joachim of Flora

tions precisely these two quaternities, or that the Naassenes knew only these, for the position of man is, in their system, closely connected with the higher Adam but is separated from the chthonic world of plants and animals, namely Paradise. Only through his shadow has he a relationship to the serpent with its dual meaning. This situation is altogether characteristic of the age of Gnosticism and early Christianity. Man in those days was close to the "kingless [i.e., independent] race," that is, to the upper quaternity, the kingdom of heaven, and looked upward. But what begins above does not rise higher, but ends below. Thus we felt impelled to symmetrize the lower Adam of the Naassenes by a Shadow Quaternio, for just as he cannot ascend direct to the higher Adam—since the Moses Quaternio lies in between—so we have to assume a lower, shadowy quaternity corresponding to the upper one, lying between him and the lower principle, the serpent. This operation was obviously unknown in the Gnostic age, because the unsymmetrical upward trend seemed to disturb nobody, but rather to be the very thing desired and "on the programme." If, therefore, we insert between Man and Serpent a quaternity not mentioned in the texts, we do so because we can no longer conceive of a psyche that is oriented exclusively upwards and that is not balanced by an equally strong consciousness of the lower man. This is a specifically modern state of affairs and, in the context of Gnostic thinking, an obnoxious anachronism that puts man in the centre of the field of consciousness where he had never consciously stood before. Only through Christ could he actually see this consciousness mediating between God and the world, and by making the person of Christ the object of his devotions he gradually came to acquire Christ's position as mediator. Through the Christ crucified between the two thieves man gradually attained knowledge of his shadow and its duality. This duality had already been anticipated by the double meaning of the serpent. Just as the serpent stands for the power that heals as well as corrupts, so one of the thieves is destined upwards, the other downwards, and so likewise the shadow is on one side regrettable and reprehensible weakness, on the other side healthy instinctivity and the prerequisite for higher consciousness.

³³   Thus the Shadow Quaternio that counterbalances man's

position as mediator only falls into place when that position has become sufficiently real for him to feel his consciousness of himself or his own existence more strongly than his dependence on and governance by God. Therefore, if we complement the upward-tending pneumatic attitude that characterizes the early Christian and Gnostic mentality by adding its opposite counterpart, this is in line with the historical development. Man's original dependence on a pneumatic sphere, to which he clung like a child to its mother, was threatened by the kingdom of Satan. From him the pneumatic man was delivered by the Redeemer, who broke the gates of hell and deceived the archons; but he was bound to the kingdom of heaven in exactly the same degree. He was separated from evil by an abyss. This attitude was powerfully reinforced by the immediate expectation of the Second Coming. But when Christ did not reappear, a regression was only to be expected. When such a great hope is dashed and such great expectations are not fulfilled, then the libido perforce flows back into man and heightens his consciousness of himself by accentuating his personal psychic processes; in other words, he gradually moves into the centre of his field of consciousness. This leads to separation from the pneumatic sphere and an approach to the realm of the shadow. Accordingly, man's moral consciousness is sharpened, and, as a parallel to this, his feeling of redemption becomes relativized. The Church has to exalt the significance and power of her ritual in order to put limits to the inrush of reality. In this way she inevitably becomes a "kingdom of this world." The transition from the Anthropos to the Shadow Quaternio illustrates an historical development which led, in the eleventh century, to a widespread recognition of the evil principle as the world creator.

404   The serpent and its chthonic wisdom form the turning-point of the great drama. The Paradise Quaternio with the *lapis,* that comes next, brings us to the beginnings of natural science (Roger Bacon, 1214–94; Albertus Magnus, 1193–1280; and the alchemists), whose main trend differs from the pneumatic not by 180° but only by 90°—that is to say, it cuts across the spiritual attitude of the Church and is more an embarrassment for faith than a contradiction of it.

405   From the *lapis,* i.e., from alchemy, the line leads direct to

the quaternio of alchemical states of aggregation, which, as we have seen, is ultimately based on the space-time quaternio. The latter comes into the category of archetypal quaternities and proves, like these, to be an indispensable principle for organizing the sense-impressions which the psyche receives from bodies in motion. Space and time form a psychological *a priori,* an aspect of the archetypal quaternity which is altogether indispensable for acquiring knowledge of physical processes.

⁶ The development from the Shadow to the Lapis Quaternio illustrates the change in man's picture of the world during the course of the second millennium. The series ends with the concept of the *rotundum,* or of rotation as contrasted with the static quality of the quaternity, which, as we have said, proves to be of prime importance for apprehending reality. The rise of scientific materialism connected with this development appears on the one hand as a logical consequence, on the other hand as a deification of matter. This latter aspect is based, psychologically, on the fact that the *rotundum* coincides with the archetype of the Anthropos.

⁷ With this insight the ring of the uroboros closes, that symbol of the *opus circulare* of Nature as well as of the "Art."

7

⁸ Our quaternio series could also be expressed in the form of an equation, where A stands for the initial state (in this case the Anthropos) and for the end state, and $B\ C\ D$ for intermediate states. The formations that split off from them are denoted in each case by the small letters $a\ b\ c\ d$. With regard to the construction of the formula, we must bear in mind that we are concerned with the continual process of transformation of one and the same substance. This substance, and its respective state of transformation, will always bring forth its like; thus A will produce a and $B\ b$; equally, b produces B and $c\ C$. It is also assumed that a is followed by b and that the formula runs from left to right. These assumptions are legitimate in a psychological formula.

⁹ Naturally the formula cannot be arranged in linear fashion

but only in a circle, which for that reason moves to the right. *A* produces its like, *a*. From *a* the process advances by contingence to *b*, which in turn produces *B*. The transformation turns rightwards with the sun; that is, it is a process of becoming conscious, as is already indicated by the splitting (discrimination) of *A B C D* each time into four qualitatively discrete units.[100] Our scientific understanding today is not based on a quaternity but on a trinity of principles (space, time, causality).[101] Here, however, we are moving not in the sphere of modern scientific thinking, but in that of the classical and medieval view of the world, which up to the time of Leibniz recognized the principle of *correspondence* and applied it naïvely and unreflectingly. In order to give our judgment on *A*—expressed by *abc*—the character of wholeness, we must supplement our time-conditioned thinking by the principle of correspondence or, as I have called it, *synchronicity*.[102] The reason for this is that our description of Nature is in certain respects incomplete and accordingly excludes observable facts from our understanding or else formulates them in an unjustifiably negative way, as for instance in the paradox of "an effect without a cause."[103] Our Gnostic quaternity is a naïve product of the unconscious and therefore represents a psychic fact which can be brought into relationship with the four orienting functions of consciousness; for the rightward movement of the process is, as I have said, the expression of conscious discrimination [104] and hence an application of the four functions that constitute the essence of a conscious process.

410   The whole cycle necessarily returns to its beginning, and does so at the moment when *D*, in point of contingence the state furthest removed from *A*, changes into a_3 by a kind of enantiodromia. We thus have:

---

100 Corresponding to the *phylokrinesis*. [Cf. supra, pars. 118, 133.]
101 I am not counting the space-time continuum of modern physics.
102 Cf. "Synchronicity: An Acausal Connecting Principle."
103 [Jeans, *Physics and Philosophy*, pp. 127, 151.—EDITORS.]
104 The immediate cause is the rightward movement of our writing. The right, so to speak, is ruled by conscious reason: the right is "right" in all senses (upright, downright, forthright, etc.). The left is the side of the heart, the emotions, where one is affected by the unconscious.

$$
\begin{array}{ccc}
& b_3 & & d \\
c_3 & a_3 = A = a & c \\
& d_3 & & b \\
& \| & & \| \\
& D & & B \\
& \| & & \| \\
& d_2 & & b_1 \\
a_2 & c_2 = C = c_1 & a_1 \\
& b_2 & & d_1
\end{array}
$$

The formula reproduces exactly the essential features of the symbolic process of transformation. It shows the rotation of the mandala,[105] the antithetical play of complementary (or compensatory) processes, then the apocatastasis, i.e., the restoration of an original state of wholeness, which the alchemists expressed through the symbol of the uroboros, and finally the formula repeats the ancient alchemical tetrameria,[106] which is implicit

in the fourfold structure of unity: $A = a \begin{array}{c} d \\ \diagup \diagdown \\ \diagdown \diagup \\ b \end{array} c$. What the for-

mula can only hint at, however, is the higher plane that is reached through the process of transformation and integration. The "sublimation" or progress or qualitative change consists in an unfolding of totality into four parts four times, which means nothing less than its becoming conscious. When psychic contents are split up into four aspects, it means that they have been subjected to discrimination by the four orienting functions of consciousness. Only the production of these four aspects makes a total description possible. The process depicted by our formula changes the originally unconscious totality into a conscious one. The Anthropos A descends from above through his Shadow B into Physis C ($=$ serpent), and, through a kind of crystallization process D ($= lapis$) that reduces chaos to order, rises again

105 Cf. "Concerning Mandala Symbolism," figs. 19, 21, 37, 60.
106 Cf. Psychology and Alchemy, pars. 189 and 209f., in relation to the four regimina and dispositiones.

to the original state, which in the meantime has been transformed from an unconscious into a conscious one. Consciousness and understanding arise from discrimination, that is, through analysis (dissolution) followed by synthesis, as stated in symbolical terms by the alchemical dictum: "Solve et coagula" (dissolve and coagulate). The correspondence is represented by the identity of the letters a, a_1, a_2, a_3, and so on. That is to say, we are dealing all the time with the same factor, which in the formula merely changes its place, whereas psychologically its name and quality change too. At the same time it becomes clear that the change of place is always an enantiodromian change of situation, corresponding to the complementary or compensatory changes in the psyche as a whole. It was in this way that the changing of the hexagrams in the *I Ching* was understood by the classical Chinese commentators. Every archetypal arrangement has its own numinosity, as is apparent from the very names given to it. Thus a to d is the "kingless race," a_1 to d_1 is the Shadow Quaternio, which is annoying, because it stands for the all-too-human human being (Nietzsche's "Ugliest Man"),[107] a_2 to d_2 is "Paradise," which speaks for itself, and finally a_3 to d_3 is the world of matter, whose numinosity in the shape of materialism threatens to suffocate our world. What changes these correspond to in the history of the human mind over the last two thousand years I need hardly specify in detail.

411   The formula presents a symbol of the self, for the self is not just a static quantity or constant form, but is also a dynamic process. In the same way, the ancients saw the *imago Dei* in man not as a mere imprint, as a sort of lifeless, stereotyped impression, but as an active force. The four transformations represent a process of restoration or rejuvenation taking place, as it were, inside the self, and comparable to the carbon-nitrogen cycle in the sun, when a carbon nucleus captures four protons (two of which immediately become neutrons) and releases them at the end of the cycle in the form of an alpha particle. The carbon nucleus itself comes out of the reaction unchanged, "like the Phoenix from the ashes."[108] The secret of existence, i.e., the existence of the atom and its components, may well consist in a continually repeated process of rejuvenation, and one comes to

107 [Cf. *Thus Spake Zarathustra*, trans. by Common, pp. 303ff.—EDITORS.]
108 Gamow, *Atomic Energy*, p. 72.

similar conclusions in trying to account for the numinosity of the archetypes.

12   I am fully aware of the extremely hypothetical nature of this comparison, but I deem it appropriate to entertain such reflections even at the risk of being deceived by appearances. Sooner or later nuclear physics and the psychology of the unconscious will draw closer together as both of them, independently of one another and from opposite directions, push forward into transcendental territory, the one with the concept of the atom, the other with that of the archetype.

13   The analogy with physics is not a digression since the symbolical schema itself represents the descent into matter and requires the identity of the outside with the inside. Psyche cannot be totally different from matter, for how otherwise could it move matter? And matter cannot be alien to psyche, for how else could matter produce psyche? Psyche and matter exist in one and the same world, and each partakes of the other, otherwise any reciprocal action would be impossible. If research could only advance far enough, therefore, we should arrive at an ultimate agreement between physical and psychological concepts. Our present attempts may be bold, but I believe they are on the right lines. Mathematics, for instance, has more than once proved that its purely logical constructions which transcend all experience subsequently coincided with the behaviour of things. This, like the events I call synchronistic, points to a profound harmony between all forms of existence.

14   Since analogy formation is a law which to a large extent governs the life of the psyche, we may fairly conjecture that our—to all appearances—purely speculative construction is not a new invention, but is prefigured on earlier levels of thought. Generally speaking, these prefigurations can be found in the multifarious stages of the mystic transformation process, as well as in the different degrees of initiation into the mysteries. We also find them in the classical as well as Christian trichotomy consisting of the pneumatic, the psychic, and the hylic. One of the most comprehensive attempts of this kind is the sixteenfold schema in the Book of Platonic Tetralogies.[109] I have dealt with

109 An anonymous Harranite treatise entitled "Platonis liber quartorum," printed in *Theatr. chem.*, V (1622), pp. 114ff.; conjectured to have been translated from the Arabic in the 12th cent.

this in detail in *Psychology and Alchemy* and can therefore limit myself here to the basic points. The schematization and analogy-formation start from four first principles: 1. the work of nature, 2. water, 3. composite natures, 4. the senses. Each of these four starting-points has three stages of transformation, which to-gether with the first stage make sixteen parts in all. But besides this fourfold horizontal division of each of the principles, each stage has its correspondence in the vertical series:

I	II	III	IV
1. *Opus naturalium*	*Aqua*	*Naturae compositae*	*Sensus*
2. *Divisio naturae*	*Terra*	*Naturae discretae*	*Discretio intellectualis*
3. *Anima*	*Aer*	*Simplicia*	*Ratio*
4. *Intellectus*	*Ignis*	*Aetheris simplicioris*	*Arcanum*

415   This table of correspondences shows the various aspects of the *opus alchemicum,* which was also bound up with astrology and the so-called necromantic arts. This is evident from the use of significant numbers and the invocation or conjuring up of the familiar spirit. Similarly, the age-old art of geomancy [110] is based on a sixteen-part schema: four central figures (consisting of Sub- or Superiudex, Iudex, and two Testes), four *nepotes* (grand-sons), four sons, four mothers. (The series is written from right to left.) These figures are arranged in a schema of astrological houses, but the centre that is empty in the horoscope is replaced by a square containing the four central figures.

416   Athanasius Kircher [111] produced a quaternity system that is worth mentioning in this connection:

I. *Unum = Monas monadikē = Deus = Radix omnium = Mens sim-plicissima = Divina essentia = Exemplar divinum.*

(The One = First Monad = God = Root of all things = Simplest understanding = Divine Essence = Divine Exemplar.)

II. *10 (1 + 2 + 3 + 4 = 10) = Secunda Monas = dekadikē = Dyas = Mundus intellectualis = Angelica intelligentia = Compositio ab uno et altero = i.e., ex oppositis.*

---

[110] Fludd, "De animae intellectualis scientia seu Geomantia," *Fasciculus geomanticus* (1687), pp. 35f.

[111] *Arithmologia, sive De abditis numerorum mysteriis* (1665), pp. 260ff. I have to thank Dr. M.-L. von Franz for calling my attention to this.

(. . . Second Monad = tenth = duality = spiritual world = intelligence of the angels = composition of the One and the Other = i.e., from opposites.)

III. 10^2 = 100 = *Tertia Monas* = *hekatontadikē* = *Anima* = *Intelligentia*.

(. . . Third Monad = hundredth = soul = intelligence.)

IV. 10^3 = 1000 = *Quarta Monas* = *chiliadikē* = *Omnia sensibilia* = *Corpus* = *ultima et sensibilis Unionum explicatio*.

(. . . Fourth Monad = thousandth = all concrete things = body = final and concrete unfolding of unities.)

7   Kircher comments that whereas the senses affect only the body, the first three unities are objects of understanding. So if one wants to understand what is perceived by the senses (*sensibilia*), this can only be done through the mind. "Everything perceived by the senses must therefore be elevated to reason or to the intelligence or to absolute unity. When in this way we shall have brought the absolute unity back to the infinitely simple from all perceptible, rational or intellectual multiplicity, then nothing more remains to be said, and then the Stone too is not so much *a* Stone as *no* Stone, but everything is the simplest unity. And even as the absolute unity of that concrete and rational Stone has God for an exemplar, so likewise its intellectual unity is the intelligence. You can see from these unities how the perceiving senses go back to reason, and reason to intelligence, and intelligence to God, where in a perfect cycle is found the beginning and the consummation." [112] That Kircher should choose the *lapis* as an example of concrete things and of God's unity is obvious enough in terms of alchemy, because the *lapis* is the arcanum that contains God or that part of God which is hidden in matter.

8   Kircher's system shows certain affinities with our series of quaternios. Thus the Second Monad is a duality consisting of opposites, corresponding to the angelic world that was split by Lucifer's fall. Another significant analogy is that Kircher conceives his schema as a cycle set in motion by God as the prime cause, and unfolding out of itself, but brought back to God again through the activity of human understanding, so that the end returns once more to the beginning. This, too, is an analogy

112 Ibid., p. 266. [The next sentence is revised and transposed from par. 418. (2nd edn.)]

of our formula. The alchemists were fond of picturing their *opus* as a circulatory process, as a circular distillation or as the uroboros, the snake biting its own tail, and they made innumerable pictures of this process. Just as the central idea of the *lapis Philosophorum* plainly signifies the self, so the *opus* with its countless symbols illustrates the process of individuation, the step-by-step development of the self from an unconscious state to a conscious one. That is why the *lapis,* as *prima materia,* stands at the beginning of the process as well as at the end.[113] According to Michael Maier, the gold, another synonym for the self, comes from the *opus circulatorium* of the sun. This circle is "the line that runs back upon itself (like the serpent that with its head bites its own tail), wherein that eternal painter and potter, God, may be discerned." [114] In this circle, Nature "has related the four qualities to one another and drawn, as it were, an equilateral square, since contraries are bound together by contraries, and enemies by enemies, with the same everlasting bonds." Maier compares this squaring of the circle to the "homo quadratus," the four-square man, who "remains himself" come weal come woe.[115] He calls it the "golden house, the twice-bisected circle, the four-cornered phalanx, the rampart, the city wall, the four-sided line of battle." [116] This circle is a magic circle consisting of the union of opposites, "immune to all injury."

419   Independently of Western tradition, the same idea of the circular *opus* can be found in Chinese alchemy: "When the light is made to move in a circle, all the energies of heaven and earth, of the light and the dark, are crystallized," says the text of the *Golden Flower*.[117]

420   The ὄργανον κυκλικόν, the circular apparatus that assists the circular process, is mentioned as early as Olympiodorus.[118] Dorn is of the opinion that the "circular movement of the Physiochemists" comes from the earth, the lowest element. For the fire originates in the earth and transforms the finer minerals and water into air, which, rising up to the heavens, condenses there

[113] Documentation in *Psychology and Alchemy,* esp. pars. 427, n. 4, and 431.
[114] *De circulo physico quadrato,* p. 16.   [115] Ibid., p. 17.
[116] Ibid., p. 19.
[117] Wilhelm, *The Secret of the Golden Flower* (1962 edn.), p. 30.
[118] Berthelot, *Alch. grecs,* II, iv, 44.

and falls down again. But during their ascent the volatilized elements take "from the higher stars male seeds, which they bring down into the four matrices, the elements, in order to fertilize them spagyrically." This is the "circular distillation" [119] which Rupescissa says must be repeated a thousand times.[120]

The basic idea of ascent and descent can be found in the *Tabula smaragdina,* and the stages of transformation have been depicted over and over again, above all in the Ripley "Scrowle" and its variants. These should be understood as indirect attempts to apprehend the unconscious processes of individuation in the form of pictures.

[119] "Physica genesis," *Theatr. chem.,* I, p. 391.
[120] *La Vertu et la propriété de la quinte essence,* p. 26.

XV

CONCLUSION

422   I have tried, in this book, to elucidate and amplify the various aspects of the archetype which it is most important for modern man to understand—namely, the archetype of the self. By way of introduction, I described those concepts and archetypes which manifest themselves in the course of any psychological treatment that penetrates at all deeply. The first of these is the SHADOW, that hidden, repressed, for the most part inferior and guilt-laden personality whose ultimate ramifications reach back into the realm of our animal ancestors and so comprise the whole historical aspect of the unconscious. Through analysis of the shadow and of the processes contained in it we uncover the ANIMA/ANIMUS syzygy. Looked at superficially, the shadow is cast by the conscious mind and is as much a privation of light as the physical shadow that follows the body. For this superficial view, therefore, the psychological shadow with its moral inferiority might also be regarded as a privation of good. On closer inspection, however, it proves to be a darkness that hides influential and autonomous factors which can be distinguished in their own right, namely anima and animus. When we observe them in full operation—as the devastating, blindly obstinate demon of opinionatedness in a woman, and the glamorous, possessive, moody, and sentimental seductress in a man—we begin to doubt whether the unconscious can be merely the insubstantial comet's tail of consciousness and nothing but a privation of light and good.

423   If it has been believed hitherto that the human shadow was the source of all evil, it can now be ascertained on closer investigation that the unconscious man, that is, his shadow, does not consist only of morally reprehensible tendencies, but also displays a number of good qualities, such as normal instincts, appropriate reactions, realistic insights, creative impulses, etc. On this level of understanding, evil appears more as a distortion, a deformation, a misinterpretation and misapplication of facts

266

that in themselves are natural. These falsifications and carica-
tures now appear as the specific effects of anima and animus, and
the latter as the real authors of evil. But we cannot stop even at
this realization, for it turns out that all archetypes spontaneously
develop favourable and unfavourable, light and dark, good and
bad effects. In the end we have to acknowledge that the self is
a *complexio oppositorum* precisely because there can be no
reality without polarity. We must not overlook the fact that
opposites acquire their moral accentuation only within the
sphere of human endeavour and action, and that we are unable
to give a definition of good and evil that could be considered
universally valid. In other words, we do not know what good
and evil are in themselves. It must therefore be supposed that
they spring from a need of human consciousness and that for
this reason they lose their validity outside the human sphere.
That is to say a hypostasis of good and evil as metaphysical entities is inadmissible because it would deprive these terms of
meaning. If we call everything that God does or allows "good,"
then evil is good too, and "good" becomes meaningless. But
suffering, whether it be Christ's passion or the suffering of the
world, remains the same as before. Stupidity, sin, sickness, old
age, and death continue to form the dark foil that sets off the
joyful splendour of life.

4   The recognition of anima and animus is a specific experience
that seems to be reserved mostly, or at any rate primarily, for
psychotherapists. Nevertheless, anyone who has a little knowledge of *belles-lettres* will have no difficulty in forming a picture
of the anima; she is a favourite subject for novelists, particularly
west of the Rhine.[1] Nor is a careful study of dreams always necessary. It is not quite so easy to recognize the woman's animus, for
his name is legion. But anyone who can stand the animosity of
his fellows without being infected by it, and is capable at the
same time of examining it critically, cannot help discovering
that they are possessed. It is, however, more advantageous and
more to the point to subject to the most rigorous scrutiny one's
own moods and their changing influence on one's personality.
To know where the other person makes a mistake is of little
value. It only becomes interesting when you know where *you*

1 The outstanding example in Swiss literature is Spitteler's *Imago*. [In English
literature, perhaps Rider Haggard's *She.*—EDITORS.]

make the mistake, for then you can do something about it. What we can improve in others is of doubtful utility as a rule, if, indeed, it has any effect at all.

425   Although, to begin with, we meet the anima and animus mostly in their negative and unwelcome form, they are very far from being only a species of bad spirit. They have, as we have said, an equally positive aspect. Because of their numinous, suggestive power they have formed since olden times the archetypal basis of all masculine and feminine divinities and therefore merit special attention, above all from the psychologist, but also from thoughtful laymen. As numina, anima and animus work now for good, now for evil. Their opposition is that of the sexes. They therefore represent a supreme pair of opposites, not hopelessly divided by logical contradiction but, because of the mutual attraction between them, giving promise of union and actually making it possible. The *coniunctio oppositorum* engaged the speculations of the alchemists in the form of the "Chymical Wedding," and those of the cabalists in the form of Tifereth and Malchuth or God and the Shekhinah,[2] not to speak of the marriage of the Lamb.

426   The dual being born of the alchemical union of opposites, the Rebis or Lapis Philosophorum, is so distinctively marked in the literature that we have no difficulty in recognizing it as a symbol of the self. Psychologically the self is a union of conscious (masculine) and unconscious (feminine). It stands for the psychic totality. So formulated, it is a psychological concept. Empirically, however, the self appears spontaneously in the shape of specific symbols, and its totality is discernible above all in the mandala and its countless variants. Historically, these symbols are authenticated as God-images.

427   The anima/animus stage is correlated with polytheism, the self with monotheism.[3] The natural archetypal symbolism, describing a totality that includes light and dark, contradicts in some sort the Christian but not the Jewish or Yahwistic viewpoint, or only to a relative degree. The latter seems to be closer to Nature and therefore to be a better reflection of immediate experience. Nevertheless, the Christian heresiarchs tried to sail

[2] Hurwitz, "Archetypische Motive in der chassidischen Mystik," ch. VI.
[3] This thema is the subject of an Oxford dissertation by Amy I. Allenby: *A Psychological Study of the Origins of Monotheism.*

round the rocks of Manichaean dualism, which was such a danger to the early Church, in a way that took cognizance of the natural symbol, and among the symbols for Christ there are some very important ones which he has in common with the devil, though this had no influence on dogma.

8   By far the most fruitful attempts, however, to find suitable symbolic expressions for the self were made by the Gnostics. Most of them—Valentinus and Basilides, for instance—were in reality theologians who, unlike the more orthodox ones, allowed themselves to be influenced in large measure by natural inner experience. They are therefore, like the alchemists, a veritable mine of information concerning all those natural symbols arising out of the repercussions of the Christian message. At the same time, their ideas compensate the asymmetry of God postulated by the doctrine of the *privatio boni,* exactly like those well-known modern tendencies of the unconscious to produce symbols of totality for bridging the gap between the conscious and the unconscious, which has widened dangerously to the point of universal disorientation.

9   I am well aware that this work, far from being complete, is a mere sketch showing how certain Christian ideas look when observed from the standpoint of psychological experience. Since my main concern was to point out the parallelism or the difference between the empirical findings and our traditional views, a consideration of the disparities due to time and language proved unavoidable. This was particularly so in the case of the fish symbol. Inevitably, we move here on uncertain ground and must now and then have recourse to a speculative hypothesis or tentatively reconstruct a context. Naturally every investigator must document his findings as fully as possible, but he should also venture an occasional hypothesis even at the risk of making a mistake. Mistakes are, after all, the foundations of truth, and if a man does not know what a thing *is,* it is at least an increase in knowledge if he knows what it is *not.*

BIBLIOGRAPHY

BIBLIOGRAPHY

The items of the bibliography are arranged alphabetically under two headings: *A*. Ancient volumes containing collections of alchemical tracts by various authors; *B*. General bibliography, including cross-references to the material in section *A*. Short titles of the ancient volumes are printed in capital letters.

A. ANCIENT VOLUMES CONTAINING COLLECTIONS OF ALCHEMICAL TRACTS BY VARIOUS AUTHORS

ARS CHEMICA, quod sit licita recte exercentibus, probationes doctissimorum iurisconsultorum. . . . . Argentorati [Strasbourg], 1566.

Contents quoted in this volume:

i Septem tractatus seu capitula Hermetis Trismegisti aurei [pp. 7–31; usually referred to as "Tractatus aureus"]
ii Tabula smaragdina [pp. 32–33]

ARTIS AURIFERAE quam chemiam vocant. . . . . Basileae [Basel], [1593]. 2 vols.

Contents quoted in this volume:

VOLUME I

i Turba philosophorum [two versions: pp. 1–65, 66–139]
i-a Allegoriae super librum Turbae [pp. 139–45]
ii Aenigmata ex Visione Arislei philosophi et allegoriis sapientum [pp. 146–54; usually referred to as "Visio Arislei"]
iii In Turbam philosophorum exercitationes [pp. 154–82]
iv Aurora consurgens, quae dicitur Aurea hora [pp. 185–246]
v [Zosimus]: Rosinus ad Sarratantam episcopum [pp. 277–319]
vi Maria Prophetissa: Practica . . . in artem alchemicam [pp. 319–24]

vii Tractatulus Aristotelis de practica lapidis philosophici [pp. 361–73]

viii Interpretatio cuiusdam epistolae Alexandri Macedonum regis [pp. 382–88]

ix Tractatulus Avicennae [pp. 405–37]

VOLUME II

x Morienus Romanus: Sermo de transmutatione metallica [pp. 7–54]

xi Rosarium philosophorum [pp. 204–384]

MANGETUS, JOANNES JACOBUS (ed.). *BIBLIOTHECA CHEMICA CURIOSA, seu Rerum ad alchemiam pertinentium thesaurus instructissimus* . . . Coloniae Allobrogum [Geneva], 1702. 2 vols.

Contents quoted in this volume:

VOLUME I

i Allegoriae sapientum supra librum Turbae philosophorum XXIX distinctiones [pp. 467–79]

ii Turba philosophorum [pp. 445–65; another version, pp. 480–94]

iii Allegoriae supra librum Turbae [pp. 494–95]

MUSAEUM HERMETICUM reformatum et amplificatum . . . *continens tractatus chimicos XXI praestantissimos* . . . Francofurti [Frankfurt a. M.], 1678. For translation, see (B) WAITE, *The Hermetic Museum.*

Contents quoted in this volume:

i [Barcius (F. von Sternberg)]: Gloria mundi, alias Paradysi tabula [pp. 203–304]

ii Lambspringk: De lapide philosophico figurae et emblemata [pp. 337–72]

iii Sendivogius: Novum lumen chemicum e naturae fonte et manuali experientia depromptum [pp. 545–600]

iv [Sendivogius:] Novi luminis chemici Tractatus alter de sulphure [pp. 601–46]

v Philalethes: Introitus apertus ad occlusum regis palatium [pp. 647–700]

vi Philalethes: Metallorum metamorphosis [pp. 741–74]

THEATRUM CHEMICUM, praecipuos selectorum auctorum tractatus . . . continens. Ursellis [Ursel] and Argentorati [Strasbourg], 1602–61. 6 vols. (Vols. I–III, Ursel, 1602; Vols. IV–VI, Strasbourg, 1613, 1622, 1661 respectively.)

Contents quoted in this volume:

VOLUME I

i Fanianus: De arte metallicae metamorphoseos ad Philoponum [pp. 28–48]
ii Hoghelande: Liber de alchemiae difficultatibus [pp. 121–215]
iii Dorn: Ars chemistica [pp. 217–54]
iv Dorn: Speculativae philosophiae, gradus septem vel decem continens [pp. 255–310]
v Dorn: Physica genesis [pp. 367–404]
v-a Dorn: Physica Trismegisti [pp. 405–37]
vi Dorn: Philosophia meditativa [pp. 450–72]
vii Dorn: Philosophia chemica ad meditativam comparata [pp. 472–517]
viii Dorn: Congeries Paracelsicae chemicae de transmutationibus metallorum [pp. 557–646]
ix Bernardus Trevisanus: Liber de alchemia [pp. 773–803]

VOLUME II

x Ripley: Duodecim portarum axiomata philosophica [pp. 123–39]
xi Hollandus: Fragmentum de lapide [pp. 142–46]
xii Dee: Monas hieroglyphica [pp. 218–43]

VOLUME III

xiii Aristoteles de perfecto Magisterio [pp. 56–118]

VOLUME IV

xiv Artefius: Clavis maioris sapientiae [pp. 221–40]
xv Duodecim tractatus de lapide philosophorum [pp. 478–502]
xvi Beatus: Aurelia occulta philosophorum [pp. 525–81]
xvii Hermetis Trismegisti Tractatus vere aureus de lapide philosophici secreto [pp. 672–797; usually referred to as "Tractatus aureus"]

VOLUME V

xvii-a Turba philosophorum [pp. 1–57]
xviii Allegoriae sapientum et distinctiones XXIX supra librum
       Turbae [pp. 64–100]
xix Platonis liber quartorum [pp. 114–208]
xx Tractatus Aristotelis alchymistae ad Alexandrum Mag-
       num de lapide philosophico [pp. 880–92]

VOLUME VI

xxi Blaise de Vigenère: Tractatus de igne et sale [pp. 1–139]
xxii Collesson: Idea perfecta philosophiae hermeticae [pp.
       143–61]
xxiii Fidelissima et jucunda instructio de arbore solari [pp.
       163–194]
xxiv Grasseus: Arca arcani artificiosissimi de summis naturae
       mysteriis [pp. 294–381]
xxv [Barchius:] Summa libri quae vocatur Gloria mundi, seu
       Tabula comprehensa [pp. 513–17]
xxvi Chartier: Scientia plumbi sacri sapientum [pp. 569–99]

B. GENERAL BIBLIOGRAPHY

ABARBANEL, ISAAC (Isḥāq Abravanel ben Jehūdā). *Mashmiʻa Ye-shuʻah* ["Proclamation of Salvation"]. (In Hebrew.) Salonica, 1526.

———. *Maʻyene ha-Yeshuʻah* ["Sources of Salvation"]. (In Hebrew.) Ferrara, 1551.

Abot de Rabbi Nathan. See NATHAN.

ADAM SCOTUS. *De tripartito tabernaculo.* See MIGNE, *P.L.*, vol. 148, cols. 609–796.

[ADAMANTIUS]. *Der Dialog des Adamantius* περὶ τῆς εἰς θεὸν ὀρθῆς πίστεως. Edited by Willem Hendrik van de Sande Bakhuyzen. (Griechischen Christlichen Schriftsteller.) Leipzig, 1908.

"Aenigmata ex Visione Arislei." See (*A*) *Artis auriferae,* ii.

AILLY, PIERRE D' (Petrus de Aliaco). *Concordantia astronomie cum theologia. Concordantia astronomie cum hystorica narratione. Et elucidarium duarum praecedentium.* Venice, 1490.

ALBUMASAR. See JA'FAR IBN MUḤAMMAD (ABU MA'SHAR) AL-BALKHĪ.

ALCIATI, ANDREA. *Emblemata*. Padua, 1621 (another edn., 1661).

ALIACO, PETRUS DE. See AILLY, PIERRE D'.

"Allegoriae sapientum et distinctiones XXIX supra librum Turbae." See (*A*) MANGETUS, *Bibliotheca chemica*, i; *Theatrum chemicum*, xviii.

"Allegoriae supra librum Turbae." See (*A*) *Artis auriferae*, i-a; MANGETUS, *Bibliotheca chemica*, iii.

ALLENBY, AMY INGEBORG. *A Psychological Study of the Origins of Monotheism*. Unpublished dissertation, Oxford University.

AMBROSE, SAINT. *Explanationes in Psalmos*. In: *Sancti Ambrosii Opera*, Pars 6. Edited by M. Petschenig. (Corpus Scriptorum Ecclesiasticorum Latinorum, 64.) Leipzig and Vienna, 1919.

ANGELUS SILESIUS (Johannes Scheffler). See FLITCH.

ANGER, RUDOLPH. "Der Stern der Weisen und das Geburtsjahr Christi," *Zeitschrift für die historische Theologie* (Leipzig), 1847, pp. 347–98.

ARATUS. *Phaenomena*. In: *Callimachus and Lycophron; Aratus*. Translated by A. W. and G. R. Mair. (Loeb Classical Library.) London and New York, 1921.

ARISLEUS. "Visio Arislei." See (*A*) *Artis auriferae*, ii.

"Aristoteles de perfecto Magisterio." See (*A*) *Theatrum chemicum*, xiii.

ARTEFIUS. "Clavis maioris sapientiae." See (*A*) *Theatrum chemicum*, xiv.

AUGURELLUS, JOANNES AURELIUS. "Chrysopoeia." See GRATAROLUS.

AUGUSTINE, SAINT. *The City of God*. Translated by John Healey and edited by R. V. G. Tasker. (Everyman's Library.) London and New York, 1945. 2 vols. (Original: *De Civitate Dei*. See MIGNE, *P.L.*, vol. 41, cols. 13–804.)

——. *The Confessions: Books I–X*. Translated by F. J. Sheed. London, 1951. (Original: *Confessiones*. See MIGNE, *P.L.*, vol. 32, cols. 659–868.)

――――. *Contra adversarios legis et prophetarum.* See MIGNE, *P.L.*, vol. 42, cols. 603–666.

――――. *Contra Faustum.* See MIGNE, *P.L.*, vol. 42, cols. 207–518. For translation, see: *Reply to Faustus the Manichaean.* Translated by Richard Stothert. (*Works of Aurelius Augustinus,* edited by Marcus Dods, 5.) Edinburgh, 1872.

――――. *De diversis quaestionibus LXXXIII.* See MIGNE, *P.L.*, vol. 40, cols. 11–100.

――――. *Dialogus Quaestionum LXV.* See MIGNE, *P.L.*, vol. 40, cols. 733–752.

――――. *De Trinitate.* See MIGNE, *P.L.*, vol. 42, cols. 819–1098. For translation, see: *Augustine: Later Works.* Selected and translated by John Burnaby. (Library of Christian Classics, 8.) London, 1955. (Pp. 37–181.)

――――. *Enarrationes in Psalmos.* See MIGNE, *P.L.*, vols. 36, 37.

――――. *Liber Sententiarum ex Augustino.* See: *Prosperi Aquitani Sententiae ex Augustino delibatae liber unus.* Being Vol. X, Part 2, of *S. Aurelii Augustini . . . opera omnia . . .* , opere et studio monachorum O.S.B. e Congregatione S. Mauri. Paris, 1835–39. 11 vols.

――――. *Retractationes.* In MIGNE, *P.L.*, vol. 32, cols. 583–656.

――――. *Sermo I.* See: *Sermones supposititii.* Being Vol. V of *S. Aurelii Augustini . . . opera omnia . . .* , opere et studio monachorum O.S.B. e Congregatione S. Mauri. Paris, 1835–39. 11 vols.

――――. *Sermo XC.* See MIGNE, *P.L.*, vol. 38, cols. 559–66.

――――. *Sermo CCXXXVII.* See MIGNE, *P.L.*, vol. 38, cols. 1122–24.

――――. *Tractatus in Joannis Evangelium.* In MIGNE, *P.L.*, vol. 35. For translation, see: *Lectures or Tractates on the Gospel according to Saint John,* Vol. II. Translated by James Innes. (*Works of Aurelius Augustinus,* edited by Marcus Dods, 11.) Edinburgh, 1874.

"Aurora consurgens." See *(A) Artis auriferae,* IV; *(B)* FRANZ, M.L. VON.

Bahman Yast. In: *Pahlavi Texts,* Part I. Translated by E. W. West. (Sacred Books of the East, 5.) Oxford, 1880.

Baruch, Apocalypse of. See "2 Baruch (The Syrian Apocalypse of Baruch)" in CHARLES, *Apocrypha*, II, pp. 470–526.

BASIL THE GREAT, SAINT. *Quod Deus non est auctor malorum.* See MIGNE, *P.G.*, vol. 31, cols. 329–54.

——. *Homiliae in Psalmos.* In MIGNE, *P.G.*, vol. 29, cols. 209–494.

——. *Homiliae in Hexaemeron.* See MIGNE, *P.G.*, vol. 29, cols. 3–208. For translation, see: *The Treatise De Spiritu Sancto, the Nine Homilies of the Hexaemeron and the Letters of St. Basil the Great.* Translated by the Rev. Blomfield Jackson. (Select Library of Nicene and Post-Nicene Fathers of the Christian Church, Second Series, 8.) Oxford and New York, 1895.

BAUER, WALTER. *Griechisch-Deutsches Wörterbuch zu den Schriften des neuen Testaments.* 3rd edn., Berlin, 1937.

BEATUS, GEORGIUS. "Aurelia occulta." See (*A*) *Theatrum chemicum*, xvi.

BENOIST, JEAN. *Histoire des Albigeois et des Vaudois.* Paris, 1691. 2 vols.

Bereshith Rabba. See: *Midrash Rabbah translated into English.* Edited by H. Freedman and Maurice Simon. London, 1951. 10 vols.

BERNARD OF CLAIRVAUX, SAINT. *Tractatus de gradibus superbiae.* See MIGNE, *P.L.*, vol. 182, cols. 957–72.

BERNARDUS TREVISANUS. "Liber de alchemia." See (*A*) *Theatrum chemicum*, ix.

BERTHELOT, MARCELLIN. *Collection des anciens alchimistes grecs.* Paris, 1887–88. 3 vols.

Bible. The following versions are cited textually:
[AV] Authorized ("King James") Version (cited unless otherwise indicated).
[DV] Douay-Reims Version. [RSV] Revised Standard Version.

BÖHME, JAKOB. "Aurora, oder die Morgenröte im Aufgang." In: *Des gottseligen, hocherleuchteten . . . Schrifften,* q.v. For translation, see: *Aurora.* Translated by John Sparrow. London, 1914.

———. "Tabula principiorum." See pp. 269–87 of *De signatura rerum* etc., in: *Des gottseligen, hocherleuchteten . . . Schrifften,* q.v.

———. *Des gottseligen, hocherleuchteten Jacob Böhmen Teutonici Philosophi Alle Theosophische Schrifften.* Amsterdam, 1682. (This edition of Böhme's works consists of a number of parts, each separately paginated, and variously bound up.)

BOLL, FRANZ JOHANNES. *Sphaera.* Leipzig, 1903.

———. *Aus der Offenbarung Johannis.* (ΣΤΟΙΧΕΙΑ, Heft I.) Leipzig and Berlin, 1914.

BOUCHÉ-LECLERCQ, AUGUSTE. *L'Astrologie grecque.* Paris, 1899.

BOUSSET, WILHELM. *The Antichrist Legend.* Translated by A. H. Keane. London, 1896. (Original: *Der Antichrist.* Göttingen, 1895.)

———. *Hauptprobleme der Gnosis.* (Forschungen zur Religion und Literatur des Alten und Neuen Testaments, 10.) Göttingen, 1907.

Brihadaranyaka Upanishad. See: Upanishads.

BRUGSCH, HEINRICH. *Religion und Mythologie der alten Ägypter.* Leipzig, 1885.

BUDGE, E. A. WALLIS. *The Gods of the Egyptians.* London, 1904. 2 vols.

———. *The Papyrus of Ani.* London, 1895.

CABROL, FERNAND, and LECLERCQ, HENRI. *Dictionnaire d'archéologie chrétienne et de liturgie.* Paris, 1907–53. 15 vols.

CAESARIUS OF HEISTERBACH. *Dialogue on Miracles.* Translated by H. von E. Scott and C. C. S. Bland. London, 1929. (Original: *Dialogus Miraculorum.* Edited by Joseph Strange. Cologne, 1851.)

CAMPBELL, COLIN. *The Miraculous Birth of King Amon-Hotep III.* Edinburgh and London, 1912.

CARDAN, JÉRÔME (Hieronymus Cardanus, Girolamo Cardano). "Commentarium in Ptolemaeum De astrorum Judiciis." In: *Opera Omnia.* Lyons, 1663. 10 vols. (Vol. V, pp. 93–368.)

CAUSSIN, NICHOLAS. [*Polyhistor symbolicus.*] *De symbolica Aegyptiorum sapientia. Polyhistor symbolicus, Electorum symbolorum, & Parabolarum historicarum stromata.* Paris, [1618 and] 1631.

CHARTIER, JEAN. "Scientia plumbi sacri sapientum." See (*A*) *Theatrum chemicum,* **xxvi.**

CHARLES, R. H. (ed.). *The Apocrypha and Pseudepigrapha of the Old Testament in English.* Oxford, 1913. 2 vols.

CHRISTENSEN, ARTHUR [EMANUEL]. *Le Premier Homme et le premier roi dans l'histoire légendaire des Iraniens.* (Archives d'Études orientales, 14.) Stockholm, 1918, 1934. 2 parts.

CHWOLSOHN, DANIEL (Khwolson, Daniil Avraamovich). *Die Ssabier und der Ssabismus.* St. Petersburg [Leningrad], 1856. 2 vols.

CLEMENT OF ALEXANDRIA. *Paedagogus* ("The Instructor"). See MIGNE, *P.G.,* vol. 8, cols. 247–684. For translation, see *Writings,* below.

———. *Stromata* ("Miscellanies"). See MIGNE, *P.G.,* vol. 8, col. 685 – vol. 9, col. 602. For translation, see *Writings,* below.

———. *The Writings of Clement of Alexandria.* Translated by William Wilson. (Ante-Nicene Christian Library, 4, 12.) Edinburgh, 1867–69. 2 vols.

CLEMENT OF ROME, SAINT (Pope Clement I). *Second Epistle to the Corinthians.* In: *The Apostolic Fathers.* With an English translation by Kirsopp Lake. (Loeb Classical Library.) London and New York, 1912–13. 2 vols. (Vol. I, pp. 128–63).

———, pseud. *The Clementine Homilies and the Apostolical Constitutions.* Translated by Thomas Smith, Peter Peterson, and James Donaldson. (Ante-Nicene Christian Library, 17.) Edinburgh, 1870.

COLLESSON, JOHANNES. "Idea perfecta philosophiae hermeticae." See (*A*) *Theatrum chemicum,* **xxii.**

Compendium theologicae veritatis. See HUGH OF STRASBOURG.

CREMER, HERMANN. *Biblisch-theologisches Wörterbuch der Neutestamentlichen Gräzität.* 10th edn. (edited by Julius Kögel), Gotha, 1915.

CUMONT, FRANZ. *Les Religions orientales dans le paganisme romain.* 4th edn., Paris, 1929.

———. *Textes et monuments figurés relatifs aux mystères de Mithra.* Brussels, 1894–99. 2 vols.

DEE, JOHN. "Monas hieroglyphica." See (*A*) *Theatrum chemicum,* xii.

DE GUBERNATIS, ANGELO. *Zoological Mythology.* London, 1872. 2 vols.

DELATTE, LOUIS. *Textes latins et vieux français relatifs aux Cyranides.* (Bibliothèque de la Faculté de Philosophie et Lettres de l'Université de Liège, fasc. 93.) Liège, 1942.

DENZINGER, HEINRICH, and BANNWART, KLEMENS. *Enchiridion symbolorum.* 6–7th edn., Freiburg, i. B., 1928.

DEUSSEN, PAUL. *Allgemeine Geschichte der Philosophie.* Leipzig, 1894–1917. 2 vols. in 6 parts.

DIDYMUS OF ALEXANDRIA. *De trinitate libri tres.* See MIGNE, *P.G.,* vol. 39, cols. 269–992.

DIETERICH, ALBRECHT. *Die Grabschrift des Aberkios.* Leipzig, 1896.

———. *Eine Mithrasliturgie.* Leipzig, 1903. 2nd edn., 1910.

DIONYSIUS THE AREOPAGITE, pseud. *De divinis nominibus.* In MIGNE, *P.G.,* vol. 3, cols. 585–996. For translation, see: *Works of Dionysius the Areopagite.* Translated by John Parker. Oxford, 1897–99. 2 vols.

DOELGER, FRANZ JOSEF. ΙΧΘΥΣ: *Das Fischsymbol in frühchristlicher Zeit.* Rome and Munster, 1910–27. 4 vols.

DORN, GERHARD (GERARDUS). See (*A*) *Theatrum chemicum,* iii–viii.

DOZY, REINHART, and DE GOEJE, M. J. "Nouveaux documents pour l'étude de la religion des Harraniens." In: *Actes du sixième Congrès international des Orientalistes (1883).* Leiden, 1885.

DRAGOMANOV, M. "Zabelezhki vrkhy slavyanskite religioznoeticheski Legendi," *Sbornik za narodnaya umortvoreniya* (Sofia), X (1894), 3–68.

DREWS, ARTHUR. *Der Sternhimmel in der Dichtung und Religion der alten Völker und des Christentums.* Jena, 1923.

DU CANGE, CHARLES. *Glossarium ad scriptores mediae et infinae latinitatis.* Paris, 1733–36. 6 vols. New edn.: Graz, 1954. 10 vols.

"Duodecim tractatus de lapide philosophorum." See (A) *Theatrum chemicum,* xv.

ECKHART, MEISTER. See: PFEIFFER, FRANZ (ed.). *Deutsche Mystiker des Vierzehnten Jahrhunderts.* Leipzig, 1845–57. 2 vols. (Vol. II.)

———. [*Works.*] Translated by C. de B. Evans. London, 1924–52. 2 vols.

EISLER, ROBERT. "Der Fisch als Sexualsymbol," *Imago* (Leipzig and Vienna), III (1914), 165–93.

———. *Orpheus—The Fisher.* London, 1921. (An unpublished second volume of this work is preserved in typescript in the British Museum, London.)

———. *The Royal Art of Astrology.* London, 1946.

ELEAZAR, R. ABRAHAM. *Uraltes Chymisches Werk.* Leipzig, 1760.

EPHREM THE SYRIAN, SAINT. *Hymni et sermones.* Edited by Thomas Joseph Lamy. Mechlin, 1882–1902. 4 vols.

EPICTETUS. *Enchiridion.* See: *Epictetus; The Discourses, etc.* Edited and translated by W. A. Oldfather. (Loeb Classical Library.) London and New York, 1926–28. 2 vols. (Vol. II, pp. 479–537.)

EPIPHANIUS, SAINT. *Ancoratus.* In: *Epiphanius,* Vol. I. Edited by Karl Holl. (Griechische Christliche Schriftsteller.) Leipzig, 1915.

———. *Panarium* [*Adversus octoginta haereses*]. Edited by Franciscus Oehler. Berlin, 1859–61. 3 parts.

ERMAN, ADOLF. *Die Religion der Ägypter.* Berlin and Leipzig, 1934.

Esdras, Second (or Fourth) Book of. In: CHARLES, *Apocrypha and Pseudepigrapha,* q.v. (Vol. II, pp. 561–624.)

EUCHERIUS OF LYONS, SAINT. *Liber formularum spiritalis intelligentiae.* See MIGNE, *P.L.,* vol. 50, cols. 727–72.

EUTHYMIOS ZIGABENOS. *Panoplia Dogmatica.* See MIGNE, *P.G.,* vol. 130 (entire).

FANIANUS, JOANNES CHRYSIPPUS. "De arte metallicae metamorphoseos ad Philoponum." See (A) *Theatrum chemicum,* i.

FERGUSON, JOHN. *Bibliotheca Chemica*. Glasgow, 1906. 2 vols.

"Fidelissima et jucunda instructio de arbore solari." See (*A*) *Theatrum chemicum,* xxiii.

FIERZ-DAVID, HANS EDUARD. *Die Entwicklungsgeschichte der Chemie.* (Wissenschaft und Kultur, 2.) Basel, 1945.

FIERZ-DAVID, LINDA. *The Dream of Poliphilo.* Translated by Mary Hottinger. (Bollingen Series XXV.) New York, 1950.

FIRMICUS MATERNUS, JULIUS. *De errore profanarum religionum.* Edited by Charles Halm. (Corpus Scriptorum Ecclesiasticorum Latinorum, 2.) Vienna, 1867.

FLITCH, J. E. CRAWFORD (trans.). *Angelus Silesius: Selections from The Cherubinic Wanderer.* London, 1932.

FLUDD, ROBERT. *Animae intellectualis scientia seu De geomantia.* In: *Fasciculus Geomanticus, in quo varia variorum opera geomantica continentur,* Verona, 1687.

FRANZ, MARIE-LOUISE VON. "Die Passio Perpetuae." In: C. G. JUNG. *Aion: Untersuchungen zur Symbolgeschichte.* (Psychologische Abhandlungen, VIII.) Zurich, 1951.

—— (ed.). *Aurora Consurgens: A Document attributed to Thomas Aquinas on the Problem of Opposites in Alchemy.* Translated by R. F. C. Hull and A. S. B. Glover. New York (Bollingen Series) and London, 1966.

FROBENIUS, LEO. *Das Zeitalter des Sonnengottes.* Berlin, 1904.

GAEDECHENS, RUDOLF. *Der Marmorne Himmelsglobus des Fürstlich Waldeckischen Antikencabinets zu Arolsen.* Göttingen, 1862.

GAMOW, GEORGE. *Atomic Energy.* Cambridge, 1947.

GARNERIUS. *Sancti Victoris Parisiensis Gregorianum.* See MIGNE, *P.L.,* vol. 193, cols. 23–462.

GERHARDT, OSWALD. *Der Stern des Messias.* Leipzig, Erlangen, 1922.

"Gloria mundi." See (*A*) *Musaeum hermeticum,* i.

GOODENOUGH, ERWIN R. *Jewish Symbols in the Greco-Roman Period.* (Bollingen Series XXXVII.) New York, 1953–68. 13 vols. (Vol. V, *Fish, Bread, and Wine,* contains two chapters on fish symbolism.)

GRASSEUS, JOHANNES. "Arca arcani artificiosissimi de summis naturae mysteriis." See (A) Theatrum chemicum, xxiv.

GRATAROLUS, GULIELMUS. Verae alchemiae artisque metallicae, citra aenigmata, doctrina, etc. Basel, 1561. (Pp. 269–86 contain Augurellus' "Chrysopoeia.")

GREGORY THE GREAT, SAINT. Expositiones in librum I Regum. See MIGNE, P.L., vol. 79, cols. 17–468.

———. In Expositionem beati Job Moralia. See MIGNE, P.L., vol. 75, col. 615 – vol. 76, col. 782.

GRENFELL, BERNARD P., and HUNT, ARTHUR S. New Sayings of Jesus and Fragment of a Lost Gospel from Oxyrhynchus. New York and London, 1904.

GUIGNEBERT, CHARLES. "Quelques remarques sur la perfection et ses voies dans le mystère paulinien," Revue d'histoire et de philosophie religieuses (Strasbourg), Année 8 (1928), pp. 412–29.

HAGGARD, H. RIDER. She. London, 1887.

HAHN, CHRISTOPH ULRICH. Geschichte der Ketzer im Mittelalter. Stuttgart, 1845–50. 3 vols.

HARNACK, ADOLF. Lehrbuch der Dogmengeschichte. 5th edn., Tübingen, 1931.

HAUCK, ALBERT (ed.). Realencyklopädie für protestantische Theologie und Kirche. Leipzig, 1896–1913. 24 vols.

HEIDEGGER, JOHANN HEINRICH. Quaestiones ad Textum Lucae VII, 12–17. 1655.

HELLWIG, CHRISTOPH VON. Neu eingerichtetes Lexicon Medicochymicum, oder Chymisches Lexicon. Frankfurt a. M. and Leipzig, 1711.

HENNECKE, EDGAR (ed.). Neutestamentliche Apokryphen. 2nd edn., Tübingen, 1924.

HERMAS. The Shepherd. In: The Apostolic Fathers. With an English translation by Kirsopp Lake. (Loeb Classical Library.) London and New York, 1912–13. 2 vols. (Vol. II, pp. 6–305.)

HERMES TRISMEGISTUS. *Tractatus vere aureus de lapidis philosophici secreto.* Opere et studio Dominici Gnosii in lucem editus. Leipzig, 1610. See also (A) *Ars chemica,* i; *Theatrum chemicum,* xvii.

HERTZ, MARTIN. *De P. Nigidii Figuli Studiis atque operibus.* Berlin, 1845.

HIPPOLYTUS. *Commentary on Daniel (Eis ton Daniel).* See: *Hippolytus' Werke,* Vol. I. Edited by G. N. Bonwetsch and H. Achelis. (Griechische Christliche Schriftsteller.) Leipzig, 1897.

———. *Elenchos.* See: *Hippolytus' Werke,* Vol. III. Edited by Paul Wendland. (Griechische Christliche Schriftsteller.) Leipzig, 1916. For translation, see: *Philosophumena; or, The Refutation of All Heresies.* Translated by Francis Legge. (Translations of Christian Literature.) London and New York, 1921. 2 vols.

HOGHELANDE, THEOBALD DE. "Liber de Alchemiae difficultatibus." See (A) *Theatrum chemicum,* ii.

HÖLDERLIN, FRIEDRICH. *Sämtliche Werke.* Berlin, 1943. 3 vols.

HOLLANDUS, JOANNES ISAACUS. "Fragmentum de lapide." See (A) *Theatrum chemicum,* xi.

HOMER. *The Iliad.* Translated by E. V. Rieu. (Penguin Classics.) Harmondsworth, 1954.

———. *The Odyssey.* Translated by E. V. Rieu. (Penguin Classics.) Harmondsworth, 1955. Also: *The Story of Odysseus.* Translated by W. H. D. Rouse. London and New York, 1937.

HONORIUS OF AUTUN. *Speculum de mysteriis ecclesiae.* In MIGNE, *P.L.,* vol. 172, cols. 807–1108.

HUGH OF STRASBOURG. *Compendium theologicae veritatis.* Venice, 1492.

HURWITZ, SIGMUND. "Archetypische Motive in der chassidischen Mystik." In: *Zeitlose Dokumente der Seele.* (Studien aus dem C. G. Jung-Institut, 3.) Zurich, 1952.

I Ching, or Book of Changes. The Richard Wilhelm [German] translation rendered into English by Cary F. Baynes. Princeton (Bollingen Series XII) and London, 3rd edn., 1967.

IDELER, CHRISTIAN LUDWIG. *Untersuchungen über den Ursprung und die Bedeutung der Sternnamen.* Berlin, 1809.

[IGNATIUS OF LOYOLA, SAINT.] *The Spiritual Exercises of St. Ignatius Loyola.* Edited and translated by Joseph Rickaby, S.J. 2nd edn., London, 1923.

"Instructio de arbore solari." See (*A*) *Theatrum chemicum,* **xxiii.**

"In Turbam philosophorum exercitationes." See (*A*) *Artis auriferae,* **iii.**

"Interpretatio cuiusdam epistolae Alexandri Macedonum regis." See (*A*) *Artis auriferae,* **viii.**

IRENAEUS, SAINT. *Adversus* [or *Contra*] *haereses libri quinque.* See MIGNE, *P.G.,* vol. 7, cols. 433–1224. For translation, see: *The Writings of Irenaeus.* Translated by Alexander Roberts and W. H. Rambaut. (Ante-Nicene Christian Library, 5, 9.) Edinburgh, 1868–69. 2 vols.

ISIDORE OF SEVILLE, SAINT. *Liber etymologiarum.* In MIGNE, *P.L.,* vol. 82, cols. 73–728.

JACOBI, JOLANDE. *The Psychology of C. G. Jung.* Translated by K. W. Bash. Revised edn., New Haven and London, 1951.

JA'FAR IBN MUḤAMMAD (ABU MA'SHAR) AL-BALKHĪ (Albumasar). *De magnis coniunctionibus.* Venice and Augsburg, 1489.

JAMES, MONTAGUE RHODES (trans.). *The Apocryphal New Testament.* Oxford, 1924.

JEREMIAS, ALFRED. *The Old Testament in the Light of the Ancient East.* Translated by C. L. Beaumont. London and New York, 1911. 2 vols.

JOHN CHRYSOSTOM, ST. *Responsiones ad orthodoxas.* (Among the works falsely attributed to St. Justin Martyr.) See MIGNE, *P.G.,* vol. 6, cols. 1249–1400.

JOSEPHUS, FLAVIUS. *Contra Apionem.* In: *Josephus.* With an English translation by H. St. J. Thackeray and R. Marcus. (Loeb Classical Library.) London and New York, 1926– . 9 vols. (not yet complete). (Vol. I, pp. 325ff.)

JUNG, CARL GUSTAV. *Alchemical Studies. Collected Works,** Vol. 13. New York and London, 1968.

———. "Answer to Job." In: *Psychology and Religion: West and East,* q.v.

———. *Archetypes and the Collective Unconscious. Collected Works,** Vol. 9, Part I. New York and London; 2nd edn., 1968.

———. Commentary on *The Secret of the Golden Flower.* In: *Alchemical Studies,* q.v.

———. "Concerning Mandala Symbolism." In: *Archetypes and the Collective Unconscious,* q.v.

———. "Concerning Rebirth." In: *Archetypes and the Collective Unconscious,* q.v.

———. "Instinct and the Unconscious." In: *The Structure and Dynamics of the Psyche,* q.v.

———. *Memories, Dreams, Reflections.* Recorded and edited by Aniela Jaffé. Translated by Richard and Clara Winston. New York and London, 1963. (U.S. and Brit. edns. separately paginated.)

———. *Mysterium Coniunctionis. Collected Works,** Vol. 14. New York and London, 1963; 2nd edn., 1970.

———. "On the Nature of the Psyche." In: *The Structure and Dynamics of the Psyche,* q.v.

———. "On Psychic Energy." In: *The Structure and Dynamics of the Psyche,* q.v.

———. Paracelsus the Physician." In: *The Spirit in Man, Art, and Literature,* q.v.

———. "Paracelsus as a Spiritual Phenomenon." In: *Alchemical Studies,* q.v.

* For details of the *Collected Works of C. G. Jung,* see end of this volume.

———. "The Phenomenology of the Spirit in Fairytales." In: *Archetypes and the Collective Unconscious,* q.v.

———. "The Philosophical Tree." In: *Alchemical Studies,* q.v.

———. "A Psychological Approach to the Dogma of the Trinity." In: *Psychology and Religion: West and East,* q.v.

———. *Psychological Types. Collected Works,** Vol. 6. (Alternate source: translation by H. G. Baynes, London and New York, 1923.)

———. *Psychology and Alchemy. Collected Works,** Vol. 12. New York and London, 2nd edn., 1968.

———. "The Psychology of the Child Archetype." In: *The Archetypes and the Collective Unconscious,* q.v.

———. "The Psychology of Eastern Meditation." In: *Psychology and Religion: West and East,* q.v.

———. "Psychology and Religion" (The Terry Lectures). In: *Psychology and Religion: West and East,* q.v.

———. *Psychology and Religion: West and East. Collected Works,** Vol. 11. New York and London, 1958; 2nd edn., 1969.

———. "The Psychology of the Transference." In: *The Practice of Psychotherapy. Collected Works,** Vol. 16. New York and London, 2nd edn., 1966.

———. "The Psychology of the Trickster Figure." In: *The Archetypes and the Collective Unconscious,* q.v.

———. "The Relations between the Ego and the Unconscious." In: *Two Essays on Analytical Psychology. Collected Works,** Vol. 7. New York and London, 2nd edn., 1966.

———. *The Spirit in Man, Art, and Literature. Collected Works,** Vol. 15. New York and London, 1967.

———. "The Spirit Mercurius." In: *Alchemical Studies,* q.v.

———. *The Structure and Dynamics of the Psyche. Collected Works,** Vol. 8. New York and London, 1960.

* For details of the *Collected Works of C. G. Jung,* see end of this volume.

———. "A Study in the Process of Individuation." In: *Archetypes and the Collective Unconscious,* q.v.

———. *Symbols of Transformation. Collected Works,** Vol. 5. New York and London, 1956; 2nd edn., 1967.

———. "Synchronicity: An Acausal Connecting Principle." In: *The Structure and Dynamics of the Psyche,* q.v.

———. "Transformation Symbolism in the Mass." In: *Psychology and Religion: West and East,* q.v.

———. "Über das Selbst," *Eranos Jahrbuch 1948* (Zurich, 1949). (Became ch. IV of the present work.)

KELCHNER, ERNST. *Der Enndkrist.* Frankfurt a. M., 1891.

Kena Upanishad. See Upanishads.

KEPLER, JOHANN. *Discurs von der grossen Conjunction.* In: *Johannis Kepleri Astronomi Opera Omnia.* Edited by Ch. Frisch. Frankfurt a. M., 1858–71. 8 vols. (Vol. VII, pp. 697–711.)

KHUNRATH, HEINRICH CONRAD. *Von hylealischen, das ist, pri-materialischen catholischen, oder algemeinem natürlichen Chaos.* Magdeburg, 1597.

KIRCHER, ATHANASIUS. *Arithmologia, sive De abditis numerorum mysteriis.* Rome, 1665.

KIRCHMAIER, GEORG CASPAR. *Disputationes zoologicae.* Jena, 1736.

KNAPP, MARTIN JOHANN. *Antiskia: Ein Beitrag zum Wissen um die Präzession im Altertum.* Basel, 1927.

KOHUT, ALEXANDER. "Die talmudisch-midraschische Adamssage," *Zeitschrift der deutschen morgenländischen Gesellschaft* (Leipzig), XXV (1871), 59–94.

[Koran.] *The Meaning of the Glorious Koran.* An Explanatory Translation. By Marmaduke Pickthall. London, 1930.

LAGARDE, PAUL ANTON DE (previously P. A. Boetticher). *Clementina.* Leipzig, 1865.

* For details of the *Collected Works of C. G. Jung,* see end of this volume.

LAIBLIN, WILHELM. "Vom mythischen Gehalt unserer Märchen," in: WILHELM SCHLOZ and LAIBLIN. *Vom Sinn des Mythos.* Stuttgart, 1936.

LAMBSPRINGK. "De Lapide philosophico figurae et emblemata." See (*A*) *Musaeum hermeticum,* ii.

LAYARD, JOHN. "The Incest Taboo and the Virgin Archetype," *Eranos-Jahrbuch* (Zurich), XII (1945). (Volume for C. G. Jung on His Seventieth Birthday.)

——. *Stone Men of Malekula: Vao.* London, 1942.

Lexicon Medico-chymicum. See HELLWIG.

LIBAVIUS, ANDREAS. *Alchymia . . . recognita, emendata, et aucta.* Frankfurt a. M., 1606.

LIGHTFOOT, JOSEPH BARBER. *Notes on Epistles of Saint Paul.* London, 1895.

MAAG, VICTOR. "Jahwäs Heerscharen," *Schweizerische theologische Umschau* (Bern), XX (1950), 27–52.

MACROBIUS, AMBROSIUS THEODOSIUS. *Commentarium in Somnium Scipionis.* In: *Opera.* Edited by F. Eyssenhardt. Leipzig, 1893.

MAIER, MICHAEL. *De circulo physico quadrato.* Oppenheim, 1616.

——. *Secretioris naturae secretorum scrutinium chymicum.* Frankfurt a. M., 1687.

——. *Symbola aureae mensae duodecim nationum.* Frankfurt a. M., 1617.

MAIMONIDES, MOSES. [*More Nebuchim.*] *The Guide for the Perplexed.* Translated by M. Friedlander. London, 1928.

MANGETUS, JOANNES JACOBUS. See under (*A*).

MARIA PROPHETISSA. "Practica . . . in artem alchemicam." See (*A*) *Artis auriferae,* vi.

MARIETTE, FRANÇOIS AUGUSTE FERDINAND. *Dendérah.* Paris (printed in Alexandria), 1875. Plates, 5 vols., Paris, 1870–74.

MASENIUS, JACOBUS. *Speculum imaginum veritatis occultae.* Cologne, 1714. 2 vols.

MECHTHILD, SAINT. *Liber gratiae spiritualis.* Venice, 1522. For translation, see: *The Revelations of Mechthild of Magdeburg, or The Flowing Light of the Godhead.* Translated by Lucy Menzies. London, 1953.

MEERPOHL, FRANZ. *Meister Eckharts Lehre vom Seelenfünklein.* (Abhandlungen zur Philologie und Psychologie der Religion, 10.) Würzburg, 1926.

MEYER, KARL H. *Altkirchenslavisch-griechisches Wörterbuch des Codex Suprasliensis.* Glückstadt and Hamburg, 1935.

Midrash Tanchuma (Shemoth). (In Hebrew.) Edited by Solomon Buber. Vilna, 1885.

MIGNE, JACQUES PAUL (ed.). *Patrologiae cursus completus.*
[*P.L.*] Latin series. Paris, 1844–64. 221 vols.
[*P.G.*] Greek series. Paris, 1857–66. 166 vols.
(These works are referred to as "MIGNE, *P.L.*" and "MIGNE, *P.G.*" respectively.)

MORIENUS ROMANUS. "Sermo de transmutatione metallica." See (*A*) *Artis auriferae,* **x.**

MUHAMMAD IBN JARĪR ABŪ-JAFAR AL-TABARĪ. *Chronique.* Translated (into French) by Hermann Zotenberg. 4 vols. Paris and (vol. 4) Nogent-le-Rotrou, 1867–74.

MUENTER, FREDERIK CHRISTIAN KARL HENRIK. *Sinnbilder und Kunstvorstellungen der alten Christen.* Altona, 1825. 2 vols.

——— (as Muenter, Friedrich). *Der Stern der Weisen.* Copenhagen, 1827.

MYLIUS, JOHANN DANIEL. *Philosophia reformata.* Frankfurt a. M., 1622.

NATHAN, RABBI. *Abot de Rabbi Nathan.* See: *The Fathers according to Rabbi Nathan.* Translated by Judah Goldin. (Yale Judaica Series, 10.) New Haven, 1955.

NELKEN, JAN. "Analytische Beobachtungen über Phantasien eines Schizophrenen," *Jahrbuch für psychoanalytische und psychopathologische Forschungen* (Vienna and Leipzig), IV (1912), 504ff.

NEUMANN, ERICH. *The Great Mother.* Translated by Ralph Manheim. New York (Bollingen Series XLVII) and London, 1955.

————. *The Origins and History of Consciousness.* Translated by R. F. C. Hull. New York (Bollingen Series XLII) and London, 1954.

NIETZSCHE, FRIEDRICH. *Thus Spake Zarathustra.* Translated by Thomas Common, revised by O. Levy and J. L. Beevers. London, 1932.

NIGIDIUS FIGULUS, PUBLIUS. See HERTZ.

NOSTRADAMUS, MICHEL (Nostredame). *The Complete Prophecies of Nostradamus.* Translated and edited by Henry C. Roberts. New York, 1949. (Original: *Vrayes Centuries et Prophéties de Maistre Michel Nostredame.* Amsterdam, 1667.)

"Novi luminis chemici Tractatus. . . ." See (*A*) *Musaeum hermeticum,* **iv.**

"Novum lumen chemicum." See (*A*) *Musaeum hermeticum,* **iii.**

ONIANS, RICHARD BROXTON. *The Origins of European Thought.* 2nd edn., Cambridge, 1954.

ORIGEN. *Commentaria in Genesim.* See MIGNE, *P.G.,* vol. 12, cols. 47–92.

————. *Contra Celsum.* See MIGNE, *P.G.,* vol. 11, cols. 641–1632. For translation, see: *Contra Celsum.* Translated by Henry Chadwick. Cambridge, 1953.

————. *De principiis.* See MIGNE, *P.G.,* vol. 11, cols. 115–414. For translation, see: *On First Principles.* Translated by G. W. Butterworth. London, 1936.

————. *De oratione.* See MIGNE, *P.G.,* vol. 2, cols. 415–562. For translation, see: *Alexandrian Christianity. Selected Translations of Clement and Origen.* . . . By John Ernest Leonard Oulton and Henry Chadwick. (Library of Christian Classics, 2.) London, 1954. (Origen "On Prayer," pp. 180–387.)

————. *In Genesim homiliae.* See MIGNE, *P.G.,* vol. 12, cols. 145–262.

————. *In Leviticum homiliae.* See MIGNE, *P.G.,* vol. 12, cols. 405–574.

————. *In Lucam homiliae.* See MIGNE, *P.G.,* vol. 13, cols. 1801–1902.

————. *In Numeros homiliae.* See MIGNE, *P.G.,* vol. 12, cols. 583–806.

————. *Selecta in Genesim.* See Migne, *P.G.,* vol. 12, cols. 91–146.

————. See also Adamantius.

Orosius. "Ad Aurelium Augustum commonitorium de errore Priscillianistarum et Origenistarum." In: *Corpus Scriptorum Ecclesiasticorum Latinorum,* Vol. XVIII. Edited by Georg Schepss. Vienna and Leipzig, 1889. (Pp. 151–57.)

Pantheus, Joannes Augustinus. *Ars transmutationis metallicae.* Venice, 1519.

[Paracelsus (Theophrastus Bombastus of Hohenheim).] *Theophrast von Hohenheim genannt Paracelsus Sämtliche Werke.* Edited by Karl Sudhoff. Munich and Berlin, 1922–35. 15 vols. (Vol. III contains: *De vita longa,* pp. 247ff.; *De mumia libellus,* pp. 375f.; *Fragmentarische Ausarbeitungen zur Anatomie,* pp. 459ff.)

————. *Volumen Paramirum und Opus Paramirum.* Edited by Franz Strunz. Jena, 1904. (*De causis Morborum invisibilium,* pp. 291ff.)

Pauli, W. "The Influence of Archetypal Ideas on the Scientific Theories of Kepler." Translated by Priscilla Silz. In: C. G. Jung and Pauli. *The Interpretation of Nature and the Psyche.* New York (Bollingen Series LI) and London, 1955.

Paulinus of Nola, Saint. See: *S. Pontii M. Paulini Carmina.* Edited by Wilhelm Hartel. (Corpus Scriptorum Ecclesiasticorum Latinorum, 30.) Vienna, 1894.

Pernety, A. J. *Dictionnaire mytho-hermétique.* Paris, 1787.

Peters, Christian Heinrich Friedrich, and Knobel, Edward Bell. *Ptolemy's Catalogue of Stars: A Revision of the Almagest.* Washington, 1915.

Petrus de Aliaco. See Ailly.

Philalethes, Eirenaeus. "Introitus apertus . . ." See (*A*) *Musaeum hermeticum,* v.

————. "Metallorum metamorphosis." See (*A*) *Musaeum hermeticum,* vi.

Picinelli, Filippo (Philippus Picinellus). *Mundus symbolicus.* Cologne, 1680–81.

Pistis Sophia. Translated by George Robert Stow Mead. London, 1896.

"Platonis liber quartorum." See *(A) Theatrum chemicum,* **xix.**

PLINY (Gaius Plinius Secundus). *Natural History.* Translated by H. Rackham and W. H. S. Jones. (Loeb Classical Library.) London and New York, 1938– (not yet completed).

PLOTINUS. *The Enneads.* Translated by Stephen MacKenna. 2nd edn., revised by B. S. Page. London and New York, 1956.

PLUTARCH. *De Iside et Osiride.* In: *Plutarch's Moralia.* With an English translation by Frank Cole Babbitt. (Loeb Classical Library.) London and New York, 1927 ff. 14 vols. (Vol. V, pp. 6–191.)

——. *Quaestiones convivales.* In: *Plutarchi Moralia.* Edited by C. Hubert and others. Vol. IV. Leipzig, 1925.

POHL, OTTO. *Das Ichthysmonument von Autun.* Berlin, 1880.

POLEMON. *De physiognomia liber.* Edited by Georg Hoffmann. In: *Scriptores Physiognomici Graeci et Latini.* Edited by P. Richard Foerster. Leipzig, 1893. 2 vols. (Vol. I, pp. 93–294.)

PORDAGE, JOHN. *Sophia: das ist Die Holdseelige ewige Jungfrau der göttlichen Weisheit.* Amsterdam, 1699.

PREISENDANZ, KARL. *Papyri Graecae Magicae.* Leipzig and Berlin, 1928–31. 2 vols.

PRISCILLIAN. *Opera quae supersunt.* (Corpus Scriptorum Ecclesiasticorum Latinorum, 18.) Edited by Georg Schepss. Vienna and Leipzig, 1889.

PROSPER OF AQUITAINE. See AUGUSTINE, *Liber Sententiarum.*

PSELLUS, MICHAEL. *De daemonibus.* In: *Iamblichus de Mysteriis Aegyptiorum,* etc. Edited by Marsilio Ficino. Venice, 1497. (fol. N–N vi^v.)

QUISPEL, GILLES. "Philo und die altchristliche Häresie," *Theologische Zeitschrift* (Basel), V (1949), 429–36.

——. "Note sur 'Basilide'," *Vigiliae Christianae* (Amsterdam), II (1948), 115–16.

RAHNER, HUGO. "Flumina de ventre Christi," *Biblica* (Rome), XXII (1941), 269–302; 367–403.

RAMSAY, WILLIAM MITCHELL. "The Cities and Bishoprics of Phrygia," *Journal of Hellenic Studies* (London), IV (1883), 370–436.

RASHI (Solomon ben Isaac of Troyes). See: *Pentateuch with Targum Onkelos . . . and Rashi's Commentary*. Translated by M. Rosenbaum and A. M. Silbermann. London, 1929–34. 5 vols.

REITZENSTEIN, RICHARD. *Poimandres*. Leipzig, 1904.

—— and SCHÄDER, H. H. *Studien zum antiken Syncretismus aus Iran und Griechenland*. (Studien der Bibliothek Warburg, 7.) Leipzig and Berlin, 1926.

RHABANUS MAURUS. *Allegoriae in Sacram Scripturam*. See MIGNE, *P.L.*, vol. 112, cols. 849–1088.

Rig-Veda. See: NICOL MACNICOL (ed.). *Hindu Scriptures*. (Everyman's Library.) London and New York, 1938.

RIPLEY, GEORGE. "Duodecim portarum axiomata philosophica." See (*A*) *Theatrum chemicum*, x.

——. *Chymische Schrifften*. Erfurt, 1624.

——. *Opera omnia chemica*. Kassel, 1649.

ROBERTS, R. "Jesus or Christ?—a Reply," *The Quest* (London), II (1911), 108–25.

Rosarium philosophorum. See (*A*) *Artis auriferae*, xi.

ROSCHER, WILHELM HEINRICH. *Ausführliches Lexikon der griechischen und römischen Mythologie*. Leipzig, 1884–1937. 6 vols.

"Rosinus ad Sarratantam." See (*A*) *Artis auriferae*, v.

ROUSSELLE, ERWIN. "Seelische Führung im lebenden Taoismus," *Eranos-Jahrbuch 1933* (Zurich, 1934), 135–99.

RULAND, MARTIN. *Lexicon alchemiae*. Frankfurt a. M., 1612. Translated as: *A Lexicon of Alchemy*. [London, 1892.]

RUPESCISSA, JOANNES DE. "De confectione veri lapidis." See GRATAROLUS, in whose work it is contained.

——. *La Vertu et la propriété de la quinte essence*. Lyons, 1581.

RUSKA, JULIUS FERDINAND. *Tabula Smaragdina; ein Beitrag zur Geschichte der hermetischen Literatur.* Heidelberg, 1926.

——. *Turba Philosophorum.* Berlin, 1931.

——. "Die Vision des Arisleus." In: *Historische Studien und Skizzen zu Natur- und Heilwissenschaft.* Festschrift für Georg Sticker. Berlin, 1930.

SCHÄRF, RIWKAH. "Die Gestalt des Satans im Alten Testament." In: C. G. JUNG. *Symbolik des Geistes.* Zurich, 1953.

SCHEFTELOWITZ, I. "Das Fisch-Symbol im Judentum und Christentum," *Archiv für Religionswissenschaft* (Leipzig), XIV (1911), 1–53, 321–92.

SCHOETTGEN, CHRISTIAN. *Horae Hebraicae et Talmudicae.* Dresden and Leipzig, 1733–42. 2 vols.

SCHREBER, DANIEL PAUL. *Memoirs of My Nervous Illness.* Translated by Ida Macalpine and Richard A. Hunter. London, 1955. (Original: *Denkwürdigkeiten eines Nervenkranken.* Leipzig, 1903.)

SCOTT, WALTER (ed.). *Hermetica.* Oxford, 1924–36. 4 vols.

SENARD, MARCELLE. *Le Zodiaque.* Lausanne, 1948.

SENDIVOGIUS, MICHAEL. "Novi luminis chemici." See (*A*) *Musaeum hermeticum,* iv.

Shaare Kedusha. See VITAL, HAYIM.

Shatapatha Brahmana. Translated by Julius Eggeling. (Sacred Books of the East, 12, 26, 41, 43, 44.) Oxford, 1882–1900. 5 vols.

Sibylline Oracles. See: *Oracula Sibyllina.* Edited by John Geffken. (Griechische Christliche Schriftsteller.) Leipzig, 1902.

SILBERER, HERBERT. *Der Zufall und die Koboldstreiche des Unbewussten.* (Schriften zur Seelenkunde und Erziehungskunst, 3.) Bern and Leipzig, 1921.

SMITH, E. M. *The Zodia.* London, 1906.

SÖDERBERG, HANS. *La Religion des Cathares.* Uppsala, 1949.

SPIEGELBERG, W. "Der Fisch als Symbol der Seele," *Archiv für Religionswissenschaft* (Leipzig), XII (1909), 574–75.

STEPHEN OF CANTERBURY. *Liber Allegoricus in Habacuc.* [Facts unavailable.—EDITORS.]

STRAUSS, HEINZ ARTHUR. *Die Astrologie des Johannes Kepler.* Munich and Berlin, 1926.

SYNESIUS OF CYRENE. *Hymni et Opuscula.* Edited by Nicholas Terzaghi. Rome, 1944. 2 vols.

TABARI. See MUHAMMAD IBN JARĪR ABŪ-JAFAR AL TABARĪ.

Tabula smaragdina. See (*A*) *Ars chemica,* ii; RUSKA.

TACITUS, P. CORNELIUS. *Historiarum Liber: The Histories.* Edited by W. A. Spooner. London, 1891. For translation, see: *The Histories.* Translated by W. Hamilton Fyfe. Oxford, 1912. 2 vols.

Talmud. *The Babylonian Talmud.* Translated into English under the editorship of Isidore Epstein. London, 1935–52. 35 vols. (Abbr.: *BT.*)

Targum. *The Targum to The Song of Songs.* Translated by Hermann Gollancz. London, 1908.

TATIAN. *Oratio adversus Graecos.* See MIGNE, *P.G.,* vol. 6, cols. 803–888. For translation, see: *The Writings of Tatian, etc.* Translated by B. P. Pratten [and others]. (Ante-Nicene Christian Library, 3.) Edinburgh, 1867.

TERTULLIAN. *Adversus Marcionem.* See MIGNE, *P.L.,* vol. 2, cols. 239–526. For translation, see: *The Five Books of Tertullianus against Marcion.* Translated by Peter Holmes. (Ante-Nicene Christian Library, 7.) Edinburgh, 1868.

————. *Apologeticus adversus gentes pro Christianis.* See MIGNE, *P.L.,* vol. 1, cols. 257–536. For translation, see: *The Writings of Quintus Septimus Tertullianus.* Vol. I. Translated by S. Thelwall. (Ante-Nicene Christian Library, 11.) Edinburgh, 1869. (Pp. 53–140.)

————. *De baptismo.* See MIGNE, *P.L.,* vol. 1, cols. 1197–1224. For translation, see: *The Writings* (as above). (Pp. 231–56.)

THEODOR BAR-KUNI. *Inscriptiones mandaïtes des coups de Khouabir.* Edited by H. Pognon. Paris, 1898–99. 3 parts (consecutively paginated).

THEOPHILUS OF ANTIOCH. *Ad Autolycum.* See MIGNE, *P.G.,* vol, 6, cols. 1023–1168.

THIELE, GEORG. *Antike Himmelsbilder.* Berlin, 1898.

THOMAS AQUINAS, SAINT. *Summa contra Gentiles.* Translated by the English Dominican Fathers. London, 1924–29. 5 vols.

———. *Summa theologica.* Translated by the Fathers of the English Dominican Province. London, 1911–22. 18 vols.

THOMAS AQUINAS, pseud. "Aurora, sive Aurea hora." In: [H. CONDEESYANUS, pseud., i.e., J. Grasseus.] *Harmoniae imperscrutabilis chymico-philosophicae, sive Philosophorum antiquorum consentientium* . . . Decas I . . . collectae ab H.C.D. . . . Decas II . . . collecta studio et industria Joannis Rhenani, M. D. Frankfurt a. M., 1625. See also (A) *Artis auriferae,* iv.

THORNDIKE, LYNN. *A History of Magic and Experimental Science.* New York, 1923–57. 8 vols.

TITUS OF BOSTRA. *Adversus Manichaeos libri III.* See MIGNE, *P.G.,* vol. 18, cols. 1069–1256.

"Tractatulus Avicennae." See (A) *Artis auriferae,* ix.

"Tractatus Aristotelis. . . ." See (A) *Artis auriferae,* vii; *Theatrum chemicum,* xx.

"Tractatus aureus." See (A) *Ars chemica,* i; *Theatrum chemicum,* xvii.

Turba philosophorum. See RUSKA, *Turba Philosophorum;* (A) *Artis auriferae,* i; MANGETUS, *Bibliotheca chemica,* ii; *Theatrum chemicum,* xvii-a.

Upanishads. See: *The Principal Upanishads.* Translated by Sarvapalli Radhakrishnan. London, 1953.

USENER, HERMANN. *Das Weihnachtsfest.* 2nd edn., Bonn, 1911.

[VAUGHAN, THOMAS.] *The Works of Thomas Vaughan: Eugenius Philaletha.* Edited by A. E. Waite. London, 1919.

VIGENÈRE, BLAISE DE. See (A) *Theatrum chemicum,* xxi.

VIROLLEAUD, CHARLES. "Note complémentaire sur le poème de Mot et Aleïn," *Syria* (Paris), XII (1931), 350–57.

———. "La Légende de Baal, Dieu des Phéniciens," *Revue d'études sémitiques* (Paris), C (1935), iii–xxi.

"Visio Arislei." See (*A*) *Artis auriferae*, ii.

VITAL, HAYIM. *Shaare Kedusha* ("The Gates of Holiness"). (In Hebrew.) Jerusalem, 1926. (Orig., Constantinople, 1731.)

VOLLERS, KARL. "Chidher," *Archiv für Religionswissenschaft* (Leipzig), XII (1909), 234–84.

WACKERBARTH, GRAF AUGUST JOSEPH LUDWIG VON. *Merkwürdige Geschichte des weltberühmten Gog und Magog*. Hamburg, 1820.

WAITE, ARTHUR EDWARD. *Lives of Alchemystical Philosophers*. London, 1888 (reprinted, 1955).

——— (trans.). *The Hermetic Museum Restored and Enlarged*. London, 1893. 2 vols. (Original: (*A*) *Musaeum hermeticum*.)

———. See also VAUGHAN.

WEISS, JOHANNES. *The History of Primitive Christianity*. London, 1937. 2 vols. (Original: *Das Urchristentum*. Göttingen, 1914–17.)

WHITE, VICTOR, O.P. "Eranos, 1947, 1948." In his: *Dominican Studies*. Oxford, 1949. 2 vols. (Vol. II, pp. 399–400.)

WICKES, FRANCES GILLESPY. *The Inner World of Man*. New York and London, 1950.

WILHELM, RICHARD. *The Secret of the Golden Flower*. With a European commentary by C. G. Jung. Translated by Cary F. Baynes. London and New York, 1932; revised edn., 1962.

WIRTH, ALBRECHT. *Aus orientalischen Chroniken*. Frankfurt a. M., 1894.

WISCHNITZER-BERNSTEIN, RAHEL. *Symbole und Gestalten der jüdischen Kunst*. Berlin, 1935.

WÜNSCHE, AUGUST. אדר' המש'ח or *Die Leiden des Messias*. Leipzig, 1870.

Zohar, The. Translated by Harry Sperling and Maurice Simon. London, 1931–34. 5 vols.

ZOSIMUS. "Rosinus ad Sarratantam." See (*A*) *Artis auriferae*, v.

INDEX

INDEX

In entries relating to the books of the Bible, the numbers in parentheses
indicate the chapter and verse(s) referred to.

A

Aaron, 107, 228
abaissement du niveau mental, 28, 202
Abarbanel, Isaac, 74, 107
Abba, Rabbi, 80
Abercius inscription, 73, 89n, 103, 115, 117
ablution, 187
Abot de Rabbi Nathan, 113n
Abraham, 59
Abraham ben Hiyya, Rabbi, 74
Abu Ma'shar/Abu Mansor, *see* Albumasar
accentuation, moral, of opposites, 70
acetum, 160; *see also* vinegar
Achamoth, *see* Sophia
act of God, 25
Acts of the Apostles, (2 : 3), 135n; (7 : 43), 75n; (17 : 29, 30), 191n
Acts of Thomas, see *Thomas, Acts of*
Adam, 199; Adam/Eve syzygy, 254; carries Eve with him, 206; Christ and, 39, 197, 232; Eve's birth from, 205f; first and second, 37; higher, 197, 214, 232, 237, 240, 248, 255; —, and lower, 227, 233; lower, 244, 255; male/female, 204; mystic, 36; original man/Anthropos/Archanthropos, 200, 203, 208, 218n; relation to creator and creatures, 189; as "rock," 88, 208; second, 201, 204; and serpent, 233, 244f

Adamantius, dialogue of, 54n
Adamas (arch-man), 208
adamas (steel), 161
Adam Scotus, 100f
adaptation, weak, and emotion, 9
Adar, month of, 119
Adech, 213
Adler, Alfred, 165
Adonis, 121, 199
"Aenigmata ex Visione Arislei," 126, 127n, 137–38, 142
Aeon: Autopator as, 191; birth from Kore, 104
aeon, Christian, ix
"aes Hermetis," 156
Aesculapius, serpent of, 245n
affects, 9; and anima/animus, 16; feeling-tone, 33
Africa, 96, 175
agape, 90
Agathodaimon, 186; serpent as, 188, 230, 245n
ages, two, in pseudo-Clement, 55
aggregation, states of, 250f, 257
ἄγνοια, 191
ἀγνωσία, 190–92, 193n; God's, 194
Ailly, Pierre d', 75n, 76n, 77n, 82, 83, 96, 97, 98n, 99
Aipolos, 216
air, 249
Akathriel, 60
albedo, 148, 235
Albertus Magnus, 77n, 80n, 87, 256
Albigenses, 150
Albumasar (Ja'far ibn Muhammad [Abu Ma'shar] al-Balkhī), 75, 76–78nn, 80n, 95n, 96, 97, 99

alchemy/alchemists, 89 *et passim;*
beginnings of, 173; Catharism
and, 150; Chinese, 264; and
Christ, 182; Christ-image in, 67;
compensation in, 124; conjunction
of opposites in, 40; dragon in,
120; eagle in, 64*n;* fish in, 126*ff;*
Latin, beginnings of, 87; motive
of, 171; and natural science, 176;
Negroes in, 210; pagan currents
in, 176; phenomenology of symbols in, 179; physical speculations
of, 249*ff;* quaternio in, 232*ff;* rise
of, 150; significance of matter in,
66; and "theoria," 179; uncon-
scious in, 142
Alciati, Andrea, 158
alcohol, 225
alembics, three, 241
Alexandria, 89, 104, 156*n*
Alexius Comnenus, 148
"Allegoriae sapientum supra librum
Turbae," 126
"Allegoriae super librum Turbae,"
125*n*, 126, 127*n*
allegories, *see* symbols
Allenby, Amy Ingeborg, 268*n*
Almaricus, *see* Amalric of Bene
Amalric of Bene, 83
ambivalence, 13; of fish symbol,
118*ff*
Ambrose, St., 88, 235*n*
Amen, 206
Amitābha land, vision of, 151*n*
Amon, 78
Amoraim, 80*n*
Amos, Book of, (5 : 26), 74*f*
Anacreon, beaker of, 211
analogy formation, 261
analysis, 260
anamnesis, 40, 180
Andrew, St., 89
androgyny, of Christ, 204, 205
angels, 146, 195
Angelus Silesius, 206
Anger, Rudolph, 74*n*
Ani, Papyrus of, 76*n*

anima, 8, 10, 13*ff*, 30*f*, 187, 266; and
Eros, 14; feeling-value of, 28;
liberty as, 30; Miriam as, 210,
228; novelists and, 267; personification of unconscious, 11*n;* possession by, 23; *see also* anima/
animus
anima/animus: appearance of contents, 19; cannot be integrated,
20; effects on ego, 16*f;* fear of,
33; feeling-value of, 28; as functions, 20; positive aspect, 268;
recognition of, 22, 267; relation
to each other, 15
anima christiana, 36
anima mundi, 136, 142, 160, 198,
242
anima rationalis, 38*f*, 212*n*
anima rerum, 157–58*n*
animals, helpful, 145, 186
animosity, 16, 267
animus, 8, 10, 14*ff*, 30*f*, 33, 266,
267; and logos, 14, 16, 21; positive aspect of, 16; *see also* anima/
animus
annunciation, of Christ-figure, 189
Anthropos, 246, 247, 259; Christ as,
204; figures, ix, 65, 204; Gnostic,
197*f;* —, names of, 189; and
Hermes, 230; king as, 198; ser-
pent/snake and, 232*f;* symbol for
God, 195; vessel as counterpart
of, 242; *see also* Adam; Archanthropos; Man, original; Protanthropos
Anthropos quaternio, 231, 233, 244,
254
Anthropus primus, Saturn as, 197
Antichrist, ix, 36, 61, 62, 63, 94,
106; astrological origin, 76; astrological prediction of, 99; as half
archetype of self, 44; as King of
the Jews, 79*n*, 107; Nostradamus
on, 101; problem of, 42*f;* prophecies of, 109; second, 96, 102; as
shadow of self, 42, 44
antimimon pneuma, 35, 42

Antony, Mark, 144
Anu, 124
Apelles, 75
Apep, 76
Aphrodite, 21, 104, 112, 217
Apocalypse, ix, 36, 90, 105–6, 110;
    see also Revelation of St. John
apocatastasis, 40, 169, 259
Apollo, 81, 252
Apollonius of Tyana, 126n
Apophis-serpent, 230
apperception, 169
aqua, 160; abyssi, 215; doctrinae,
    159, 180, 185, 187, 188, 215, 241;
    permanens, 88, 150, 158, 187n,
    235, 239n, 241; roris nostri, 158
Aquarius (♒), 82, 87, 91, 92, 93
Aquilo, 100, 125
Arab tradition, fish in, 123
Aratus, 92n
arcane substance/arcanum, 152, 157,
    159, 160, 163, 187n; artifex as,
    155; fishes as, 150; healing power
    of, 180; called lapis, 236; mag-
    nesia as, 156; in man and with-
    out, 162; refers to self, 145
Archanthropos, 197, 203, 209; see
    also Adam; Anthropos; Man, or-
    iginal; Protanthropos
Archegonos, 201n
archetic appetite, 133, 134
archetype(s), 8, 16f, et passim; in
    art history, 68; assimilation of,
    222; autonomous factors, 21; de-
    notes completeness, 68; good and
    bad effects of, 267; image of in-
    stinct, 179; numinosity of, 184n,
    196; self as, 167, 169; of the Spirit,
    85; totality of, 196; unconscious
    organizers of our ideas, 179; see
    also anima; animus; brothers,
    hostile; Christ; God-man; mar-
    riage quaternio; mother, chthon-
    ic; mother-son marriage; Re-
    deemer; self; shadow; spirit of
    gravity; wholeness; wise old man
Archeus, 133n, 213

archon(s): Christ and, 65; demiurge,
    190; of future/this Aeon, 254;
    Gnostic, 57, 230; Ialdabaoth, 75,
    208; Sabaoth, 76
argument, animus and, 15
Aries (♈), 74n, 82, 90n, 98, 103;
    see also Ram
Arisleus, 143; vision of, 130n; —,
    see also "Aenigmata ex Visione
    Arislei"
"Aristoteles de perfecto Magisterio,"
    156
Aristotle, 51
Armilus, 107
Ars chemica, 187n
art, history of, archetype in, 68
Artefius, 132n
Artis auriferae, 126n, 130n, 197n,
    238n, 240n, 241n
"as if," 203
ascendent, 82n, 148
ascension, 65
Ascension of Isaiah, 57
aspersion, 187
ass, 75f
assimilation, 189; ego/self, 24f; by
    projection-making factor, 24
Assumptio Mariae, see Mary
assumptions, 15
Astarte, 112
astrology, 262; Fishes in, 111; Ori-
    ental, 93; Saturn in, 75ff
Atargatis, 73, 104, 111, 112, 121
atheism, 109
Athens: Little Metropolis, 91; St.
    Paul and, 176, 191
atman, 32, 69, 144, 167, 194, 222
atom, 237, 242, 249, 260
attention, 24
Attis, 213, 217n; as Ichthys, 152n;
    "holy shepherd," 89n; polymor-
    phous, 199; Shepherd and, 103
Augurellus, Joannes Aurelius, 232n
Augustine, St., 38–40&nn, 46, 49–51,
    52, 72n, 79n, 80n, 90n, 100, 113,
    120, 147, 158, 182
Augustus, 144

Aurelia occulta, 187*n*
Aurora consurgens, 88*n,* 156*n,* 220*n,*
  238*n,* 239*n,* 241
aurum nostrum, 127
Authades, 197*n*
authority, inner, 25–26
autism, 9
autoerotism, projections and, 9
Autogenes, 197*n*
autonomy: of anima/animus, 20, 28;
  of archetypes, 21; of characteristics of shadow, 8
Autopator, 190*f*
Autun, 89
avatar, 176
Aztecs, 144

B

Baal, 119
Baba Bathra, see Talmud
Baba Kamma, see Talmud
Babylon, 121
Babylonian tradition, 124
Bacchus, 199
Bacon, Roger, 87, 97, 256
Bactria, 74
Bahman Yast, 108
Balaam, 59, 117
Balak, 59
baptism, 89, 90, 88; *see also* font
Barabbas, 91
barbel, 122
Barbelo, 195, 197*n;* Barbelo-Gnosis,
  196*n,* 197*n*
Bardesanes, 54
Bar-Kuni, *see* Theodor Bar-Kuni
Baruch, Apocalypse of, 115, 116,
  118
Basil the Great, St., 46–48, 82, 129
Basilides/Basilidians, 64, 66, 185*n,*
  190, 230, 234*n,* 269
Basilius (Bogomil bishop), 148
bath kol, 106
Baubo, chthonic, 13
Bauer, Walter, 213*n*

bear, as symbol, 226
Bear, Great, *see* Great Bear
Beasts, Lady of the, 116
Beatus, Giorgius, 187*n*
beetle, 226
Beghards, 84, 150
Beguins, 150
Behemoth, 115*n,* 118, 120, 121, 123,
  147*n;* battle with Leviathan, 80,
  118; eucharistic food, 116
being, in God, 193
Belinus, 126*n*
beloved, 12, 13
Benat na'sh, 124
Benedict, St., 82–83, 85
Benoist, Jean, 145
Berakoth, see Talmud
Bereshith Rabba(ti), 59*n,* 106
Bernard of Clairvaux, St., 125
Bernardus Trevisanus, 143, 239*n*
Berthelot, Marcellin, 65*n,* 127*n,*
  143*n,* 156*n,* 159*n,* 238*n,* 264*n*
Bethlehem, 106
Bible, Protestants and, 178
bīn, 121
bird(s): allegory of Christ, 72; two
  fighting, 150; white and black,
  226
body, 64–65; in Basilides, 66
body/spirit triads, 55
Bogomils, 58, 147, 150
Böhme, Jakob, 61, 125, 171, 252*n*
Boll, Franz Johannes, 81*n,* 90*n,*
  91*n,* 104*n,* 105
Bouché-Leclercq, Auguste, 75*n,* 76*n,*
  81*n,* 104*n,* 112*n*
Bousset, Wilhelm, 75*n,* 108*n,* 109,
  197*n,* 198*n,* 208*n,* 219*n,* 220*n*
Brahe, Tycho, 81*n*
brahman, 222
"Bread through God," 84
breasts, Christ's, 205
Brethren of the Free Spirit, 84, 150
brh, 119
Brihadāranyaka Upanishad, 223
Brimos, 217
brother-sister pair, 31, 210

brothers, hostile, 80n, 81, 87, 254; monsters as, 119
Brugsch, Heinrich, 207n
Buddha, symbol for God, 195
Buddhism, 136; and yoga, 176; see also Zen
Budge, Ernest Alfred Wallis, 88n, 122n, 123, 207n
bull: Behemoth as, 120; Mithras and, 124; one-horned, 199; as symbol, 226
Bundahish, 246n

C

Cabala/cabalism/cabalists, 58, 61, 125, 173, 218n, 268
Cabiros/Cabiri, 201, 212
Cabrol, Fernand, and Leclercq, Henri, 89n
Caesarius of Heisterbach, 239n
calendar, revolutionary, 98
Caligula, 144
Campbell, Colin, 198
Cana, miracle of, 211
Canopic jars, 122
Canticles, see Song of Solomon
Capricorn (♑), 92, 111
caput corvi, 210
carbon-nitrogen cycle, 260
Carcassonne, 145
Cardan, Jerome, 76n, 77n, 82, 95n
Carthage, 121
Carus, C. G., 6
Cassino, Monte, 83
castle, as symbol, 224
Castor, 81
cat, black, 30
Cathari/Cathars, 58, 83, 146ff; and alchemy, 150
causation, psychological, 62
causes, 165
Caussin, Nicholas, 128, 192
Celsus, 75
centre, 224; in alchemy, 169; in man, and God-image, 171; in one-

self and environment, 170; in Plotinus, 219; psychic and alchemical, 171
cerebellum, "Son" and, 186
cerebrum, "Father" and, 186
Chaldaeans, 111
chalybs, 132
chaos, 79, 148, 155, 194, 234, 236–37; and cosmos, 32; magnesia as, 156; see also massa confusa
Charles, R. H., 115n, 118n, 147n
Chartier, Jean, 139n
chemical processes, alchemy and, 157
cherub/cherubim, 123, 241
child: divine, 31; symbol for God, 195
China: circular opus in, 264; dragon symbolism in, 245; religions of, 70
"chirographum," 230 & n
Chiun, 74, 75n
choice: four elements and, 56; free, 5
Christ, 32, 255; and age of fishes, 92, 114; as Anthropos, 204; and Antichrist, 61, 115; archetype of self, 37; — of wholeness, x, 40; assimilation into psyche, 221; attributes of, and self, 44; as avatar of Vishnu, 176; childhood of, 103; common symbols with devil, 72; and contents of unconscious, 181; death of, 35; descent into hell, 39; dualistic aspects, 111; both ego and self, 110; as fish, see fish(es); and horoscope, 136–37; horoscopes of, 77n; human soul of, 39; as inner man, 203; as king and priest, 39, 147; lamb and, 105–6; male/female, 205; and Mary, in Gnostic legend, 202; as new aeon, 90; the perfect man, 69; pre-existent, 148; as quaternion of opposites, 63; as rock, 88; scriptural symbols of, 221; second, 65; and self, parallel,

Christ (*cont.*):

42, 44; and serpent, 186, 232; and shadow, 41*n*, 110; spouse of the Church, 21; subjective parallel of, 182; symbol for God, 195; — of self, 36*ff*, 62*n*; synoptic and Johannine, 72; transfiguration of, 122*n*; "uncomeliness" of, 140; "within," 183; as younger son of God, 57, 147; *see also* Adam; androgyny; Ichthys

Christ-figure: annunciation of, 189; significance of, 203–4

Christ-image: anthropomorphic, 67; perfection of, 68–69

Christensen, Arthur, 77*n*, 246*n*

Christian doctrine: and nature, 173; and the psyche, 174

Christianity: astrological origin, 76; divine syzygy in, 21; Germanic acceptance of, 175; myths underlying, 179; place in Western life, 175

Christmas Eve, 111

Chronos, 139

chthonic world, shadow and, 34

Church: as Bride of Christ/Lamb, 21, 204; as female, 21*n*; in modern world, 176; soul as, 206; as symbol, 224

Chwolsohn, Daniel, 75*n*, 197*n*

cinedian fish/stone, 138–39

circle(s): character of wholeness, 224*n*; God as, 153; magic, 32; in Maier, 264; soul as, 219; and square/squaring of, 224–25, 239, 241, 264; squared, of self, 204; symbols, 194; — of God, 195; —, self in, 190

circumambulation, 224

citrinitas, 127

city: heavenly, 37; in Oxyrhynchus sayings, 145; as symbol, 224

Clement of Alexandria, 22, 113*n*, 121, 222, 234*n*

Clement of Rome, 125; Second Epistle to Corinthians, 21*n*; for

pseudo-Clement, *see* Clementine Homilies

Clementine Homilies, 54*ff*, 101*n*, 192*n*, 254

cloud, 155

Cnidaria, 128

Codex Ashburnham 1166, 232

cognition, 61, 69

collective unconscious, 7, 164, 223, 234; archetypes and, 8; autonomy of, 20; dogma and, 174–75; and mythology, 179

Collesson, Johannes, 160, 162

collision, of conscious and unconscious, 194

collyrium, 127

Colossians, Epistle to the, (2 : 14), 230*n*

commissure, 93, 148

compass, 134

Compendium theologicae veritatis, 80*n*

compensation: function of unconscious, 20; in man and woman, 14

completeness: and perfection, 68, 69, 111; voluntary, 70; *see also* wholeness

complexio oppositorum, 61*n*, 225, 267; see also *coniunctio oppositorum*

compulsion, 140; c. neurosis, 10

concept, 33; merely a name, 32; metaphysical, 34

Concorricci, 83, 146*n*

concupiscentia, 112, 129

confusion, 194

coniunctio, of Adam and Eve, 206

coniunctio(nes) maxima(e), 82, 96, 97, 98, 111

coniunctio oppositorum, 31, 152, 159, 167, 268; *see also* opposites, conjunction of

conscientiousness, 24

consciousness: in Autopator, 191; broadening of, and *opus*, 148; cannot comprehend whole, 110–11; and causes and ends, 165;

differentiation of, 191; and discrimination, 260; ego and, 3, 24; ego as subjective, 164; founded on unconsciousness, 30; God-image and, 194; limits of its field, 3; monsters and development of, 121; myths and coming of, 148; relation of unconscious manifestations to, 225; and splitting of Original Man, 204; threshold of, 4; *see also* ego

consensus omnium / consensus generalis, 29, 30, 47, 178

constellations, 29

consummation of universe, 254

conversion, 40

copulation, 206; self-, 207

coral, 125*n*

Corinthians, First Epistle to, (5 : 2), 23*n*; (10 : 4), 88; (10 : 16), 115*n*; (15 : 47), 39*n*; Second Epistle to (Clement of Rome), 21*n*

Cornarius, 191

corpus mysticum, 32

correspondence: in *opus alchemicum,* 262; principle of, 258; *see also* synchronicity

cortex, 127, 137–38

corybants, 211

Corybas, *see* Korybas

cosmos, and chaos, 32; *see also* chaos

Cramer, H., 213*n*

crazes, 169

creation: Heliopolitan story of, 207; and *opus,* 148; of world by devil, 146

creator: as dreaming, 192; Gnostic symbols for, 196

creed, 174, 179

crocodile, 244

cross, 65*n*, 182, 189; as quaternity symbol, 204, 224; and snake, 78*n*; as symbol of God, 195

crucifixion, 69, 70; punishment for slaves, 78*n*

crystal, 224

culture hero, Christ as, 36

Cumont, Franz, 91*n*, 115*n*, 121

Curetes, 211

Cybele, 121

Cyprian, St., 112*n*

Cyranides, 138

D

Dactyls, 212

Dagon, 115*n*, 121

daimon(ion), 27, 199, 226

Damdad-Nashk, 246*n*

damnation, eternal, 61*n*

Daniel, Book of, 74; (2 : 34), 208*n*; (2 : 35), 209*n*; (2 : 45), 88*n*; (3 : 24*f*), 199; (3 : 25), 123*n*; (11 : 36*ff*), 36*n*

Dardaris, 250

daughter, 12; and father, 14, 16

David, 79

dawn-state, 148

dealbatio, 148

Dee, John, 221

Degenhardus, 139

De Gubernatis, Angelo, 114

"De igne et sale," 132*n*

deliberation, 16

Demeter, 12

demiurge, 110, 230; Basilidian, 190; devil as, 150, 232; Esaldaios, 208; Gnostic, 150, 196, 197–98; ignorant, myth of, 189; Satanael as, 147–48; son of, 190

Democritus (alchemist), 143*n*, 159

Denderah, 76*n*, 91

Denzinger, Heinrich, and Bannwart, Klemens, 52*n*, 83*n*, 253*n*

Derceto, 73, 104, 111

descensus ad inferos, 39

Deus absconditus, 135

Deussen, Paul, 152*n*

Deuteronomy, (32 : 17), 107; (32 : 39), 55

devaluation, of sexuality, 226

devil: as Adversary, 42; his body of fire, 132n; in Christian dogma, 124; counterpart of God, 61; as demiurge, 150, 232; and evil, 48; fourth person, 208; God ruling world through, 254; in Joachim of Flora, 86; Origen and fate of, 110; in Protestantism, 41; serpent as, 188, 230; symbols, in common with Christ, 72; world created by, 146; see also Satan

dharma, 217n

Didymus of Alexandria, 235n

Dieterich, Albrecht, 89, 124n

dilemma, of one and three, 195, 224, 225

din, 58

Diodoros (Megarian philosopher), 76n

Diodorus, 76

Dionysius the Areopagite, 46, 49, 51

Dionysus, 81, 158

Diorphos, 121

Dioscorides, 156n

Dioscorus, 159n

Dioscuri, 81

Diotima, 27

discrimination, 121, 258, 260; of the natures, 79

distillation, circular, 265

disturbance, symptoms of, 29

divisio, 168, 187; see also separatio

doctrinairism, 86

doctrine, Christian, see Christian doctrine

Doelger, Franz Josef, 73, 89, 113n, 114n, 115, 121

dog, 150

dogma(s), 169, 174–75; barbarian peoples and, 175; "belief" in, 178; believers and, 178n; drift from, 179; prejudice against, 175; reason for insistence on, 179; and "sacred history," 179; see also doctrine

Dominican order, 83

Domitian, 110

Dorn, Gerhard, 157, 159, 160–64, 166, 169–71, 174, 181, 187n, 197n, 220, 221n, 239, 264

dove, 115n, 139, 197

Dozy, Reinhart, and de Goeje, M. J., 75n

drachates / draconites / dracontias, 138, 139, 140

draconite, see drachates

Dragomanov, M., 147n

dragon, 155, 197; in China, 245; head of, 100; and snake, 233n, 244; stone of, 138f; winged and wingless, 120; and woman, 12, 103–4; see also snake

dream-analysis, 203

dreams, 25, 30, 35, 142, 223, 243; anima/animus in, 19; childhood, 190; of disoriented student, 134; fire in, 137n; of fishes, 151–52; image of self in, 67; instinctual foundation of, 203n; mandalas in, 31; of Passion play and snake, 78n; quaternary symbols in, 132n; shadow in, 120; symbolism in, 202

Drews, Arthur, 90n

dualism: in archetypal self, 42; in Christ-figure, 111; God's humanity and, 110; Manichaean, 49, 55, 57n, 58, 61, 269

duality: man's, 255; symbol for God, 195

du Cange, Charles, 128n, 138n, 154n

"Duodecim portarum axiomata philosophica," 131n

"Duodecim tractatus," 156n, 158

duty, conflicts of, 25, 45

dyad, 194

Dyophysites, 110

E

Ea, 121

eagle, 64, 72, 120

earth, 264

East, Philosophical, 132

Ebionites, 44, 81, 147, 197

Ecclesiasticus (9 : 18[25]), 135; (48 : 1), 129

echeneis, 140–42, 144, 145, 154–55

echinus, see *echeneis*

Eckhart, Meister, 87, 135, 189, 193–94, 206, 219

ecliptic, 93, 124

Eden, 225, 234; *see also* Paradise

education, modern, and dissociation, 181

egg, 220*n*, 239*n*

ego, 190; acquired during lifetime, 5; approximation to self, 23; archetypes and, 8; as centre of personality, 6; Christ's correspondence to, 110; complex nature of, 3; conscious and unconscious in, 4; dependence on unconscious, 7; effects of anima/ animus on, 16; exponent of self, 223; individuality of, 6; inflation of, 23–24; its knowledge of itself, 163–64; and metaphysical ideas, 34; not coincident with conscious personality, 4; overpowering of, 23; perplexity of, 189; relative abolition of, 45; somatic and psychic bases of, 3, 4; subjective consciousness, 164; subordinate to self, 5; as total consciousness, 5; what it is, 3; *see also* assimilation; personality

ego-consciousness: differentiation from unconscious, 24; and psyche, 164; shadow and, 28

Egypt, 209*n;* fish-cult in, 121; flight of Christ to, 103; and Israel, common symbols, 123; Jews in, 78; slaying of firstborn in, 58*n*

eidos, 34

eight, 224

Eisler, Robert, 90*n*, 91*n*, 103*n*, 104*n*, 116*n*, 121*n*

Eleazar, Abraham, 131

electron, 187*n*

elements, four, 251, 254, 264*f*, Plate I; contained in *lapis,* 166, 237 & *n;* hate and love of, 17; quaternity of, 86, 197*n;* as stages of fire, 249

elephant, 226

Elephantine, 121

Eleusis: mysteries of, 217; priests of, 217*n*

Elias, 106, 122*n*

elixir vitae, 127, 180

Elogabal, 89*n*

Elysian Fields, 30

Emmaus, 113

emotion: not an activity, 9; and the shadow, 8–9

emotionality, female, 55

Empedocles, 17

enantiodromia, ix, 43, 93, 95, 102, 108, 149, 225, 258

ends, 165

energy, 251

enkekalymmenos, 18

Enlightenment, the, 43, 150

ἔννοια, 191, 197*n; see also* consciousness

"Entkrist," 101

Enuma Elish, 124

environment: influence of, 21; projections and, 9–10

Ephesians, Epistle to the: (3 : 18), 88*n;* (4 : 23), 193*n;* (5 : 14), 208

Ephrem the Syrian, St., 140

Epictetus, 213*n*

Epidaurus, 188

Epiphanius, 44*n*, 57, 66, 72*n*, 76*n*, 81*n*, 88, 104, 114, 147, 159*n*, 190*n*, 197, 202, 208*f*

Epiphany, 104

epiphenomenon, psyche as, 174

equation, quaternio as, 257*ff*

equinoctial point, 77&*n*

Erman, Adolf, 78

Eros, 11, 12, 19; anima and, 14, 16, 21; a mighty daimon, 27

Esaldaios, 197; "the fourth," 208

eschatological state, 169

eschatology, in New Testament, 36

Esdras II, 121*n;* (6 : 49*ff*), 147*n;* (13 : 2*ff*), 120; (13 : 25), 115*n*

"Ethiopian woman," 228, 251, 252

Ethiopians, 210

Eubulides, 18*n*

eucharist, fish and, 113, 115*n*, 121, 152

eucharistic: act of integration, 144; feast, of Ophites, 188; food, Leviathan as, 119*f*

Eucherius, 72*n*, 100

Euchites, 44, 148

Euphrates, 104, 184–85, 199*f*, 211, 225, 235, 251, 252

Euthymios Zigabenos, 148

evangelists, four, 36, 195; symbols of, 123

Eve, 204, 205*f*, 206, 235; *see also* Adam

Everlasting Gospel, *see* Gospel

evil, 41, 46*ff*; absolute, 10; anima/animus and, 267; Christianity and, 109; and disposition of soul, 61; Gnostics and, 230; and good, 44–45*n*, 46*ff*, 267; and the north, 124; principle of, as creator, 256; shadow and, 266–67; *see also privatio boni*

evolution, 180

exaltatio, of Aphrodite, 112

exaltation, 156*n*

Exodus, Book of: (2 : 4*ff*), 210; (12 : 22), 58; (15 : 6), 59; (15 : 20*f*), 210; (18 : 27), 229*n;* (33 : 5), 58

experience: intersexual, 21*n;* sensory and immediate, 3

extrasensory perception, 184*n*

eyes, seven, 105*n*

Ezekiel, 101, 105*n*, 124, 132, 195, 241; (1 : 22), 123; (1 : 26), 123

F

factors: causal and final, of psychic existence, 165; *see also* subjective factor

fairytales, 149, 169, 180

faith: is absolute, 174; crumbling away of content, 178; and dogma, 178; rift from knowledge, 173*f*

Fall, the, 37, 39

Fallopius, Gabriel, 158

Fanianus, Joannes Chrysippus, 157

Farnese Atlas (Naples), 91

father: and daughter, 14; demiurge as, 190; in female argumentation, 15; God as, 193; idea of, 18*f;* in Moses quaternio, 227; "signs of the," 190; as unconscious, 191

father-animus, 210

father-mother, symbol for God, 195

fear, of unconscious, 33

feeling, 31, 178; function of value, 32

feeling-tones, 28, 33; subjective and objective, 29

feeling-value, 28, 31

female, *see* male and female

femininity, man's, 21*n*

Ferguson, John, 133*n*

"Fidelissima et jucunda instructio de arbore solari," 140*n*, 154

Fierz-David, Hans Eduard, 251*n*

Fierz-David, Linda, 13*n*

fifth, the, 225

filius macrocosmi, 66, 127, 155, 237

filius philosophorum, 66, 127, 155, 213

fire, 101, 264; in alchemy, 130*ff*, 252; as dream-symbol, 132*n*, 137*n;* four aspects of, 132, 249*ff*; and water, 225

firmament, 164

Firmicus Maternus, Julius, 88

firstborn, slaying of the, 58*n*

fish(es): 189, 244; aeon of the, 62; allegory of the damned, 122; in Arab tradition, 123; assimilation

of Christ-figure, 182; Atargatis cult and, 121; bad qualities of, 112; beneath the earth, 145; Christ and, 92, 113, 120; Christ and age of, 92, 111; and Christ as Ichthys, 115; Christian significance of, 114; direction of, 91; "drawn from the deep," 79n, 120; eaten by Christ, 121n; and fire, 135–36; golden, dream of, 151–52; great, as shadow of God, 119; —, splitting of, 119; historical significance of, 103ff; in Jewish symbolism, 115, 121; Lambspringk's symbol of reversed, 150; and Leviathan, 120; miraculous draught of, 89; as mother and son, 111, 114; originally one, 111; pagan symbolism, 115f; Platonic month of, ix, 149; in primitive Christianity, 188; "round," 127ff, 137–38, 140, 144; as ruling powers, 147, 149; as sepulchral symbol, 115; and serpent, 186; sign (♓) of the, 72ff, 91; —, a double sign, 111; —, twelfth, of zodiac, 118; Southern, 111n, 112; symbol, ambivalence of, 118ff; —, of Christ, 67, 72ff, 89; —, in Eastern religions, 73; —, of love and religion, 129; —, of self, 226; —, of soul, 122; symbolism of, and self, 183; yoked, 145, 147, 148–49; zodiacal, in Lambspringk, 145
fish-deities, Semitic, 121
fisherman, 112
fish-glue, 127n
five, 224
fixation, 168
Flaccianus, 72n
flatus vocis, 32
"flesh," the, 233
flood, god who dwells in, 211
flower, as symbol of self, 226
Fludd, Robert, 262n
Fomalhaut, 111n, 112
font, baptismal, 73

formlessness, 66
four, see elements s.v. four
"fourth," the, 184, 252
Franciscan order, 83 ·
Franz, Marie-Louise von, ix, 88n, 210n, 220n, 262n
Free Spirit: Brethren of the, 84, 150; and Eckhart, 194
freedom: of ego, limited, 7; moral, 26; subjective feeling of, 5
French Revolution, 43, 98, 233
Freud, Sigmund, 165, 203n; sexualistic approach to psyche, 226
frivolity, and evil, 61–62
Frobenius, Leo, 111n
fructificatio, 83
functions: anima/animus as, 20; differentiated and undifferentiated, 195; four, of consciousness, 258, 259; quaternity of, 196; rational, 28; reflex, 233; sensory, rivers as, 199; and space-time quaternio, 253

G

Gaedechens, Rudolf, 91n
Galileo, 34
gall, fish's, 137
Gamaliel the Elder, 113n
Gamow, George, 260n
garbha griha, 217n
Gargaros, 206n
Garnerius, 100, 125n
gate, narrow, 200
Gayomart, 246
Gehenna, fire of, 131
Gemini (♊), 77, 80n, 81, 83n
Genesis, Book of, 204, 235; (1 : 2), 148, 237; (1 : 7), 184n; (18 : 23), 59; (28 : 17), 214n; (44 : 5), 211n
Genesis, Johannine, 80
"genius," man's, 45
geomancy, 261
Gerard of Borgo San Donnino, 82
Gerhardt, Oswald, 74n, 75n, 77
Germanic peoples, 175

Geryon, 211
Gihon, 199, 225, 235
"Gloria mundi," 88n, 130
Gnosticism/Gnostics, 58, 93, 181, 192, 196ff, 269; and alchemy, 173, 232; Christ-figure in, 203; and demiurge, 150n; Eckhart and, 194; and evil, 41, 46, 109f; and Holy Ghost, 86; and magnetism, 154; and psyche, 174; as psychologists, 222; quaternio among, 242ff, 254ff; and symbols of self, 184ff; and unconscious, 190–91; and water, 159n
god: dying, 206; "earthly," Mercurius as, 232
God: absolute, 143; of Basilidians, 190; fish as shadow of, 119; and man, affinity, 209; in Old and New Testaments, 192; pneuma and soma in, 254; quaternary view of, 253n; symbols for, 195; threefold sonship, 64; two sons of, 147; union of natures in, 110; will of, 26f; without consciousness, 192; of wrath and of love, 192
God-eating, 144
Godhead: in Eckhart, 193; Second Person of, 196; unconscious, 193
God-image: alchemy and, 125; anthropomorphic, 55, 67; centre as, 219; in Christ and man, 38; Christian doctrine as expressing, 174; an experience, 194; human element in, 121; incomplete, 120; reformation of, 40; results of destruction of, 109; self as, 63, 109; and transcendent centre in man, 171; transformations of, and changes in consciousness, 194; and wholeness, 198; Yahwistic, 58; see also Imago Dei
God-man, archetype, 181–82
"gods": anima/animus as, 21; ithyphallic, 211; theriomorphic attributes of, 29

goddess, heavenly, 13
Goethe, J. W. von, 208, 234
Gog and Magog, 79, 80n, 107
gold, in alchemy, 264
good and evil, see evil
Goodenough, Erwin R., 73n, 90n, 113n, 115n, 117, 120n, 122n, 145n
Gospel, Everlasting, 82, 85, 88
gospels: miraculous element in, 177; synoptic, 93
grace: divine, 129; restoration through, 39; state of, 34
grape, 200
Grasseus, Johannes, 139
Gratarolus, Gulielmus, 146n, 232n
gravity, spirit of, 116n
Great Bear, 123, 124
Great Mother(s), 89n, 112, 199, 210
green/greenness, 30, 245
Gregory the Great, St., 101, 205n, 206n
Grenfell, B. P., and Hunt, A. S., 37n
ground, universal, 195, 200; Gnostic symbols for, 196ff
Guignebert, Charles, 213n
gyne (woman), 104n

H

Habakkuk, Book of, (2 : 3), 60
Haggard, H. Rider, 267n
Hahn, Christoph Ulrich, 84, 145n, 146n
Haly, 239n
Hanan ben Tahlifa, Rabbi, 80n
handwriting, 230
Hapi, 123
Harnack, Adolf, 54n, 254n
Harran, 126
Hartmann, E. von, 6
Hathor, Temple of, 91
heaven(s), 155; in Ascension of Isaiah, 57; four pillars of, 123; iron plate in, 122–23; kingdom of, 145; lapis in, 170; northern, 123

Heb-Sed festival, 198
Hecate, 21
Heidegger, Johann Heinrich, 76*n*
Heimarmene, 93*n*, 137*n*
Helen (Selene), 21
Helen (in Simon Magus), 197*n*
Heliogabalus, 89*n*
hell, 135; St. Basil on, 129; eternity of, 110; fire of, 131, 132; God's love in, 125
hemispheres, 134
hemlock, 217*n*
Hennecke, Edgar, 57*n*
Henry II, of France, 95
heptad, 197*n*
Hera, 206*n*; Babylonian, 116
Heracles, 81
Heraclitus, 219, 250
heresies, 150
hermaphrodite, 159, 211, 234, 248; and elevated places, 206; Original Man as, 204; stone as, 246; symbol for God, 195
Hermaphroditus, 127
Hermas, "Shepherd" of, 88*n*, 103, 224*n*
Hermes, 21, 155, 209, 234, 245; bird of, 221; ithyphallic, 230; Kriophoros, 103; Kyllenian/Kyllenios, 201, 211, 212, 232; Naassene view of, 208; "Ter Unus," 177; *see also* Mercurius/Mercury
Hertz, Martin, 136*n*
Heru-ur, 78, 122–23, 132*n*
hesed, 58
hexad, 228
hexagrams, 260
Hiddekel, 225, 235
hieros gamos, 12, 39–40, 89*n*, 206
Hierosolymus, 76*n*
Hinduism, and Buddhism, 176
Hipparchus, 81, 91
Hippocrates, 201*n*
Hippolytus, 1, 64, 65*n*, 66, 75*n*, 88*n*, 114, 139, 173, 184, 186, 187, 191, 198, 199, 200, 201, 202, 208*ff*, 222, 223*n*, 226, 230*n*, 233, 254

hiranyagarbha, 246
Hitler, Adolf, 102
Hoghelande, Theobald de, 137, 239*n*, 240
Hölderlin, Friedrich, 29
Hollandus, Johannes Isaacus, 235*n*
Holy Ghost, 135, 162; age of, 82–83, 85–86; espousal of, 86; fire of, 129, 131; indwelling of, 88; movement, 85–86, 87, 89, 150
Homer: *Iliad*, 206*n*, 218*n*; *Odyssey*, 208*n*, 209, 216
homo: altus, 232; *coelestis*, 39; *maximus*, 198; *quadratus*, 264
homosexual, 12
homunculus, 232, 246
Honorius of Autun, 101*n*
hook, fish-, 112*n*
horos, 65*n*
horoscope, 136–37, 224; zodia in, 148
horse, 226
Horus, 104, 122; four sons of, 122, 123, 124, 132, 240, 243; "older," 78; quaternio, 243; *see also* Heru-ur
house, as symbol, 224*f*
Hugh of Strasbourg, 80*n*, 102*n*
human figure, as symbol of self, 225, 226
Hurwitz, Sigmund, 226*n*, 268*n*
hyacinth, 139
hydromedusa, 134
hyle, 79
hypochondriac ideas, 169
hysteria, 203*n*; collective, 181

I

Ialdabaoth, 75, 208
Ibn Ezra, 108
I Ching, 118*n*, 260
Ichthys: Adonis as, 121; Christ as, 183; Christ or Attis as, 152*n*; Christian, 112, 119–20, 121; son of Derceto, 104, 111; *see also* fish(es)

315

ideals, collective, 29
Idechtrum, 213
Ideler, Christian Ludwig, 124*n*
identification, with intellectual standpoint, 31
identity, 18; of hunter and prey, 112; of lowest and highest, 246
Ides/Ideus, 213
idiosyncrasy(-ies), 169, 200
Ignatius Loyola, St., 165
ignis, see fire
ignorance, 191
illusion, 11, 16; see also *maya*
image of God: Christ and the soul as, 37; see also *imago Dei*
imagination, active, 19, 223, 243
imago, of mother, 11, 12, 14
imago Dei, 31, 37, 38*n*, 41, 260; *see also* God-image; image of God
Imhullu, 120
"immutability in the new rock," 84, 87
impulses, 27
"In Turbam philosophorum exercitationes," 126
incarnation, 179; fish and, 121
incest, 206, 210, 228, 229
incomplétude, sentiment d', 9
increatum, 237
India: development of symbol in, 176, 217*n*; Eckhart and, 194; fish in, 114; religions of, 70; thought of, 175
Indian influences, 223
Indies, 133–34
individuality, and ego, 6
individuation, 39, 40, 45, 200; apocatastasis in, 169; Christianity and, 70; as *mysterium coniunctionis,* 64; *opus* and, 264; repressed, 70; self and, 167; stone compared with, 170; symbolized in dreams, 153
infans, 127
infection, psychic, 248*n*
inferiority, 9, 17
inflation, 25; of ego, 23–24; nega-

tive, 62; peril of, 24; religious, 84
inhabitant, of house, 225
initiation, in mysteries, 261
Innocent III, Pope, 83, 99
innocents, massacre of, 103
Inquisition, 145
insight, intellectual, insufficiency of, 33
instinct(s), 21, 26, 31, 40–41, 145, 179, 234; archetype image of, 179; individual and common, 7; snake symbol of, 244
"Instructio de arbore solari," 140*n*, 154
integration, 30, 40, 200; of collective unconscious, 39; of contents of anima/animus, 20; mandala and, 32; of shadow, 22; of unconscious contents, 23
intellect, and values, 32
intellectualism, 86, 150
intensity, of idea, 28
"Interpretatio . . . epistolae Alexandri," 167*n*
Interrogationes maiores Mariae, 202, 207
Irenaeus, 41*n*, 45–46, 54, 65*n*, 66*n*, 110*n*, 150*n*, 196, 197*n*, 218*n*, 219*n*
Iron Age, fourth, 108
iron-stone, magnetic, 156*n*
irrationality, 17
Isaac, 90*n*
Isaiah, Ascension of, see *Ascension of Isaiah*
Isaiah, Book of: (14 : 12*ff*), 100; (14 : 31), 101*n*; (26 : 20), 59; (27 : 1), 118, 119; (28 : 10), 210*n*; (30 : 18), 60; (33 : 14), 144*n*; (66 : 7), 105
Ishmael, Rabbi, 60
Ishtar, 112
Isidore of Seville, St., 154*n*
Isidorus (Gnostic), 234
Isis, 104
Islam, 54*n*, 76, 95*n*, 99, 176
Israel and Egypt, common symbols, 123

J

Jacob, 214
Jacobi, Jolande, 253n
Ja'far ibn Muhammad (Abu Ma'-shar) al-Balkhī, see Albumasar
James, Epistle of, 135; (3 : 5), 135n; (3 : 6), 135
James of Sarug, 75
James, Montague Rhodes, 37n, 197n
Jeans, Sir James, 258n
jelly-fish, 128, 134, 137–38, 154n
Jeremiah, Book of: (1 : 13), 101; (1 : 14), 100
Jeremias, Alfred, 73n, 74, 112, 124n
Jesuits, 58
Jesus, 1, 65, 144, 201; faith and personality of, 178–79; as God-man, 35; Makarios, 200; Passion of, 64, 65, 67; in Pistis Sophia, 78–79; relation to Christ, 67; and separation of categories, 64; as third sonship, 67; a trichotomy, 65; as "truth sprouting from earth," 79; see also Christ
Jethro, 209n, 210, 228f, 244
Joachim of Flora, 82–83, 84, 86, 87, 149, 150, 253, Plate II
Job, 60, 108, 120
Job, Book of, 42, 58, 118; (26 : 7), 100; (26 : 12), 120; (26 : 13), 120n; (27 : 21), 101; (41), 119n
Jochanan, Rabbi, 60
Johannes de Lugio, 146n
John, St., 145; Epistles of, 43, 68; First Epistle of (4 : 3), 36n; Revelation of, see Revelation
John, Gospel of, 148; (1), 218n; (1 : 1ff), 211; (1 : 2), 148; (1 : 4), 211; (3 : 12), 202, 203; (4 : 10), 184n, 185, 199n; (5 : 2), 131n; (6 : 53), 202; (7 : 38), 214; (10 : 9), 185n; (10 : 34), 89, 209n; (14 : 6), 200; (18 : 36), 37n
John the Baptist, 192n
John Chrysostom, St., 48f

John of Paris, 80n
Jonah, 117; sign of, 111
Jonathan, Rabbi, 60
Jordan, 210–11
Joseph (father of Jesus), 78–79
Josephus, 76
Joshua, 111
jot, 218
Jothor, 209, 210
Judaeus (son of Set), 76n
Judaism, 58ff; Messianism in, 107
judgments: good/evil as, 53; moral, 47–48
Jung, Carl Gustav:
  CASES: student who dreamed of jelly-fish, 134; young woman with intense inner life who dreamed of fishes, 151–52
  WORKS: "Answer to Job," 87n; Commentary on The Secret of the Golden Flower, 182n; "Concerning Mandala Symbolism," 40n, 219n; "Concerning Rebirth," 111n; "Instinct and Unconscious," 8n; Memories, Dreams, Reflections, 134n; Mysterium Coniunctionis, 13n, 235n; "On the Nature of the Psyche," 4, 8n, 24n, 164n, 174n, 179n; "On Psychic Energy," 29n; "Paracelsus the Physician," 133n, 213n; "Paracelsus as a Spiritual Phenomenon," 211n, 214n, 239n, 242n; "The Phenomenology of the Spirit in Fairytales," 55n, 85n, 99n, 159n, 203n, 224n, 229n; "The Philosophical Tree," 235n; "A Psychological Approach to the Dogma of the Trinity," 37n, 86n, 152n, 153n, 224n, 246n, 253n; Psychological Types, 28n, 116n, 159n, 223n, 224n, 253n; Psychology and Alchemy, 31n, 37n, 40n, 63n, 64n, 67n, 78n, 87, 116n, 125n, 134n, 136n, 140n, 152n, 155n, 182, 190n,

Jung, Carl Gustav (*cont.*):
   197*n*, 199*n*, 237*n*, 239*n*, 241*n*,
   243*n*, 245*n*, 259*n*, 262, 264*n*;
   "The Psychology of the Child
   Archetype," 31*n*; "The Psychology of Eastern Meditation," 135*n*, 151*n*, 204*n*;
   "Psychology and Religion,"
   87*n*, 182*n*; "Psychology of the
   Transference," 13*n*, 22*n*, 64*n*,
   159*n*, 167*n*, 209*n*, 225*n*, 228*n*,
   229*n*, 242*n*, 243*n*; "The Psychology of the Trickster Figure," 203*n*; "The Relations
   between the Ego and the Unconscious," 21*n*, 23*n*, 63*n*,
   182*n*; "The Spirit Mercurius,"
   43*n*, 86*n*, 136*n*, 152*n*, 168*n*,
   203*n*, 212*n*, 232*n*, 235*n*, 253*n*;
   "A Study in the Process of Individuation," 65*n*, 67*n*, 190*n*,
   204*n*, 219*n*, 253*n*; *Symbols of
   Transformation*, 101*n*, 111*n*,
   132*n*; "Synchronicity," 184*n*,
   258*n*; "Transformation Symbolism in the Mass," 144*n*, 220*n*,
   238*n*; "Über das Selbst," 23*n*

Jupiter (♃), 74, 76, 77, 78, 81, 82,
   83*n*, 95, 97; moons of, 34
jurisprudence, and consciousness, 5
justice, of Yahweh, *see* Yahweh
Justin Martyr, 173, 177, 230

K

Ka-mutef, 206
Kant, Immanuel, 6
karma, 140*n*, 271*n*
Kaulakau, 210
Kelchner, Ernst, 102*n*
Kena Upanishad, 223
Kepler, Johann, 77*n*, 173, 207
kerygmatics, 177
Keshava, 114
Kewan, 75*n*
Khidr legend, 111
Khunrath, Heinrich Conrad, 88,
   156, 220

kibla, 124
king(s), deification of, 198; divine
   right of, 177
kingdom(s), heavenly/of God, 37;
   two, in pseudo-Clement, 55
"kingless race," 260
Kings, First Book of, 59; (22 : 19),
   59
kingship, and self, 198
Kircher, Athanasius, 262*f*
Kirchmaier, Georg Caspar, 116*n*
Klaus, Brother, 25
Knapp, Martin Johann, 81*n*
Kohut, Alexander, 246*n*
Kolorbas, 195
Korah, children of, 106
Koran, 111*n*
Kore, 104
Korion, 104
Korybas, 199, 211–12
krater, 65*n*, 191*n*
Kurma, 176
Kyrios, 182

L

lac virginis, 160
"Ladder of the Twin Gods," 122
Lagarde, Paul A. de, 56*n*
Laiblin, Wilhelm, 149*n*
lake, as symbol of self, 226
Lamb, 103; in Apocalypse, 90*n*,
   105*f*; Church as Bride of, 204;
   marriage of the, 12, 36, 268
Lambspringk, 92*n*, 145, 150
lamp, 112
lapis (philosophorum), 68, 87, 127,
   139, 143, 155, 159, 182, 208, 236*ff*,
   247*ff*, 263; fish as symbol of, 126*ff*;
   found only in heaven, 170; parallel of Christ, 237; quaternio,
   238*ff*; as rock, 88; and serpent,
   245; symbol of self, 268; thousand
   names of, 182, 189; "uncomeliness" of, 140; union of opposites
   in, 247*f*; *see also* stone
lapis angularis (Christ), 208
lapis animalis, 157

lapis exilis, 30
lapis vegetabilis, 159
Lateran Council, Fourth, 52*n*, 82, 83*n*, 253*n*
lawlessness, man of, 36*n*
Layard, John Willoughby, 242*n*
lead, 139
Leda, 81
left, *see* right and left
legends, 169
Leibniz, Gottfried Wilhelm, 6, 164*n*, 258
lethargia, 208*n*
Lethe, and unconscious, 208*n*
Leto, 104
Leviathan, 123, 147*n*, 182; battle with Behemoth, 80, 108; eucharistic food, 112, 120; fish and, 120; male and female, 118
Lévy-Bruhl, Lucien, 29
Lexicon medico-chymicum, 154*n*
Libavius, Andreas, 158
liberty, idea of, 29
libido, 132*n*, 256; kinship, 243
Libra (♎), 77*n*, 83
Libya, 138
life-process, psychic interpretation of, 4
light, transcendent nature of, 63*n*
Lightfoot, Joseph Barber, 213*n*
lime, unslaked, 130; *see also* quicklime
lingam, 217*n*
lion(s), 120; Michael and, 75; symbol of Christ, 72; of the tribe of Judah, 105; two, 150
lodestone, 189*n; see also* magnet
Logos, 148, 187*f*, 201, 252; animus and, 14, 16, 21; cosmogonic, 211; Gnostic, 202; Hermes as, 201; as magnetic agent, 188; Protanthropos as, 209; serpent as, 188, 232
λόγος σπερματικός, 207
love: fish as symbol of, 129; at first sight, 15; God's, in hell, 125; language of, 15

love-magic, 140
love-potion, 138
Loyola, *see* Ignatius
Lucian, 212
lucidus, 138*n*, 139*n*
Lucifer, 72, 125
Lugio, Johannes de, 146
Luke, Gospel of: (5 : 10), 89; (6 : 35), 89, 209*n;* (11 : 29*f*), 111*n;* (16 : 8), 146*n;* (16 : 17), 218*n;* (17 : 20*ff*), 37*n;* (19 : 12*ff*), 166; (19 : 27), 106*n;* (24 : 42), 121*n;* (24 : 43), 113
Lully (Lull), Raymond, 239*n*
Luna, 235; *see also* moon
Luther, Martin, 89, 235; as Antichrist, 102
Lycia, 121

M

Maag, Victor, 182*n*
Macrobius, Ambrosius Theodosius, 219*n*
macrocosm, 214
Magi, 89, 132
magic, 140, 242
magnesia, 155–57, 159, 160
magnet, 133, 154*ff*, 184, 187*n;* of the wise, 142, 155
magnetic agent, three forms of, 188
magnetism, 133*n;* of fish, 154; Gnostics and, 184*ff*
Magog, *see* Gog and Magog
Magus, 167*n*
Mahomet, 97; *see also* Mohammed
Maier, Michael, 187*n*, 220, 249, 252, 264, pl. I
Maimonides, Moses, 116*n*, 119*n*
Mainyo-i-Khard, 246*n*
Majui, 80*n*
maladaptation, 27
Malchuth, 268
male and female, 55
man: complete, water as, 200; higher, in Moses quaternio, 228;

man (*cont.*):
    inner, 208*f*, 228; One, 205; Original, 198, 200, 201, 203, 204, 211, 214, 216, 237, 239, *see also* Adam, Anthropos, Archanthropos, Protanthropos; perfect, 212*f;* pneumatic, 256; primordial, 36
"man," in II Esdras, 120
mana, 251*n*
Mandaeans, 124
mandala(s), 64, 152, 219, 241, 253; Christ in Christian, 36; rotation of, 259; in student's dream, 134; symbols of order, 31*f*, 135; totality images, 40, 268; and unconscious personality, 204; vessel as, 240
Manget, Jean Jacques (Joannes Jacobus Mangetus), 126*n*
Manichaeans/Manichaeism, 48, 49, 55, 57*n*, 58, 61*n*, 99, *see also* dualism
Manu, 73; fish of, 113*f*
Marcionites, 49
Marduk, 120, 124
Maria, axiom of, 153, 251
Maria the prophetess, 240
Mariam, *see* Miriam
Mariette, François A. F., 76*n*
Marinus, 54
Mark, Gospel of, (10 : 18), 58*n*
marriage: of Christ and the Church, 39; classes, 22; as conscious relationship, 243; constellation of unconscious in, 242; cross-cousin, 22, 209*n*, 229, 242*f;* mingling of subtle with dense, 167*n;* of mother and son, 12; quaternio, 22, 64, 209, 210, 229, 242, 252
Mars (♂), 79*n*, 95
Marxism, 181
Mary: as fountain, 116; in Gnostic symbolism, 202, 204, 205; in *Pistis Sophia,* 78
Mary, the Virgin, 205; Assumption, 87; Immaculate Conception, 87*n;* as substitute for Church, 21*n*
masculinity, woman's, 21*n*

Masenius, Jacobus, 154*n*
mass man and evil, 166
massa confusa, 148, 155, 234, 236
Mater Alchimia, 173, 232
materialism, 109, 150, 176, 181, 233, 257, 260
mathematics, 261
Matsya, 176
matter, numinosity of, 66, 260
Matthew, Gospel of, 101*n*, 201*n;* (2 : 1*ff*), 89; (3 : 2), 192*n;* (4 : 19), 89; (5 : 3), 193; (5 : 8), 217*n;* (5 : 18), 218*n;* (5 : 48), 69*n;* (7 : 14), 200*n;* (10 : 34), 187; (12 : 39), 111*n;* (13 : 24), 37*n;* (13 : 45), 37*n;* (16 : 4), 111*n;* (17 : 4), 122*n;* (18 : 23), 37*n;* (19 : 17), 58*n*, 201*n;* (21 : 19), 106*n;* (22 : 2), 37*n;* (22 : 7), 26*n;* (27 : 15*ff*), 90
maya, 11, 13
meaning, 27
Mechthild of Magdeburg, St., 205*f*
mediator, 237*n*, 239; animus as, 16; man as, 255*f*
medicament, incorrupt, 170
medulla, 205, 233
medusa, 126*ff*
Meerpohl, Franz, 219
megalomania, 17
Meir ben Isaac, 118
Melusina, 235
memory, 4
mendicant orders, 82, 83
Mephistopheles, 234
Mercurius/Mercury (☿), 76, 77*n*, 78, 95, 97, 130, 131, 161, 171, 187, 232, 249*f*, 252; as *anima mundi,* 136; and double aspect of water, 180; double/duplex nature of, 150, 252*f*, 254; "non vulgi," 155, 234; philosophical, *see* Mercurius "non vulgi"; and the Pole, 133, 135; synonyms for, 241; as tree-numen, 235; as trickster, 203*n;* as Virgo, 127
mercy, of Yahweh, 59, 60

Mesopotamia, 74, 214
Messahala, 82n
Messiah(s), 106ff, 121; ben Joseph and ben David, 107; birth of, 105, 149; coming of, 74, 118; two, 107, 108; in Zohar, 214
Mestha, 123
metals, 246
μετάνοια, 192
metaphysical ideas, 34, 35
metaphysics: Jung and, 195n; psychology and, 54, 61, 67, 194, 198
Metatron, 214
Meyer, Karl H., 146
Michael (angel), 75
Michaias, 57
microcosm/microcosmos, 155, 164, 214; wandering, 213
microphysics, 174
Midrashim, 59; Midrash Tanchuma (Shemoth), 59n, 118n, 119n
mind, transformation of, 192
Miriam, 209, 210, 228, 244
Mithraic: liturgy, 124; monuments, 91
Mithras, 121, 124
modesty, 25
Mohammed, 102; see also Mahomet
molecular movement, 250f
mollusc, 128
monad(s), 189, 218f; Kircher's, 262–63; in Sabellius, 253n
monasticism, 82f, 85, 89
monks, as fishes, 113
Monoïmos, 218f, 222f
Monophysites, 110
monotheism, 268
monsters: attributes of death, 120; horned, 105; sea, see Behemoth, Leviathan; splitting of, 119f
moods, 17
Moon (☽), 76, 77, 155, 249; celestial horn of, 211
morality, 25
Morienus Romanus, 166, 168
morphomata, 81

Moses, 74, 107, 122n, 209n, 210, 227ff, 244
Moses quaternio, 227ff, 243f, 251, 254f
Moses ha-Darshan, 106
mother, 155; chthonic, 22; higher, in Moses quaternio, 228; search for, 11; as symbol, 11; and son, 12; see also Great Mother(s); imago
mountain, 203, 209; as symbol of self, 226
Muenter, Friedrich, 74
mumia, 213f
mummy, 122; see also mumia
Mundus, 137
Musaeum hermeticum, 88n, 130n, 131n, 133n, 145n, 150n, 221n, 241n
mussel-shell, 127f
Mut, 206
"mutilation of the soul," evil as, 48
Mylius, Johann Daniel, 88n, 139, 156n, 187n, 197n, 221, 235n, 237n, 239n
mysteries, Eleusinian, 217
mysterium coniunctionis, 64
mysterium iniquitatis, 44, 86
mysticism, Jewish, 108
mythologem: of Amen, 206; dying god, 206; fish as, 138
"mythological" aspects, 30
mythology, 35; comparative, 34; and dogma, 179
myths, 35, 149; cosmogonic, 148; gods in, 177; and unconscious processes, 180

N

Naas, 199, 230, 232
Naassenes, 64, 75, 88, 89, 184f, 197, 198, 199, 200, 201, 208f, 241, 226f; see also quaternio
name, and thing, 32
Nanni, Giovanni, 102n

naphtha, 185
Naples: Farnese Atlas, 91
Nathan, Rabbi, 113*n*
nature: Christianity and, 174; improvement of, 143; individual, of Christ's disciples, 211; rejoices in nature, 159; two powers of, 123
natures, changing of the, 166
Nazis, 102
necromancy, 262
negligence, evil and, 62
Negroes, 210
nekyia, 209
Nelken, Jan, 33*n*
Nematophora, 128
Neoplatonists, 126
Nero, 102
Neumann, Erich, 116*n*, 148*n*, 183*n*
neurosis(es), 20, 180, 181, 189
neurotic disturbances, 169
New Testament: devil in, 86; eschatology, 36; Jesus in, 179; snake in, 245; *see also names of individual books*
Nicholas of Cusa, 225*n*
Nietzsche, Friedrich Wilhelm, 260
night-heron, 72
night sea journey, 111
Nigidius Figulus, Publius, 136
nigredo, 148, 149, 194, 210; *see also* chaos
Nina, 121
Nippur, 124
nirdvandva, 191
nodes, 253
North, the, 99*ff*; in ancient history, 125; Ezekiel and, 124; King of the, 125; Mithras and, 124
North Star, 133
Nostradamus, Michel, 95*ff*, 125, 126
"nothing but," 179
nous, 21; descent to Physis, 233; krater filled with, 191*n*; Mercurius symbol of, 168; serpent as, 186, 188, 230, 232; unconscious, 203*n*

"Novi luminis chemici Tractatus alter de sulphure," 131*n*
Numbers, Book of: (12 : 10), 210; (16), 106*n*; (24 : 16), 59*n*; (24 : 17), 117
Numbers, *see* dyad; triad; quaternity; heptad; ogdoad; three; four; five; eight; twelve
Nun, 111, 121

O

Oannes, 73, 112, 121, 201
observation, uncertainty of, 226
obsessions, 169
obsidian, 138, 139*n*
ocean/Oceanus, 209, 212, 214, 218
Oehler, Franciscus, 191
ogdoad, 110, 196, 197*n*, 226; archon of the, 190
Old Testament, 70; *see also names of individual books*
olive, 200
Olympiodorus, 239*n*, 264
Olympus, 164
omega element, 238
Onians, Richard Broxton, 212*n*
Ophites, 188
Ophiuchus, 111
opinionatedness, 16
opinions, 21: archetypes and, 17; Logos and, 15
opposites: alchemical, linked together, 244; anima/animus, 268; annihilation of, 70; Christ/Satan, 44–45*n*; cinedian stone and, 139; coincidence of, 124; —, in Godhead, 193; conjunction of, 40, 70, 194, see also *coniunctio oppositorum*; day/night, 123; equivalence of, 61; Father as without, 191; good/evil, 47, 123; Heru-ur/Set, 123; husband/wife, 204; identity of, symbols and, 129*f*; kosmos/chaos, 123; life/death, 123; light/darkness, 223; moral

accentuation of, 70; never unite at own level, 180; pairs of, *see also* syzygy(ies); problem of, and neurosis, 180; serpents, 118*n*; tension of, 31, 91, 247*f*; union of, 264; —, in astrology, 77, 87; —, and salvation, 195; —, in stone, 170; —, and unconsciousness, 193
opsianus, 138
opus, 237; as apocatastasis, 169; and creation of world, 148, 234; and individuation, 264
Oracula sibyllina, 73*n*
order: mandalas symbols of, 31; principle of, 195
Origen, 37, 38*n*, 41, 44–45*n*, 75, 81, 90*n*, 114*n*, 204*f*, 215, 234; and the devil, 110
Orion, 136
Orosius, 230*n*
Orpheus, 103
Orphos, 121
Osiris, 122, 123, 198, 199, 201
Osob, 146, 147*n*, 200
Ostanes, 159*n*, 237*n*, 245*n*
oxen, fishes and, 145, 147, 148*f*
Oxford English Dictionary, 25
oxyrhynchus (fish), 122
Oxyrhynchus, fish-worship at, 121
Oxyrhynchus fragments, 37*n*, 144, 145

P

paganism, 96; return of, in Europe, 176
pair, royal, in Moses quaternio, 228
Palestine, 74, 138
Pan, 199
Pandolfus, 156
Pandora, 241
panic, 33
panspermia, 200
Pantheus, Joannes Augustinus, 139*n*
Papa, 213
Papyri Graecae Magicae, 126

Paracelsus, 164, 181, 213, 214, 237
para-da, 152
Paradise: four rivers of, 184, 199, 215, 227, 235, 243; Garden of Eden, 254*n*; Leviathan eaten in, 113; quaternio, 234*f*, 236*f*, 243, 245, 254; as symbol, 189
paradox, 70
Parmenides, 137*n*, 143
parthenogenesis, 35
Parthenon, 203*n*
Passion, of Jesus, *see* Jesus
Passover, 119
Patarenes, 83
patience, 24
Paul, St., 39, 174, 176, 177, 178, 191; Epistles of, 68; *see also names of separate Epistles*
Pauli, W., 207*n*
Paulicians, 148
Paulinus of Nola, 65*n*
pearl, round, 127*n*
Pectorios inscription, 89*n*, 113, 116*n*
pelican, 239
penetration, 120*n*
Pentecost, 129
Pepi I, 88*n*, 122
Peratic doctrine, 185*f*
perception(s): conversion of stimuli into, 4; endosomatic, 3; psyche and, 32
Perdition, Son of, 36
peregrinatio, 133
perfection: Christ as, 39; and completeness, 68*f*; evil as lack of, 41
perforation, 120*n*
Pernety, Antoine Joseph, 155, 160*f*
Perpetua, St., Passion of, 210
Persephone, 12, 21, 217
personality: changes of, 6; dissociation of, 180; double, 120; ego as centre of, 6; inferior, *see* shadow; of Jesus, 178*f*; not coincident with ego, 5; self as total, 5; total description of, impossible, 5
perversions, intellectual, 169
Pesahim, see Talmud

Peter, St., 89; in Clementine Homilies, 56
Peter, First Epistle of; (2 : 4), 88; (2 : 4*f*), 171*n;* (2 : 5), 88
Peter Damian, St., 113
Peter Lombard, 253*n*
Peters, C. H. F., and Knobel, E. B., 77*n*, 93*n*
phallicism: Gnostic, 232; unconscious, 226
phallus, 201*f*, 226
pharmakon athanasias, 116
phenomenology, individual, and collective unconscious, 179
Philalethes, Eirenaeus, 132, 133*n*, 241
Philippians, Epistle to the (3 : 12), 212
phlogiston theory, 250*f*
phobias, 169
Phrat, *see* Euphrates
Phrygians, 198, 213; *see also* Naassenes
phylokrinesis, 64, 79, 258*n*
physics: collision of psyche with, 174; nuclear, 261; and psychology, 261
Physis, 198, 233, 247, 249, 259
Phyton, 131
Picinellus, Philippus, 112*n*, 113*n*, 122*n*, 129, 135
Pisces: aeon, middle of, 150; zodiacal sign for, 91, 114; *see also* fish(es)
pisciculi Christianorum, 103
piscina, 89
Piscis Austrinus, 111*n*
Pison, 199, 225, 235
Pistis Sophia, 75*n*, 78*f*, 93*n*, 122*n*, 137*n*, 197*n*
Pius IX, Pope, 87*n*
planets, influence of, 148
Plato, 246; *Phaedrus,* 64; *Timaeus,* 136
Platonic Tetralogies, Book of, see "Platonis liber quartorum"

"Platonis liber quartorum," 197*n*, 238, 261*n*
Pleiades, 136
pleroma, 41*n*, 46, 66*n*, 219*n*
Pliny, 128, 138, 144, 156*n*, 177
Plotinus, 219
plough, 148*f*
Plutarch, 76, 121, 122*n*
pneuma, 21, 83; and Barbelo, 197*n;* feminine, 206; in God, 254; hidden in stone, 245; of Jesus, 79; winged beings as, 120
πνευματικόs (-οί), 212&*n,* 219*n*
Pohl, Otto, 113*n*
Poimandres, 103
Poimen, *see* Hermas
point, 189, 198*f*, 218, 222; in alchemy, 220*f*
pole, 133–34; centre in North, 171; heavenly, 123*f*, 224; North, hidden God at, 135; —, magnetism of, 154
Polemon, 76*n*
Pollux, 81
polydemonism, 175
polytheism, 175, 268
Poor Men of Lyons, 83, 146, 150
Pordage, John, 163*n,* 235
Poseidon, 216
Prajapati, 207*n*
precession of equinoxes, 81, 92, 95
prefigurations, 261
Preisendanz, Karl, 126*n*
Priapus, 230
prima materia, 132, 142, 161, 162, 237; alchemical laborant as, 168; anima and, 187; lapis as, 127, 236, 264; production of, 155; as psychic situation, 155; synonyms of, 160
primum mobile, 131
principium individuationis, 64
Priscillian, 88, 136, 230*n*
privatio boni/privation of good, 41, 45*n*, 46, 48, 50, 52, 54, 58, 61, 62*n*, 110, 269; *see also* evil
problems, moral, 25*f*

projection(s): anima and, 13; anima/animus, 17, 242; dissolution of, 18f; effect of, 9f; impersonal withdrawal of, 23; mandala and, 32; in Mary, 204; and mother-imago, 12; reality of factor making, 24; and reality of psyche, 66n; shadow and, 9

Protanthropos, 213; and Korybas, 211; as Logos, 209; Sophia and, 197; see also Adam; Anthropos; Man, original; Archanthropos

Protestantism/Protestants, 150, 178

Proteus, 216f

Protoplast, 214

Protothoma, 213

Prunicus/Προύνικος, 196n; see also Sophia

Psalms: (2 : 9), 105; (82 [81] : 6), 209n; (89), 108f

Psellus, Michael, 44n, 148n

psyche, 142, 255; aspects of, 32; begetter of all knowledge, 173; ego-consciousness of, 164; and evil, 62; field of consciousness, 6; horoscope and, 136; and life-processes, 4; man's knowledge of, 165; and matter, 261; objective reality of, scientists and, 174; outside consciousness, 6; reality of, 66n; reasons for undervaluation of, 62

"psychic," use of term, 4

psychoanalysis, 203n

psychology, and good/evil, 53

psychopathology, 30

psychopomp(os): anima as, 30; animus as, 16; fishes as symbols for, 145; Proteus as, 216

psychosis, 33; mass, 248n

psychotherapy: and anima/animus, 267; and problem of opposites, 180

Ptolemy, 74n, 94n

puer, 127

"puffed-up-ness," 24; see also inflation

pulmo marinus, 128

punctum/punctus solis, 220n; see also point

purusha, 167, 194

Pyramid Texts, 122

Python, 104

Q

Qazvini, 123

Qebhsennuf, 123

'qltn, 119

quaternio/quaternity, 159, 194, 210, 211, 226ff; its character of wholeness, 224; of Christ, 204; Christian, 253; and circle, motif, 224; defective, three as, 224; in fire, 132; in Irenaeus, 197n; Kircher's, 262f; in man, 22; Naassene, 22n, 79n; of opposites, in self and Christ, 63f; as organizing schema, 242; Osiris and, 123; self as, 42; static quality of, 257; as symbols, 31, 195; —, for God, 195; —, self in, 190; unity complement of, 224; see also Anthropos quaternio; Horus quaternio; lapis quaternio; marriage quaternio; Moses quaternio; Paradise quaternio; shadow quaternio; space-time quaternio

quick-lime, 158

quicksilver, 139, 155

"quicksilver system," Indian, 152

quid/quis distinction, 164, 169

Quinta Essentia, 159n

Quispel, Gilles, 66 & n, 190, 191

R

Ra, 122

Radhakrishnan, Sarvapalli, 223n

radius, see ray

Rahab, 120

Rahner, Hugo, 215*n*, 235*n*
Raison, Déesse, 98
Ram (♈), 77*n; see also* Aries
ram: Christ as, 90, 92; daemonic, 105*f;* symbol of Christ and Attis, 103; *see also* lamb
Rameses II, 78
Ramsay, William Mitchell, 73*n*
Raphael, 113
Rashi, *see* Solomon ben Isaac
Ras Shamra, 119
rationalism, 86, 150, 221
rationality, 248*n;* male, 55
raven, 72
ray, 187*n*
realism, 150, 176, 233
reality: psychic, 48; requires polarity, 267
realization, conscious, 239*n*
rebirth, 212
Rebis, 159, 268
Red Sea, 74
Redeemer: archetype of, 183; as fish and serpent, 186; Gnostic/ Gnosticism and, 79, 184; and unscious, affinity of, 181
redemption, 35, 70, 175, 191, 256; of the dead, 39
reflection, 16
Reformation, the, 93, 102, 178; Holy Ghost movement and, 87
reformation, of God-image, 40
Reguel, 229; *see also* Jethro
Reitzenstein, Richard, 75*n*, 103; and Schäder, H. H., 246*n*
relationship, 17; function of, 14, 16; inadequate, 19; to partner, 22
remora, 140*f*, 144, 154*n*
Rempham, 75*n*
Renaissance, the, 43, 94, 98
renovatio, 98*n*
renovation of the age, 98
repentance, 192
représentations collectives, 29
repression, 226
resentment, 16

resistances, shadow and, 9
responsibility, in jurisprudence, 5
Revelation of St. John: (5 : 5), 105; (5 : 6), 105*n;* (5 : 6*ff*), 105; (6 : 15*ff*), 105; (12 : 1), 103; (12 : 9), 230*n;* (14 : 4), 217; (17 : 14), 105; (20 : 7*f*), 79*n; see also* Apocalypse
revolution, 98*n*
Rex gloriae, 195, 204
Rhabanus Maurus, 100
Rhea, 199
Rhine, J. B., 184*n*
right and left, 54, 59, 258*n*
righteousness, 70
Rig-Veda, 192*n*
Ripley, Sir George, 131*n*, 139, 144, 148*n*, 149, 235*n*, 249
Ripley "Scrowle," 235, 265
ritual, 256; Protestantism and, 178
rivers, four, of Paradise, 184, 199, 215, 225, 227, 235, 243
Roberts, R., 221*n*
rock: Christ as, 87*f;* inner man as, 208
roes, two, 107
Romans, Epistle to: (7 : 21), 69*n;* (12 : 2), 40
Romulus, 107*n*
room, as symbol, 224*f*
Rosarium philosophorum, 156*n*, 197*n*, 239*n*, 245*n*
Roscher, Wilhelm Heinrich, 211*n*, 212*n*
Rosenkreutz, Christian, 210
Rosinus, 156, 157, 167*f*
rota nativitatis, 136
rotation, 246*n*, 257
rotundum, 238, 239*n*, 246, 248*f*, 257
Rousselle, Erwin, 11*n*
Ruland, Martin, 133*n*, 138*n*, 139, 156*n*
Rupescissa, Johannes de, 146, 241, 265
Ruska, Julius, 126*n*, 130*n*, 137*n*, 220*n*

S

Sabaeans, 75, 124, 197*n*
Sabaoth, 76
Sabbath, 75
Sabellius, 253*n*
Sagittarius, 74*n*
sailor, 112
sal ammoniac, 154*n*
sal sapientiae, 133, 161
Salmanas, procedure of, 127*n*
salt, 133, 157; in alchemy, 161; "of the metals," 139
salvation, 195
Salvator mundi, 127
Sammaël, 57
Samothrace, 211, 212
Sanhedrin, see Talmud
sapientia, 160, 220
Sapientia Dei, 127
Sassanids, 116
Satan, 43*f*, 105*n*; as elder son of God, 57, 61; in Old Testament, 192; state before fall, 145; and two fishes, 148
Satanaël, 43, 147
satori, 169
Satorneilos, *see* Saturninus
Saturn (♄), 74*ff*, 77*n*, 81, 82, 83, 96, 97, 98, 99; and Esaldaios, 208; as Gnostic symbol, 197; Jewish thought and, 74*f*; and quicksilver, 139; stone and, 138*f*
Saturnia (plant), 139
Saturninus, 219
Saulasau, 210
Saviour, compounded of four things, 197*n*
Schärf, Riwkah, 42*n*, 121*n*, 192, 245*n*
Scheftelowitz, I., 113*n*, 116, 117, 118*n*, 119
Schelling, F. W. J., 6
schizophrenia, 33
Schoettgen, Christian, 107*n*, 214*n*
scholasticism, 172
Schopenhauer, Arthur, 6

Schreber, Daniel Paul, 33*n*
Schwestrones, 84*n*
science: alchemy and, 176; and faith, 173*f*; natural, 27; —, rise of, 150; modern, 89; trinity in, 258
scintilla vitae, 219
Scott, Walter, 191*n*
sculptures, obscene, 217*n*
scurrility: in dreams, 203; of Gnostic nomenclature, 230 ·
scyphomedusa, 128
sea, 155; "our," 142
sea-hawk, 187*n*; centre of the, 189
seal, seventh, opening of, 82
seals, 216
sea-nettle, 128*n*
sea-urchin, 154*n*
Second Coming, ix; expectation of, 256
Secret of the Golden Flower, 182*n*, 224, 264
secret of the wise, 143
sects, 96*f*
Secundus, 110*n*
Selene, 21
self, 23*ff*, 33, 34; Anthropos and, 189; antinomial character, 225; apotheosis of individuality, 62; appearance of in unconscious products, 190; appears in all shapes, 226; as archetype, 167; as brahman and atman, 222; Christ as archetype/symbol of, 36*ff*, 62*n*, 182; Christ's correspondence to, 110; dream-symbols and, 132; "fixation" of, in mind, 168*f*; Gnostic symbols of, 184*ff*, 226*ff*; a God-image, 22, 205; impersonal unconscious and, 169; lapis as, 127, 167; a product of cognition, 69; as quaternion of opposites, 63*f*; relation to ego, 6; religious mythologem, 30; round fish as, 142, 144; supraordinate to ego, 3; as total personality, 5; transcendent(al), 62*f*, 170; union of con-

self (*cont.*):
scious and unconscious, 268; *see also* assimilation; atman; God-image
self-aggrandizement, 24; *see also* inflation
self-criticism, 25
self-fertilization, 207
self-knowledge, 16, 162*ff*; 222; and alchemy, 166*ff*; and ends, 165*f*; increased, 19, 23*ff*; and knowledge of ego, 164; shadow and, 8
Senard, Marcelle, 92*n*
senarius, 228, 230
Sendivogius, Michael, 131*n*
Senior, 240
sense-perception, *see* perception
sentimentality, 16
separatio/separation, 168, 170; *see also divisio*
Sephiroth, Tree of the, 58
Sephora, 209, 210
septenarius, 240
serpens mercurialis/*Mercurii*, 160, 234, 245
serpent(s), 111, 189, 232, 255; fighting, 118; as magnetic agent, 188; Naas, 199; in Peratic doctrine, 185*f*; in shadow quaternio, 230, 244; and stone, 245; and tension of opposites, 247; *see also* dragon; snake; uroboros
Set, 76, 78, 99, 122*f*, 124, 132
Sethians, 186*f*, 219
sexual theory, of psychic substance, 201*n*
sexuality, 90–91*n*; undervaluation of, 226
Shaare Kedusha, 218*n*
shadow, 8–10, 17, 30, 33, 155, 233*f*, 255, 259, 260; Antichrist as, 41; of arcane substance, 187*n*; assimilation into conscious personality, 9; in Christ's birth, 41*n*, 110; consciousness of, 8; doubling of, 120; fear of, 33; fish as shadow

of God, 119; good qualities of, 266; integration of, 22; and Moses quaternio, 228, 244; has negative feeling-value, 28; personal unconscious and, 169; quaternio, 229*n*, 230*f*, 233*ff*, 244, 255*f*, 260; represents chthonic world, 34
Shatapatha Brahmana, 113*n*, 114*n*
sheep, land of, 16
Shekinah, 268
shepherd, 103; good, 103
Shu, 207
Shulamite, 210
Sibyls, Erythraean, 72*n*
Silberer, Herbert, 164*n*
Simon Magus, 197, 220
sister, 12
skull, 238
slave's post, 76*n*, 78
Smith, E. M., 92*n*, 94*n*
smoke, 101
snail, 226
snake, 72, 233*ff*; Aesculapian, 188; allegory of Christ, 233, 245, 247; on cross, 78*n*; Mercurius as, 232; in New Testament, 245; signifies evil/wisdom, 234; and Son, 188; symbolism of, 186; as symbol, of instinct, 244; —, of self, 226; —, of wisdom, 245
Söderberg, Hans, 147*n*
Sodom, 59
sol niger, Saturn as, 197
Solomon ben Gabirol, 74
Solomon ben Isaac, 80, 81
solvents, 160
soma, in God, 254
son, 185, 186; as Father's thought of own being, 193; and mother, 11*f*; symbol for God, 195
son of God, serpent as, 188
son of Man, 203, 218; pictures of, 195
sons of God, two, 42*f*, 57, 58
Song of Solomon: (1 : 1), 205; (1 : 5), 210; (4 : 5), 107; (8 : 7), 129

sonship, threefold, of God, 64f
Sophia, 65n; Achamoth, 197n; Prounikos, 54, 196f
"Soul, My Lady," 13
soul: 64, 142; and anima, 13; animal, 11n; as bride of Christ, 39; "excrescent," 234; fish as symbol of, 122; human, of Christ, 39; as second Eve, 206; as sphere, 136; "twittering," 209; world-, see anima mundi
"soul in fetters," 197n, 208n
space-time continuum, 24, 258n
space-time quaternio, 251, 252, 253, 257
spark, 219f
Sphere, the, 93n; soul as, 136
spider, 226
Spiegelberg, W., 122n
spinal cord, 233
Spinning Woman, 11
spirit, 64, 142; animus and, 16; archetype of, 85f; of the world, 142
"Spirit in the Bottle, the," 235
spirits, seven, 105n
spiritus, 160, 187
Spitteler, Carl, 13, 267n
splitting, 119f, 120n; of conscious/unconscious, 247–48n; of Original Man, 204
spondilo, 138
spring-point, 93
square, and circle, 224f, 264
stabilization, 243
stag, 150
Stahl, G. E., 251
star, rising of, and birth of hero, 117
"star of the sea," 128
starfish, 128f, 154n
steel, 133; alchemical, 161; see also chalybs
stella marina, 128f
stella maris, 135, 137
Stephen, St., 75n

Stephen of Canterbury, 112
sterility, feeling of, 9
stimuli: endosomatic, 3; unconscious, 4
stone: animate, 159; as Christ-image, 67; cinedian, 138f; complement of serpent, 245; derived from circle and quaternity motif, 224; dragon's, 138; Heracleian, 185; inner man as, 208; making the, a "human attitude," 166; projection of unified self, 170; psychic relationship to man, 167; symbol of self, 246; unity of, 170; see also lapis
Strauss, Heinz Arthur, 82n
subject, necessary to consciousness, 3; and object, differentiation in consciousness, 193
"subjective factor," 223
sublimation, 259
subliminal, see unconscious
substance, metaphysical, 161
sucking-fish, 140
sulphur(s), 171, 239n, 250
Summa Fratris Reneri, 146n
Summum Bonum, God as, 45f, 52
sun, 249, 260
Sutech, 78
swan, 81
Swedenborg, Emanuel, 198
Switzerland, 225
sword, 187
Syene, 121
symbol(s): in alchemy, 179; autonomous, 31; of Christ and the devil, 72; dogma as, 175; Gnostic, 196ff; for God, 195; Indian, 175; meaning of, 73; of opposite sex, 10; pictorial, psychology and, 194; polarity of, 129f; quaternary, in dreams, 132; theriomorphic, 186; triadic, 243n; uniting, 194; of unity and totality, 31; see also anima; animus; mandala
symbolism: sexual, Christ and, 202; theriomorphic, of self, 226

"symbolum": as *aqua doctrinae*, 180; creed as, 174

symptoms, localization of, 186

synchronicity, 85, 150, 168, 258; of archetype, 184

Synesius, 159*n*

Synesius of Cyrene, 116

synthesis, 260

Syria: cult of fish in, 121; dove and fish in, 115; round fish in, 138

syzygy(-ies), 33, 191, 254; Adam/ Eve, 254; anima/animus, 11*ff*, 266; in Clementine Homilies, 54; divine, in Christianity, 21; proto- type of divine couples, 34; Valen- tinian, 228; wholeness superior to, 31; *see also* opposites

T

Tabari, *Chronique* of, 79*n*, 107

Tabula smaragdina, 126, 265

Tacitus, 76

talents, parable of the, 166

Talmud, Babylonian, 58*n*, 59*n*, 60*n*, 79, 80*n*, 83, 107, 116, 117, 118, 149; and astrology, 81

Tanit, 121

tanninim, 79, 80, 81

Tantrism, 217*n*

Tao, 58, 69; symbol for God, 195; as "valley spirit," 180

Targums, 107*n*

Tatian, 46

tebūnā, 120

Tefnut, 207

Tehom, 237

τέλειος, 212, 213*n*

τελείωσις, *see* completeness

temperature, Arctic, 52

tension: conscious/unconscious, 20; signified by Christ's advent, 44; in uroboros, 248*f*; *see also* oppo- sites

tentacles, 128

teoqualo, 144

Tertullian, 37, 76, 90*n*

tetrads, 191

tetrameria, 254; alchemical, 259

Tetramorph, 36

Thabit ibn Qurrah, 126

Thales, 157, 199

Theatrum chemicum, 130*n*, 131*n*, 132*n*, 137*n*, 139*n*, 140*n*, 143*n*, 156*n*, 157*n*, 158*n*, 160*n*, 163*n*, 187*n*, 197*n*, 220*n*, 221*n*, 235*n*, 237*n*, 238*n*, 239*n*, 240*n*, 261*n*, 265*n*

thema, 136

Theodor Bar-Kuni, 197

Theologia Germanica, 89

Theophilus of Antioch, 46

Theophrastus, 141, 222

theoria, 142, 171, 179, 181

Thessalonians, Second Epistle to the: (2 : 3*ff*), 36*n*

Thiele, Georg, 91*n*

thieves, two, at crucifixion, 44, 69, 255

thinking, 32

third, superordinate, 180

Thomas, Acts of, 116, 197

Thomas Aquinas, St., 51*f*, 87, 178*n*

Thorndike, Lynn, 96*n*, 98*n*, 102*n*

Thracian riders, 73

three: as defective quaternity, 224; and one, motif, 225, 253; *see also* dilemma

Tiamat, 120

Tifereth, 268

Tigris, 199

Timaeus, 136

Timochares, planisphere of, 91

tincture, synonyms for, 137

Titus of Bostra, 48

Tobit, 113

tongue(s), 135, 137; fiery, 129, 135*n*

tortoise, 226

totality, 34, 143*f*; becoming con- scious, 259; Christ as divine, 37, 39, 41; chthonic, 224; idea of,

62*n;* images of, 40; spiritual, 224; symbols of, 31, 190; *see also* wholeness

"Tractatulus Avicennae," 167*n*

"Tractatus Aristotelis . . .," 235*n*

Tractatus aureus, 187*n,* 220, 237*n,* 239

tradition, 181

transference, 229

transformation: Christian, 169; formula of, 259; prefigurations in, 261; skull as vessel of, 238; tree as symbol of, 235

transition, from waking to sleeping, 28

treasure, guarded by dragon/snake, 234

tree: philosophical, 235; and serpent, 235; as symbol of self, 226

Trevisanus, *see* Bernardus Trevisanus

triad: lower, 99, 224; male and female, in pseudo-Clement, 55; in man, 22; Naassene, 209; opposed to trinity, 224

trichotomies, 65*f*

trickster, Mercurius as, 203*n*

Trinity, the, 35, 131, 253, Plate II; devil lacking in, 86; divine sphere of, 57; dogma of, 177; Jesus' soul as, 201; Kepler and, 207; Naassene, 197, 226; space/time/causality, 258; spiritual totality, 224; triad opposed to, 224

Troad, the, 156*n*

truth(s), 171; first, 178; psychological, 27

Tuamutef, 123

Tuat, 122

Turba philosophorum, 126, 137, 143, 220*n,* 250

Turukalukundram, 217*n*

twelve, 224

Twins, the, *see* Gemini; Saviour of the, 79*n,* 122*n*

Typhon, 99, 121, 122

U

Ugarit, 119

Uhlhorn, 254*n*

umbra Jesu, 106

Unas, 122

uncertainty relationship, between conscious and unconscious, 226

uncomeliness, outward, 140

unconscious: alchemy and symbolism of unconscious processes, 179; cannot be "done with," 20; collective, *see* collective unconscious; compensation in, 124; contents of, and man's totality, 140; contents of ego, three groups, 4, 7; dawn-state and, 148; fear of, 33; fishes as product of, 149; frightening figures in, 225; Gnostics and, 190; in Hippolytus and Epiphanius, 66; importance of, 5; integration of contents, 23; organizing principle of, 204; "our sea" symbol of, 142; personal and impersonal, 7, 169; problems of integration of, 181; processes, compensatory to conscious, 204; Proteus personifying, 216; self and the, 3; soul as projection of, 142; theriomorphism and, 145; as the unknown in the inner world, 3; without qualities, 191

unconsciousness: and proneness to suggestion, 247–48*n;* sin of, 192*n*

uncontrollable natural forces, action of, 25*f*

underworld, gods of, 224

unicorn, 150

unity, 31, 34; complement of quaternity, 224; in Kircher, 263; as symbol of self, 226; transcendent, stone as, 170

Unknown, the: ego and, 3; two groups of objects in, 3

Upanishads, see *Brihadāranyaka* and *Kena*

Urania, 89*n*

uroboros, 190, 246, 248, 257, 259, 264

V

Valentinians, 65*n*, 190, 191, 197*n*, 228
Valentinus, 41*n*, 110, 234*n*, 269
value, 27*ff*; feeling as function of, 32
value quanta, 29
values, reversal of, 233
Vamana, 176
vas, 238; *naturale*, 241; *see also* vessel
Vaughan, Thomas, 133*n*
Vedas, 204
"veiled one," 18
Venus (♀), 76, 77*n*, 112, 155
veritas, 160, 161, 171, 181; *prima*, 178*n*
vessel: in alchemy, 238*ff*; Hermetic/ nigromantic, 240; as symbol, 224*f*
Vigenère, Blaise de, 132, 139, 197*n*, 250
vinegar, 239*n*; see also *acetum*
viper, 72
Vir Unus, 205
virgin, mother-goddess as, 104
Virgo (♍), 77*n*, 80*n*, 104*n*, 105; Mercurius as, 127
Virolleaud, Charles, 119
virtues, 24, 25
Vishnu, 113, 114*n*, 176
"Visio Arislei," *see* "Aenigmata ex Visione Arislei"
visions, 223
Vitus, Richardus, 13*n*
voice, fourfold, of Christ, 206
"volatile," winged beings as, 120
Voltaire, 98*n*
Vollers, Karl, 111*n*
Vulcan, 249*f*, 252

W

Wackerbarth, Graf August J. L. von, 80

Waite, Arthur Edward, 133*n*
Waldenses, 83, 150
wand, golden, of Hermes, 208
water: in alchemy, 159*f*, 180, 249; baptismal, 180; bright, 139; in dreams, 225; of life, 155; living, 184, 199*f*, 207; magical, 187; as magnetic agent, 188; prime substance, 199; real, used in ritual, 188; of rivers of Paradise, 199*f*; symbol and, 180
"wedding, chymical," 40, 268
Weiss, Johannes, 213*n*
Werblowsky, Zwi, 58
West, and Eastern thought, 176
whale-dragon, 111, 118
wheat-sheaf, 105
wheel: as symbol, 224; of birth, 136, 137, 224; of heaven, 136
White, Victor, O.P., 61*n*, 178*n*
whitening, 148; see also *albedo*; *dealbatio*
whole: present in ego, 111; procreative nature of, 201
wholeness, 169, 183; archetype of, 40; in Christ, 41, 62*n*; empirical, 31; image of, x, 24; of individual, 195; knowledge as, 222; paradoxical, 145; psychic, and God-image, 198; restoration of, 259; symbols of, 40, 171, 194, 195, 198; —, and God, 195; *see also* completeness; totality
Wickes, Frances G., 220*n*
Wilhelm, Richard, 264*n*
will: free, 5*f*; of God, 26*f*; and impulses, 27; omnipotence of, 26; and psyche, 4
wind, north, 100, 120, 125*n*
wine, 225
Wirth, Albrecht, 116*n*, 117*n*
Wischnitzer-Bernstein, Rahel, 115*n*
wise old man, 22, 152, 210, 229
witches, 175
wolf, 150
woman: in Apocalypse, 105; clothed with the sun, 103; image of, 13;

from side of Christ, 204; star-crowned, 12, 103*f*
Word, the, 200; *see also* Logos
world situation, present, 70
world-soul/world spirit, *see anima mundi*
world-views, parallel, 173
World War, second, 36
wrath, of Yahweh, *see* Yahweh
"wrath-fire," God's, 61
Wünsche, August, 106*n*, 107*n*

Y

Yahweh, 46, 229; changing concept of, 192; demiurge, 65, 75; injustice of, 55; justice of, 59; monsters of, 116, 118, 123, *see also* Behemoth, Leviathan; Saturn and, 197; unreliability of, 108; wrath of, 58*f*, 105
Yajñavalkya, 223
Yajui, 80*n*

Yama, 217*n*
yang/yin relationship, 58, 180
year: Christ as, 204; Platonic, 81*n*
Yehoshua/Yeshua, *see* Joshua
Yima, 246*n*
yod, 218*n*
yoga, Buddhism and, 176

Z

Zarathustra, 246*n*
Zechariah, Book of: (4 : 10), 105*n*
Zeesar, 210–11
Zen Buddhism, 169
Zeus, 206*n*
Zipporah, 209*n*, 227*f*, 244, 251, 252
zodia, 118, 148
zodiac, 94*n*; signs of, 81, 230*n*
Zohar, 107*n*, 117, 214
Zoroaster, 220*n*
Zosimos, 65*n*, 157*n*, 182, 197*n*, 237*n*, 238, 245*n*

THE COLLECTED WORKS OF

C. G. JUNG

T HE PUBLICATION of the first complete edition, in English, of the works of C. G. Jung was undertaken by Routledge and Kegan Paul, Ltd., in England and by Bollingen Foundation in the United States. The American edition is number XX in Bollingen Series, which since 1967 has been published by Princeton University Press. The edition contains revised versions of works previously published, such as *Psychology of the Unconscious*, which is now entitled *Symbols of Transformation*; works originally written in English, such as *Psychology and Religion*; works not previously translated, such as *Aion*; and, in general, new translations of virtually all of Professor Jung's writings. Prior to his death, in 1961, the author supervised the textual revision, which in some cases is extensive. Sir Herbert Read (d. 1968), Dr. Michael Fordham, and Dr. Gerhard Adler compose the Editorial Committee; the translator is R. F. C. Hull (except for Volume 2) and William McGuire is executive editor.

The price of the volumes varies according to size; they are sold separately, and may also be obtained on standing order. Several of the volumes are extensively illustrated. Each volume contains an index and in most a bibliography; the final volumes will contain a complete bibliography of Professor Jung's writings and a general index to the entire edition.

In the following list, dates of original publication are given in parentheses (of original composition, in brackets). Multiple dates indicate revisions.

*1. PSYCHIATRIC STUDIES

On the Psychology and Pathology of So-Called Occult Phenomena (1902)

On Hysterical Misreading (1904)

Cryptomnesia (1905)

On Manic Mood Disorder (1903)

A Case of Hysterical Stupor in a Prisoner in Detention (1902)

On Simulated Insanity (1903)

A Medical Opinion on a Case of Simulated Insanity (1904)

A Third and Final Opinion on Two Contradictory Psychiatric Diagnoses (1906)

On the Psychological Diagnosis of Facts (1905)

†2. EXPERIMENTAL RESEARCHES

Translated by Leopold Stein in collaboration with Diana Riviere

STUDIES IN WORD ASSOCIATION (1904–7, 1910)
The Associations of Normal Subjects (by Jung and F. Riklin)

An Analysis of the Associations of an Epileptic

The Reaction-Time Ratio in the Association Experiment

Experimental Observations on the Faculty of Memory

Psychoanalysis and Association Experiments

The Psychological Diagnosis of Evidence

Association, Dream, and Hysterical Symptom

The Psychopathological Significance of the Association Experiment

Disturbances in Reproduction in the Association Experiment

The Association Method

The Family Constellation

PSYCHOPHYSICAL RESEARCHES (1907–8)
On the Psychophysical Relations of the Association Experiment

Psychophysical Investigations with the Galvanometer and Pneumograph in Normal and Insane Individuals (by F. Peterson and Jung)

Further Investigations on the Galvanic Phenomenon and Respiration in Normal and Insane Individuals (by C. Ricksher and Jung)

Appendix: Statistical Details of Enlistment (1906); New Aspects of Criminal Psychology (1908); The Psychological Methods of Investigation Used in the Psychiatric Clinic of the University of Zurich (1910); On the Doctrine of Complexes ([1911] 1913); On the Psychological Diagnosis of Evidence (1937)

* Published 1957; 2nd edn., 1970.　　　　† Published 1973.

*3. THE PSYCHOGENESIS OF MENTAL DISEASE
  The Psychology of Dementia Praecox (1907)
  The Content of the Psychoses (1908/1914)
  On Psychological Understanding (1914)
  A Criticism of Bleuler's Theory of Schizophrenic Negativism (1911)
  On the Importance of the Unconscious in Psychopathology (1914)
  On the Problem of Psychogenesis in Mental Disease (1919)
  Mental Disease and the Psyche (1928)
  On the Psychogenesis of Schizophrenia (1939)
  Recent Thoughts on Schizophrenia (1957)
  Schizophrenia (1958)

†4. FREUD AND PSYCHOANALYSIS
  Freud's Theory of Hysteria: A Reply to Aschaffenburg (1906)
  The Freudian Theory of Hysteria (1908)
  The Analysis of Dreams (1909)
  A Contribution to the Psychology of Rumour (1910–11)
  On the Significance of Number Dreams (1910–11)
  Morton Prince, "The Mechanism and Interpretation of Dreams": A
      Critical Review (1911)
  On the Criticism of Psychoanalysis (1910)
  Concerning Psychoanalysis (1912)
  The Theory of Psychoanalysis (1913)
  General Aspects of Psychoanalysis (1913)
  Psychoanalysis and Neurosis (1916)
  Some Crucial Points in Psychoanalysis: A Correspondence between
      Dr. Jung and Dr. Loÿ (1914)
  Prefaces to "Collected Papers on Analytical Psychology" (1916, 1917)
  The Significance of the Father in the Destiny of the Individual
      (1909/1949)
  Introduction to Kranefeldt's "Secret Ways of the Mind" (1930)
  Freud and Jung: Contrasts (1929)

‡5. SYMBOLS OF TRANSFORMATION (1911–12/1952)
    PART I
  Introduction
  Two Kinds of Thinking
  The Miller Fantasies: Anamnesis
  The Hymn of Creation
  The Song of the Moth   (continued)

* Published 1960.   † Published 1961.
‡ Published 1956; 2nd edn., 1967. (65 plates, 43 text figures.)

5. (*continued*)

PART II

Introduction

The Concept of Libido

The Transformation of Libido

The Origin of the Hero

Symbols of the Mother and of Rebirth

The Battle for Deliverance from the Mother

The Dual Mother

The Sacrifice

Epilogue

Appendix: The Miller Fantasies

*6. PSYCHOLOGICAL TYPES (1921)

Introduction

The Problem of Types in the History of Classical and Medieval Thought

Schiller's Ideas on the Type Problem

The Apollinian and the Dionysian

The Type Problem in Human Character

The Type Problem in Poetry

The Type Problem in Psychopathology

The Type Problem in Aesthetics

The Type Problem in Modern Philosophy

The Type Problem in Biography

General Description of the Types

Definitions

Epilogue

Four Papers on Psychological Typology (1913, 1925, 1931, 1936)

†7. TWO ESSAYS ON ANALYTICAL PSYCHOLOGY

On the Psychology of the Unconscious (1917/1926/1943)

The Relations between the Ego and the Unconscious (1928)

Appendix: New Paths in Psychology (1912); The Structure of the Unconscious (1916) (new versions, with variants, 1966)

‡8. THE STRUCTURE AND DYNAMICS OF THE PSYCHE

On Psychic Energy (1928)

The Transcendent Function ([1916]/1957)

A Review of the Complex Theory (1934)

The Significance of Constitution and Heredity in Psychology (1929)

* Published 1971.   † Published 1953; 2nd edn., 1966.
‡ Published 1960; 2nd edn., 1969.

Psychological Factors Determining Human Behavior (1937)
Instinct and the Unconscious (1919)
The Structure of the Psyche (1927/1931)
On the Nature of the Psyche (1947/1954)
General Aspects of Dream Psychology (1916/1948)
On the Nature of Dreams (1945/1948)
The Psychological Foundations of Belief in Spirits (1920/1948)
Spirit and Life (1926)
Basic Postulates of Analytical Psychology (1931)
Analytical Psychology and *Weltanschauung* (1928/1931)
The Real and the Surreal (1933)
The Stages of Life (1930–1931)
The Soul and Death (1934)
Synchronicity: An Acausal Connecting Principle (1952)
Appendix: On Synchronicity (1951)

*9. PART I. THE ARCHETYPES AND THE
  COLLECTIVE UNCONSCIOUS
Archetypes of the Collective Unconscious (1934/1954)
The Concept of the Collective Unconscious (1936)
Concerning the Archetypes, with Special Reference to the Anima
    Concept (1936/1954)
Psychological Aspects of the Mother Archetype (1938/1954)
Concerning Rebirth (1940/1950)
The Psychology of the Child Archetype (1940)
The Psychological Aspects of the Kore (1941)
The Phenomenology of the Spirit in Fairytales (1945/1948)
On the Psychology of the Trickster-Figure (1954)
Conscious, Unconscious, and Individuation (1939)
A Study in the Process of Individuation (1934/1950)
Concerning Mandala Symbolism (1950)
Appendix: Mandalas (1955)

*9. PART II. AION (1951)
    RESEARCHES INTO THE PHENOMENOLOGY OF THE SELF
The Ego
The Shadow
The Syzygy: Anima and Animus
The Self
Christ, a Symbol of the Self
The Sign of the Fishes   (*continued*)

* Published 1959; 2nd edn., 1968. (Part I: 79 plates, with 29 in colour.)

9. *(continued)*

    The Prophecies of Nostradamus
    The Historical Significance of the Fish
    The Ambivalence of the Fish Symbol
    The Fish in Alchemy
    The Alchemical Interpretation of the Fish
    Background to the Psychology of Christian Alchemical Symbolism
    Gnostic Symbols of the Self
    The Structure and Dynamics of the Self
    Conclusion

*10. CIVILIZATION IN TRANSITION
    The Role of the Unconscious (1918)
    Mind and Earth (1927/1931)
    Archaic Man (1931)
    The Spiritual Problem of Modern Man (1928/1931)
    The Love Problem of a Student (1928)
    Woman in Europe (1927)
    The Meaning of Psychology for Modern Man (1933/1934)
    The State of Psychotherapy Today (1934)
    Preface and Epilogue to "Essays on Contemporary Events" (1946)
    Wotan (1936)
    After the Catastrophe (1945)
    The Fight with the Shadow (1946)
    The Undiscovered Self (Present and Future) (1957)
    Flying Saucers: A Modern Myth (1958)
    A Psychological View of Conscience (1958)
    Good and Evil in Analytical Psychology (1959)
    Introduction to Wolff's "Studies in Jungian Psychology" (1959)
    The Swiss Line in the European Spectrum (1928)
    Reviews of Keyserling's "America Set Free" (1930) and "La Révolution Mondiale" (1934)
    The Complications of American Psychology (1930)
    The Dreamlike World of India (1939)
    What India Can Teach Us (1939)
    Appendix: Documents (1933–1938)

†11. PSYCHOLOGY AND RELIGION: WEST AND EAST
    WESTERN RELIGION
    Psychology and Religion (The Terry Lectures) (1938/1940)

* Published 1964; 2nd edn., 1970. (8 plates.)
† Published 1958; 2nd edn., 1969.

A Psychological Approach to the Dogma of the Trinity (1942/1948)
Transformation Symbolism in the Mass (1942/1954)
Forewords to White's "God and the Unconscious" and Werblowsky's "Lucifer and Prometheus" (1952)
Brother Klaus (1933)
Psychotherapists or the Clergy (1932)
Psychoanalysis and the Cure of Souls (1928)
Answer to Job (1952)

EASTERN RELIGION

Psychological Commentaries on "The Tibetan Book of the Great Liberation" (1939/1954) and "The Tibetan Book of the Dead" (1935/1953)
Yoga and the West (1936)
Foreword to Suzuki's "Introduction to Zen Buddhism" (1939)
The Psychology of Eastern Meditation (1943)
The Holy Men of India: Introduction to Zimmer's "Der Weg zum Selbst" (1944)
Foreword to the "I Ching" (1950)

*12. PSYCHOLOGY AND ALCHEMY (1944)
Prefatory note to the English Edition ([1951?] added 1967)
Introduction to the Religious and Psychological Problems of Alchemy
Individual Dream Symbolism in Relation to Alchemy (1936)
Religious Ideas in Alchemy (1937)
Epilogue

†13. ALCHEMICAL STUDIES
Commentary on "The Secret of the Golden Flower" (1929)
The Visions of Zosimos (1938/1954)
Paracelsus as a Spiritual Phenomenon (1942)
The Spirit Mercurius (1943/1948)
The Philosophical Tree (1945/1954)

‡14. MYSTERIUM CONIUNCTIONIS (1955-56)
AN INQUIRY INTO THE SEPARATION AND
SYNTHESIS OF PSYCHIC OPPOSITES IN ALCHEMY
The Components of the Coniunctio
The Paradoxa
The Personification of the Opposites
Rex and Regina   (continued)

* Published 1953; 2nd edn., completely revised, 1968. (270 illustrations.)
† Published 1968. (50 plates, 4 text figures.)
‡ Published 1963; 2nd edn., 1970. (10 plates.)

14. (*continued*)
Adam and Eve
The Conjunction

*15. THE SPIRIT IN MAN, ART, AND LITERATURE
Paracelsus (1929)
Paracelsus the Physician (1941)
Sigmund Freud in His Historical Setting (1932)
In Memory of Sigmund Freud (1939)
Richard Wilhelm: In Memoriam (1930)
On the Relation of Analytical Psychology to Poetry (1922)
Psychology and Literature (1930/1950)
"Ulysses": A Monologue (1932)
Picasso (1932)

†16. THE PRACTICE OF PSYCHOTHERAPY
GENERAL PROBLEMS OF PSYCHOTHERAPY
Principles of Practical Psychotherapy (1935)
What Is Psychotherapy? (1935)
Some Aspects of Modern Psychotherapy (1930)
The Aims of Psychotherapy (1931)
Problems of Modern Psychotherapy (1929)
Psychotherapy and a Philosophy of Life (1943)
Medicine and Psychotherapy (1945)
Psychotherapy Today (1945)
Fundamental Questions of Psychotherapy (1951)
SPECIFIC PROBLEMS OF PSYCHOTHERAPY
The Therapeutic Value of Abreaction (1921/1928)
The Practical Use of Dream-Analysis (1934)
The Psychology of the Transference (1946)
Appendix: The Realities of Practical Psychotherapy ([1937] added,
    1966)

‡17. THE DEVELOPMENT OF PERSONALITY
Psychic Conflicts in a Child (1910/1946)
Introduction to Wickes's "Analyse der Kinderseele" (1927/1931)
Child Development and Education (1928)
Analytical Psychology and Education: Three Lectures (1926/1946)
The Gifted Child (1943)
The Significance of the Unconscious in Individual Education (1928)

* Published 1966.
† Published 1954; 2nd edn., revised and augmented, 1966. (13 illustrations.)
‡ Published 1954.

The Development of Personality (1934)
Marriage as a Psychological Relationship (1925)

18. THE SYMBOLIC LIFE
Miscellaneous Writings

19. GENERAL BIBLIOGRAPHY OF C. G. JUNG'S WRITINGS

20. GENERAL INDEX TO THE COLLECTED WORKS

See also:

C. G. JUNG: LETTERS
Selected and edited by Gerhard Adler, in collaboration with Aniela Jaffé.
Translations from the German by R.F.C. Hull.
 VOL. 1: 1906–1950
 VOL. 2: 1951–1961

THE FREUD / JUNG LETTERS
Edited by William McGuire, translated by
Ralph Manheim and R.F.C. Hull

C. G. JUNG SPEAKING: Interviews and Encounters
Edited by William McGuire and R.F.C. Hull

C. G. JUNG: Word and Image
Edited by Aniela Jaffé

Supplementary Volume A:
THE ZOFINGIA LECTURES
Edited by William McGuire, translated by Jan Van Heurck,
introduction by Marie-Louise von Franz

SELECTED LETTERS OF C. G. JUNG, 1909–1961
Selected and edited by Gerhard Adler, in collaboration with Aniela Jaffé
Translations from the German by R.F.C. Hull

DREAM ANALYSIS
Notes of the Seminar Given in 1928–1930
Edited by William McGuire

THE ESSENTIAL JUNG
Selected and introduced by Anthony Storr